A DAY TO DIE FOR

A DAY TO DIE FOR

1996: EVEREST'S WORST DISASTER
One Survivor's Personal Journey
to Uncover the Truth

GRAHAM RATCLIFFE

MAINSTREAM
PUBLISHING

EDINBURGH AND LONDON

First published in Great Britain in 2011 by
MAINSTREAM PUBLISHING COMPANY
(EDINBURGH) LTD
7 Albany Street
Edinburgh EH1 3UG

ISBN 9781845966386

A catalogue record for this book is available
from the British Library

Printed in Great Britain by
Clays Ltd St Ives plc

3 5 7 9 10 8 6 4

For Catherine, Angela, Amy and Sophia

And in memory of friends lost in pursuit of their dreams

Facts are stubborn things; and whatever may be our wishes, our inclinations, or the dictates of our passions, they cannot alter the state of facts and evidence.
– Joey Adams (Joseph Abramowitz, 1911–99)

Disclaimer

It was MacGillivray Freeman Films, as producers, who organised the shooting of the IMAX documentary film *Everest* in the spring of 1996. The IMAX Corporation were not involved in the planning of the Everest expedition to shoot the film, or in any of its decision-making.

Within the text of this book, the IMAX Corporation and the films shown in their large-screen cinemas are referred to using capitals (as in their trademark) and the Imax expedition, as it was known, with a capital letter and the rest in lower case.

The fact that the expedition was called the 'MacGillivray Freeman IMAX/IWERKS Expedition', which is referred to as the Imax expedition in this book, does not mean they and the IMAX Corporation are one and the same. Any references in the book to the Imax expedition are not referring to the IMAX Corporation or indeed to IWERKS Entertainment, Inc.

Where this book quotes directly from other authors, there may be occasions where IMAX or IMAX/IWERKS is used to refer to the Imax expedition. This is beyond the author's control and we apologise for this overlap in the adopted method.

Acknowledgements

There are many people I wish to thank for so generously giving their time to assist me on this personal journey over the last five years. More than anyone, I would like to thank my wife Catherine for showing such patience and understanding, as well as being the voice of reason in difficult times.

Others to whom I wish to extend my sincere gratitude include: Geoff Scarth and Olwyn Hocking for their belief in the difficult task they knew I had set myself, for their continued support and sound advice based on professional experience, which guided me along a logical path.

Dr Henrik Jessen Hansen for the considerable amount of time he has taken to respond to my numerous questions, and whose answers have helped provide an important insight into the days leading up to the tragedy of 10 May 1996.

The many meteorologists who have assisted with my investigation and without whom I would have been totally lost.

Mike Harrison, who has made countless enquiries on my behalf and who must have spent untold hours behind the scenes or at his computer answering my continual questions; for making the time, along with his colleague, to read the archives that would prove so invaluable in my research.

Søren Olufsen from the Danish Meteorological Institute, whose excellent recall opened the way for me.

Bob Aran and Martin Harris for the thoughtfulness they displayed as I tested their memories on the events of so long ago.

Joey Comeaux, Will Spangler, Leslie Forehand, Jan Carpenter and William Brown from the National Oceanic and Atmospheric Administration (NOAA). David Ucko, Valentine Kass, Robert Robinson and Hyman Field (retired) from the National Science Foundation (NSF). Fiona Gedge, Marion Archer and Kate Strachan from the UK Met Office. Keith Fielding from the European Centre for Medium-Range Weather Forecasts (ECMWF). And the many other members of staff from meteorological institutions around the globe who were so helpful in assisting me with my enquiries.

Henry Todd for his generosity, patience and understanding over several Everest expeditions. Iswari Paudel for dealing with safety in the most difficult of circumstances. My fellow climbers Neil Laughton, Paul Deegan, Brigitte Muir, Nikolai Sitnikov and Crag Jones.

The other people who have helped along the way: Gladys Hayles, Michael Dunn, Ben Bradfield, Colin Westland, Hazel Morton, Peter Molnar, Harry Taylor, Ed Douglas, Lindsay Griffin, Geoff Birtles, John Traynor, Simon Manns and Roger Southcott to name but a few.

There are many more people than I have listed here. Five years is a long time. To all who helped me along my way: thank you. For without the help of so many individuals this book would have never been completed.

I would like to conclude by thanking my agent, Andrew Gordon of David Higham Associates, for showing faith in my work and for understanding that this needed to be published. To Bill Campbell of Mainstream Publishing for taking the book on, to my thoughtful and meticulous editor Ailsa Bathgate, to whom I am indebted, and Amanda Telfer for her sound advice; to Kate McLelland for the excellent graphics, and to Graeme Blaikie and all the other staff at Mainstream who have assisted with the publication of this book.

Contents

Introduction: Ascending into Turmoil

It was late afternoon on 10 May 1996. The winds on Everest's upper reaches, which had been gradually building up over the preceding days, took a sudden turn for the worse. Descending from the summit were two guided teams. Having become dangerously spread out along Everest's South East Ridge, they found themselves fighting for their very survival. Bolts of lightning flashed eerily in the dark clouds that had blown in with the storm; thunder clashed terrifyingly close overhead. The wind brought with it a blizzard of driving snow that would change the landscape out of all recognition for the descending climbers, who became hopelessly lost in near white-out conditions.

Meanwhile, the team I was with was climbing up from Camp 3 on the Lhotse Face to Everest's South Col, from where we planned to launch our own summit bid later that same evening. During this upward move, we were sheltered from the winds. The light overhead disappeared into swirling misty cloud; there was a sense of foreboding in the air. It was only when I emerged out of the lee and onto this desolate rocky plateau, just as darkness was settling over the mountain, that I was struck by the rising storm. I bowed my head against the relentless onslaught of the horizontal blizzard ripping across from Tibet.

Totally unaware of the struggle for survival of the two guided teams, I dived into our tent to join my fellow climbers. They were preparing to settle down for the night. We now knew fine well there would be no summit bid that night and questioned what we were doing there in the first place in such conditions.

We had no clue that by the following day five people would be dead, others close to death itself. One, a diminutive Japanese lady, lay 150 yards from our tent, across the flat expanse of the South Col. As shocked awareness dawned, we could not understand why no one had told us what was happening outside our tent or asked us for help.

But more than this, I had been wrestling with a nagging doubt. During the climb, I had questioned over the radio the decision to go; I felt it had been obvious that the conditions were not settled enough.

There were many questions that plagued me, but immediately

afterwards was not the time to ask. I returned home that year and re-entered my normal life, and in the end the questions were never addressed. I even avoided all the books and accounts that followed . . . that was until 2004.

Finally, I was compelled for my own peace of mind to search for an understanding of the events that had led to the deaths of eight people on Everest that night. I turned to published accounts, some of which had become international bestsellers, and to the films that had been made in the intervening time. I hoped that I might find the answers I was looking for, but that was not to be the case. Instead, they only served to raise more questions in my mind. And so began my personal journey, one that would span the next five years.

It was only once I had uncovered the staggering, and hitherto unpublished, circumstances that had led to Everest's worst-ever disaster that I could truly come to terms with what happened that fateful day.

The Meaning of Life

Hanging in the garage was the motorcycle petrol tank I had painted emperor purple. The year was 1970 and it was my 15th birthday. I'd bought myself the 200cc Triumph tiger cub for the princely sum of £5. The engine didn't run, but I wasn't bothered. How it was going to look was all-important. I wouldn't be able to ride it on public roads for another year anyway, not until I turned 16.

I shut the garage door to stop dust landing on the lovingly applied paint and grasped the small gold-coloured carton deep in my trouser pocket. It was a pack of ten Benson and Hedges Sovereign cigarettes. I'd bought them because the friends I hung around with had started to smoke. The choice of brand had been made because gold looked more sophisticated to me than the mundane colours of other makes displayed in the newsagent shop.

My parents didn't smoke, and I'd had to find a place where the smell would not be detected. In recent weeks, I had located the perfect spot. Rushing up the winding staircase of our large three-storey Edwardian house, I made my way to the attic rooms. Next to my bedroom was the playroom, with two large windows separated by a column of brick. I looked out at the narrow lead-lined veranda enclosed by an ornate wrought-iron balustrade. This was not my chosen place. The veranda was at the front of the building, and I knew I could be seen from the street, three floors below. But it was my route to a safe hiding place. Through a daredevil antic, I had discovered that if I climbed over the left-hand side of the balustrade and stood on the four-inch-wide sandstone edge, I could launch myself up the smooth slate roof. With a hard push off, the crepe soles of my shoes and the palms of my hands gave me enough grip, provided I was quick, to reach the top of the attic's large dormer window.

From this point, the central ridge of the main roof was within reach. On the far side, some eight feet down, stood a tall, narrow chimneystack. I clambered over the top ridge and slithered down to it. Now free of the parental restrictions that lay far below, I rested against this brick structure, opened my cigarettes and lit one up. The taste was repulsive, and when I inhaled it made my head spin. However, I was sure if I persevered I would begin to enjoy these nauseating sensations.

Surveying the land round about, rooftops dominated the skyline; far beyond, I caught a glimpse of the North Sea. In each direction, tall chimneystacks stood like sentinels in this alien world. Forty feet below, the neatly manicured gardens held no interest for me, except that is for the reinforced concrete air raid shelter at the bottom of our rear garden, a relic from the Second World War. My brothers and I had managed to excavate it from beneath several tons of earth, much to our mother's consternation. Built by a previous owner of the house who had worked for the War Department, it had a small but very thick metal door with a sabre painted on the inside surface, wood-panelled walls and even bunk beds. The seemingly unyielding nature of this wartime structure had sparked our imaginations.

High on the rooftop, I felt untethered. The breeze at this lofty height stimulated my senses. Spurred on by this elation, I wondered what excitement I might feel if I moved out from behind the stack and onto the main roof, where I would have less control and no support. My heart began to beat faster as I edged away from the chimney. Once I was beyond arm's length, exhilaration spread from my stomach throughout my whole body, my arms tingled and the hairs on the back of my neck stood on end. I had never felt so alive. That was, until I slid forward about three inches. On this the northern side of the chimney, a thin layer of lichen covered part of the roof. Beneath the palms of my hands and soles of my shoes, it was beginning to detach from the slates. In an instant, extreme pleasure turned into abject fear as I began to inch downwards. Carried by tiny balls of lichen, I gradually picked up speed. Between me and the edge of the roof, which was getting ever nearer, there was nothing I could grab to halt my descent. Far below, across the rear of the house, were a flight of concrete steps, a garden rockery and a holly tree with gnarled branches pointing upwards. If I fell, there seemed little chance of escaping death, and serious injury appeared certain.

I pushed my hands flat against the roof, the soles of my shoes also. The denim on my backside scraped across the dusty surface, but still I continued down. Less than six feet from the edge, I ground to a halt. Fortune had saved me. The tongue of lichen stretching down the surface of the roof had come to an abrupt end. I froze, not sure what to do next. I was terrified that if I relinquished any of my contact with the roof I would simply slide over the edge. I did my utmost to control the panic that was welling inside. Twisting my head around, I could see the marks where I had slid down. There was no way I was going to risk trying to climb back up the same way. Inch by inch, I shuffled left along the roof, further still from the now distant chimneystack. Here, it appeared to be clear of the lichen that had launched me down this deadly slope. I manoeuvred myself backwards up the roof. It took me two heart-pounding minutes to regain the centre ridge.

The familiar slope on the other side, which led back to the veranda, now held nothing but fear for me. My nerves were shredded. I slid precariously over the slates with my eye firmly fixed on the ironwork I needed to grab on the way past. Within moments, I was kneeling on the playroom floor, my hands trembling. The initial exhilaration I had felt by moving out across the roof was undeniable, but so was the fear that followed the audacious manoeuvre.

However, I was still young and my memory short-lived. The carefree and experimental nature of youth had still to run its course. My appetite for thrill-seeking adventure was undiminished.

I had yet to learn to curb this reckless risk taking, to maintain an element of control over the objective dangers. If I did not, life could end up being far shorter than I had expected.

Tibet

May 1995

Ahead, the expansive snowfield rose at an angle of 45 degrees. Hanging down over its glistening surface was a length of 9mm climbing rope. To the left of this single strand was a trail of footprints heading up. I leant forward and pulled at a short section of the rope. It had been buried by the light breeze and gently drifting snow. Breaking through the crust of this frozen wasteland was the occasional dark outcrop of crumbling weathered rock. In the distance, I could make out the tents at 27,200 feet. They were still some half an hour away. I was high on the North Face of Everest. The date was 16 May 1995. Far below and out of sight were the two Russian climbers, Anatoli Boukreev and Nikolai Sitnikov, with whom I was climbing. We were on our way to our top camp. From here, we'd make our summit push in the early hours of the next day. I'd been on the mountain once before, but this was my first realistic shot at reaching the top.

As I slid my jumar up the cord, it wiped clean the snow that had frozen to the woven outer layer. A fine coating of this crystalline spray covered my right glove and forearm. I placed my boot firmly onto the next foothold and pulled on my jumar. The sprung-loaded quadrant with its serrated metal surface gripped hard against the rope. I heaved myself up and lifted my other foot into the next placing, then slid the jumar up once more. Ten steps in a row were as much as I could manage before having to rest for a moment so that the oxygen level in my muscles could catch up. Four hours had passed since I had left Camp 2, 1,300 feet below. In that time, I had hauled myself up this slope with what seemed an agonisingly slow and protracted effort.

Taking my last few paces into Camp 3, I wearily dumped my rucksack onto the soft snow. I strained to give a grateful smile through hacking coughs and gasps for air. The recipients of my appreciation were our three Sherpas. Having positioned a second tent for us, they were eagerly preparing to descend to a far more comfortable altitude. They too were feeling the debilitating effects of this elevation. All summit attempts this year, by our eleven-strong team, would be without Sherpas – hence their rapid departures back down.

Over the preceding weeks, they had made trip after trip up the mountain to place and supply three camps, each higher than the one before. Due to their hard work, the chances of our success had been greatly improved. However, because they covered the ground so quickly, none would need to sleep higher than the North Col: the first of the three camps, located at 23,000 feet.

I watched with some envy as our Sherpas scampered down the steep slope and out of sight. Then, turning my attention, I began to protect the two well-positioned tents with extra rocks and guy ropes. It was impossible to make the tents overly secure. The North Face of Everest had a notorious reputation for wind.

A few hundred feet below, another expedition was placing a small number of tents. They too were planning to begin their summit attempt that night.

We had no weather forecast of what lay ahead. Although we'd been enjoying clear skies and minimal winds for several days, conditions could turn with little or no warning. Instincts, experience and a watchful eye would be our guardians.

A week earlier, we'd listened in Base Camp to the radio calls of those attempting Everest from the Nepalese side of the mountain. Normally, we were unable to receive these transmissions, as they were blocked out by the huge snow-covered ridges several thousand feet high that separated Nepal from Tibet. However, as the climbers got higher on the mountain, this restriction no longer applied.

It had been a gloriously sunny morning when we picked up the calls of New Zealander Rob Hall, owner of a company called Adventure Consultants: an outfit that specialised in upmarket guided expeditions. He was accompanied by four of his clients, one of whom was an American postal worker by the name of Doug Hansen. They were attempting Everest via the South East Ridge. In support were Sherpas and professional guides including the highly experienced Ed Viesturs.

I remember hearing that they were progressing well and hoped to be on the summit within the hour. All we could do was stare upwards, wishing it had been us. We hovered around the radio as these climbers started to make their way over the relatively short distance to the top. The next communication expressed frustration. They had encountered deep snow that had dramatically slowed their progress. Every 30 minutes, they made contact with their team lower down the mountain. On each occasion, they extended their expected arrival time at the summit.

Eventually came the despondent radio call: 'OK, we're turning around and heading back down.' The voice was that of Rob Hall.

Due to both the time of day and deep snow, they were abandoning their attempt. While this decision must have been difficult to make, given that they could actually see their goal so tantalisingly close, it was nevertheless the correct choice. We understood the immense disappointment they must have been feeling. With hindsight, we were glad it had not been our attempt.

Now, several days on, it was our turn to test our luck but by a different route.

My fellow aspirants arrived into camp mid-afternoon. Anatoli, aged 37, was a tall, blond, wiry climber of international acclaim, who had been born in Korkino, a mining area in Russia's southern Ural Mountains. He now hailed from Alma-Ata (Almaty) in Kazakhstan, where he had taken up citizenship in 1991 following the break-up of the Soviet Union. Prior to this upheaval, he had held the honour of Master of Sport and a place on Russia's national high-altitude climbing team. He was a man of relatively few words. Those he did use were carefully thought through. Not a person to suffer daydreamers, he would come straight to the point.

When we'd first met as a team, he'd asked others the direct question: 'Tell me what you have climbed. Do not tell me about the Alps; I want to know about high altitude, over 20,000 feet.'

This year he was working for our expedition run by Henry Todd. He was not employed as a guide in the Western sense of the word, rather as a 'rope bullet', as Henry described him. Should anything go wrong, or a member of the team find themselves in trouble, he was there to cover ground quickly and sort matters out.

Nikolai, in his 30s, spoke virtually no English and also came from the Urals. He was a distinctively muscular man with a round face and shaven head. What had particularly caught the attention of others on our team was the stylish way in which he strutted between Base Camp and Advanced Base Camp. He would set off on this 12-mile hike wearing tight-fitting shorts, a checked shirt with the sleeves rolled up, and a handkerchief placed over his exposed scalp. Proud of his own strength, he'd held his head high, taking the required effort in his stride. He was a very likeable character who'd apparently had his place on the expedition paid for in full by Ural Electrochemical Integrated Plant: the world's largest uranium enrichment enterprise and manufacturer of advanced process control technology for the nuclear industry. Quite how he'd managed this, nobody was sure. We were, however, highly impressed that he'd pulled it off.

I sat outside the tents and watched as Anatoli and Nikolai mustered the effort to drag themselves up the last section of the fixed rope and into camp. Our two tents had been erected on precariously small pieces of flat ground excavated out of the mountainside. Differing in size, they had been placed about 15 feet apart. As Nikolai and I struggled with a language barrier, we decided my two companions should share the bigger of the two. The final planning for our summit push would be made by calling to each other from our respective accommodation.

During the afternoon, we each began to prepare our personal equipment. It was at this point that I came across an unexpected problem.

We had two types of oxygen cylinders with us. The steel ones, weighing in at a rather heavy 13 lb each, were for sleeping. They had a valve that could be turned by hand and to which the regulator could be directly fitted. The other, much lighter, Poisk cylinders were for climbing. These had a thin metal lining surrounded by a thick resin and fibre wrapping and weighed a more enviable 5.5 lb. However, this type required a spanner to remove a threaded hexagonal cap before the regulator could be fitted to the fixed valve to allow the flow of oxygen. Only then could it be turned on. The Poisks were the ones Nikolai and I needed for our ascent. We were going to climb using supplementary oxygen. Anatoli was climbing without gas.

After I'd laid out my equipment, I turned my attention to the oxygen I was going to use during the attempt. Looking around the tent, I realised the spanner wasn't packed with the equipment I'd brought with me.

I shouted across to Anatoli: 'Can you ask Nikolai if I can have the spanner for the Poisk bottles?'

A conversation ensued in Russian between my fellow climbers. Moments later came the mortifying words from Anatoli: 'Nikolai says you must have it.'

My heart sank. Looking back now, I find this hilarious, but at the time it seemed somewhat less amusing. All the careful checking of equipment I had carried out in preparation for my summit attempt and I had forgotten to bring the one item I needed to turn the oxygen on!

In such a harsh environment, overlooking the smallest detail can have dire consequences. We were responsible for the error and had no one to blame but ourselves. The solving of this problem was up to us.

Tentatively, I made an attempt to loosen the hexagonal cap from one Poisk bottle by tapping it with my ice axe. However, tackling an oxygen cylinder charged to 2600 psi with an ice axe seemed a slightly dangerous option. An image flashed through my mind, rather as the oxygen cylinder would have done, of the outcome if my improvisation went wrong. My concern was not just for myself but also for anyone within 300 feet. This included those below us on the mountain who might be hit by falling debris. Sheepishly, I put my ice axe down as common sense prevailed, and I sank back on my sleeping bag to further ponder this unexpected complication.

The term 'using oxygen' is one that conjures up an image in the public mind of climbers making their ascent breathing pure bottled oxygen. This is not the case. A manually operated regulator sets the volume of oxygen being supplied from the bottle to the climber. This is set in increments of half a litre per minute, up to a maximum of four litres per minute. The gas is fed via a narrow rubber tube to a bladder on the fighter pilot mask that is worn over the climber's mouth and nose. The oxygen being supplied in this manner mixes with the rarefied air being breathed in through the front of the mask. At over 26,000 feet, the effort required to climb is immense; the breaths taken are deep and rapid: up to 30 per minute. With each breath, the painfully thin ambient air is exhaled and then inhaled, into which a small quantity of oxygen is fed. This effectively raises the amount of oxygen within the air the climber is breathing from one-third of that found at sea level to just under half. The biggest benefit is that it makes for a warmer climb and reduces the chance of frostbite. This injury occurs under low oxygen levels because the body constricts the vessels carrying blood to the surface in an effort to maintain core temperature. With warm blood not reaching the outer layer, both hands and feet are far more susceptible to cold injuries. The use of supplementary oxygen significantly lessens the risk of this happening.

The method of raising the oxygen level through an artificial supply seems straightforward; it's easy to assume that if the climber ran out, the effort to continue would simply become marginally more tiring. However, this is the area in which the danger lies. The consequences of a climber running out of oxygen at high altitude can vary enormously. Some continue on at a slightly reduced pace but with little other effect. Others slow dramatically and their thought processes become impaired. In the most serious cases, the climber can collapse into a heap as the body and mind begin to shut down in response to the sudden change in the oxygen levels. The problem lies in not being able to predict how either yourself or a fellow climber might react to this eventuality. This is complicated further by the fact that the effect it has on one occasion does not mean you can guarantee the consequences of future occurrences. These can vary according to the level of acclimatisation at the time, fitness, health, state of exhaustion and even the climber's age.

When climbing with the use of supplementary oxygen, it is

imperative that climbers know the exact number of hours their total supply will last. At the flow rate they have set, there must be a safety margin built in for their return to the top camp. To move beyond this time frame is courting disaster.

Nikolai and I were faced with three options. We could climb without using oxygen. We could abandon our ascent that night and try again in a few days. Or we could use two steel bottles for our summit attempt instead of the much lighter Poisk bottles. We mulled over our individual options and each decided, independently, to go for number three. The weight of the two steel cylinders, regulator, mask, Thermos of water, spare gloves, goggles, camera, rucksack and other equipment was going to give us 44 lb each to carry to the summit of Everest. This was half as much again as we'd been expecting to shoulder. A daunting prospect!

That problem dealt with, in theory anyway, we now needed to decide at what time we should depart for the summit.

Anatoli called to me from the other tent: 'Graham, I think we should leave at midnight.'

In quick response I replied, 'Can we agree on two o'clock? I was hoping for a lie-in.'

I heard Anatoli translating this for Nikolai. There followed a roar of laughter from the two Russians. Two o'clock in the morning it was for our departure towards the summit of Everest.

As the evening light began to fade, I ventured out of my tent to gaze upon the Himalaya, most of which lay far below. It was as though I had stepped out into the firmament. Through gaps in the clouds that gently blanketed the valley floors, glaciers could be seen as rivers of flowing ice. They twisted and turned on their creeping downward journey. Huge crevasses looked like small splits in their fractured surfaces. Majestic snow-capped peaks reached skywards through billowing clouds, their upper reaches bathed in infinite soft pastel shades of red and orange cast by the setting sun. High on Everest, I stood amongst the very phenomenon I'd observed so many times from far below. I felt humbled by what I was witnessing. Yet, at the same time, my spirit was lifted by the sense of being unbelievably privileged to glimpse such a vista.

With the diminishing light, the Himalayan summits that still managed to reach through the layers of cloud took on a colder, darker and more sinister appearance. They reminded me I was in a place where I should not exist. I was surviving on little more than borrowed time.

As the last remnants of the day departed from the evening sky, my thoughts had been wiped clean of our climb ahead, now only a matter of hours away. As the temperature plummeted, I slipped back inside the tent. Wrapped in the warmth of my goose-down sleeping bag, I rolled slightly inwards. The sensation was that of being embraced. Although I knew this was in my imagination, the feeling of security was almost overwhelming. The platform had probably been hacked out of the slope many years earlier by a previous expedition. Either by chance or design, it sloped gently into the face of the mountain. Wearing my oxygen mask, with my regulator set at a rate of one litre per minute, I enjoyed the best night's sleep I have had on any climb. There was no fear or apprehension. A complete sense of calm wafted over me as I slept.

Summit Day

17 May 1995

I was woken from my unexpectedly comfortable sleep by the continual bleeping of my Timex Indiglo watch. This had been given to me as a Christmas present a few months earlier. My mother-in-law had purchased it, not because it was hi-tech but rather for its good alarm and the face that lit up brightly at the touch of a button. It was simple to use, robust and weighed little: factors that were essential up here.

The time was just after midnight. As ever with these early starts, my mind tried to convince me to remain in the relative comfort of my bed a while longer. Five more minutes, I thought. However, in fear of nodding off again I knelt up. I was still cocooned in my sleeping bag. Anatoli and Nikolai would be relying on me being ready at the agreed time. If I was not, they couldn't stand around getting cold while waiting.

As my head brushed against the roof of the tent its icy lining showered down. The fine particles melted instantly on my warm face. The intense tingling sensation woke me abruptly from my soporific state and into reality. Everything I did from that moment on would have a direct effect on my chances of reaching the summit of Everest. There was no one looking over my shoulder to check the equipment, set oxygen flow rates or steady the last-minute jitters. I was alone. Logical, calm preparation was required. My nerves hid just beneath the surface.

I'd been on the north side of Everest once before, without success. In the year and a half that had passed since that time, I'd spent many a waking hour dreaming of this opportunity. The glorious fantasy of those musings seemed very distant. The apprehension I felt in my tent over the potential dangers that lay ahead was far more real. I also knew that once we started the climb this would pass.

I switched on my head torch. My first priority was to light the gas stove. It was imperative I made myself a hot drink before our scheduled departure in little more than an hour and a half's time. Unzipping the entrance to my tent slightly, I could see that Anatoli and Nikolai were also awake. The beams from their two torches flashed erratically against the side of their tent as they shuffled around.

'Morning!' I shouted in a deliberately cheerful voice.

The mutterings I heard back were those of acknowledgement. The Russians were as reluctant as myself to emerge from the warmth of their slumbers.

Looking around, my vision was swallowed up by the night sky. The moon was so small and cast such little light that it took on the appearance of a distant planet. High above, I could make out the North East Ridge, distinguishable as a solid black outline contrasted against a sky filled with pinpricks of light from innumerable stars. This ridge would lead us to the summit. I listened carefully. There was no wind. The air was still.

I withdrew my head back inside the tent and knelt over my freshly brewed yet already lukewarm cup of tea. I sipped reluctantly at this tepid fluid, knowing it was essential for the climb ahead. As the time moved all too quickly from midnight to after one o'clock, I slid into my down suit and neoprene inner boots, each warmed in my sleeping bag over the last half-hour. My rucksack lay ready, carefully packed with my supplies and oxygen cylinders the previous afternoon.

As the agreed departure time of two o'clock approached, my controlled calmness began rapidly to disappear. I pulled on my outer climbing boots in preparation for stepping outside. My crampons were the last items to be fitted, once I had stuck my legs out of the tent.

As I stood upright, the sensation of being engulfed by the pitch black came as a shock. I looked down at the pitiful puddle of light provided by my head torch. It shone a few feet onto the ground ahead. I stared anxiously upwards at the distant vague outline of the North East Ridge stretching towards the summit of Everest.

The slope I was standing on gave an indication of up from down. But which way we had to climb through the mass of rocks that lay ahead was not so obvious. I had perused the ground above on my arrival into camp the previous afternoon. In the dead of night, what little I could make out seemed eerily different.

Finding our way was one concern. The other was the weather. We needed to keep a constant eye on it, to watch and listen for changes. Especially for the danger of the wind catching us out high up.

As I stood transfixed by the darkness, I had the forethought to take a photograph. At two o'clock in the morning! I wanted to capture the moment, or should I say the fear of that moment. Nowadays, whenever I give a presentation I show this slide. I have yet to find an audience that does not gasp with an understanding that the obvious should have been so unexpected. The sensation each member of the audience feels is one of actually being within the image or strongly connected to it. This is brought about by the fact the audience is sitting in a blacked-out room.

Once Anatoli and Nikolai had emerged from their tent, I cleared my thoughts of the sight of the ground ahead, or the lack of it, and prepared to depart. Heaving the rucksack up, I slid the straps over my shoulders and took the full weight for the first time. It felt as though my spine was being compressed. I heard the sound of my crampons being forced deeper into the frozen crust. I had no illusion that this was going to be anything but hard work.

Three or four hundred feet above and far to the right, I saw three quick flashes of light against the otherwise dark outline of the mountain. Not everyone had had a lie-in. The expedition camped below had set out a couple of hours ahead of us. They were making steady progress. Only the occasional flicker of a head torch gave away their location.

Carrying no rucksack, Anatoli took the lead. I was envious of his attempt without oxygen. I pondered the wisdom of my 44 lb load.

Turning the wheel on the regulator, I set the flow rate at two and a half litres of supplementary oxygen per minute. Pulling the mask over my nose and mouth, I breathed deeply.

Directing my torch into Anatoli's shallow footprints, I followed his tracks up the snow slope. As we entered the towering rocks above, our dim lights cast ghostly shadows across the gloomy form. The points of our crampons scraped painfully across the impenetrable surface.

Glancing back after ten minutes, I could see that Nikolai, now some way behind, had not yet left camp. I wondered what apprehension he must have been feeling as he saw us disappear into the night. Looking again a short while later, I was relieved to see the beam of light was moving. He'd begun to trace our steps.

Anatoli and I kept moving higher, rarely separated by more than a few feet. No longer did I notice the weight of my rucksack. As I focused on the climb, my apprehension had given way to concentrated effort.

It was at this time I remembered Harry, a Finnish friend of mine, with whom I'd climbed on Everest in the autumn of 1993. 'Graham,' he'd said to me, 'the worst part of any climb is the first half-hour.' His wise words brought my only comfort that dark night.

Nikolai, despite making steady progress, dropped slowly behind. We were not unduly concerned. Time was on our side, for the moment at least.

Within range of my head torch, Anatoli stopped to sit on a rock. Catching his breath, he asked, 'Graham, what height do you think we are at?'

I carefully considered his question, but with nothing much to actually gauge it by I gave my best estimate.

Pulling my mask slightly to one side, I replied, 'Around 27,500 feet.'

Anatoli looked at me, doing his best to muster a smile. 'You go first, Graham.'

So I took the lead. We moved ever upwards.

As night progressed towards the end of its natural cycle, the utter darkness began to fade into a deep grey. The sky above took on a grainy appearance as the first signs of the dimmest light tried to pierce their way through. The already frigid air dropped several degrees, as though millions of minute airborne ice particles had suddenly evaporated. I shuddered with this sudden change, one that signalled the coming of dawn.

By the time we broke onto the crest of the North East Ridge, night had slipped away. It had done so almost unnoticed. The sun had not risen over the horizon, yet the arrival of this subdued light brought with it a sense of security. This was more a perception than reality. The main difference was that we could now see where we were going. No longer was our view limited to the beams of our torches. It took a while for us to realise they were still on and that we could switch them off.

Directly in front of us, the ground dropped away for 10,000 feet. The North Face is steep, but on the other side of this knife-edged ridge the Kangshung Face of Everest is near vertical. Beyond stretched the view of two Himalayan giants, Makalu and in the far distance Kangchenjunga, the fifth- and third-highest summits in the world, respectively. Ten thousand feet below, at the bottom of the Kangshung Face, lay a thick blanket of cloud. Holding my camera over the edge, I took a photograph. It looks as though it has been taken from a cruising jetliner.

As I glanced left down the ridge, its jagged edge appeared as a row of sharks' fins, each one set at a slightly different angle from the vertical. Looking right, in the direction we needed to move, an upward traverse of half a mile or more stood between us and our goal. On the ground ahead, two sections of rock barred the way: the First and Second Steps. Both would have to be negotiated before we could gain access to the final snowfield. We still seemed a long way off.

The angle eased significantly towards the First Step. This section gave me the first real opportunity to survey our surroundings. I had the sensation we were leaving one world and entering another.

As we navigated along the ridge, Anatoli and I soon caught and passed two of the climbers whose head torches, only a matter of a few hours earlier, had seemed so far above us. We were now at a height of about 27,800 feet.

Anatoli, climbing without oxygen, was beginning to feel the increase in altitude. His pace slowed. Each step I took increased the distance between us. Within what seemed like a few minutes, we moved from climbing as a pair to climbing alone. We were both comfortable with that.

The snow-covered First Step posed no real problem. By comparison, the onward traverse towards the Second Step was far more precarious. Lying at an angle of 50 degrees, the slope consisted mostly of small pieces of rock little bigger than sugar lumps. When weight was placed on either foot, the ground began to gently slip away. On my left, a jagged rock face jutted upward 30 or 40 feet. Made up of thousands of smaller pieces that were held together like a three-dimensional jigsaw, it had been shattered by the snow and ice continually melting and re-freezing over countless years. To my right, the North Face plummeted away steeply. A short distance away, the Second Step loomed menacingly. Glancing back, I could see Anatoli as a small lone figure on the vastness of the North East Ridge.

Hanging down to the base of the Second Step were ropes left by previous expeditions. Directly in front of me towered 20 feet of vertical rock that I needed to climb. Although this would not have been difficult at sea level, I needed to consider that I was at 28,200 feet, the height of K2; I was carrying a 44 lb rucksack and wearing huge down mittens. The task ahead was somewhat like trying to tune a piano while wearing a pair of boxing gloves: difficult but not impossible.

Removing my rucksack, I jammed it securely between the rock face and myself. The instructions Henry had given me two days earlier rang through my mind.

Henry Todd, aged 50, was a tall, burly and bearded Scottish gentleman who lived in Edinburgh, and leader of our expedition. He came across as an imposing character with a high level of self-confidence and a well-spoken English vocabulary to match. For some time, he'd been organising commercial expeditions that were a mixture of invited friends and climbers who paid for their place; 1995 was the first of these ventures on Everest. Henry considered the small details often overlooked by other expeditions. He went to great lengths to give his climbers a realistic chance of reaching the summit, provided they were up to the task.

'Graham,' Henry had said, 'when you get to the base of the Second Step, I want you to turn your oxygen flow to maximum. Climb the Second Step, but you must not forget to then turn your oxygen back down to the slower rate once this has been done.'

We both knew that it would be all too easy to increase the flow and then forget to adjust it back down once the Second Step had been climbed, with potentially deadly consequences. If the flow rate were left turned up, my oxygen supply would run out.

When we got back down, I would have to admit to Henry that we'd forgotten to bring up the spanner to open the lighter-weight Poisk bottles. I didn't expect much sympathy.

With the rate duly turned up, I heaved the rucksack back over my shoulders. Then I clipped my jumar and karabiner onto the rope that looked in the best condition. As insurance, I took hold of a couple of the others in my left hand, in case the first rope had been frayed by rubbing on the edge of the rock above. Pushing the front points of my crampon into a fracture line in the rock to gain purchase, I hauled myself upwards. The sharp steel tips scratched against the limestone's hard surface as my feet sought the subsequent footholds.

Within minutes, I had pulled myself up onto the small patch of angled snow that defines the mid-point of this obstacle. I had seen photographs of this place. A short distance away, an aluminium ladder was fastened into the corner. Leaning onto a rock face, it reached to all but the last few feet of the Second Step's upper section. Placed there many years ago by a Chinese expedition, it had become a permanent fixture on the mountain. As I had just dragged myself up a rope, this looked quite a luxury.

With each step, my crampons clashed against the aluminium rungs. Several old ropes, which dangled over from the top of the Second Step, were wrapped around the upper end of the ladder. As there was virtually no wind, I slid the down mitten and woollen inner glove off my right hand to unravel them. This in itself wouldn't have been a problem had I then not rested my hand on one of the rungs. My palm froze instantly to the metal. To release it as quickly as possible I pulled my hand away briskly. Left behind was a thin layer of skin as evidence of my mistake. Smiling at my avoidable blunder, I put my glove and mitten back on. Grabbing several of the ropes – about five, I think – I pulled myself off the ladder and up over the edge.

Standing upright, it took a moment for both my glasses and eyes to adjust to the light reflected off the snow. I had, without realising, been climbing in the shadow of the North East Ridge. I was now bathed in dazzling sunlight.

For me, this was the most magical point of the whole climb. Maybe it was because I'd been concentrating so intently on each step that the thought of reaching the summit of Everest hadn't properly entered my mind. At the exact moment I pulled myself up over the top of the Second Step, to be welcomed by the brightness and warmth of a new day, I knew beyond any doubt I was going to reach the summit – even though there was another 700 feet in altitude for me to climb.

I vividly recall looking up towards the remaining ground with what seemed to be tunnel vision, through my glasses and past the oxygen mask that bridged the top of my nose. The hood of my down suit blinkered my view on either side. It felt as though I was looking through a large pair of binoculars that gave no extra magnification.

Although the feeling of excitement was electric, I had an equally powerful understanding of my own insignificance on this huge mountain. I felt no bigger than a speck of dust.

Not wanting to have my thoughts swamped by the euphoric anticipation of what lay ahead, I calmly focused on the task in hand. Reaching for my regulator, I turned the dial back down to its previous rate: two and a half litres of supplementary oxygen per minute.

Next to the fixing point for the ropes that hung down over the Second Step I saw a single set of fresh footprints in the snow. They led off towards another rock mass about 300 feet away. This is often referred to as the Third Step, but it's merely a steep scramble when compared with the rock face I had just scaled. A climber from another expedition was hidden from view somewhere on this outcrop. Not higher, as there were no telltale tracks in the steep snowfield that lay above.

As I climbed up through the Third Step, my pace suddenly slowed even though the effort I was making remained constant. This was a sure sign my first bottle had run out. I stopped to make the changeover, and I plead guilty to removing the empty cylinder from my rucksack and wedging it under a rock. The temptation to lose 13 lb from my overweight rucksack was too much to resist.

Once above this section, I shadowed the deep tracks of the unknown climber up the slope. My legs sank to midway up my thighs in the soft snow. Each step required me to lift my knee to chest height, employing both arms and legs in each movement. Progress was slow and required a concerted effort. This short snowfield of less than a hundred yards took half an hour to wade through.

During my last Everest expedition, post-monsoon in 1993, I'd sat at Advanced Base Camp watching two of our team through a pair of high-powered binoculars on the limit of the available magnification. The climbers could be picked out as distant specks of colour moving agonisingly slowly on their upward traverse of this final snowfield, eventually disappearing out of view as they began the last undulating ridge that led towards the summit. Their final tortuous steps, and moment of joyous relief, were hidden from view. The line of sight, rising ever upwards and along the North East Ridge towards the summit of Everest, was approximately three miles from Advanced Base Camp. So remote were these ghostly figures set against the snow-encrusted background that I'd felt as though I was watching climbers on the moon. Now, nearly two years on, the thought that I'd swapped roles was difficult to comprehend.

Ahead of me lay that gently undulating ridge. The summit was still out of sight. Maybe from overconfidence or through having my thoughts distracted by being so close, I stumbled on the ridge. Only with the aid of some quick foot shuffling did I regain my balance. The moment I relaxed, felt safe and had become complacent, fate had tested me out.

As I approached the final stretch of the ridge, the summit came into view. I could pick out the other climber wearing a red down suit crouching at the top. With each step, I appeared to get no nearer. Although in sight, it seemed to take an eternity to reach. It was like a dream when the person being chased can never be caught, each step ponderous, heavy and almost futile. I could see my observer watching my slow progress, no doubt understanding exactly what I was going through, having just suffered the same anguish.

Through my struggle, I could hear the radio conversation ahead. Raising my head, I pulled my mask to one side and gave an exhausted smile. The waiting climber shouted into his radio, 'It's Graham.'

Before me sat George Kotov, a Russian from St Petersburg with whom I'd climbed two years earlier while attempting this same route. A slight man with thinning hair and a moustache, he was blessed with the enviable sure-footed agility of a mountain goat. George was on a different team this year.

I'd reached the summit of the world and found a friend sitting there. Life really doesn't get much better than that.

The time was 8.30 a.m. on 17 May – some six and a half hours after we'd left the top camp. I had had no sense of time or of how long the climb had taken me. My only reference points were a glance at my watch when I reached the summit and the earlier appearance of daylight.

It was with great relief that I took off my rucksack and oxygen mask. I sat in the snow next to George. He was on the radio to Jon Tinker, another acquaintance from that same climb two years ago. George handed me the radio, and I heard Jon's voice crackle through the silence: 'Congratulations, Graham. Now get down safely.'

His words brought home a reality. Getting to the top was less than half the job. Going back down did not have the overwhelming draw of the summit. In simple terms, this was an easy time to make a mistake – especially for those who'd overstretched themselves in reaching the summit without giving thought to their descent. If exhaustion started to set in, oxygen supplies could easily run out if a close eye was not kept on the time.

George and I sat savouring the moment. Much to my surprise, he pulled out a packet of cigarettes and lit one up. He revelled at the look of horror on my face. With a wry smile, he explained that on every summit he enjoyed a cigarette. Everest was going to be no exception.

I pulled a thin cotton banner from my pocket. Printed on it were the words 'Muscular Dystrophy Group' and a stylised logo of one person comforting another. Holding it taut, I asked George if he would take my picture.

My cousin, Dr John Muse, a specialist in laser technology, had died from this hereditary muscle disease six years earlier at the age of thirty-four. We had been the same age. At the time, a charitable organisation called the Muscular Dystrophy Group had given tremendous support to his parents in coping with the loss of their only child. This was our way of acknowledging their kindness.

It also transpired that George and I had each climbed with a lucky mascot. Both were in the form of a soft toy about 12 inches tall that we'd placed in our rucksacks. George's was a small teddy bear that belonged to his daughter. Mine was modelled on Barnaby, the canine cartoon character. I'd bought him from the PDSA (People's Dispensary for Sick Animals) as a way of contributing to their funds. With refreshing humour, George and I took each other's photograph. I would later send a copy of the picture of Barnaby and myself to the PDSA, to show what adventures he'd been on. They were astounded.

After 20 minutes, George packed up his equipment and headed down. I stood up and slowly turned full circle to take in my surroundings. The view of the Himalaya reflecting the morning sunlight was breathtaking. Jagged snow-capped summits rose for two vertical miles above the valley floors. The clear, windless sky bathed everything in an ethereal blue light. Chilled early-morning clouds, lying as a thick blanket many thousands of feet below, gave the impression that they bore these mountains upwards.

With my feet still firmly on the ground, I was, out of the whole of humanity, the highest on the planet. For a brief few minutes of my life, this is exactly how it felt. The warmth of the natural world lay far below me. From where I stood, the Earth's curvature was visible. The horizon was nearly 200 miles away. The snow-laden summits of the Himalayan Range that separated the Indo-Gangetic Plain from the Tibetan Plateau stretched as far as the eye could see, both east and west. My mind struggled to grasp the enormous scale of my observations.

The summit of Everest, although very real, was a momentary existence. My life, family and everything I knew lay far below. It felt as though I was on the edge of another world, a place where lethal mistakes in judgement are made. The thread that attached me to reality seemed very thin indeed, yet within me, the understanding that it was imperative I leave this magical place was very strong.

Cranking my oxygen back on, I heaved up my rucksack once more. Pulling the mask back over my mouth, I began to descend. I felt compelled to glance back, once. I needed to cast my eyes over the deserted summit. I tried to imagine what horrifically ferocious weather the pinnacle of our planet must endure in the depths of its worst storms. In the exact place where I had momentarily stood.

At the end of the undulating ridge was the beginning of the deep snowfield. Here, I came across Anatoli leaning against a rock.

'How far to summit, Graham?' he asked in his wonderful Russian accent.

'About 20 minutes,' I replied.

Removing my mask, I sat down next to him. We chatted in a relaxed manner about the weather and condition of the route. It was as though we'd bumped into each other in a cafe in Kathmandu rather than on a rock at the top of the North Face of Everest, at nearly 29,000 feet. It was so matter-of-fact and showed the level of confidence and self-reliance we each had in that situation. To me, it was a very special few minutes. It is an episode that I will not forget.

The final piece of humour between us happened moments after I had pulled on my mask and started down the deep snow slope. Facing inward, I punched my hands and feet into the snow alternately from side to side as I descended.

I heard Anatoli shout from above, 'I like the way you go down, Graham.'

I smiled without looking up and kept going.

I passed Nikolai some time later, at the top of the Second Step. We didn't speak. He raised his head and held his hand up in acknowledgement. He moved on, slowly and inexorably upwards.

As I retraced the route back down, I looked back towards the summit. I could see the weather was beginning to change. Clouds were forming and the wind was starting to pick up. Hurrying on, I reached the camp we'd left in darkness some ten hours earlier. It was now around midday. Collecting my personal equipment, I continued my descent to our next camp at 25,900 feet. Here, the expedition had a single tent, known affectionately as the 'Anatoli tent'. The Sherpas had placed it there three weeks earlier for acclimatisation runs. However, Anatoli, fully aware of the north side's reputation for wind, had decided it needed to be bulletproof. He'd fastened it down with rope, like a cargo net, to the point that it could withstand some fearsome winds.

When I was within sight of this tent, my second oxygen bottle finally ran out. Tiredness filled my whole body as my pace slowed over the last 50 yards. I was drained of energy, not only from the physical effort but also the mental concentration. I now felt a sense of release.

Surveying the route I'd descended, I could see no signs of Anatoli or Nikolai. I unpacked my sleeping bag and settled on top of it. I had no wish to move another inch. Here, I lay motionless for a good two hours, recuperating from the day's toil, and there I could have quite happily remained until the following morning. However, logic had to take control. Work needed to be done. Being first back, it was up to me to prepare for the possible arrival of Anatoli and Nikolai. Like myself, I knew they might choose not to spend the night at the top camp. Instead, they could head further down to the tent I now occupied. I went outside and collected snow to start boiling water.

It was four hours after I'd reached the tent that Nikolai arrived. He unzipped the tent and threw himself in, landing on top of me in the process. Looking at his face, I could see no expression. His eyes spoke for him, saying, 'Thank God I'm back.'

I handed him a hot drink. He sat there watching the steam rise from his lukewarm tea, the effort to sip being too much for him to contemplate. After a while, he managed to tell me, in the handful of English words he'd mastered, that Anatoli was going to spend the night at the top camp.

The weather continued to deteriorate. By late evening, the wind was blowing full force, horrendous. The flapping of the tent was so loud that it was painful to the ears. My recurring thought was, 'Thank goodness Anatoli spent so much time fastening down the tent.' However, the fact the tent was well secured didn't mean that it couldn't rip apart. As we lay there during the hours of darkness, the furiously gusting wind kept bending in the sides of the tent, distorting the structure into unnatural shapes. Despite our success in reaching the summit, things could still go terribly wrong. We were not off the mountain yet. We were under the control of Everest, Chomolungma, the Tibetan Mother Goddess of the World. I couldn't help but think of the consequences if the tent ripped apart or, worse, the fastenings came loose. Although well placed, it was only about twenty feet from the edge of a steep 5,000-ft drop to the glacier far below. If the tent failed, we would have been ill prepared and had little chance of controlling what might follow. Clambering out of my sleeping bag, I got dressed into my full climbing equipment. Once ready, I encouraged a dazed Nikolai to do the same. I don't think he was really aware of what was happening or of the potential danger we were in. Now both fully dressed, I urged Nikolai to sit alongside me. We placed our backs to the side of the tent that was being forced inwards by the fiercely gusting wind. We sat there for hours, protecting our shelter, ready to abandon it should it start to rip or, worse still, begin to move. Shortly after dawn, around 6 a.m., the wind suddenly abated. Seizing the opportunity,

I grabbed my already packed rucksack. I signalled to Nikolai that I was heading down without delay. Within moments, I was gone.

One hour later, I was on the North Col, bathed in the warmth of the morning sun: a stark contrast to the night before. Here, two other members of our expedition, Crag Jones and Michael Jörgensen, were preparing to move up for their attempt. Michael, aged 28, was from Denmark, a humorous yet quietly driven and very capable climber. Crag, aged 33, was a proud Welshman who wore his heart on his sleeve, a wonderful character with a wealth of climbing experience.

Within ten minutes of meeting Crag for the first time, back in late March of that year, I discovered he'd been at Bangor University in North Wales with my younger brother Adrian. The two of them had been good friends. Small world!

At the time I arrived back on the North Col, Crag was busy assisting Leo Dickinson with his filming. Leo, one of the world's leading adventure filmmakers, was present on Everest that year to shoot a documentary. The subject matter was British-born American Tom Whittaker. Some 16 years earlier, Tom had been involved in a serious car accident in the US. This had resulted in his right foot being amputated and left him with two badly damaged knees. Fitted with a prosthetic specially designed for climbing, he was attempting to make the first disabled ascent of Everest. For this he had joined a commercial expedition led by seasoned operator Russell Brice.

Crag, swept up by his impending stardom in Leo's footage, almost forgot why we were there. In a slightly embarrassed Welsh accent he complimented me on reaching the summit. 'Sorry, I nearly forgot, well done, mate. Congratulations.'

I explained to Crag that Anatoli had spent the night in the top camp and that Nikolai, although tired, should be on his way down from the camp above.

After abseiling over the edge of the North Col, I was back in Advanced Base Camp for breakfast. Wearing his bright-red down jacket, Henry was waiting for my arrival. His eyes let slip his feelings.

'Hey, man, well done,' were Henry's opening words. I received a crushing hug. 'Come and get some tea, Graham,' he said, leading the way to our green canvas cook tent. 'I want to hear about your climb.'

He was justifiably proud of how his climbers were performing. More were heading up. His hard work, all his careful planning, was paying off.

Our Sherpas had also come out to welcome me back. This was a dangerous game we played; they worried for our safety. With their generous smiles, they shared in my joy and relief at returning from a successful climb. Only one of them, Neema, had been to the summit before, but this had been from the other side of the mountain. The others hoped one day that they might get their turn. Such an accolade increased their chances of future employment. Each year, expeditions went out of their way to secure the services of those who had been to the top. They were paid more. The Sherpas were well aware of this fact – and of the greater risks they would need to take to earn the extra money.

Anatoli got back to Advanced Base Camp later that morning. It would be another 24 hours before an extremely tired Nikolai would arrive.

Never a Dull Moment

The next morning, with equipment packed, I said my farewells to the Sherpas and my fellow teammates. I departed from Advanced Base Camp on the 12-mile trek over the ice and moraine of the East Rongbuk Glacier. It would be the last time I would need to make this tortuous journey. Four thousand feet lower down, the relative comfort of Base Camp beckoned.

A sense of relief and renewed strength accompanied me on this journey. I felt a huge weight had been lifted, as though I didn't have a care in the world. Ambling rather than striding out, I took time to absorb the splendour of the frozen world that surrounded me. I now appreciated it as a natural wonder rather than as an obstacle to overcome.

My arrival at Base Camp came several hours later, around mid-afternoon. Here, an American expedition led by Paul Pfau was in the process of taking down its communications tent: a luxury that our team couldn't afford. Their encampment was adjacent to ours. His climbers had summited a day or two before me. They were preparing to leave for home. Seizing the opportunity, I rushed across to ask if I might make a phone call before it was finally dismantled. I would pay, of course. I hadn't spoken to my wife, Catherine, in over two months. I was eager to tell her of my success.

'No problem,' was the reply.

As the person in charge of the satellite phone tapped in my number, I got a horrible feeling I'd get the dreaded answerphone. It was a weekday and there might be no one at home.

The phone rang four or five times before I heard Catherine's faint voice: 'Hello.'

'Hi, it's Graham here,' I replied.

'Hi, how are you?' came Catherine's excited voice.

'Now listen carefully,' I said, 'I'm on a satellite phone and I can't stay on for long. I reached the summit of Everest on the morning of 17 May. I'm back in Base Camp now. I want you to book a flight on Biman Airlines and meet me at the Gauri Shankar Hotel in Kathmandu in one week's time, on Saturday, 27 May.'

'What about work?' Catherine asked.

She must have sensed how I felt about that because she paused.

'Who gives a stuff about what work thinks? This is once in a lifetime. This is not up for negotiation,' were my instant thoughts. Luckily I didn't have to spell it out.

'OK, I'll sort that out,' was the next thing Catherine said. 'I'll see you on Saturday.'

'Remember, Biman Airlines. They'll do you the best deal on a flight and will almost certainly have spare seats at short notice. Look forward to seeing you on Saturday,' were my parting words.

The gentleman in the communications tent exuded a glorious smile. These were the calls that made his position worthwhile: the pleasure of witnessing people break such unique news to their families.

Calls from satellite telephones in those days were expensive, as was the equipment. The briefest of conversations had cost me $45. It was worth every penny, and a lot more.

Henry's philosophy with regard to his climbers once they'd either summited or had decided to make no further attempt was that from then on they became little more than a drain on resources. This was not an uncaring attitude, rather a practical one. Henry was not there to hold people's hands; he found those who expected constant attention irritating. He preferred those with a degree of independence. My equipment would be taken back to Kathmandu for me when the expedition finally broke camp. Meanwhile, it was up to me to sort out my personal transport arrangements.

I rose early the next day to find the American expedition pulling down the remainder of their tents. They were preparing for an imminent departure. Pre-arranged trucks and Land Cruisers had gathered nearby. These were being loaded with several tons of equipment. Spotting an opportunity for a lift across the Tibetan Plateau into Nepal and on to Kathmandu, I approached Paul Pfau. I enquired if there might be any chance of hitching a ride. I was told to pack my things and stand by. He wasn't sure but was hopeful that there might be space. One by one, these four-wheel-drive vehicles departed. Each of their available seats was filled by an awaiting climber. Then came the call: 'OK, Graham, we can fit you in.'

All I had time for was a hurried goodbye to our Base Camp Sherpas. Eagerly I dragged my rucksack and holdall across to the nearby truck to be loaded. With a renewed liveliness, I clambered into the rear of their last Land Cruiser to begin my journey home.

Soon Base Camp began to fade into the distance. Clouds of dust were thrown up in our wake as the convoy made its way along the dirt road. Laughter, the talk of modern comforts and our recent climbs occupied the conversation.

I was fascinated to find out that amongst their number was the grandson of George Leigh Mallory of 1924 fame. He'd also been named George Mallory and had reached the summit of Everest three days before me. His family had long since moved from his grandfather's beloved England and now resided in the southern hemisphere. He'd signed up with this American expedition to enable him to tread in his grandfather's footsteps.

It was not lost on me, this bizarre situation. There I was being transported across Tibet, the landscape looking more or less the same as it did in 1924, save a few minor additions such as the dirt road. Sitting next to me was a pleasant young gentleman by the name of George Mallory. I was discussing with him the condition of the route we'd both climbed and our respective times from the top camp to the summit. The latter I found particularly amusing. George had been half an hour quicker than me. Particularly apt, I thought, given his lineage and the legendary name he bore.

Reaching the top of the Pang La Pass, we stopped to look back. The view of Everest dominated the skyline. Swathes of Himalayan summits occupied the entire length of the horizon from east to west. The land we'd travelled over was the drier, brown, mountainous landscape of Tibet. The peaks nearer Everest and the border with Nepal were heavily capped with snow.

The sound of our engine revving in a low gear and the smell of brakes filled the vehicle as we descended the steep, tortuous switchback road on the other side. Here we passed through small settlements where the white flat-roofed homes displayed numerous Buddhist prayer flags, each one about A4 in size in a single colour of red, blue, green, white or yellow. They were held high by the many long willow shoots placed above the four corners of the buildings.

A few miles further on we turned in a more southerly direction, towards Nepal. A short distance brought us to the first of several military checkpoints. Here we needed to stop in order to produce our documents containing the 60-day Chinese visas we'd been issued in advance of entering the country.

When I'd entered Tibet some six weeks earlier, this particular checkpoint had produced a couple of interesting episodes, one of which was rather amusing, but the other depended on your point of view. Our team, Henry Todd's, had arrived here mid evening back in early April. As this was either the third or fourth such outpost we'd encountered that day, we'd got used to the time-consuming bureaucracy of the officials posted here by Beijing. Each climber produced a passport when signalled to do so and was then gestured to stand to one side until beckoned back to collect it a while later. When I handed mine across, the guard opened the page bearing my details. What had otherwise been a rather stoic and expressionless face now registered interest. My passport, originally a joint one with Catherine, contained her photograph. Intrigued by the picture of an attractive 35-year-old Western woman, he used his hands to ask where she was. I explained to a slightly disappointed guard that she was not travelling with us. Undeterred, he stepped into the guardroom, where his colleagues were, and shut the door. We could hear talking and laughter emanating from the officials as they passed the photograph of my wife around. The sight of a Western woman's face and shoulders must have seemed somewhat erotic when compared to the Communist literature supplied from Beijing. Their curiosity satisfied, the guard came out, handed me my passport and signalled I could go. My fellow climbers who'd been waiting considerably longer than me muttered something about my apparent queue-jumping tactics, to which I responded, 'You should have brought a photograph of your wife.'

The second episode I was not witness to but heard about some hours later. This I luckily missed. Once there were enough of us who'd had our passports inspected to fill the first vehicle, we drove on to our overnight stop at the town of Xegar. The other four-wheel-drive would catch us up. At least that was the plan. As they stood around in the cold night air, Mozart, one of our Brazilian climbers, decided he needed the toilet. He could have walked the mere 50 yards into the pitch dark to relieve himself. Instead, he decided to urinate against the checkpoint, the only building for miles around. Unfortunately, he was spotted in the act by one of the Chinese soldiers. Not surprisingly, they took this as an insult to their importance and a demonstration of our total lack of respect. The single-storey concrete building, painted white to contrast with the brown arid landscape, carried all the weight of Beijing. The authority of its incumbents was not to be messed with. The feeble barrier barring the single-track dirt road that wound its way over this high alluvial plain was our only way through. No insult would go unpunished. If the guards chose, entry could be refused without any reason being given.

All the remaining climbers were ordered to stand outside, away from the building and their awaiting vehicle. The temperature was well below zero. Here they spent four hours shivering away in a freezing Tibetan night. Once the guards were satisfied that an appropriate punishment had been dealt out for this act, they signalled that the travellers could collect their passports and leave. Not a word was spoken.

I vividly remember Crag at breakfast the following morning, cursing away in his Welsh accent. 'Bloody Mozart, he went and pissed on the checkpoint. He could have pissed anywhere and he had to bloody go and do it there!' Mozart sat sheepishly, more than a little embarrassed at the unscheduled and rather cold delay he'd caused. Now, on our way home, the American team and I passed through this checkpoint with minimal delay.

A few miles further on, we came across a lone Chinese figure standing at the side of the road. He was dressed in combat fatigues, wearing a bright red bandana and carrying a sub-machine gun. He waved down the vehicle I was in.

'Oh, great,' was my exasperated thought.

Once this man had had a short conversation with our driver in Chinese, I was signalled to shuffle across and let the guy in. His appearance was of someone who'd watched too many Rambo movies, or others of that genre. The macho image of some as yet undiscovered hero was apparent. Of all the people in the world, I had to be sat next to some nutcase with a loaded machine gun and a bullet belt over his shoulder. There he sat, with his gun held at the ready, staring blankly forwards. There was no expression on his face, no attempt to smile or acknowledge us. He tried his utmost to portray a steely image.

It was much to my relief, as I'm sure it was to the rest of the passengers in the vehicle, that when we reached the town of Nylam our fellow traveller signalled to the driver that this was where he wanted to be dropped off.

Nylam was a place my fellow American travellers wanted to forget due to their previous experience here.

At the beginning of the expedition, the official guide appointed to us had suggested that our team stay overnight at Nylam. Unfortunately for him, I'd passed through the town in 1993. I informed Crag, who was temporarily in charge because of Henry's absence, that the place was a bit of a dump and that we'd be far better heading further on. Our guide's reluctance to comply with our wishes led us to suspect he was going to earn a good bonus by getting us to stay at one of the town's dubious-looking hotels. However, we stood our ground. Our convoy moved on. The American team, also passing through Nylam on the same day, had accepted the recommendation to stay overnight. To compound this mistake tenfold, they had actually eaten in one of the local restaurants. Sometime during the course of the night, their intestines reacted to the food they'd eaten. Frantically rushing around the hotel, they soon realised there was in fact no toilet in the establishment and, to make matters worse, the front door was locked. In total desperation, and with moments to spare, they pushed their backsides out of the windows of the upper rooms they occupied. Not a pleasant experience!

Now, on our homeward journey, my travelling companions were understandably reluctant to stop any longer than was necessary.

From here, we travelled south in a relaxed atmosphere. Our next stop was the town of Xangmu, lying on the Tibetan side of the border with Nepal. Beyond this point, our Chinese drivers and vehicles were not allowed to go.

As we arrived late in the afternoon, there was no chance of crossing into Nepal that day. With little option, we checked into the overpriced and uninviting but officially authorised Zhangmu Hotel. Positioned next to the 'China Customs', it had the appearance of a rundown office building that had been hurriedly constructed in the '70s. Its flat roof, large metal-framed windows and solid floors foretold of a cold night. However, in the hotel's singular defence, its location would enable us to make a relatively rapid departure the following morning, which in the end is what we wanted.

By the time we'd had breakfast, the Sherpas from the American expedition had already completed the arduous task of manhandling several tons of equipment. They had loaded it into Nepalese trucks for its onward journey to Kathmandu. Having spent two months away from home, they too were keen to get back to their families.

Chinese military personnel dressed in immaculate mid-green uniforms with bright-red epaulettes browsed over official paperwork. The matching green flat-topped officer hats they wore curved up at both the front and rear. Pulled tightly onto the head, they were decorated with a gold braid that ran around the circumference. The black shiny peak covered the upper part of the soldiers' faces. No eye contact was made. The display indicated that they would see to us when they were ready, and not before. Compliance with this unspoken but transparent requirement was the only way to make a quicker than average departure from the Autonomous Region of Tibet. Any objection to this wait would bring either long delays or a comprehensive baggage search. The reason: they could if they chose to.

The border itself is defined by a structure called the 'Friendship Bridge' that spans a deep gorge and fast-flowing river below. It was a relief to be leaving such a strictly controlled area.

At the opposite end of the 85 yards of roadway that sits atop of the single reinforced concrete arch lies the town of Kodari: a ramshackle group of buildings that clings precariously to the narrowest strip of land between the road and the abrupt slope of eroded shale that plummets to the river below. Facing this human habitation on the other side of the road is an alarmingly steep mountainside, scarred with the signs of previous landslides and gushing streams. Here, Nepalese passport control and our awaiting vehicles welcomed us.

With our overnight bags stowed onboard, we drove off down the 'Friendship Highway', the name given to this road's entire length from the border to Kathmandu, where we were to arrive some six hours later.

When dropping me off, my American companions generously invited me to be their guest at the 'end of expedition' evening meal in the restaurant of the Yak and Yeti Hotel. Set in large, resplendent gardens, complete with swimming pool and a quartet that played during afternoon tea, this establishment was at the upper end of the accommodation available in Kathmandu. It was a place steeped in history; the older parts of the building had been converted from what had once been a Rana palace.

I checked into the more modest Gauri Shankar Hotel, from which my team had departed less than two months earlier. At that time I had been preoccupied with high hopes and dogged determination. Now, a hot shower, a shave and clean clothes were top of my list. These simple luxuries were a stark contrast to the more basic amenities I'd endured for the intervening period.

It was when I was about to leave the Gauri Shankar to join the American team for the evening meal that I met Alison Hargreaves. Little more than a week earlier, at the age of 33, she'd completed an outstanding and largely independent ascent of the North Ridge of Everest. This she had done without the use of supplementary oxygen.

Standing about 5 ft 6 in., with shoulder-length wavy brown hair and a soft complexion, there was a quiet confidence about her: one that can only be found in those who have achieved a long-held goal. She had arrived in Tibet nearly two months earlier deliberately carrying extra body weight: fuel that would aid her with the ambitious undertaking. Now she had the appearance of a well-honed athlete in peak physical condition.

I'd seen Alison several times on the route. We had exchanged greetings as we passed each other. Although I recognised her in the hotel, I doubted the reverse was true. I had, in the last half-hour, shaved off the beard I had grown during the course of the expedition. I smiled and told her I'd just got back from the north side myself.

Maybe it was because she felt vulnerable or because she was a rising star in a sport mostly dominated by men that she felt she had to display her confidence. Her response was, 'When did you summit?'

I suspected she half hoped I would say I hadn't and go on to make some excuse, so strengthening her position. I merely answered, '17 May.'

I think the fact I left it at that and said no more surprised her slightly. Alison was in a world where people boasted of exploits, one in which she had to undertake climbs much harder than her male counterparts just to be an equal. She was naturally defensive but had no need to be. The more we spoke over the coming days, on matters not related to climbing, the more comfortable and relaxed she became.

As I stepped out of the well-lit Gauri Shankar, my eyes struggled to adjust to the lack of street lighting. The sound of beeping horns and the glare of dazzling headlights confronted me as I turned left up the short alley that led to the main road. Clouds of fumes and dust filled the beams of light from thundering trucks, cars, motorcycles and the small three-wheeled tuk-tuks that wove their way through the slow-moving throng. All this was interspersed by incredibly brave souls on bicycles.

A quick wave of an arm followed by the briefest of negotiations and my 30-rupee (35 pence) transport to the Yak and Yeti was obtained. With the skill and precision of a go-kart racer, my tuk-tuk driver wound the two-stroke machine through pedestrian-filled streets. He skimmed past people with little more than a whisker to spare. I winced each time this occurred, half expecting to hear a thud or scream of pain from some person we'd injured. It was with some relief that I paid the driver at the end of my journey: a point at which I no longer felt that any collision might somehow end up being my responsibility.

At the Yak and Yeti, I was escorted to the dining room in the older part of the hotel. Here we passed through a grand entrance hall with a broad mahogany staircase that led off to an upper balcony. Around the edges of the ceramic tiled floor, the walls were decorated with photographs of yesteryear. Images of maharajas, princes, kings and foreign dignitaries sporting their guns hung on the wall. Stretched out at their feet, in each case, were the carcasses of several magnificent Royal Bengal tigers, an animal that now typifies nature's struggle to survive. Each picture showed the same. To my shame, my countrymen had more than played their part.

In the dining room, my hosts had already gathered. Long tables had been formally laid out on three sides. Drinks were being served at a nearby bar. I gazed admiringly at the high ceilings, with their ornate cornices. These, along with the dark panelling and generous dimensions of the room, gave clues to its regal past.

Soup and main course came and went as the evening progressed. The whole place buzzed with conversations of our recent endeavours. The drinks that flowed further cemented the sense of camaraderie.

One by one my American friends stood up to give a short speech. Each thanked their colleagues for their hard-fought success, commending the virtues that individuals had brought to the team. The audience revelled in descriptions of all the planning and struggles they'd gone through to bring their expedition from an idea into reality. During these orations, there was much laughter but many ended in the speaker becoming emotional. This whole experience had, understandably, become a huge personal achievement in their lives. They were not embarrassed to shed a few tears in front of the friends with whom they'd endured so much.

One gentleman gave a heartfelt speech about a team member who'd been tragically killed only a matter of months before their departure from the US. He described how out of respect for their friend they'd brought some of his ashes, which they'd carried to the summit of Everest. Once the speaker reached this point, most of his audience were either standing next to him consoling his open grief or were crying themselves.

When the tears were in full flow, one of my American friends sitting next to me said, 'Go on, Graham, stand up and do a "John Cleese".'

If I could have carried this off without causing offence, I would have loved to oblige. The moment passed.

The grief subsided and laughter once again returned to the celebrations. I know it's not seen as 'British' to display feelings so openly, but I couldn't help but admire their genuine concern for one another while retaining their sense of humour. Paul and the rest of his team showed me genuine friendship. I felt privileged to share in their private celebration.

The Paths We Choose

It was at breakfast the next day in the Gauri Shankar that I met Alison again. Sitting with her were Cindy Whittaker and Cindy's four-year-old daughter Lizzy, a wonderfully gregarious little blonde girl who had a sparkling personality and intelligence to match. She was the sort of child who decided almost instantly whether she liked you or not. We got on like a house on fire.

Cindy had been in Nepal for several weeks. She was waiting for her husband Tom, who was attempting the North Ridge of Everest with Russell Brice's expedition.

As I eagerly awaited Catherine's arrival in the next few days, the company of Alison, Cindy and Lizzy came as a refreshing change from the all-male expedition with which I'd spent the last two months. Each morning we met up for breakfast, although we soon discovered that Lizzy was not content with merely having this at the same table. Much to the amusement of the hotel staff, Alison and Cindy, she was insistent on sitting next to me.

Socialising gathered pace as more climbers began to arrive back in Kathmandu from their respective expeditions. Apart from two Brazilians, Waldemar Niclevicz and Mozart Catao, I was the only one from our team to have returned. Aware of this, Alison invited me to join her and a few friends for an evening meal at Rum Doodles, an establishment that was a favoured gathering spot for climbers. We made arrangements to meet in the lobby of the Gauri Shankar that evening.

In the meantime, I had things to do. A regional broadsheet newspaper back in the UK, the *Newcastle Evening Chronicle*, had covered my place on the expedition. The reporter assigned to the story was Alastair Leithead. In future years, he would become a reporter for the regional BBC, then a fully fledged BBC foreign correspondent. In time, he'd cover world news such as the destructive floods in New Orleans, Robert Mugabe's exploits in Zimbabwe, the war in Iraq, and report live while accompanying British troops in Afghanistan's dangerous Helmand Province. Early in 2009, Alastair would take on the position as the BBC's correspondent for South-East Asia.

With Catherine due soon, I was planning to stay in Nepal for the next two weeks. Alastair would want to go to print well before my return home. He would need photographs. To overcome this last problem, I decided to have my summit photographs developed in Kathmandu, copies of which I'd have couriered back to him.

I nervously entrusted the films to the most respectable-looking establishment I could find. These were the only shots I had. If lost or damaged, they couldn't be replaced. I pleaded with the shop owner to take extra care, exaggerating their importance. I was assured they would be perfectly safe and ready for collection the next day.

At the appointed time of 7.30 p.m., I was standing with a small group in the hotel lobby. Alison came skipping down the stairs. Wearing a white-buttoned top and flouncy white skirt, she looked as though she was dressed suitably for a birthday party: probably a rebellion from the unfashionable climbing equipment that she'd worn over the last two months. This was an opportunity for her to dress up and display her femininity. She looked happy and relaxed.

Rum Doodles, a short walk from the hotel, was where 15 of us gathered. Once the barman realised we were recently back from Everest, all summiteers were requested to sign one of the large boards displayed behind the bar. They bore the names of legends; those of Edmund Hillary and Reinhold Messner were easily spotted. Hundreds of signatures of climbers both alive and deceased adorned this Everest archive. Half the fun was to try to pick out who else had stood in the same place over decades of climbing. Alison, given the magnitude of her recent ascent, was asked to go first: a signing that was accompanied by rapturous applause.

I sat next to Alison during the meal. Our conversation covered many topics but quite naturally moved to her planned climb of K2 in Pakistan, where she would be heading in a few weeks' time. She informed me that she was going back to the UK for 12 days before flying out to Karachi. Curious as to why she was not flying directly from Nepal, I asked her why she was returning home first. Alison looked at me, not quite sure what to say. Her eyes filled with tears. With great decorum she got up and quietly left the table. She did not want me to see her upset.

While she was away, someone nearby explained to me that Alison was trying to find a way to leave her husband. He was at home looking after their two children. She was going back to the UK principally to move out of the family's temporary accommodation. Alison had found herself and the children a new home; matters were complicated.

Her tears brought with them a stark reminder that those on expeditions to these remote locations had private lives that had been momentarily interrupted. Alas, such personal matters as Alison now faced had only been delayed from their inevitable conclusion. The escape from them had at best been temporary.

I felt terrible for causing her distress, but I'd had no idea of the circumstances. When Alison returned a short while later, we resumed our conversation but on a different subject. The redness of her eyes soon disappeared into laughter as the evening wore on.

The next morning, I met Alison in the hotel lobby. Her climbing equipment was piled up in the reception area in readiness for her departure. She looked uneasy. Whether it was her trip back to the UK or the onward journey to K2 that was the cause, I couldn't tell. Saying my farewell to Alison, I wished her luck on K2 and told her to keep herself safe.

Alison was to reach the summit of K2 on 13 August 1995 and die the same day. It was three months exactly from her ascent of Everest on 13 May. She was blown off the mountain by hurricane-force winds while making her descent. This I would hear of over the radio as my family and I were driving home from a visit to the south of England. I remember being shocked into disbelief by this tragic news.

I would, in time, discover the sequence of events that had led to her death. She had joined an American expedition, led by Rob Slater, for her attempt on K2. After several weeks of bad weather, which had thwarted them getting to the top of the mountain, half the team packed up and went home. Alison too was coming to the same conclusion and had arranged porters for her imminent departure. She had gathered up her equipment in readiness to leave. However, some 15 minutes before she was due to depart she changed her mind. There seemed to be a glimmer of hope that the weather might be improving. Teaming up with two New Zealand and two Canadian climbers, Alison and Rob Slater decided to give it one last-ditch attempt. Amongst the group was Peter Hillary, son of the late Sir Edmund Hillary.

On 13 August, they left the top camp for the 12-hour climb to the summit. It was mid morning that they approached a steep chute known as the Bottleneck: considered to be something of a point of no return, it involves an exposed ice traverse. Here they met a team of Spanish climbers who were also heading up. According to Peter Hillary, in an article entitled 'The Last Ascent of Alison Hargreaves' by Greg Child for *Outside* magazine, it was at this juncture that the weather, which had been reasonable for the past four days, started to change: 'Big altostratus clouds were moving in, and a strong wind was blowing snow. I saw everyone crossing the traverse. Then they disappeared in clouds.'

Concerned that a storm was approaching, Hillary and another climber Kim Logan turned back. Both survived unscathed. Alison and the other climbers continued up.

Her ascent of K2 was part of a well-publicised project to climb the world's three highest mountains, Everest, K2 and Kangchenjunga, all without the use of supplementary oxygen. Alison had started to make her living as a climber. Such an achievement would catapult her into the higher echelons of the sport and secure her position as the world's best female mountaineer; it would give her the recognition from the wider climbing community that she felt had been a long time coming. This in turn would bring her valuable sponsorship and hopefully a degree of financial security that might help resolve more personal issues.

The problem was that mixed up with this was her marriage to a man who was emotionally and physically abusive. She appeared to struggle with his stronger personality; he sought to control her career. Alison seemed to lack self-esteem and kept talking to others about trying to break free from the bondage of this unhappy union; although closer, she was yet to take that last determined step. The problem deepened as she tried to work out how she could bring up her two children and continue with a climbing career without her husband. In climbing, she found the control she did not have in her personal life. She was under both professional and emotional pressure.

On K2, Alison was losing that control. In desperation, she was letting outside worries influence her crucial decisions. The correct choice would have been to turn back, but this brought other pressures. She must have known from her experience she was taking an incredible risk; in light of K2's savage reputation, no significant deterioration in the weather could be ignored. But Alison was trying to climb free of the personal problems she faced.

As the sun began to set on 13 August 1995, Alison reached the summit of K2 at 6.45 p.m. The conditions at the top were reported to be good during the radio calls that were made. Within an hour, winds well in excess of 100 mph struck the upper reaches of the mountain. The descending climbers did not stand a chance. Six people, including Alison, died on K2 that night. A seventh, Canadian Jeff Lakes, was to die of exhaustion the following night after an epic descent. He had turned around before the top. It would be described as the worst season in K2's history.

Several miles away, on the neighbouring 26,000-ft Broad Peak, Seattle-based climber Scott Fischer had watched the events unfold. In an article that appeared in *Outside Online*, he said: 'When we were coming off of Broad Peak, the winds were brutal, and the difference between Broad Peak and K2 is about 3,000 feet. That was the difference between life and death.'

Although K2 is actually only 1,837 feet higher than Broad Peak, the figure Scott gave is the exact differential that separates the summit of Everest and the South Col on the southern route of the world's highest mountain. His words would hold significance for the following year.

Ultimately, the dangers of climbing are controlled very much by the vagaries of the sport: the overwhelming consequences of nature extracting the ultimate price from an unwary participant caught out in the open. Even for those acting with circumspection, there are no guarantees of safety. There is a fine line separating what we perceive as failure and success, between which life and death is sometimes decided. Failure to reach one's goal does not lead to death, or the success in doing so to life; the two are often reversed by the unwise forging ahead.

The last sight I had of Alison was of her waving from the hotel minibus as she departed for Kathmandu airport that morning. Her smile was full of hope.

Catherine was scheduled to arrive at 5 p.m. the following afternoon. I hadn't seen her for over two months. I wanted to get as much of my work out of the way as I could before she landed; my summit photographs were top of the list.

On my arrival at his shop, the proprietor presented the package to me with due reverence to indicate the care with which he'd handled my precious images. With great anticipation, I opened the small folder. The pictures had good definition and colour but were not quite what I'd expected. Yet I couldn't actually say why. The gentleman looked at me to observe my satisfaction but soon picked up that I wasn't, for some reason, showing the appropriate positive and grateful response. Much to his dismay, I informed him there was something wrong with his work. Affronted by this slur, he quickly defended his position, telling me he'd done exactly as instructed. At that moment, while holding one of my summit photographs, I glanced up at the wall behind him. Like many shops in the tourist area of Kathmandu, he sold panoramic posters with views from the summit of Everest. I held up my photograph so I could observe it and the poster at the same time. A smile of understanding spread across my face. I asked the shopkeeper if he could explain to me why, according to his poster, Makalu, the fifth-highest mountain in the world was to the right of Everest, while in my photograph, taken from the same position, it appeared on the left. There was a perplexed silence from the gentleman.

I explained, 'I think you might have put the negatives the wrong way up in your machine.'

A rather embarrassed owner asked if I could come back in a couple of hours, by which time he would have rectified the problem.

My next task was to call Alastair Leithead, primarily to let him know I'd summited. I also had to inform him that some photographs were being sent by courier that afternoon. Catherine and my family had been sworn to secrecy; he had not yet been told. We wanted the news to come out properly, once everything was ready, in order to promote the Muscular Dystrophy Group we were supporting. I telephoned him from the reception desk of the Gauri Shankar.

'Hi, Alastair, it's Graham. I'm back in Kathmandu,' was my opening remark.

'How did you get on?' he asked.

'I topped out,' I replied.

'What, you've dropped out?' was his muffled query.

I realised I needed to choose my words more carefully on this far from perfect phone line. 'No, I topped out. I reached the summit at 8.30 a.m. on 17 May. I'm sending a few summit shots by courier this afternoon. You should hold the story until you get them.'

A few pleasantries and Alastair was gone.

I now learnt a valuable lesson about journalists. Asking them to hold back a story until they got the corresponding photographs when they already had enough information to go to print was a waste of time, especially if they thought that another publication might beat them to the story.

Alastair wrote the article probably as soon as I'd put the phone down. However, he did us proud. The story occupied the full front cover of our regional broadsheet newspaper; inset was a picture of Everest, but not mine. We'd even reached the heady heights of the newspaper billboards. More importantly he'd not forgotten to make a sizeable reference to the Muscular Dystrophy Group.

It turned out, in the intervening time, that Catherine's week had been almost as eventful as mine.

After my satellite telephone call, she'd been granted time off work, not by requesting it but by informing her employer that, unbeknown to her, I'd booked flights for her to join me in Nepal. Consequently she was forced into taking unpaid leave, a supposed reluctant traveller.

Her next stop had been the local travel agent. However, during my phone call from the Tibetan Plateau to north-east England she'd misheard my instructions. She told the lady sitting behind the desk that she wished to book flights to Nepal on Demon Airlines rather than Biman Airlines as I'd indicated. I can picture the look of bewilderment that must have appeared on the travel agent's face. With a great deal of laughter, the confusion was overcome.

Catherine had arrived at Heathrow Airport at the allotted time only to be told there would be a short unscheduled detour via Paris. It would just cause a slight delay. What had surprised Catherine was how few people actually boarded the plane at Heathrow: barely 50 or so. She assumed the flight to Paris was to pick up more travellers for the onward journey.

As they sat on the tarmac at Charles de Gaulle Airport, she could hear the cargo hold being loaded. However, what perplexed her was that only two or three extra people joined the aircraft. The pilot's voice came across the public-address system requesting all passengers move to the seats in the rear of the plane. He explained that Biman's other aircraft, which flew out of Heathrow, was stranded in Bangladesh. They had been instructed to fly out a spare engine. This had now been loaded. Having all the passengers seated at the rear of the aircraft would assist greatly with take off.

Catherine arrived at Kathmandu airport on time. We met with a huge embrace. A sometimes-fiery redhead, 5 ft ¼ in. tall – she was proud of the extra quarter inch – she was a foot shorter in height than me. We'd been married for more than eighteen years and had two teenage daughters, Angela and Amy, aged seventeen and fourteen respectively. Apart from running the family home, professionally Catherine cared for the elderly: demanding work that she found rewarding. She often regaled the family with stories of incredible journeys that some of these older men and women had undertaken in their youth. The adventures of our generation paled in comparison.

We both relished the outdoor life and often went walking in the hills together at home. For Catherine, the higher mountains held no attraction. The effort to reach these lofty summits seemed to require all too much energy and misery for her liking. She was quite happy for me to undergo that by myself.

For more than two months, since we'd last seen each other, we'd led completely different lives – each responsible for everything that happened within them. Although excited about seeing each other, we were aware that there would be a period of adjustment. Each would have to relinquish some of the recently acquired responsibilities. Nearly every person who goes away on long expeditions finds it difficult to settle back into normal everyday life. This takes quite some time and the process can often remain incomplete. Simmering away in the background is usually the urge to seek further adventure.

As our taxi drove through the dusty streets, Catherine couldn't stop laughing. With tears rolling down her cheeks, she recounted the epic saga from our satellite phone call to her eventual arrival in Kathmandu. Her smile was what I had missed.

Catherine and I left Kathmandu and flew down to the Terai, the lowland area of southern Nepal where the Royal Chitwan National Park is located. For five days, we swapped the dust and fumes of the capital for the unbearable humidity of the period leading up to the monsoon.

By the time we returned, most climbers were back from Everest. The party atmosphere was accentuated by the mounds of expedition equipment that now occupied every square inch of available space in the Gauri Shankar.

We received a rapturous welcome from Lizzy, but her mood contrasted with that of her father, Tom Whittaker. He had come back bitterly disappointed. Russell Brice, who'd been climbing with him, had turned him around on their summit attempt. Although they'd reached the Second Step, at over 28,000 feet Russell had decided if they didn't turn around there might not be enough time to make a safe descent before nightfall. Tom had initially been against retreating. Only after Russell stood his ground in the ensuing argument did Tom concede. Such difficult decisions always leave 'what ifs' hanging in the air. In the final analysis, the right choice in these situations has to be the safe one. For those with determination, the mountain will be there another year.

Now, several days later, Tom was back in Kathmandu. The disappointment hadn't subsided. His talk was of organising his own expedition from Nepal to attempt the South East Ridge in a year or two. He'd started to make enquiries.

Anatoli and Nikolai had also returned. As Anatoli was working for Henry, he had needed to wait until the last of our team's summit attempts had taken place. Only then could he leave Tibet.

Both Russians had checked into the Gauri Shankar. Anatoli subsequently moved to a different hotel after one night. Not because he wanted to be away from us but because the alternative was less than half the price. Ours was $10 per night and his new accommodation $4. Even though Anatoli had earned good money from the last two months' work, he'd no indication of the next employment he would find. His Soviet background had taught him that the US dollar was a valuable asset that was hard to come by. He was not about to spend the money he'd earned on something that cost more than twice as much but ultimately provided the same facility: a bed.

The recent break-up of the USSR worried Anatoli. The rush in certain quarters to earn personal wealth without any regard for others was of particular concern. He openly said he preferred the order that had been abandoned, where at least the elderly had been looked after rather than being cast aside by others' greed. It was not that he had objections to a free-market economy – one that he'd recently entered into. Rather, he disliked the avarice and criminality the former Soviet Union was now witnessing, with the accompanying rise in Mafia-style businesses.

Anatoli had been honoured as one of the USSR's Masters of Sport, for which he'd been presented with a bright-red cloak bearing the insignia of the hammer and sickle with star above. He'd brought this garment with him on our expedition, one that might shelter him from the icy Tibetan wind. Inner strength, humility and principles were an important part of who he was.

Catherine and I joined Anatoli and Nikolai each morning for breakfast in a restaurant only five minutes' walk from our respective hotels. This new venue had a garden area overlooked by a balustraded veranda that caught the warmth of the morning sun. Here, over a leisurely meal, taking an hour or more, we'd sit and discuss all manner of topics. Every now and again Anatoli halted the conversation to explain, in Russian, to Nikolai those parts he'd been unable to follow.

Anatoli spoke with passion about his home city of Alma-Ata in Kazakhstan. He asked if we might come to visit him there, with a view to going climbing. He was aware that I had visited his country before. As is often the case, having recently finished one expedition we were immediately starting to plan the next adventure. Such is the addictive nature of the sport.

One morning, after a leisurely breakfast, Catherine and I returned to find a light-blue VW Beetle parked near the hotel entrance. Sitting in the reception area talking to Henry was American expatriate Elizabeth Hawley.

Liz had arrived in Nepal in September 1960 at the age of 36, as a reporter for *Time*. Initially here to send back political dispatches from the Kingdom, she had never left, once describing herself as 'a refugee from the Manhattan rat race'. Realising the potential of Himalayan climbing, which was in a golden era, Liz began reporting for Reuters. It wasn't long before she became recognised as the unofficial chronicler of Himalayan expeditions. Although she has never climbed a single mountain herself, Liz has meticulously recorded the details of every expedition ever since. She rapidly earned a reputation for rigorous interviewing, mercilessly weeding out those who made false claims. Standing about 5 ft tall, wearing dark-rimmed glasses and with permed hair, she was a lady who could make mountaineers more than twice her size and less than half her age squirm uncomfortably if they weren't telling the truth. For those who were, Elizabeth Hawley was an absolute delight.

'Graham, could you join us for a moment?' asked Henry.

Sitting down beside them, I was introduced to Elizabeth Hawley for the first time. I'd not met her when I'd been here in 1993.

Henry had been discussing with Liz the climbers from his team that had summited from the north side that spring. They'd been about to start on the day Anatoli, Nikolai and I had made our attempt when I'd walked through the door.

'On 17 May, Graham, Anatoli and Nikolai reached the top,' Henry continued.

Liz at this point was writing the details down. Well aware of Anatoli's reputation as a strong and fast climber, she replied, 'Anatoli got there first. Who was second?'

'Graham got to the top first, Anatoli was second, then Nikolai,' was Henry's correction.

Liz lifted her head slightly and looked over the top of her glasses at Henry. Then she turned and focused on me for my reaction.

'I got to the summit about an hour before Anatoli' – her stare had required a response.

Feeling almost embarrassed about this fact, I blurted out what felt like an excuse, 'I was using oxygen, Anatoli was not.'

Liz continued to look at me for a moment, made a slight noise that indicated her surprise and then continued to make her notes.

'Graham was first, then Anatoli, followed by Nikolai,' she repeated back.

Once Liz had collected the remaining information she needed with regard to the other ascents from our team, she stood up and thanked us for our time.

This was the busiest period for her as teams began to arrive back in Kathmandu. Her difficulty was she had to catch them all before they departed the country; otherwise, her undertaking became far more problematic.

Within a matter of days, the time came for Catherine and me to fly home. Leaving the Gauri Shankar at 5.30 a.m., we were driven in the hotel minibus along deserted streets. Numerous dogs slept by the roadside. Cows grazed on piles of rubbish that steamed in the cool morning air. It was a stark contrast to the daytime chaos.

Once through airport security and check-in, we made our way via passport control to the departure lounge. It was while seated here that we heard a scream of delight from across the expanse of the seating area. Lizzy had spotted us. About 30 feet behind her was Tom. On witnessing her joy, his face mellowed with a smile. From that moment on, we became good friends. He was starting to recover from his recent disappointment. Tom would go on to organise his own expedition in 1998, achieving his goal, to great international acclaim, of making the first disabled ascent of Everest.

Of the other climbers on our expedition in 1995, there was a notable ascent by Crag Jones and Michael Jörgensen. On reaching the summit, they made the first Welsh and Danish ascents of Everest respectively. What made their achievement all the more remarkable was that they had done this after being pinned down by very strong winds for three days at the top camp, 27,200 feet. The two Brazilians, Mozart Catao and Waldemar Niclevicz, also summited, as did Polish climber Ryszard Pawlowski.

Eight out of our eleven-strong team reached the summit and there were no injuries. Prior to 1995, little more than 50 climbers had reached the summit of Everest via the North Ridge route in its entire history. This made our expedition one of the most successful to date.

I flew out of Nepal with Catherine in 1995 delighted and very grateful for both my success and safe return. My mind was focused on scuba diving, a beach and a cold beer. I'd finished my Everest adventure (or so I thought) – one that would stay with me for the rest of my life.

Tyneside to Argentina

It was late summer 1995, a few months after my return from Everest. The location was my home on Tyneside in north-east England.

I could hear a faint ringing in my head. A few seconds passed before my eyes sprang open. It was not in my dreams. The sound was coming from the telephone downstairs. I glanced at the clock. The display read five in the morning.

'Who the hell would be calling at this time?' was my first thought.

I leapt out of bed. Unsure as to how long the phone had been ringing, I held on to the banister and bounded down the stairs five steps at a time. My fear was that something terrible had befallen a family member. Catching my breath, I picked up the phone. 'Hello?' I said in a quizzical, wary voice.

'Hi, Graham,' came the reply, 'it's Torgeir here. Two of my friends and I are going to Argentina in late December to climb Aconcagua via the Polish Glacier. I was wondering if you would like to join us?'

Up to this point, all I had uttered was the word 'hello'. My eyes were open, but the brain was lagging behind. It struggled to formulate thoughts as to what I had just heard. However, my sense of relief was palpable as I heard Torgeir spout forth his invitation. The fear of receiving some devastating news disappeared as quickly as it had come. To this day, this has to be the most unusual early-morning phone call I have ever received. It is undeniably the one with the best opening gambit.

Torgeir, aged 30, was a sports officer in the Norwegian Air Force. I'd spent a month with him in the Tien Shan Mountains on the Kazakhstan–China border back in 1992. A year later, I'd visited him in northern Norway to go climbing. We got on extremely well. Even at five o'clock in the morning, this was an easy decision to make.

'Yes, I'd love to go,' I replied with hardly a thought.

The commitment I was making was based on the fact I would like to go rather than a considered decision. Often choices were made on the spur of the moment; only later did I work out how to make them happen.

There I was sitting in my pyjama bottoms answering an unexpected phone call at an unearthly hour. The next thing I knew I had agreed to go to Argentina over Christmas and New Year. The whole event had taken me by surprise.

We spoke for a while about the dates, agreeing to meet up in Santiago, the capital of Chile. From there we would travel by bus into the Andes and over the border into Argentina. The arrangements were being made so quickly that it was more akin to two young boys planning a harebrained adventure in their secret den.

We concluded our conversation by me telling Torgeir I'd phone him back at a later date, once I'd booked my flights. On that note, I went back to bed.

As I slipped back under the covers, Catherine asked in a sleepy voice, 'Who was that on the phone?'

'It was Torgeir,' I replied. 'I won't be here for Christmas or New Year. I'm going to Argentina.'

My tone could not have been more matter-of-fact. I was hoping to avoid her justifiable wrath. There was a stony silence – a very long one. Oops! Maybe I should have at least checked with Catherine first before making such a promise. Having made the commitment, I didn't want to go back on my word. In fairness, Catherine was very good about it. She didn't give me a hard time for my selfishness and total lack of thought – one that I deserved.

Autumn came and went. Time slipped by, easing past our 19th wedding anniversary in late November. The days on the calendar moved ever closer to my next adventure. I busied myself by laying out my expedition equipment in the front room of our house. Decisions had to be made on what I should take with me and what should be left behind. Weight was the deciding factor. In Argentina, we would not enjoy the luxury of having Sherpas. This time, we'd have to carry everything on our own.

I began thumbing through photographs of the route we intended to climb. The plan was to approach Aconcagua via the Vacas Valley. This more picturesque and quieter side of the mountain was away from the 'normal' route. The earth-brown landscapes reminded me of Tibet. The thought of visiting a country I had not been to before added to my anticipation. The sense was of the unknown lying ahead. I could hardly wait to get there.

Meanwhile, Catherine had begun to gather together the required ingredients for the family Christmas. The sight of her starting to wrap the children's presents made me feel uncomfortable. I'd never missed Christmas before. The pangs of guilt had me doubting that I'd made the right decision in saying that I would go. However, by this time flights were already booked, climbing insurance sorted and arrangements made. It was with some regret that I waved goodbye to Catherine and my two daughters when I left for South America.

Late December 1995, some 40 hours after I'd left the UK, the plane touched down in Santiago. Here, as arranged, Torgeir and his two Norwegian friends met me.

From Santiago, the four-hour bus journey took us via the spectacularly wild Trans-Andean Highway over the border into Argentina. Our destination was Puente del Inca, a small settlement that consisted of a few buildings sparsely spread out along the barren roadside. Our simple timber-framed accommodation was clean but basic. Nearby stood the office from where we would obtain our climbing permits the next day. Adjacent was the Parque Provincial Aconcagua.

We spent two days acclimatising, scrambling up the lower peaks that rise on either side of this strip of black tarmac: a road that tortuously winds its way through what is an otherwise rugged and occasionally snow-capped landscape. It is a safe passage through this hostile environment that in Argentina is referred to as Ruta Nacional No. 7.

It was while I was alone during one of these acclimatisation days that my mind began to wander. Clear of normal everyday trivia, the mental images I had were of summit day on Everest several months earlier. As though wafted in by the fresh mountain breeze or inspired by the warm Andean rock, my next thought came out of the blue. No British climber had reached the summit of Everest from both Nepal and Tibet. In fact, no British climber had reached the summit twice. I could, if I went to Nepal this coming spring, be the first.

This was just too tempting. I couldn't ask Catherine because she wasn't with me, therefore I couldn't be blamed. The plan was near perfect in every respect, except for a few small details. First, such an expedition would leave from the UK in about ten weeks and I wasn't on one. Second, I was in Argentina and wasn't due to return home for another four weeks. Third, I had to think of some way of getting the money together to go on such an adventure. The permit fee alone, charged by the Nepalese Government, was $10,000 for each climber. In all, this was really just a list of minor points. It was decided. I had to go.

I said nothing about my plans to my Norwegian friends. Although I knew I intended to return to Everest in a matter of weeks, I needed to make it happen. Speaking too soon was tempting fate.

On Aconcagua, we reached a little over 19,700 feet before atrocious weather descended onto the upper part of the mountain. We had no option but to retreat. Other expeditions on the mountain in January of that year suffered a similar fate. The weather closed in solidly for a three-week period. Thwarted by these continuing unsettled conditions, our climb was unsuccessful. Our planned time there had run its course. We packed up and headed out.

Leaving Base Camp at midday, I strode out ahead of my friends. I was a man on a mission. My thoughts were of Everest and the preciously short time I had left to make arrangements. I just kept on walking, following the well-established but sometimes precarious path that traces the river along the valley floor. From Base Camp I walked clean out of the Vacas Valley that afternoon.

At the valley's northern entrance to the park, I managed to hitch a lift. When asked where I was going, my reply was simple: 'The nearest hotel.' The local driver obliged by dropping me off at the first reasonable-looking place we came across. This six-storey modern concrete building was in a different league from the accommodation we had first occupied on our arrival at Puente del Inca. By nine o'clock that evening, I was showered and sipping a cold beer at the virtually deserted but quite luxurious hotel bar. I remember sitting there thinking my calf muscles felt as though they'd done some work, so I rewarded myself with another beer. On reflection, I suppose I'd walked around 30 miles out of the valley in little more than an afternoon. Probably best described as 'driving ambition'.

I arrived back on Tyneside on 23 January 1996. The overriding feeling was that the clock was ticking. There was no time to waste.

The enthusiasm with which I explained my plan to Catherine demonstrated the passion, the commitment, I was giving to this endeavour. She knew only too well that trying to talk me out of this would have been tantamount to cruelty. As she put it, 'It would be like caging a wild animal, asking you not to go.'

Her agreement came with the understanding that I made sure there was enough money in the bank to keep the family afloat while I was away. Our fragile family income was made up of several sources. Catherine had her part-time job working in care for the elderly and we had a modest rental income from two floors of a commercial property we owned. I was in the process of converting other parts of this building to try to increase the return we saw for our investment. We always seemed to have a plan for other ventures that might boost our income in the coming year, one that would lift us out of the typical financial rut in which the family seemed to scrape along. In truth, I could afford the time to go climbing, but to any sane person with a growing family to maintain it was unaffordable. Only determination and a huge dose of over-optimism made it happen. With Catherine's agreement came her dark sense of humour, one that manifested itself more as an instruction than a request: 'Mind, I don't want bits of you coming back. It's all or nothing!'

I knew Henry was planning an expedition on the Nepalese side of Everest that spring. He was my best, if not only, chance of making this happen at such short notice. Fortunately, Henry lived not much more than a hundred miles north of me. So within two days of getting home I found myself driving the short distance between Newcastle and Edinburgh in the knowledge that the next few hours would decide if my hurried departure from Argentina/Chile, all the plans I'd made, would mean anything. The difference between dreams and reality hung in the balance. I tried not to think about possible disappointment as I drove north. The final decision was out of my hands.

Sitting with Henry over a coffee, I explained my plans, hopeful but not sure whether he could, or more importantly would, make this happen. There was precious little time left before his own departure to Nepal. A more positive, accommodating and helpful response I could not have asked for. We hadn't even finished our coffee and the deal was done. I was going back to Everest.

In the six weeks before I needed to be in Nepal, there was a considerable amount to be organised: flights to be booked, insurances to be arranged, my equipment to be sorted. Pieces that were worn out or missing had to be replaced. Then there was the mammoth task of washing and cleaning all the equipment that had just been halfway around the world. This left one last small detail. How would my place on the expedition be paid for?

There was no cash left in the bank. My recent trips to Everest and Aconcagua had put paid to that. Looking around, the only obvious way to raise sufficient money quickly enough was to sell our one-year-old family car. I placed a 'for sale' advert in the local newspaper. A week later, a rundown replacement vehicle worthy of being owned by an impoverished college student stood in our driveway.

Arrangements needed to be made for me being away for 'yet another three months'. Mundane matters took on a much greater significance. I had to make sure everything was in place, that bills would be paid. Very generously, my younger brother Adrian and his wife Carolyn stepped in to fill the financial void. They lent me their entire, and not inconsiderable, family savings. It was a vote of confidence that said I would be coming back. The alternative was to return from an expedition to find an unholy state of affairs that would take months to put right.

When preparing for a longer expedition, I usually find this the most hectic and stressful time. This is probably true for Catherine as well. Relief can be found when I'm on the aeroplane and there is no more that I can do; for Catherine, it's when I've finally gone and she can find some peace.

High Rollers

While I'd been making my last-minute and rather hurried arrangements to return to Everest, other expeditions which would also be making an attempt from Nepal that spring had already been in the planning for a considerable time.

Three were to be crucial. One was the MacGillivray Freeman Imax/Iwerks expedition, there to shoot an ambitious movie using their 'Image MAXimum' technology to film the most dramatic vistas on offer. The other two were guided expeditions run by the highly respected mountaineers Rob Hall (New Zealand) and Scott Fischer (United States). Their companies were called Adventure Consultants and Mountain Madness respectively.

I was already aware that Rob Hall would be bringing a team to the mountain that spring, and Henry had told me Anatoli was going to be working for a company run by Scott Fischer. But as far as the Imax team was concerned, I would only find out about their attempt once I got to Base Camp.

The MacGillivray Freeman Imax/Iwerks expedition, or the Imax expedition as those on the mountain would refer it to that spring, was there to make a large-format documentary film. This was to be about the placing of a global positioning system and weather station on the South Col of Mount Everest by an international team of climbers. If conditions allowed, they would then try to summit and bring back footage from the roof of the world using the same sizeable IMAX camera. They'd originally hoped to carry out the filming in the spring season of 1995 but had delayed this by one year until 1996 in order to finish pulling together the $7 million budget.

The Imax expedition was to be led by 40-year-old American David Breashears from Boston, Massachusetts. David was no stranger to Everest; he'd broadcast the first live television pictures from the summit in 1983. On reaching the top again in 1985, he became the first American to summit the mountain twice. As a young man, he'd first sprung to the attention of the climbing fraternity for his technical free-climbing on some of Colorado's difficult rock walls. Soon he was combining his love of climbing and adventure with that of cinematography, working in many remote locations around the globe. His undoubted ability soon caught the attention of others, and this led to him working on such feature films as *Cliffhanger* (1993) starring Sylvester Stallone, and the Public Broadcasting Service Frontline documentary *Red Flag Over Tibet* (1994), which received awards for its excellence.

Joining David would be 36-year-old American Ed Viesturs from Seattle, who was highly regarded as one of America's top altitude climbers. He'd worked as a professional guide for Rob Hall's Adventure Consultants in the spring of 1994 and 1995. On the 1995 expedition, Ed had been amongst those on Rob's team near the summit whose transmissions we'd overheard. At the time, we'd been relaxing at Base Camp on the Tibetan side of Everest. We had listened to their frustration with the deep snow and precarious-looking cornices they'd encountered, until finally they'd abandoned their attempt.

Ed had originally qualified as a doctor in veterinary medicine from Washington State University in 1987. It was while studying here that he was drawn to the nearby Mount Rainier: a mountain that he'd both climbed and guided more than 150 times before he'd completed his degree. After graduating, he practised for two years in clinics operated by friends. However, he found it progressively difficult to balance the long spells on expedition climbing with the commitment to work. Eventually, a choice had to be made. Ed chose climbing. He reached the top of his first 26,000-ft (8,000m) mountain, Kangchenjunga, in 1989. A few years later, in 1992, he'd climbed K2 with Scott Fischer. Now, having sufficient experience, he became an International Mountain Guide, seeking sponsorship to enable him to pursue mountaineering full-time. By 1996, he was well under way with his goal to be the first American to summit the 14 highest mountains in the world, which tower more than 26,000 feet above sea level. He'd climbed nine out of the fourteen. To add further difficulty, he intended to climb them all without supplementary oxygen. He would go on to fulfil his ambition in the spring of 2005 with the ascent of Annapurna.

Also on the Imax team was 30-year-old Jamling Tenzing Norgay from Darjeeling, the son of Tenzing Norgay, who'd made the first ascent of Everest with Edmund Hillary. Owner of Tenzing Norgay Adventures, a travel company started by his late parents, he was there to follow in his father's footsteps.

Rob Hall ran a guided expedition to Everest and had done so for several years: a period during which he'd achieved a reputation of running a slick and rather successful operation. In consequence, he had attracted a number of clients from the US. The price of $35,000, initially charged in 1992, had risen somewhat because of these results. Adventure Consultants could now charge up to $65,000 for a place on one of its trips.

This high-dollar guiding on Everest had caught the attention of Scott Fischer, who ran a company called Mountain Madness out of Seattle. Scott had decided he wanted to try to break into this lucrative market; 1996 was going to be his first year. No doubt he considered that if successful he could capture much of the future business as, unlike Rob, he lived in the US, which is where most of their customers appeared to reside. This might give him home advantage.

With this now competitive market, their eyes were firmly set on the future. Both Rob and Scott realised that a favourable press in the US, reporting on their respective operations this current year, could well be the key to securing clients for subsequent expeditions.

Through a twist of fate, both Rob and Scott would end up offering their own separate deals to *Outside* magazine: a publication that was considering sending Jon Krakauer to Everest that spring. He would be there to write a first-hand article about the mushrooming commercialisation of the mountain and the attendant controversies.

Jon had first been asked by *Outside* magazine to report from the Tibetan side, in the spring of 1995. Although initially agreeing, he pulled out at the last minute, as they were only prepared to cover the cost of a trip to Base Camp, not his place on an expedition to climb Everest. They would see what could be arranged for the following year. In 1996, by all accounts Jon had initially been pencilled in to go with Scott's team, after *Outside* had managed to secure a substantial discount. However, the magazine then struck a late deal with Rob Hall whereby they only had to cover Jon's part of the permit and his flight to Nepal. For a much-reduced fee of only $10,000 plus a valuable advertising deal, Jon would be included in Rob's team.

Irrespective of such deals, these two expeditions must have had a total budget in the region of $400,000 each: approximately three times that of Henry's expedition, which would have more than half its money swallowed up by the permit fee alone.

With round one having been won by Rob, the stakes had been raised. Getting clients successfully to the summit had now taken on a completely new meaning. Rob hadn't managed to get any of his clients to the summit in 1995. Now, with Scott close on his heels, he needed 1996 to be a good season. This, augmented by a quality advertising campaign in *Outside* magazine, could greatly benefit his business.

Although he had lost out on securing this deal for himself, Scott had on his team Sandy Hill Pittman. She would be filing reports back to NBC Interactive Media during the course of the expedition.

Both teams would be under the scrutiny of the press. This was a self-imposed pressure that could only be detrimental to the clear and rational decisions they would need to make. Every day was destined to bring Rob and Scott new problems. The worries and pressures of dealing with this competitive market they'd helped to create were fuelled by the daily reports sent back to an awaiting, and much coveted, media in the US.

The other dilemma that both Rob and Scott would face was that they were two passionate mountaineers who, over the years, had turned their personal climbing into a business. They were not alone in spotting the opportunity to make a living from the sport they'd dedicated their lives to – a trend that was driven by an international appetite for extreme adventure. The mountaineering ethos of national teams, or teams grouped by invitation only, was rapidly changing to one driven by the supply and demand of the free-market economy. This change brought with it completely different pressures and decisions compared to my own more straightforward approach. Mine was a climb with a personal goal that I wanted to achieve: a much simpler role in so many ways. I had to consider, and get on with, the others on our expedition while conducting myself in a safe and sensible manner. To me, money was a means to an end and not the prime objective. Hopefully I'd be successful, but I was also aware that at the end of the expedition my purse would be empty. Rob and Scott, on the other hand, were looking for a handsome return for all their efforts in striving to bring success to their paying clients: ones who already had their hopes pinned so very high. The risks were increased slightly because a number of those who could afford the sums Rob and Scott charged for a place on their expeditions were often older climbers with more disposable income. This in itself had the potential to put extra demands on Rob, Scott and the guides they employed should the line of command become strained or communications falter.

These three teams that assembled in Nepal that spring would include the following (ages given where known):

MacGillivray Freeman Imax/Iwerks Expedition
David Breashears, aged 40, USA, expedition leader, film
  director
Jamling Norgay Sherpa, aged 30, India, deputy leader
Ed Viesturs, aged 36, USA, climber
Robert Schauer, aged 42, Austria, climber, cameraman
Araceli Segarra, aged 25, Spain, climber
Sumiyo Tsuzuki, aged 28, Japan, climber
Paula Viesturs, USA, Base Camp manager

Liz Cohen, USA, film production manager
Liesl Clark, aged 30, USA, film producer and manager
Audrey Salkeld, aged 60, UK, journalist

Adventure Consultants Guided Expedition

Rob Hall, aged 35, New Zealand, expedition leader. He was married to Dr Jean Arnold, who was expecting their first child. Owner of Adventure Consultants, a company he'd started in 1992 with his late friend and business partner Gary Ball. Between 1990 and 1995, he'd guided 35 people to the top of Everest. He had summited Everest himself on four occasions: 10 May 1990, 12 May 1992, 10 May 1993 and 9 May 1994.

Michael Groom, aged 33, Australia, guide. Living in Brisbane, he worked as a plumber and once in a while as a guide. In 1987, he'd become the first Australian to summit Kangchenjunga, a climb during which he suffered frostbite, losing all his toes on both feet. In 1990, he'd summited Cho-Oyu; 1993 Everest; 1994 K2; and 1995 Lhotse – all without the use of bottled oxygen.

Andy Harris, aged 31, New Zealand, guide. A mountain and helicopter skiing guide, he'd previously climbed lesser but more technically challenging Himalayan peaks.

Helen Wilton, New Zealand, Base Camp manager. She had been Base Camp manager for Rob Hall's Adventure Consultants in 1993 and 1995.

Dr Caroline Mackenzie, late 20s, New Zealand, Base Camp doctor.

Frank Fischbeck, aged 53, Hong Kong, client. Owner of a publishing business in Hong Kong, he'd attempted Everest three times before, reaching the South Summit in 1994.

Doug Hansen, aged 46, USA, client. An American postal worker, he'd been with Rob Hall in 1995 when he'd reached the South Summit.

Dr Stuart Hutchison, aged 34, Canada, client. A cardiologist and mountaineer.

Lou Kasischke, aged 53, USA, client. An attorney from Bloomfield in Michigan, he was on the seven summits trail, which covers the highest mountain on each of the seven continents, and had climbed six so far. Everest was still on the list.

Jon Krakauer, aged 42, USA, client. An experienced climber, author and journalist from Seattle, he'd joined the expedition to write an article for *Outside* magazine about the commercialisation of Everest.

Yasuko Namba, aged 47, Japan, client. Personnel director in the Tokyo branch of Federal Express, she had climbed six of the seven summits. Everest would complete the set.

Dr John Taske, aged 56, Australia, client. An anaesthetist from Brisbane, he'd taken up climbing after retiring from the army.

Dr Seaborn Beck Weathers, aged 49, USA, client. A pathologist from Texas with a passion for climbing.

Mountain Madness Guided Expedition

Scott Fischer, aged 40, USA, expedition leader. Married to Jean Price, a captain on Alaskan Airlines, they had two children aged nine and five. He was the owner of the Seattle-based company Mountain Madness. Scott had attempted Everest four times before, having reached the top in 1994 without the use of supplementary oxygen. His first guiding of a 26,000-ft peak had been on Broad Peak in Pakistan the previous year; 1996 would be his first as leader of a guided expedition to Everest. He'd first met Rob Hall in the '80s, a friendship that was reaffirmed in 1992 when Scott, Ed Viesturs and another American climber, Charlie Mace, aided Rob Hall with a fast-ailing Gary Ball very high on K2.

Anatoli Boukreev, aged 38, Kazakhstan, guide. He'd been selected as part of the Russian national team for the first traverse of Kangchenjunga in 1989. Anatoli had climbed Everest twice before, 1991 and 1995, both times without the use of supplementary oxygen. He'd also summited several other peaks over 26,000 feet – Dhaulagiri in 1991, K2 in 1993 and Makalu in 1994 – all without the use of bottled oxygen.

Neal Beidleman, aged 36, USA, guide. An aerospace engineer, he'd been on a trip to K2 with Scott Fischer in 1992 and had already climbed Makalu, the world's fifth-highest mountain.

Dr Ingrid Hunt, aged 32, USA, Base Camp manager and doctor.

Jane Bromet, USA, journalist. Scott's publicist and friend,

this Seattle-based writer was there to send reports back for *Outside Online*.

Martin Adams, aged 47, USA, client. From Aspen, Colorado, he'd been on several Himalayan trips.

Charlotte Fox, aged 38, USA, client. A ski patroller from Aspen, Colorado, she'd already summited two 26,000-ft peaks, Cho-Oyu and Gasherbrum II.

Lene Gammelgaard, aged 35, Denmark, client. A graduate in law, she lived in Copenhagen and had considerable experience in the Alps.

Dr Dale Kruse, aged 44, USA, client. A personal friend of Scott's, he was a dentist from Colorado who'd been on several Himalayan trips.

Tim Madsen, aged 33, USA, client. A ski patrolman from Aspen, Colorado, he climbed extensively in Colorado and the Canadian Rockies.

Sandy Hill Pittman, aged 41, USA, client. This was her third attempt on Everest, one of which had been an attempt on the treacherous Kangshung Face with David Breashears. She too was attempting the seven summits, of which Everest was the last. During the course of this expedition, she would be sending back reports to NBC Interactive Media.

Klev Schoening, aged 38, USA, client. A construction worker from Seattle and a former member of the US downhill ski team.

Pete Schoening, aged 68, USA, client and Klev's uncle. A highly respected Himalayan climber, who in 1953 was catapulted to fame after he single-handedly saved the lives of five climbers by arresting their fall high on K2.

By deciding to return to Everest in the spring of 1996, I'd unwittingly signed up as a witness to the events yet to unfold. The radio calls of Rob Hall's team that we'd listened to back in 1995 were a portent of things to come.

Kathmandu

22 March 1996

I stepped out from the shade and relative calm of Kathmandu's international airport into the subsiding heat of late afternoon.

Within five paces of the exit, I was swamped by the usual mass of eager taxi drivers and touts. This all-male throng, seemingly aged from seven to seventy, jostled as they vied for my custom, each member hoping that they might provide the transport for my twenty-minute ride into the city.

With outstretched arms, imploring brown eyes and well-rehearsed lines, they tried their utmost to persuade me to hand over part of my luggage, hopeful I might relinquish some of the burden and assent to their services. If successful in this manoeuvre, the unmistakable sign to their competition was that the business was won. The pandemonium would cease as abruptly as it had begun.

The more confident of these competitors took on the mantle of overpowering salesmen, pushing their way to the front and trying to take control of my luggage before a fare had been agreed. At the time, the going rate was 200 rupees, about £2.30. To each outstretched hand and eager face, I repeated, 'Two hundred rupees.' The first to agree to this figure was the one who got my custom. The whole process of arranging my transport took less than 30 seconds.

However, the next problem was how to hang on to the rest of my luggage. It was piled high upon an ancient and rather worn-out airport trolley that chose its own direction of travel. I struggled hopelessly to master the art of steering this unpredictable rusting mechanical aid. At the same time, I had to avoid the scam that any person lifting one of my bags, or in some cases just touching them, expected some payment. This perceived assistance could be as little as lifting a bag three feet in distance or one foot up onto the back seat of the car. Nevertheless, the ever-expectant open palm would be thrust out, foreign currency in the form of a note being the preferred recompense.

The entire ritual was far less intimidating than it sounds. The art was to remain in control, a smile or polite 'no' the most useful tools.

Having secured my ride, I was escorted to my taxi. It had been parked on the opposite side of the unnecessarily large official car park: oversized through aspirations of future airport expansion or as a statement of the country's ambitions in the modern world. The distance between the negotiations and provision of service had been wisely played by my driver to his best advantage. It meant I had not been able to set eyes on the 20-year-old burgundy-coloured Nissan saloon, which was heavily dented from end to end. Neatly positioned within the white lines of a designated parking space, it had the requisite four wheels and almost as many doors. To my optimistic eyes, it looked as though, once started, it might be capable of moving in a forward direction.

With my rucksack loaded onto the back seat of the sun-bleached interior, and two large expedition bags protruding from the strapped-down boot lid, we departed from the airport grounds. Passing the armed military checkpoint, we joined the public road where rules and rights of way seemed less well defined. The gearbox whined incessantly and clunked loudly with every change. The suspension, what little there was of it, rattled as though it were about to part company with the vehicle. The fuel gauge read empty.

To possess a vehicle in Nepal was a means to earn a precious living. The owners kept them going in their battle-scarred states as long as humanly possible. Nothing was wasted.

My worryingly young-looking driver was unperturbed by the abnormal sounds emanating from the car. He must have instinctively known which rattles might be terminal – that or he was just waiting for something to drop off. Accompanying him was one of his friends. This extra passenger, who had managed to squeeze alongside my rucksack in the rear of the car, just happened to be going into Kathmandu. He needed a lift. After only a few minutes, it became apparent that this extra occupant was hoping to steer me in the direction of a trekking company or hotel from which commission might be earned. It was done very nicely, in a typically Nepalese way: friendly and without the hard sell. Once they realised I'd been to Nepal before, on more than one occasion, it relaxed into an easy-going conversation of why I liked Nepal so much. They were proud that I should choose to keep coming back to their country. I was a Westerner after all, and in their eyes I had the whole world to choose from.

As the dilapidated taxi rattled its way through the narrow streets, the aromas of sweet-smelling incense mingling with that of rotting rubbish wafted through its open windows. The warm air blowing over me felt soothing after the long flight.

We passed row after row of ramshackle buildings with corrugated metal roofs that lined the streets. The goods displayed outside shops were a sea of colour and ranged from cheap plastic items of every description to earthenware pottery, chillies and spices. The constant sound was of car and motorcycle horns beeping as they all competed for what little room there was to squeeze through. Cows grazed on decaying refuse piled high at the side of the road awaiting the infrequent collections; children played happily nearby. An old bicycle tyre propelled along with a stick appeared a popular toy and prized possession. Whole families sat out in front of their simple homes, enjoying the subdued warmth of the early-evening sun. They were constantly being covered in the dust thrown up by the passing traffic and left in the clouds of choking fumes being emitted. This scene was repeated time after time as the taxi wound its way down narrow, worn streets. Overhead, innumerable power cables and telephone wires spanned the route. They drooped wearily under their own weight in what appeared to be a dangerous mess. Hand-painted signs surrounded many a doorway, advertising the businesses that occupied the upper floors of the taller and more permanent concrete buildings. Barber shops with their wooden hardback chairs offered haircuts for only a few rupees, alongside vendors carefully attending three-foot-wide hot pans of boiling oil. These sizzled with samosas, which danced in readiness across the bubbling surface.

After 20 minutes, we entered into an altogether much quieter world as the taxi turned left down a small, unmetalled side street. With a shudder from the brakes, the driver pulled up outside my hotel, the Gauri Shankar. The establishment was a favoured haunt for climbers at that time, though it has since closed down. In the years to come, customer requirements would change from clean, simple and inexpensive hotels to ones with all the modern comforts and facilities of their Western counterparts. Bookings dropped and the hotel ceased to be viable.

Above the entrance, an imposing 20-ft white banner with large blue lettering welcomed our Everest expedition to Nepal. Underneath, on the broad hotel steps, stood two traditionally dressed members of staff who only ten months earlier had bade me farewell. They had been anticipating my arrival.

This five-storey hotel was built as three equal-sized sections facing a small central entrance courtyard, the edges of which were lined with a well-watered variety of exotic plants whose flowers brought dazzling colours to this otherwise dusty urban environment. A large broad-leafed tree generously offered welcome shade from the searing heat of the midday sun. All guest rooms opened onto a concrete walkway that overlooked this small oasis set within a chaotic concrete jungle. Blue plastic storage barrels, highly favoured for expedition supplies and equipment, were spread throughout the establishment. They overflowed into the reception area and onto the large walled veranda located directly above it. Climbing equipment, clothing, tents and harnesses were strewn over every available balcony, airing in the warmth of the sun.

Hanging on the walls of the two concrete stairwells that wound their way to the upper floors were large, dramatic photographs of highly respected Himalayan climbers, both men and women. Underneath each picture was a list of their continued achievements on the 26,000-ft peaks, though several noted an untimely demise of the person in recent years.

It was a climber's paradise. The air was charged with the excitement and expectations about what lay ahead. Many were not going to Everest but to lower Himalayan peaks that often presented much harder and more dangerous technically difficult climbs.

All the expeditions gathered at the Gauri Shankar that year shared great camaraderie in their hopes and aspirations for their imminent adventure. The place was buzzing with the very essence of feeling alive.

Over the next few days, my hotel room took on the appearance of a storeroom from a climbing equipment shop. I set out, on any available surface, everything that had been so painstakingly packed at home. The floor was littered with neat piles of climbing hardware, boots, sunscreen, thick woollen socks and even a couple of tents. The dressing table and bedside cabinet were covered in piles of batteries, sewing kit, music tapes, medical supplies and every other conceivable item that I thought might be necessary for my comfort and well-being over the next two months. I made a request for the hotel staff not to clean my room; other guests were doing the same. There was no point in them attempting this impossible task. My down suit, highly insulated sleeping bags and thermal underwear, which lay airing on my half-made bed, were seemingly out of place in the rapidly rising springtime temperatures of this capital city, a place where shorts, T-shirts and sandals were far more suitable attire.

With great care, I repacked the blue plastic barrel and two large holdalls with the majority of my equipment. These would be taken by helicopter to the mountain airstrip at Lukla and from there by yak to Everest Base Camp. I would not see them again for at least two weeks. Other essentials such as a sleeping bag, waterproofs, umbrella, changes of clothes, walking poles and suncream were packed into a rucksack that would remain with me. These I needed for the ten-day acclimatisation trek from Lukla up to Everest Base Camp. I felt a nervous excitement as I sorted through the equipment and supplies that were spread out before me. The plans I had dreamt up in Argentina little more than two months earlier appeared to be coming together. Not wanting to tempt fate, I tried to deny myself the thought that I could actually pull this off – that I might summit Everest two years in a row. Too much could happen to dash my hopes and aspirations. In the intervening period between my arrival in Kathmandu and the two-month gruelling expedition to the towering heights of the lofty Himalaya that lay ahead, there was an endless list of things that could go wrong. From now on, one step at a time was the way forward.

Daytimes were spent in the many outdoor cafes and small restaurants that line the narrow bustling streets of Thamel, the hectic tourist quarter of Kathmandu: a place that draws travellers like a magnet and from where they radiate across the globe on their onward journeys. While here, they momentarily slip into a worldly melting pot of humanity: one that contains a wide spectrum of ages, cultures, nationalities and experiences.

I also idled away time browsing the large number of climbing and trekking shops. These were full of equipment that had been sold off at the end of expeditions in previous years; their sponsors' stickers adorned the windows of these overstuffed establishments. Not that I needed anything extra. Rather, I suppose, I was hoping for inspiration or for something to jolt my memory to recall that vital piece I might have forgotten. There was always the chance that I might spot some hitherto unknown piece of equipment that could aid in my forthcoming endeavour.

It was after breakfast in the large and dimly lit wood-panelled hotel restaurant that Henry and I set out to scour Thamel. Our objective was to find the best exchange rate we could, to maximise a sizeable chunk of the expedition funds. The best rate to be found in those days was not given by the licensed moneychangers but on the black market. Surprisingly, these could be found in carpet shops, which went a long way to explaining their prolific number. A discreet enquiry with the proprietor, who actively sought his next customer, and one would be ushered to the more private area to the rear of the establishment. A brief discussion concerning the amount to be changed and size of the bills would determine the rate to be offered. While this was happening, the shopkeeper's assistant would warily stand guard at the front door. Everyone knew it was going on, and no one wanted to be caught red-handed. The current daily newspaper, which lay conveniently to one side, was always referred to for the bank rate of that particular day. The rate the shopkeeper offered was always better than the banks, in order to secure this precious foreign currency; US $20 and $50 bills were preferred to the bulk of smaller notes, reflected by the amount given in return.

In the years that followed, the Nepalese government, well aware that this was going on, decided to offer a preferential exchange rate that exceeded that on the open international market, but only through authorised moneychangers. This shrewd move forced the carpet shops to close in large numbers, as they were now forced to make a living from actually selling carpets.

It was while Henry and I were passing between these carpet shops on our fact-finding tour that I spotted the tall lean figure of Anatoli walking towards us. His height, blond hair and bold blue-checked shirt made him stand out from others in the street. The welcoming smile of renewed friendship that spread across Anatoli's face was accompanied by his outstretched hand as we met. I'd heard he was working for Scott Fischer's Mountain Madness expedition this year, and I was delighted to see him.

Placing his hand on my shoulder, and with a concerned expression, Anatoli said, 'Graham, I hear you climb Everest again. Why do you not climb Lhotse?'

I was on the verge of giving a lengthy explanation as to my reasons when out of the corner of my eye I caught Anatoli trying to wink at Henry. I burst into laughter, realising I was being wound up. Quite obviously he'd spoken with Henry in the last day or two and knew of my plan. It was good to be amongst friends.

As we laughed and joked in the side-street cafes of Kathmandu, our helicopter flight to the small airstrip at Lukla, which marked the beginning of the expedition, seemed a lifetime ahead. In reality, it was only a day or so away.

The Mountain Airstrip at Lukla

Late March 1996

The down draught from the colossal 70-ft diameter rotor blades of the Russian-built Mi 17 helicopter blasted dust and small stones in every direction as it came in to land at Lukla. The gathered throng turned their backs to this rushing cloud of debris. They stood as close to the landing helicopter as the officials would allow them and then tried to shuffle closer still. These were local porters: men and women of all ages who gathered for the work brought by expeditions, which provided incomes that had become so important to the poorer inhabitants of this region of Nepal. The labour from such landings was usually handed out to those at the front of the queue. Being at the back could mean missing out on several days' employment in an area where work can be both scarce and poorly paid.

As soon as the engines stopped, but with the blades of the blue and white Asian Airlines helicopter still turning, the two curved doors that formed the very rear of the aircraft fuselage were flung open, allowing the tons of clearly marked cargo to be unloaded. Porters clambered over bags and barrels that they then either threw or passed down neatly formed lines. Large red gas cylinders, 25-litre plastic containers of cooking oil, trays of eggs stacked 10 deep in purpose-made steel meshed containers, and large 90-lb bags of vegetables that would not be available from the crops grown at these higher elevations: all were lifted clear. Expedition Sherpas carefully watched to make sure nothing was damaged or placed into an incorrect pile.

Soon this apparent chaos moved towards what was evidently an organised and well-rehearsed routine. Nearby, herds of longhaired yaks displaying impressive horns had been waiting in readiness. These sturdy animals, which stand no more than 5 ft high, are very much the Himalayan beast of burden because of their agility, strength and endurance under harsh conditions. Their insulation is so good that after a heavy snowfall they can often be seen with unmelted snow piled several inches thick on their backs and heads.

With little fuss, the huge mounds of supplies and equipment that spread out behind the fuselage were divided into individual and roughly equal loads for each beast. Centrally positioned across the back of each animal was a thick woollen blanket on top of which a small wooden-framed saddle was placed. Ropes and broad straps were employed to firmly secure each load, restraining the side-to-side movement the precious cargo would experience as the yak made its way along the uneven path.

Less than an hour after landing, the Mi 17 stood empty, its massive rotor blades drooping wearily groundwards under their own weight. The load that appeared to have been randomly stacked in its cargo hold was now moving slowly away on a long train of yaks. They faded into the distance as they made their way through the town of Lukla and up the steep valley path that winds its way towards Namche Bazaar.

Following behind was a stream of porters, each carrying an individual load that had been organised with the expedition Sherpas. All were being paid according to the weight they carried. The bigger the load, the more they earned. This system they operate unfortunately encourages porters to carry loads that are far too heavy. The weight of the burden is supported by a broad and tightly woven strap placed across the front of the head. Short ropes are attached to this and pass behind to their upper backs where the load is placed. As they bend forward, some of the weight falls directly onto their back. The neck muscles and spine take the rest of the strain.

The strength and stamina they displayed was humbling. They are a proud people and this was wonderful to see, but we knew they were carrying far too much. Should we have interfered with a system that existed long before expeditions came here? I don't know the answer.

The long trail of yaks and porters disappearing into the distance carried the equipment and supplies we would not see for another ten days, until we reached Everest Base Camp. Placed on the lateral moraine of the Khumbu Glacier at 17,000 feet above sea level, it is some 7,000 feet higher than Lukla. In the intervening time, we had to gain altitude slowly, allowing our bodies to adjust to the considerable change in elevation and thinning air. This process is essential. If rushed, it can give rise not only to dehydration and severe headaches but also to the life-threatening complications of high-altitude pulmonary and cerebral oedemas. In the case of pulmonary oedema, the lungs fill up as fluid leaches into them. Severe shortness of breath while resting, gurgling sounds from the lungs and blood in the sputum are some of the recognised symptoms. If the sufferer is not quickly removed to a lower altitude they can drown in their own bodily fluids. With cerebral oedema, the layers surrounding the brain swell up as fluid builds up in this area, causing confusion and severe mental impairment. This can rapidly lead to the person's death if lower elevations are not reached without delay. Both sets of symptoms can fade as quickly as they appear, provided prompt action is taken. Neither must ever be ignored.

No matter if we were here to climb Everest or just go trekking in the foothills, everyone has to adhere to the acclimatisation process. The recognised method is a slow and steady pace combined with drinking plenty of water, up to five litres a day.

With that approach in mind, we collected our rucksacks from beside the helicopter and walked the hundred yards across the landing area to the aptly named Paradise Lodge: a large stone building situated just down from the fifteen-foot-by-fifteen-foot, two-storey 'airport control tower'.

The lodge's veranda overlooked the 100-yd-square 'airport' area where the aircraft were both boarded and alighted. To our left rose a near-vertical cliff face, above which towered a daunting mountain many thousands of feet high. The upper reaches were still clad in winter snow. It was only one of the numerous Himalayan summits we had glimpsed through the small round Perspex windows on the Mi 17 as it came in to land. To our right, the dirt runway, one of the steepest in the world, disappeared down the mountainside at an angle of approximately 15 degrees. It came to an abrupt end at a vertical drop-off. Far below, at the bottom of the steeply sided V-shaped valley, lay the Dudh Kosi river, its raging torrents winding their way past the dark-green conifers that clung tightly to the bases of the imposing mountains.

It was from our comfortably seated vantage point that we enjoyed an early lunch from a surprisingly extensive menu, while pondering over a number of aircraft fuselages that littered the side of the runway after less-than-successful landings. The names of their operators were painted out so as not to deter potential passengers with the negative advertising this wreckage provided. Their current use was as wood stores.

Far away from the chaos and dust of Kathmandu, this was an ideal place to unwind and my first real opportunity to begin to get to know the climbers with whom I'd be spending the next two months. A few I already knew and had climbed with before.

Henry had brought the team together as a commercial expedition. He'd selected applicants based on their previous climbing experience and how he felt they would fit into the team. There were no guides. Each climber paid for his or her place. The team, apart from myself at the age of 41, consisted of:

Henry Todd, aged 51, UK, expedition leader. This was Henry's second Everest expedition, he having organised the successful climb from Tibet the previous spring. Although he would move up to some of the higher camps during the course of the expedition in support of his team, he would make no summit attempt. He had never been to the summit of Everest. He was not a person that led from the front but one who kept overall control of operations from a strategic location, where risks could be assessed and decisions clinically taken.

Kami Nuhru Sherpa, Nepal. Kami was the expedition Sirdar, our head Sherpa. He came from the village of Pangboche in the Solu Khumbu, about 15 miles from Everest. In charge of hiring our staff, their wages and welfare, he oversaw everything from logistics to the placing and supplying of all camps on the mountain. His role was pivotal. Kami had been with us the previous year, as had many of the climbing Sherpas and expedition staff.

Paul Deegan, aged 26, UK. Paul was an aspiring writer who worked in the outdoor industry. He had been with us in Tibet the previous spring but had not reached the summit. He was back to finish the task.

Neil Laughton, aged 32, UK. A businessman and former officer in the Royal Marines, he had climbed throughout the world. His sights were now firmly on Everest.

Brigitte Muir, aged 38, Australia. Along with her husband, Jon Muir, she ran an outdoor company called Adventure Plus based at Natimuk near Mount Arapiles in western Victoria. Jon had summited Everest back in 1988 with an Australian national expedition. This was Brigitte's third Everest expedition; her attempt the previous year had been thwarted because her head torch failed during the night, leaving her stranded in darkness. Waiting for dawn, she had become too cold and had to descend. Brigitte was hoping to be the first Australian woman to climb Everest.

Thomas and Tina Sjogren, aged 36 and 37 respectively, Sweden. As a husband and wife team, they ran a business together and climbed together. They were to all intents and purposes a team of their own on this expedition.

Mark Pfetzer, aged 16, USA. The youngest member of our team by far and, I'm pretty sure I would be right in saying, the youngest of any team on Everest that year. Although only 16 years old, he was solidly built and about 6 ft tall. He'd been on Everest the year before, reaching a height of 25,000 feet on the North Ridge.

Michael Jörgensen, aged 29, Denmark. Michael was part of the UN peacekeeping force in Sarajevo. Along with Welshman Crag Jones, he had summited Everest the previous spring after being pinned down by strong winds in the top camp at 27,200 feet for three days. Michael was going to join us slightly later this spring because of his commitments with the UN. He would catch up with us at Base Camp a week behind.

Ray Dorr, USA. Ray, in his 30s, worked behind the scenes in the theatres of New York. He'd attempted Everest from Tibet the previous year, on the same expedition as Mark Pfetzer.

After lunch, our climbers shouldered their modestly weighted rucksacks and set off from the Paradise Lodge at their chosen pace.

The broad stone-flagged pavement of Lukla's main thoroughfare was lined with moneychangers and shops selling an array of goods from souvenirs to trekking equipment. They were there to service the many thousands that pass through this gateway to the Everest region each year. Brightly coloured signs advertising lodges, porter and guiding services were fastened to the outer walls of the older and more permanent stone buildings that bordered this route. Two small wooden bridges in the middle of town spanned fast-flowing and unpredictable streams draining from the hillside above.

In less than a quarter of a mile, the town petered out. Marking the edge of the settlement, a white stupa bearing copper prayer wheels straddled the route. Beyond, a well-trodden dirt path had been muddied by the spring melt. Shadowing the course of the Dudh Kosi from high above, it passes through prolific vegetation before gradually winding its way down to the valley floor. Here, tall conifers, clinging to the rocky sides, filled the warm air with the fragrance of their exuded resins.

We crossed and re-crossed the wide river gorge and its many narrow tributaries over cable-slung bridges suspending wooden-planked walkways that had over the years been patched and re-patched. Each repair indicated the spot where the leg of the occasional yak or porter had plunged through. The cables themselves were adorned with coloured prayer flags that flapped timelessly in the mountain breeze.

The longest of these rickety bridges spanned 250 to 300 feet across. Here it was often necessary to pause for 'traffic' coming in the opposite direction, usually in the form of yaks and their attendant herders. Taking on the role of heavy commercial transport, they supplied the villages and tourist lodges of the region. Porters generally took on the lighter, or in some cases more awkward, loads, such as sheets of 8-ft by 4-ft plywood or the occasional 6-ft tall fridge-freezer.

These narrow mountain paths and river crossings were the nearest thing to a road system it was possible to have without adversely impacting on the dramatic environment – and it was all the people of the area could afford. Sturdy ankles were a distinct advantage as we made our way along the ever-changing surface.

To the Nepalese villagers, walking was the accepted way of travel. Distances were measured in hours and days rather than miles, which have no real meaning in such terrain. A man riding a horse was a rare sight indeed.

Where it had been possible to cultivate modest areas, villages had become established. Potatoes and barley appeared to be the staple crops. These, along with livestock, provided the mainstay of the area's economy. That was until tourism in the form of climbing and trekking had come along. These brought with them the opportunity of a life with rather less hardship and the possibility of a more formal education for their children, who otherwise would have been compelled from an early age to help the family scrape a meagre living from this harsh environment. However, these new opportunities came at a price: one being the loss of isolation that had to a certain degree protected their Buddhist values and culture. The other was the significant risks the Sherpas would undertake in these new endeavours.

After a four-hour walk, I arrived at a simple stone-built lodge called 'Toktok'. With a green corrugated metal roof, it stands alone about half an hour past the riverside village of Phakding. This building, precariously positioned high on the slope that rises precipitously from the river's edge, was where we'd arranged to spend the night. It was by now late afternoon. The open wood-burning fire used to cook the food I ordered produced copious amounts of acrid smoke that struggled to find its way up the primitive chimney. Even though my eyes stung painfully, the warmth from the fire felt welcoming as the daylight faded. My bed for the night, the sleeping bag and thin foam pad I carried, unrolled onto a wooden-boarded frame that did little to aid my slumber.

The next morning was bright and crisp as we emerged from our overnight accommodation. The clear night sky had given rise to a heavy frost. Every blade of grass and leafy surface was adorned with delicate but perfectly formed ice crystals. The soft boggy section of the path that led uphill away from the lodge, which bore the deep footprints of yesterday's travellers, was frozen solid.

Mark Pfetzer, no doubt buoyed by the exuberance of youthful infallibility, left slightly before the rest of us and strode out – as we all did at some point during the expedition in our own competitive way. His intention was presumably to be first to arrive at Namche Bazaar, the largest settlement and trading post in the Khumbu region and our next overnight halt.

Our way led ever upwards, through villages, between small stone-walled fields and along steep forested hillsides to the gated entrance of the Sagamartha National Park. With passports and climbing permits duly produced for the armed park officials, we passed through. An area set aside in 1976 by the Nepalese government, it was given the status of a World Heritage Centre by UNESCO just three years later.

After picking my way along the boulder-strewn sides of the Dudh Kosi's white-water rapids, I clambered up to the final stretch of the day. A lengthy sagging footbridge suspended 200 feet above the river spanned a vertical-sided gorge. Beyond lay the infamous Namche hill. For the porters and yaks carrying a heavy load, this next section is torture, as it was for an un-acclimatised would-be mountaineer with a more modest burden. It rises for well over an hour as it switchbacks its way across the precipitous sides. Above lie the sanctuary and comforts of Namche Bazaar.

Mark, now some way ahead, was unaware that as you enter Namche there is the normal footpath into town but also a steeper and much shorter one. I'd given no thought to how far ahead Mark might be. So, when I came to this point, I took the quicker but slightly more painful second option. This route took me along the narrow earthen alleyways that separated the simplest of houses. I squeezed past sweet-smelling bakeries and the bright displays of souvenir shops that had set up makeshift wooden benches to maximise the narrow space outside each establishment. The added temptation of 'morning price', the ultimate weapon in their arsenal to lure a would-be customer, accompanied the eager eyes and broad smiles of the proprietors. Wearily I made my way along this passage. The modest rucksack I was shouldering seemed to increase in weight with every step that brought me nearer to our pre-arranged destination: a lodge called Kalipatar.

Covering its narrow inconspicuous entrance, one that I nearly walked straight past, hung a traditional white door curtain that bore a dark-blue Buddhist image of Shirivasta: the interwoven endless knot of life. Made of cotton and edged with a two-inch-wide band of matching blue, this flimsy curtain separated the street from the interior. It bore grubby marks on either side where those entering had lifted it out of the way.

Slightly to my left, a narrow wooden staircase rose to the floor above.

Here, the half-glazed door that cast just enough light to guide me up from the gloomy entrance signalled the end of my journey for the day. On opening it, I was greeted by a large rectangular room, approximately 40 feet in width and 13 feet deep. Bathed in warm sunlight that streamed through the full-width row of windows, it overlooked the sloping town of Namche Bazaar. The walls, lined with varnished plywood, had glazed cabinets that displayed Mars bars, Snickers and bottles of spirits and beer to tempt the weariest of travellers. Underneath the windows, a long built-in bench softened by thick hand-woven Tibetan rugs offered my first comfort of the day. In the middle of the room stood a cast-iron cylindrical wood-burning stove. Its tubular chimney exited through the timber ceiling.

Dumping my rucksack unceremoniously onto the floor, I proceeded to order two milk teas and a bowl of rara noodle soup. The ordering of more than one drink at the same time was not an uncommon practice, especially in the early days of acclimatisation, when the need for the continual drinking of fluids was foremost in the mind. Infrequent visits to the toilet and anything but light-coloured urine were sure signs that I was not drinking enough. The bodily requirement during this period is so much that thirst alone cannot be used as a measure.

Hearing a squeak from the door handle, I looked up. Standing in the doorway was Mark, busily unfastening his rucksack with a look of triumphant relief plastered across his face. At this point, he had not seen me.

When Mark stepped into the room, he assumed he was first there. No one had passed him on the way. Yet in front of him he found me sitting at the table tucking into my second milk tea and a half-finished bowl of rara noodle soup. His totally bewildered expression was priceless.

Mustering the only question he could think of, he asked, 'When did you get here?'

Not wanting to spoil the moment, I didn't let on about my short cut but simply replied, 'Oh, I've been here for ages.'

As I continued with my soup, Mark stood there with a blank look on his face. Tired from the long slog up the hill, he shrugged in resignation and sat down, his rucksack still half dangling from one of his shoulders.

Throughout the afternoon, the rest of our team members arrived in ones and twos, some having stopped for lunch on the way. This was not a race; everyone had to find a pace that suited them. Some, like myself, preferred to walk without stopping; others enjoyed eating en route. This did not make one strategy better than any other, just different. Mark was doing very well. It was still early in the expedition, and he had plenty of time to learn these finer points, although he was to learn another lesson sooner than expected.

Mark was of an age where bragging rights had their importance; not so with the rest of the team. That evening, he couldn't resist telling us how good looking his girlfriend was and that this ravishing beauty was waiting for him to return. I know he didn't mean it, but many of us had partners at home that we would miss in the coming weeks. This was dangerous territory for Mark when he knew little about our individual circumstances.

Retiring to one of the modest dormitories, Mark, Paul, myself and three others who had joined our group to make a documentary film about Mark's attempt settled down for the night. After a few minutes, Paul's voice broke through the pitch black: 'Mark, have you any pictures of your girlfriend?'

Mark, delighted that we were so obviously impressed by the description of his gorgeous girlfriend, had a swagger in the tone of his reply: 'Nah, unfortunately not.'

Silence once again descended, that was until about 30 seconds later when Paul's voice whispered, 'Would you like to see some?'

I tried not to explode with laughter; as I pinched my nose, my cheeks ballooned out forcing the air to snort out in bursts through my nasal passages. Others in the room were also trying, hopelessly, to stay in control.

That was the last time we heard anything about Mark's girlfriend.

The next day the morning sun shining through the thinly glazed window, milky in appearance from its rarely cleaned outer surface, dragged us reluctantly from our sleeping bags.

Built on the slopes of a natural hillside amphitheatre, Namche is where a Saturday market is held, a bustling event that brings a hive of activity. Here, colourful market traders, a good number of whom are hardy weather-beaten Tibetans adorned with necklaces strung with turquoise and red coral beads, peddle their wares.

These enterprising men and women regularly cross the high passes via trade routes that have existed for centuries, escorting long-haired yaks loaded with ornately woven traditional woollen rugs, replica artefacts, clothing and a vast array of low-quality goods from the Chinese market. Still protected from the bitter wind by their traditional thick felt clothing, these modern-day travellers are more likely to be sporting Reebok or Nike trainers than the traditional hand-made footwear. The Sherpa people, native to this area, are themselves descended from Tibetans. Their ancestors came to Nepal many hundreds of years ago to settle in this mountainous but more fertile region, using the same paths that give access to these southern markets.

After an early breakfast of scrambled eggs on toast, two milk teas and cup of strong coffee, the latter to act as a laxative to stave off the other ghastly effect of dehydration, I decided to climb up one of the steep paths that rise up behind the town. This was mainly for exercise and would allow me to catch my first glimpse of Everest that season.

I panted and wheezed as I stumbled up the incline of the awkward stony path that threads its way up through the town. Nearing the edge of habitation I veered left alongside a colossal granite boulder embedded deep into the hillside. Towering some 40 feet up the slope, its entire surface was exquisitely carved with sacred Buddhist mantras. Underfoot changed to a dry and dusty dirt track that pushed a fine billow of powder into the air each time my foot struck the ground.

I snaked my way through hardy alpine shrubs and stunted woody-stemmed vegetation towards the top of the hill some 800 feet above. Sweat poured off my brow from my feeble exertion in the rising temperature of the morning sun. I heard shrill laughter and chattering voices coming up behind me. Looking over my shoulder I was greeted by the sight of a throng of schoolchildren aged around seven. Dressed in uniforms and carrying satchels, they were skipping and hopping their way up the same path as me. The difference was they weren't sweating profusely and didn't appear to be out of breath at all, unlike the climber they romped past – the one who was here to climb Everest. This humbling episode served to underline how much acclimatisation I needed to undertake before I could hope to match a seven-year-old schoolchild whose physiology was accustomed to this altitude.

As the children raced ahead and out of sight, I continued up at my much slower but steady pace. Far below, a cacophony of sound emanated from craftsmen working on the construction of several lodges that were being built to satisfy the recent increase in tourist demand. Each new building was strategically placed on one of the many small terraces that provided level ground on Namche's steeply rising slopes, where not so long ago potatoes and other hardy crops had been planted. Echoes rose of the timeless sound of stonemasons' hammers and chisels chipping away at blocks of hewn granite and that of carpenters' hand-held saws and planes rasping against rough-cut timber. The sounds bounced back over the deep chasm that fronted Namche Bazaar, echoing from the precipitously rising ground on the other side where conifers clung on tightly to their rocky holdfasts and through which a waterfall of ice, still in winter's grip, drove a stark crystalline divide. As spring temperatures rose, the water would once again be released from this suspended form, allowing the meltwater from the expansive snowfields of the mountain high above to drain into the Dudh Kosi that coursed along the valley floor.

Reaching the top of the hill, I paused for a moment before I looked up and far into the distance. About 15 miles away, as the crow flies, I could make out the 25,600-ft high Nuptse Wall with the dark rock pyramid of Everest's upper reaches protruding from behind. Her summit was being battered by the jet stream that left a long plume of ice crystals extending far to the east. The powerful nature of this vision took me by surprise. This was the place George Kotov and I had sat and chatted only ten months earlier, while he lit a cigarette. Now, early in this spring season, it looked terrifying. The savagery of our intended goal appeared beyond hope. However, this aspiration was nearly two months away. Much would happen in the intervening time.

After two days acclimatising at this altitude, our onward journey took us past the spectacularly positioned and deeply atmospheric Tengboche Monastery, the focal point for the Buddhist faith of this region. Set on a broad grassy hilltop, the sanctuary this location affords is unmistakable. This fertile vantage area is where the Sherpa people have built the holiest of places to them outside Tibet or Sikkim.

We ended the day at the Rhododendron Lodge, an aptly named establishment sheltering alone about 20 minutes further on from the monastery. With its off-white walls and bottle-green window frames, this two-storey stone building sits comfortably amongst a forest of rhododendron trees. These were in bud as we passed through in late March but their prolific flowers would have come and gone before I returned this way in May.

The lady who owned the lodge, Ang Kanchi Sherpa, was a long-time friend of the late Sir Edmund Hillary and more recently of Reinhold Messner: arguably the two most important figures in Himalayan climbing. She was far more worldly wise and well travelled than her appearance indicated: her list of foreign excursions included the US, Vienna and, more than once, Dharamsala in the north Indian state of Himachal Pradesh to witness the Dalai Lama speak. She was a delightful character who had an enviable and insatiable appetite for news.

Once Ang Kanchi discovered we were on Henry's expedition, employing Kami and most of our Sherpas from the nearby village of Pangboche, the welcome she'd already extended to us moved to one you would have shown a close friend. We were brought hot drinks that were accompanied by the words *che-che* (shay-shay), meaning drink-drink, for which she would take no payment. She invited us to sit nearer to the stove, which stood in the centre of the room, while she fuelled it up with even more dried yak dung. Soon we had to slide our white plastic patio chairs backwards across the wooden-boarded floor because of the amount of heat the burning excrement was throwing out.

Ang Kanchi was a deeply religious person: a trait strongly rooted in the Sherpa people. She looked upon her responsibility to others within the community, and to those visiting the area, as her social duty bound by the teachings of her Buddhist faith. Her brother, who lived in the same property, was a monk at the nearby monastery. His daytime hours were seemingly divided between his religious and commercial commitments, as he was often to be found ensconced in the kitchen wearing his burgundy monastic robe.

The lodge, through Ang Kanchi, offered emergency, albeit basic, medical facilities. A Red Cross and Himalayan Rescue Association sign was prominently displayed outside. Amongst the equipment and medications she held to aid with the more serious problems of altitude sickness was a Gamow bag. This was a manually inflatable compression chamber that could effectively reduce the height a person was at by a considerable margin; it was equipment that had to be used with caution, knowledge and expertise. The main medical centre for treating such life-threatening ailments in the area is that of the Himalayan Rescue Association clinic at Pheriche, manned by volunteer doctors. This better-equipped facility is some three to four hours further up the valley: a distance that in certain circumstances might be too far when more immediate treatment is required to stabilise a patient's condition.

It was around 10 a.m. the next day when Paul and I set out from the Rhododendron Lodge towards Pangboche. The conversation between us centred on other members of our expedition. In all fairness, it was probably me that steered the topic in that direction. I confided in Paul that I had an uneasy feeling about Ray. I couldn't really rationalise or explain, but I felt that I would rather not climb with him.

In an expedition, you cannot reasonably expect to be friends with everyone; rather, you build safe working relationships. Not wanting to climb with a particular person didn't present any real problem. As a matter of course, the team would be split up at various camps on the mountain throughout the expedition. In climbing, instincts and gut feelings are normally best not ignored, although usually these are more to do with your surroundings than other climbers.

I'd been in a situation three years earlier, during a post-monsoon expedition on the North Ridge of Everest, that had firmly taught me to trust my instincts. They had saved the life of a French climber and possibly my own.

It was early in the season when Thierry Renard and I were descending towards the North Col from a foray up to 24,500 feet on the North Ridge. With Thierry leading, we were struck by an unexpected squall that reduced visibility to almost nothing. The ground and the sky merged. It was impossible to distinguish where one finished and the other began.

As we crept slowly down to escape from the clutches of the blizzard, through a dense mist of fine swirling snow, my senses and instincts told me something was very wrong. Rather than ignoring them I shouted to Thierry over the howling wind, 'I think we've gone much too far to the right!'

These words must have confirmed a doubt that Thierry was already having in his mind. His ghostly white figure, covered in a layer of fine snow, stopped dead in its tracks. As he turned his head, which had been stooped to lessen the pain from the biting particles of snow and ice being driven forcibly by the wind, the look of confusion on his heavily bearded face was all too apparent.

'Graham, you take over!' he screamed back.

Looking down at my feet I was alarmed to find myself straddling a fresh crack in the surface of the snow, about half an inch wide. To make matters far worse than just being disorientated, we had managed to get ourselves onto a high-risk avalanche slope. Our problems now had to be dealt with in terms of priority. First we had to get back onto more solid footing. I turned almost 90 degrees to the left of our current course, and my instincts led us back up onto the centre of the ridge and safer ground. Taking account of which side of the ridge these avalanche-risk areas existed, I steered us on a downward course.

As we reached the North Col, the squall cleared as quickly as it had arrived. What we saw in the snow higher on the ridge was more than just a little bit sobering. When I'd shouted to Thierry and he'd asked me to take the lead, he had been no more than five or six steps from walking off the edge of the North Ridge: an edge we couldn't see in the white-out conditions. With the broad ridge curving gently down on the right-hand side for the first 80 feet, Thierry, in the poor visibility, had been drawn, almost sucked, in that direction. We'd actually walked onto the overhanging cornice, hence the tell-tale crack in the snow. He'd been seconds away from taking a 2,500-ft plunge to almost certain death. I may well have unwittingly followed, or if the cornice had broken off it would have taken us both at the same time. The footprints in the snow bore witness to how close we'd come – tracks that remained untouched by the weather for at least two weeks, ones that everybody saw.

My instincts were not something I was about to ignore. For the duration of the expedition, I would not climb with Ray. Anyone else in the team was fine. Once said, I didn't raise the subject again, not even with Ray, as this would have caused bad feeling from which no one would benefit.

No sooner had I told Paul my concerns about Ray than Brigitte caught up with us. Unaware of the conversation Paul and I'd just had, she announced there was one person on the expedition she did not want to climb with. I knew exactly what she was going to say.

Brigitte paused for a moment and said, 'Graham, I'm surprised you haven't had the same feeling.'

I didn't reply but turned briefly and looked at Paul. I didn't need to say anything.

Within our team in the spring of 1996, Paul, Brigitte, Michael and I knew one another from previous expeditions. I'd climbed with each of them at different times and got on well with all three. The mutual respect between us was coupled with an understanding of one another's backgrounds. I suppose it was easier for us in this regard. Among those who'd only met one or two of the other climbers on the team before, new friendships and understandings had to be forged.

Paul had a passion for the Everest region that was beyond question. At the age of 18, he had proposed, co-organised and co-led a 47-strong team in an attempt to clean up much of the rubbish and debris that had been wantonly discarded around Everest Base Camp over the previous decades. A well-read and youthful-looking man with an infectiously amusing personality, he was prone to becoming exuberant during his conversations. Despite being only 26, Paul could spin a yarn or tell a story to match the best of them. Beneath this, his self-confidence levels waned at times, as though he felt overshadowed by some of the 'superstars' present at Base Camp. He was always a pleasure to have around, an asset to any group.

Michael, in 1995, had been catapulted to fame in Denmark by becoming the first person from his country to climb Everest. Although a very capable climber, he was a modest person who kept his private thoughts to himself. Socially, he came across as an uncomplicated, affable person, who, as far as I could tell, was both liked and respected by nearly everyone.

Brigitte, who had long, straight blonde hair, was originally from Belgium but had taken Australian citizenship some years earlier. Plain speaking and volatile at times, she took no nonsense from anyone. She was a strong climber with a personality to match, and I liked her immensely. If Brigitte had any fears, she certainly didn't show them; she was both determined and focused.

At the grand old age of 41, I was the oldest climbing member of the team and the only one, apart from Henry, with children of my own. The family circumstances that I held in common with many of our Sherpas undoubtedly brought with it their respect. This was not least because several of them, including Kami, had been introduced to Catherine in Kathmandu at the end of our 1995 expedition. Having reached the summit that year, a few weeks after my 40th birthday, my age, experience and family life were hopefully considered an asset for the proposed undertaking.

Being surrounded by such companions on the ten-day trek to Base Camp brought with it the sense of an extended social gathering, which helped to distract us from the necessary and sometimes uncomfortable chore of acclimatisation. Having sufficient time for old friends and new acquaintances is something that seems so difficult to find back at home, where the ever-present pressures of work lurk in the back of your mind. Such demands didn't exist out here. The climb, the common cause and the summit were the binding focus.

By lunchtime, Paul, Brigitte and I had arrived on the outskirts of Pangboche, a small village high in the Solu Khumbu where most of our Sherpas lived. The dry-stone walls on either side guided our narrow trail alongside traditional stone buildings. They were roofed with the nearly ubiquitous corrugated metal sheets that in bygone days would have been inch-thick slabs of overlapping stone. A few homes still retained this original feature.

Kami's house, set slightly back from the main path, had a 20-ft high flagpole embedded in the ground outside. To this, a single one-foot-wide white prayer flag, of almost the same height as the pole, had been fastened. The cotton flag, hand-printed in black with Buddhist prayers, emitted snapping sounds as it tightened and slackened against the continual changes in the wind. Inside, the blessing of our expedition by monks from the nearby Pangboche monastery was well under way. For Kami, this five-day ceremony was a great honour and a sign of the respect he now commanded within his village.

As Sirdar of an Everest expedition, he was in a position to offer well-paid employment to those in the area: a responsibility he took very seriously. This work, which was highly paid in comparison with many alternatives in the area, did not come without risk. The Sherpa people, through the previous loss of friends and family in pursuit of this line of work, were well aware of this fact. The appeasement of the gods through dedication, offerings and prayer brought protection from the dangers they knew lay ahead. The custom, in return for this blessing, was for the Sirdar and his wife to provide the monks with a continuous supply of food and tea: a costly and time-consuming undertaking for this rural family.

As Paul, Brigitte and I entered the upper floor of Kami's house we could see, in the half-light, ten or more Buddhist monks clad in burgundy robes. They were sitting cross-legged on the built-in bench that ran around two sides of the room and on which thick woollen rugs had been placed. Directly in front of them, several long tables draped with cloths had been arranged end to end. Before each monk lay an open book of prayers from which he recited in a low continuous chant that fitted perfectly with the moment. The air was heavy with the fragrance of burning incense. The curling white trails of smoke rose through beams of sunlight that entered via small rectangular panes of glass that occupied part of one wall. Large beaten-copper vessels and cooking pots, blackened over many decades by smoke escaping from the poorly ventilated stove, hung from rafters; the level below us was occupied by livestock – similar to the rural houses of Britain in medieval times.

I had the sensation of time standing still. My thoughts were that if this scene had been transported back a thousand years or more, the only real inconsistencies would have been the modern packaged food and our presence.

As guests, we were offered tea. We sat motionless for almost an hour, entranced by the mysterious atmosphere. Although we were made very welcome and invited to stay longer, this ceremony was for the Sherpa people and their deep-rooted Buddhist beliefs. It was their time not ours.

Over the next two days, our team moved up to the sparsely populated outpost of Chukung. Situated several miles further on, near the head of the valley, this sprawling settlement was more importantly 1,200 feet higher in altitude than Pangboche. Here we found accommodation in a simple stone lodge with dried-turf floors and a dormitory constructed almost exclusively from plywood. The purpose for our visit to this somewhat uninviting and windswept location was an acclimatisation scramble planned for the following morning up Chukung Ri, a modest rocky peak of 17,700 feet, about 2,600 feet higher than the lodge we now occupied.

During our extended lunch, which spread well into the afternoon, Henry turned to me and asked quietly, 'Graham, can you go up and see if we will be needing plastic boots on Chukung Ri tomorrow?'

Under normal dry conditions, strong walking boots would have been enough. However, early in spring, Henry's concern was there might still be a considerable amount of snow or ice on Chukung Ri's slabby ridge. If this were the case then climbing boots and crampons would have been needed for a safe ascent and descent.

Henry's request didn't require a second thought. I was happy to have something useful to do rather than sitting around forcing down gallons of tea to stave off the ever-present possibility of a headache. With windproofs, water, a couple of Mars bars and a head torch stuffed into my rucksack, I headed off up the hill. It's times like this that I enjoy the most: the space to think, content with my own company and the remoteness of my surroundings.

It seemed no time at all before I was standing on top of Chukung Ri's rocky summit, gasping for breath at this new-found altitude. In front of me, a couple of miles away, stood the South Face of Lhotse, towering two miles vertically upwards from my current location. This view came as a stark and sobering reminder of the height we had yet to gain over the coming weeks. Lhotse, although the fourth-highest mountain in the world, is still 1,000 feet lower than Everest: a margin that put our goal at the very limit humans could survive, and then only for a few hours. Fortunately, our planned ascent of Everest, via the South Col, was nowhere near the technical difficulty of the face that stood before me: one that was classed by many as being amongst the most difficult and dangerous climbs in the world.

The sight of a thick damp mist rolling in along the valley floor brought an abrupt end to my distant thoughts. Gathering myself up, I turned and made a quick but surefooted descent back to the lodge.

I arrived to find my companions still drinking tea and warming themselves around a hot stove. In all, the round trip had taken me a little over two hours. Sitting down next to Henry, I said, 'We don't need plastics.'

'Not even on the top section?' he asked.

'No, it's clear all the way to the top,' I replied.

Brigitte, having caught our conversation, looked at me in a rather surprised manner: 'You've just been all the way to the top and back?'

Henry, while trying to keep a straight face, turned to Brigitte and said, 'Absolutely, I always like to check such matters thoroughly.'

None of us were able to control our urge to roar with laughter.

In only a matter of days, we would be at Base Camp. The innocence of these happy times would slowly begin to drift into the past.

Everest Base Camp

April 1996

Everest Base Camp resembled an undulating disused rock quarry interspersed with small half-frozen lakes and blocks of ice. Set in a natural amphitheatre enclosed on three sides by the imposing Himalayan peaks of Nuptse, Lingtren, Pumori, the West Ridge of Everest and the Khumbu Icefall, this was to be home for the next two months. Within this mass of ice and glacial moraine, embryonic base camps had begun to appear. Approximately ten expeditions would be attempting Everest from Nepal this spring season.

Over the coming days, as more climbers began to arrive, the number of multi-coloured tents rose accordingly. Soon, each individual expedition's base camp would be defined by the concentration of these conspicuous nylon domes placed within easy striking distance of their mess tent. Well-trodden paths developed between neighbouring camps as alliances and friendships between expeditions were formed or acquaintances renewed.

While our team members had been lounging at home or in their hotel in Kathmandu, the Sherpas had already been hard at work. For over a month, they had been preparing Base Camp for our arrival. A skilfully constructed stone-walled kitchen built from the rocks that lay around about stood on top of the glacier. To roof this temporary building, poles and tarpaulins had been employed. Measuring about 20 foot by 12, it was complete with seating benches, tables and work surfaces, all built from the same random stone collected from the copious amounts of glacial moraine.

By early April, another group of Sherpas, organised through Scottish climber Mal Duff's commercial expedition, had undertaken a far more treacherous task. Fixing a sequence of ropes and aluminium ladders, they had forged a route up through the notorious Khumbu Icefall. This mass of ice, several hundred feet thick and a quarter of a mile wide at its upper reaches, becomes the Khumbu Icefall when the glacier flows out over the lip of the Western Cwm. At this point, the ice fractures, forming huge ice blocks the size of large buildings separated by seemingly bottomless crevasses. This colossal volume of ice fans out on a continual downward journey of up to three feet per day. At its lower end, two and a half thousand feet below, it is more than a mile wide. Here, Base Camp is located.

It was all too easy for climbers such as myself to arrive full of personal ambition, rather than appreciating how much difficult and dangerous work the Sherpas had already undertaken on our behalf. Consciences were absolved by the $2,500 each expedition had paid towards the cost of fixing the Icefall: a sum that also guaranteed its continual maintenance throughout the season. The latter task was taken on by two or three designated Sherpas known to the climbers as 'Icefall doctors'. This was business; those who undertook this perilous task saw only a small part of the money collected. Although comparatively well paid, they had the unenviable responsibility of entering this labyrinth during the searing heat of the day. Their job was to check the fixings. Ladders could be twisted and bent, ice-screws loosen, ropes snap or complete sections, sometimes 250 feet in length, suddenly collapse, necessitating a completely new section to be fixed to re-establish the way through. Everyone knew, beyond any doubt, that they undertook the most hazardous work of anyone on the mountain.

My infinitely safer and much simpler task was to make a level platform on which to pitch my tent. There was an art to choosing the right sort of ground. Those less in the know often pitched their tents in small hollows, in the hope that this might offer some protection from the wind. However, only a matter of inches below all the tents lay the solid ice of the Khumbu Glacier. Experience had taught me that as time moved on and the temperature rose, the surface of the ice would melt, filling these small hollows with water. A better choice was on slightly raised ground, from which meltwater drained away. I also understood that the more time and attention I gave to preparing this platform, the proportionately better sleep I'd have during the several weeks of occupation. Almost three hours was given to this self-indulgent task.

Inside my newly erected tent I placed two full-length foam mats, a large top-quality pillow and a down sleeping bag, followed by the rest of my personal possessions. This temporary home was small and a little cramped yet undeniably comfortable. It contained everything I had brought with me except for my climbing equipment, which was stored in a large three-foot-tall weatherproof plastic barrel that stood next to the entrance of my tent. These sturdy blue barrels are more commonly used by industry for the storage and transport of chemicals and powders. Once sealed with the lid and its metal collar, they are airtight: a factor that, combined with their almost indestructible nature, had made these containers not only the preferred option for expeditions but also a prized and highly sought-after family possession among the Sherpa people.

Sitting outside my new accommodation, I watched the Sherpas as they moved large boulders, weighing many hundreds of kilos, using their combined strength, a sturdy pole and a small rock as a fulcrum point. They sang and laughed as they toiled, typical of their amazingly positive attitude to arduous tasks: an approach that had become an integral part of coping with the hardships in their everyday lives. They in turn admired strength, honesty and morality in those around them. Attributes not always shown by climbers coming to Everest.

Column after column of yaks arrived each day, bringing both equipment and supplies to this temporary settlement perched on top of the Khumbu Glacier – yaks that once unburdened turned around and disappeared down the same way they'd come only an hour or two earlier. Even these humble beasts of burden had more sense than to hang around any longer than was absolutely necessary in this harsh and inhospitable environment.

By the end of the first week in April, all our climbers, including Michael Jörgensen, had arrived. Life was beginning to settle into a peaceful routine. That was until we received a stark reminder of what dangers lay ahead.

There was news of an accident involving one of Rob Hall's Sherpas. While travelling up the Western Cwm towards Camp 2 with some fellow Sherpas, Tenzing either neglected to clip into the fixed rope or had not been roped up to those he was with. Breaking through the fragile surface, he had plunged into a hidden crevasse. His fall to almost certain death had been halted by him luckily landing on a ledge of ice some way down. In the process, he'd shattered his knee. After being rescued from the depths of this icy tomb, he was tied flat onto a short section of aluminium ladder and evacuated back to Camp 1, situated at the lower end of the Western Cwm. The next day, he was to be stretchered down from here by a large number of Sherpas.

Watching from Base Camp, we could make out the 30 or so Sherpas high in the labyrinth of the Khumbu Icefall. They resembled a caterpillar of tiny dots. They slid, dragged and lowered the makeshift stretcher over the edges of huge towering blocks of ice, disappearing out of view for long periods at a time only to then emerge again around or over the next seemingly impossible obstacle. The rescue party arrived in Base Camp shortly before nightfall. It had taken them all day.

At 8 a.m. the following day, we were woken by the sound of an approaching helicopter. The injured Tenzing was being airlifted out for urgent medical treatment in Kathmandu. The whole incident came as a sombre warning to those who chose not to clip into a fixed rope because it appeared 'safe'. Such decisions came with dire consequences. Safety, although always at the back of our minds, had been brought to the fore and with it my thoughts about the worry endured by those waiting back at home. The conclusion I came to was that we had to trust our judgement, as did they, otherwise neither could function effectively.

The episode brought poignancy to our team's imminent Puja, for which preparations were complete. This Buddhist ceremony was to seek the blessing and safety of everyone involved, from cook boy through to the Sirdar and expedition leader: an inclusive event in the true sense of the word.

In readiness, the Sherpas had painstakingly built a square altar from random stone. It was about six feet high and three across, with a central hollow. During the course of the ceremony, the Puja pole would be lifted upright into this central space. About 25 feet in height, the pole had fastened to it, near the top, five ropes, each about 100 feet long with prayer flags tied down their entire length. Made out of thin cotton about twelve inches by eight inches, each flag, in a single colour of red, green, blue, yellow or white, had printed on it either an auspicious image or the script of a significant Buddhist prayer. These were also attached down the length of the Puja pole and on straight slender willow branches placed next to it. The ropes were secured at the other end to large boulders. These, along with stones jammed around its base, held the Puja pole upright. The end result resembled a maypole. Wafting proudly at the very tip of this sea of colour was the Nepalese flag.

An elderly monk had trekked, over a two-day period, all the way up from the monastery at Pangboche to perform the ceremony. Draped in the traditional deep-burgundy Buddhist robe and a not-so-authentic bright-yellow woollen hat, he sat cross-legged at a low table with an open prayer book in front of him. The low drone of his voice echoed around camp as he recited the script of ancient prayers. Every so often, the chants reached a crescendo, at which point he and the Sherpas sitting on either side of him would throw an offering of sampa (a finely ground wholemeal flour) and rice into the air.

The altar was both covered and surrounded by sweets, bottles of whisky, breads, tins of food and vegetables all placed there as offerings. Equipment such as ice axes and crampons were leant against the altar so as to be included in the blessing. A good Puja, with the due respect shown to the gods, would bring a successful and, more importantly, safe expedition for both Sherpas and climbers alike. The reverence shown by the climbers and their proper involvement in the Puja was expected.

No sooner had the Puja pole been hoisted upright than a red-billed Himalayan chough settled on top of it. A member of the crow family that normally feeds on insects and fallen grain, it was drawn to Base Camp by an easy meal. The food displayed around the altar played no small part in attracting this bird that spent the summer months in the high Himalaya. An aerial acrobat whose tumbling displays were a wonder to behold, its distinctive call of *kee-aw, kee-aw, kee-aw* was a regular daytime sound that echoed around Base Camp. A careful eye had to be kept on food, as unattended it would quickly fall prey to these wily opportunists.

As the ceremony moved towards a climax, everyone faced the altar holding a handful of sampa. The chants reached a series of concluding crescendos. On each occasion, sampa was thrown into the air, covering everyone in this dusty flour. The offerings were complete.

Our Sherpas, lifted by the celebrations, began to drink some of the customary and much-awaited *chang*: a home-brewed rice-based drink that tastes not dissimilar to cider. This and cups containing whisky were proffered to all present. Now came the chance to celebrate, for our Sherpas to unwind. This was not a time for them to look towards all the hard work that lay ahead. The headaches from the excesses of chang would be enough to do that in the cold morning light of the following day.

One by one, the climbers retired for a late lunch. The Sherpas carried on into the afternoon and early evening. Nepalese folk songs rang through Base Camp, full of a sense of joy and happiness. The relaxing fragrance of burning juniper wafted easily in the air.

Circumstances had dictated that Henry needed to fly back to Kathmandu. Our oxygen supplies, and those that Henry was supplying to some of the other teams, had been held up in Customs over some paperwork. Other expedition leaders, most notably Rob Hall and Scott Fischer, had put pressure on him. They were beginning to worry about the oxygen they had been promised. Henry, concerned that bureaucracy could bog down these essential supplies, decided it was best to head back down to sort matters personally.

It was early one morning when Kami came to my tent with a worried look on his face. A meeting had been called at the Imax Base Camp, which all expedition leaders and their Sirdars were requested to attend. With Henry being away, Kami wanted to ask if I would accompany him. He was uneasy about going by himself and was looking to me for support.

As Kami and I entered the green Imax mess tent, the official manner of the proceedings was immediately apparent. At the far side was a long rectangular table at which David Breashears, Ed Viesturs, Rob Hall and Scott Fischer were seated as though in readiness for a formal inquiry. Around the edge of the tent sat various expedition leaders and their Sirdars, waiting for matters to commence. Most were unsure as to why they had been summoned to this unusual gathering. I was similarly perplexed.

The meeting began by the expedition leaders being asked if they could, in turn, introduce themselves and their Sirdar to all those present and to very briefly explain the nature or nationality of their expedition.

Rob went first, introducing himself as the leader of Adventure Consultants. His lanky appearance, dark beard, authoritative tone and self-assurance belied his 35 years. Scott soon followed with his own introduction, stating he was there in a similar role for Mountain Madness. Scott's manner was more laid-back. His muscular stature, blond hair and clean-shaven, chiselled good looks brought with them a quiet confidence; this he was more than comfortable with.

One by one, the expedition leaders made their introduction, until it came to my turn. I briefly explained that I was standing in at the meeting for Henry Todd and that the nature of his expedition was commercial.

Looking slightly confused, Rob interrupted. 'I know you?' he said, his statement quite clearly quizzical.

He knew we'd met before but couldn't remember where or when. I jolted his memory. I'd trekked up to Everest Base Camp on the Nepalese side the previous year, for acclimatisation before travelling into Tibet to make my attempt with Henry from the north. At the time, Base Camp had been devoid of climbers, apart from Rob and a few others who were making preparations for their clients' arrival. He'd very kindly offered me refreshments, and I'd spent an hour or two talking with him, finding him excellent company. His parting words that year had been: 'Pass my regards on to Henry.'

Although I didn't mention it at this impromptu meeting in the Imax tent, I also recalled asking Rob in 1995 if he'd considered running expeditions elsewhere, such as Aconcagua in South America. His reply had been 'I wouldn't get out of bed for $2,500', which was the approximate cost of joining a commercial expedition on Aconcagua at that time. I'd laughed at his reply. He clearly knew his worth and had set his sights accordingly.

With a smile, Rob acknowledged our previous meeting and his own visual recall. 'I thought so,' he said.

Once the introductions were complete, an explanation was given by those from the Imax team as to the reason for the meeting. Crampons, purposefully left at the bottom of the Icefall, had been stolen. The culprit was most probably another climber or Sherpa, and, although unlikely, a trekker coming into Base Camp could not be ruled out. It was stated in no uncertain terms that this was not acceptable; that anyone caught stealing equipment would be immediately reported to the authorities. Theft such as this could place climbers or Sherpas in danger, especially if it happened higher on the mountain. This had to stop here and now. The warning was absolutely clear.

Rob followed, using this opportunity to assume a position of authority. He touched on the issue of expeditions not clearing up properly when they'd finished. Waste should be taken away from Base Camp and disposed of in the correct manner. He was looking towards sustaining his expeditions in the coming years without having to observe an ever-growing rubbish tip around Base Camp.

The humiliation to the climbing world of the media highlighting the expanse of the South Col littered with oxygen cylinders, broken tents, tin cans, gas cylinders and other refuse was not lost on Rob. The public's attention had been further focused by reports of frozen corpses lying amongst this thoughtlessly discarded debris. Full-colour photographs had been spread across the entire centre pages of national newspapers. This was an embarrassment for all mountaineers, from which no climbing generation on Everest could escape.

Rob had already joined a scheme to make headway into this high-altitude rubbish dump, paying the Sherpas a bonus for every empty oxygen cylinder they brought down from the South Col. The reward was in the region of $20 to $30 for each one. Sherpas descending carrying rucksacks bulging with up to five old cylinders at a time would turn out to be a common sight. These extra bonuses could significantly increase their pay.

In 1994, the Sagamartha Environmental Expedition, led by Scott Fischer, had begun this clean-up operation by offering the Sherpas a similar bonus. Others had continued to embrace this successful scheme during the intervening period.

With regard to the current year, Rob was making full use of the respect and status he'd earned from his operations on Everest. He announced his intentions towards offenders trying to depart Base Camp at the conclusion of their expedition without clearing up. He was not trying to make friends, just to influence people. His message was clear in its intent. If any expedition left their Base Camp area in a mess, he would photograph that area and supply the Nepalese authorities with both the photographs and full details of those concerned. This was quite clearly not an idle threat and neither was it an unreasonable one. Rob found debris left in such a manner distasteful, and he had a considerable vested interest in improving the current situation.

Warnings had been given on both thefts and clearing up. Lines had been firmly drawn. The meeting ended in an air of apparent control and committed endeavour. As far as I am aware, this turned out to be the only theft that spring season. At a later date, I would be informed that the missing crampons had in fact belonged to David Breashears, Ed Viesturs and Robert Schauer from the Imax team.

Kami, sitting beside me throughout these proceedings, had not said a word. Without doubt he'd absorbed all that had been said, assimilating the extra responsibilities this might place on him as Sirdar of our expedition. In truth, little if anything needed to change, as he oversaw the expedition in a thoughtful and responsible manner. However, I felt such a forthright meeting had left Kami and the other Sirdars slightly uneasy due to its formal nature. I was glad I'd attended with Kami in Henry's absence. It would have been unfair and intimidating for him to be the sole representative of our expedition.

A short time after the meeting, I bumped into Rob. With a smile beaming through his thick beard, he opened the conversation: 'So, you didn't summit from Tibet last year?'

My reply took him by surprise: '17 May.'

Rob, rather puzzled by my response, asked, 'What are you doing back this year?'

I explained that no British climber had summited Everest from both north and south sides, from both Nepal and Tibet. That's why I was back.

Rob smiled, pondered for a moment or two, then looked at me with a glint in his eye and said, 'No Kiwi has ever done that.'

Maybe I'd planted a seed.

Through the Khumbu Icefall

10 April 1996

Within our expedition, climbing partnerships were beginning to form. Thomas and Tina were unquestionably a team of their own. Paul and Neil were friends at home and had arranged to climb together. Michael Jörgensen, like me, was attempting Everest from the south after his successful ascent from the north the previous year. The two of us, along with Brigitte, were given a long leash. Henry allowed us to choose our individual climbing schedules during the acclimatisation period, provided we agreed this in advance. However, it was apparent at certain stages in the climb that Henry wanted me to keep an eye on Mark Pfetzer, mainly because of his age. I wasn't sure how Ray would fit in, but no doubt at various stages during the expedition he would tag along with other members of our group.

Most of the movement in the Icefall appeared to take place in the early hours, usually between 2 and 4 a.m., as the ice contracted. Each night, lying in the dark solitude of my tent, I would hear sharp cracking sounds often followed by deep rumblings as the ice scraped over the bedrock far below, or the thunder of an occasional avalanche as it cascaded down onto the Icefall from the West Ridge of Everest or Nuptse, which flanked it on either side. None of these sounds filled me with much confidence.

The norm for our group was to depart from Base Camp at around 5.30 a.m. to climb through this frozen labyrinth to Camp 1, which lay just beyond, at the beginning of the Western Cwm. This would be a journey that would take somewhere between one hour thirty minutes and four hours, depending on an individual climber's ability and stamina once he or she was acclimatised.

Like many, my preference was to make my way through as quickly as possible, following the example of the Sherpas. The theory being: the longer you took, the greater the chance that something could happen. This was best described to me by Henry as a game of Russian roulette.

My first climb through the Icefall to Camp 1 was to be made alone. I remember lying in my tent the night before, trying not to think about the possible dangers ahead. The problem was, each time I calmed my apprehension, there came, like some sadistic reminder, another unnerving and resonating crack as the ice moved once more. I was grateful to be rescued from my fitful sleep by the alarm on my watch.

Half an hour later, I was standing alone at the bottom of the Icefall, in the cold pre-dawn light. Embedded in the snow next to me was a single marker wand that indicated the beginning of the route. My breathing was rapid. Each time I exhaled, the moisture in my warm breath billowed in the frigid air. Perspiration from the effort to walk the short distance from my tent had already caused a damp sensation in the deepest layer of my clothing.

The noise of the ice moving had ceased, replaced by an eerie lack of sound. It was as though this maze, through which I would gain 2,500 feet in altitude, was welcoming in another potential and unsuspecting victim. The quietness seeming to say, *Enter if you dare.*

After clipping onto the fixed rope, I began to climb. The noise of my crampons broke through the silence as they bit rhythmically into the brittle ice. Nerves were soon overcome by the pounding of my heart, the gasping for each breath, as my body tried to extract the meagre oxygen from the depleted air. Each inhalation, which contained half the oxygen of sea level, struggled to supply my muscles with the required amount.

I took no breaks but continued on at a steady pace. Each time I turned a corner or reached the top of another house-sized sérac, I was welcomed by one breathtaking sight after another. The unparalleled splendour occupied my mind. Curtains of crystal-clear icicles hung along the edges of tilting séracs that appeared in infinite shades of blue.

Aluminium ladders that had been laid flat and lashed together with rope spanned the crevasses. Stepping onto the first of these, the clash of my steel crampons against the metal rungs gave an indication of their makeshift nature. Each awkward step tested the flexibility of my ankles. Sheer sides of ever-darkening blue ice drew my eyes into the forbidding bowels. The tenebrous chasm disappeared into obscurity, its furthest reaches hidden by the blackness of this hellish slot. A fall un-roped into such a place would leave a climber completely out of sight, wedged in the narrowest of confines hundreds of feet below, prey to a slow and very cold death; yet all I could see was beguiling splendour.

In places where it was not possible to circumnavigate the séracs, ladders lashed together in a similar fashion had been fastened upright against faces of pale sapphire ice. Debris fields usually preceded these vertical sections, formed where one or more séracs, weighing hundreds of tons, had toppled over and splintered into countless shards. The soaring daytime temperatures, augmented by reflection off the brilliant surface, had sculpted these varying-sized pieces into innumerable three-dimensional shapes. Translucent icicles hung down from these forms; hollows and apertures had melted within them. These were masterpieces that would have enhanced the finest of galleries. More recent sérac falls appeared glass-like, the pieces sharp and angular.

The route, indicated by a single line of rope, also threaded its way through narrow passages. On either side, soaring ice tilted menacingly overhead; the variations in its shade and clarity gave me the sensation of being in a mystical realm of ice through which I had to pass. However, the Icefall was a place that in the blink of an eye could crush or swallow a passing Sherpa or climber. Many had been lost over the years. No one knew when or whereabouts on the route it would happen again. It was just down to a matter of time and a stroke of bad luck.

I arrived at Camp 1 around 8.30 a.m., minutes before the rays of the sun touched the entrance to the Western Cwm. Here, I would spend the day by myself. Others from our expedition, mostly climbing in pairs, were due up in the next few days. For the moment, they were patiently waiting their turn.

I was by myself 'in person' but surprisingly not alone. For part of the time I had a small Himalayan visitor. This unexpected but welcome addition came in the form of a bird slightly larger than a sparrow: a small creature that had quickly realised I could supply a free lunch in this harsh environment. The share of the meal I provided was in proportion to our relative size and was consumed over several visits from my avian companion.

My sleep at Camp 1 was restless, interrupted by a mild headache that was typical of the first night spent at a higher altitude. As the wind gusting down the Western Cwm buffeted the tent, the warmth of my sleeping bag brought security. Outside, I could hear the familiar sounds of moving ice and small avalanches as they fell from the steep faces on either side. The noises seemed perilously close.

The reassuring light of dawn penetrated my frozen tent around 5 a.m. My first halt at Camp 1, at around 20,000 feet, had been served. It was one of two overnight stays I would make here. On all but the next climb through the Icefall, I would progress directly up the Western Cwm to Camp 2, some two miles further on and 1,000 feet higher in elevation.

I emerged from my tent to a clear blue sky without a breath of wind. High above, the snow-clad summits dazzled intensely in the sunshine. However, the thought firmly imprinted on my mind was of the comparative luxury of Base Camp. A hot breakfast followed by a morning relaxing in my tent listening to music beckoned far below.

The climb back down through the Icefall was much quicker and easier than my ascent just 24 hours earlier. It took little more than 40 minutes. The reward was Base Camp, with its daytime temperatures that reached 25°C and where the strong sunlight burnt harshly as its ultraviolet radiation penetrated the thin air.

The time spent at Base Camp was to make up a significant proportion of the expedition. It was important for rest and recuperation between climbs up the mountain and for the opportunity it gave individuals to focus on the task ahead. Ninety per cent of the climb is in the mind. I had, on previous expeditions, sat at Base Camp and watched people convince themselves they weren't going to reach the summit or find some pressing reason they'd just thought of that necessitated their leaving for home. I have even heard of people deliberately injuring themselves with an ice axe rather than admit either their fear or fear of failure. I can only conclude that to some the romantic notion of climbing Everest disappears when faced with the stark reality of the undertaking.

Days were largely built around a routine that began at 7 a.m. with a mug of hot tea being brought by one of the kitchen staff to each of the climbers' tents. Still embedded in my sleeping bag, I relished this early-morning brew, sipped at whilst I listened to news from the BBC World Service on my shortwave radio. I would watch as the sun's first rays crept across the roof of my tent above my head. The advancing light melted the inner tent's frosty lining and delineated the point the warmth had reached on the outer layer. This in itself would send me diving under the covers as the newly formed liquid coagulated into drops that began to rain down on me.

The loud banging of a spoon against a large aluminium bowl would signify that breakfast was ready, normally around 8.30 a.m. Slowly, all would emerge from their individual tents and make their way to the mess, although at times some would decide that the early-morning tea was enough, continuing their slumber late into the morning, occasionally up to lunchtime at around midday.

Days passed by at a leisurely pace. Nothing at Base Camp was hurried. It was surprising how a few chores completely filled the time. Cleaning a small number of clothes, having a wash, shaving, reading a book, listening to music, checking equipment, an afternoon snooze – the list of arduous tasks seemed endless. Somehow even going to the toilet felt like an appointment that took up part of the day.

Situated a short distance away, the toilet facility was a tall, narrow tent, similar in shape to a sentry post. It had been positioned at the edge of some raised ground. The lower area, immediately behind, had been boxed in with a newly constructed wall, and then a blue plastic barrel was positioned in the enclosed space. At the upper level, two flat pieces of rock had been placed on the floor inside the tent. Bridging the three-foot gap between solid ground and the wall behind, they gave the occupant footholds and a dubious sense of security from what lay below.

Paul, myself and a few others were enjoying a mid-morning coffee in the shade of our mess tent. The entrance flaps were fastened back to let the warm air percolate through. Paul was busy writing and I was staring blankly into space when something caught my eye.

'Paul,' I said, trying to catch his attention.

'What?' he responded without looking up, slightly irritated at the interruption.

'Some guy has just jumped into our toilet,' I said in a nonchalant fashion.

Paul looked up, his eyes wide with bewilderment. He turned to look in that direction. The sides of the toilet tent had been lifted back. Sticking up above ground level, a man's head could be seen bobbing about.

Paul, in an overstated theatrical voice, shouted, 'Oh my God!' The others crowded round. We all stared in total disbelief, wondering what on earth had driven some poor soul to this desperate course of action.

The sight of a second person appearing into view carrying an empty barrel gave a clue. It dawned on us that the first gentleman, now standing in the bowels of our less than fragrant toilet, must be an employee of Sagamartha Pollution Control. His job: to change the barrel we had already half-filled, before it became too heavy to move. This would presumably be transported back down the valley by yak, so that its contents could be disposed of properly. Our genuine sympathy went out to this poor man who was squeezed alongside the current container.

We had been instructed to urinate to one side; only the solids were to be collected. The problem was that the barrel had been placed some three feet below the point of release. Not everybody's aim was that good, especially if the occupant was suffering from a bout of diarrhoea. Excrement in various states of solidity had slid its way down the outside of the container. On the list of the worst jobs in the world, this particular guy's had to be pretty high up. We couldn't see if he was wearing gloves. None of us had the courage to go and find out.

The opportunity to socialise with climbers on other expeditions played an important role that filled many an hour. Our most frequent visitor by far was Anatoli. He knew all our Sherpas, our Sirdar Kami, Henry, and had climbed with Michael, Paul and myself only ten months earlier. He'd also met Brigitte the previous year when she'd been climbing on the north side of Everest with her husband Jon Muir. Anatoli got on well with all of us; he felt relaxed in our company. His presence, when he was not away busy fulfilling his duties for Scott Fischer, had a natural feel to it. He knew none of us possessed fat chequebooks and that we had all made considerable sacrifices to be there. He also understood we each showed a degree of independence and self-reliance in our climbing, that we enjoyed the mountains. However, all these friendships paled in comparison to the budding and rather serious relationship he had struck up with Linda Wylie. When they had first met, this spring season, the chemistry between them had been unmistakable. Linda and her 16-year-old son Jake had joined up with us in Kathmandu. They were accompanying Mark Pfetzer to Base Camp along with a documentary film crew. Mark's mother, who had commitments back in the US, would be joining us later on in the expedition.

Once the general routine of day-to-day living had been accepted and slipped into, I found Base Camp a pleasant place to relax, to contemplate quietly what really mattered in my life. Time so rarely found in my busy and sometimes stressful everyday life at home. I found it surprising how certain aspects that seemed so crucial at home and usually to do with business were in fact not important at all. What really mattered were family and friends and, above all else, their safety and well-being. Money, success and the like seemed irrelevant in the grand scheme of things. I counted on one hand what was important to me. What I found most enlightening was the personal strength and determination this time to contemplate afforded me.

Once in a while, minor frictions would appear between members of the team: not an unusual occurrence when people are thrust together for a two-month period in such a harsh environment. I remember one such episode. Neil, both tall and good looking, was by all accounts a bit of a ladies' man: a reputation he rather enjoyed. His sometimes brash manner, although never intended as more than a bit of fun, did not sit well with Brigitte. On one occasion while Brigitte, Paul and I were sitting together, she asked, 'So, does Neil have a girlfriend at home?'

'No,' replied Paul.

'I'm not surprised!' she exclaimed.

Paul paused, allowing a tantalising moment or two of silence, and then followed with, 'He has about 12.'

I remember doubling up with laughter. Paul's timing had been perfect. Brigitte, despite looking slightly exasperated, managed a smile. She too saw the funny side and quick-wittedness of Paul's reply.

Sunset came each evening around six o'clock, accompanied by the fragrance of juniper being burnt on the Puja altar. With Pumori standing immediately to the west of Base Camp, we were always shaded from the last rays of the sun, whose golden colours lit up the snow on the upper reaches of Nuptse and the West Ridge of Everest. As quickly as the heat of the day had arrived came the cold sub-zero temperatures of the night. These usually sent me scurrying to my tent and into my down sleeping bag for an hour prior to our evening meal at 7 p.m., which once again was signalled by the familiar loud banging of spoon on bowl.

So each day at Base Camp passed in this peaceful and sedate routine, the relative silence only momentarily interrupted by a loud crack followed by the roar of an avalanche cascading off the surrounding mountains of Pumori, Lingtren and Nuptse, or nearby rockfalls as they tumbled downwards, kicking up clouds of dust.

Into the Western Cwm

14 April 1996

Through the night, noise from movement within the Icefall had been particularly prevalent. Sleep was scarce, as I lay awake nervously listening to every sound. It was shortly after 4 a.m. that I heard other climbers preparing to leave. The clanking of their equipment as they set off raised the apprehension about my own departure.

I left Base Camp around 5.30 a.m. A short ten-minute walk took me to the familiar marker wand. For the second time I entered the Khumbu Icefall just as the half-light of morning appeared.

After about 30 minutes of listening to my crampons crunch into the crystalline surface, I came across Rob and his clients. They were sitting on a small snowfield, resting and chatting to one another. I didn't know any of those with him but waved to Rob as I passed through. None of them were carrying rucksacks as far as I could see. As they were travelling light, I deduced they were intending to climb through the Icefall and return back to Base Camp later that same morning.

Pressing on at a steady pace, I'd reached the midway point when little more than 130 feet to my right a block of ice about the size of a family house toppled forwards. With a thundering crash, it sent shards of ice splintering into the air. My stomach shrank instantly. Fear welded me to the spot. I waited to hear, or feel, what happened next. Absolutely nothing – only a deathly silence followed the incident. A fine cloud of ice particles settled from the surrounding air. With my heart pounding, it took several minutes to regain my composure. Apprehensively, I moved forward to continue my journey through this captivating yet very deadly mass of blue ice.

I reached Camp 1 around 8 a.m. as the sun's rays edged towards the top of the Icefall. Soon the temperatures within this maze would begin to spiral upwards. Solar radiation and the light reflected back from the icy surface would sap the strength from those climbing later.

Sitting outside my tent at Camp 1, it was some time before I heard voices in the Icefall immediately below. Over the top appeared Rob with three or four of his clients close behind – but not all.

Those who'd made it thus far looked as though they were vying for position within their team. They were keen for Rob to both notice and acknowledge their efforts. He understood well how to manage his clients. Despite having paid considerable sums for their place on his high-profile guided expedition, none were guaranteed a shot at the summit. If they weren't up to an attempt, or might put themselves or others in danger, then the final decision was entirely up to Rob. This meant for the whole expedition his clients toed the line, wanting to be noticed as capable, going out of their way to be 'best buddies' with him. In equal measure, Rob was no doubt instilling confidence by praising their efforts: telling them they were one of the strongest teams on the mountain.

After what seemed no more than a 15-minute rest, Rob said, 'OK, time to head back down.' It was apparent that those who'd not made the top of the Icefall would be collected on the descent. They would be turned around regardless of how far up they'd climbed.

Both that day and my second night at Camp 1 passed by in quiet contemplation, and I got a reasonable night's sleep. Not wanting to be caught in the intense daytime temperatures, I rose early the following morning and got ready to move on.

Throughout my time at Camp 1, the dry ambient air had sucked moisture from my body. Each exhaled breath had carried with it vital fluid, which my drinks had not sufficiently replenished. Standing outside the orange nylon tent, I bent forward and coughed repeatedly towards the ground. Desiccated phlegm had formed as a thin carapace on the roof of my mouth. Curling my tongue across my palate, I was unable to budge this irritation. In frustration, I removed my glove and resorted to running my forefinger hard across the surface to dislodge the brittle layer – an action that caused me to both gag and salivate. As I pushed the contents of my mouth out with my tongue, a glutinous dribbling mass dangled from my lips. Pursing my lips and pinching two fingers together across them, I freed myself from this light brown crusty sputum, which I flung down into the snow. I wiped my fingers clean across the rubber side-covering of my boot. Rinsing my mouth, I gargled repeatedly with warm water from my Nalgene bottle, spitting it out onto the pristine surface. Only then did a feeling of normality return.

After departing from my overnight accommodation, I zigzagged my way up the Western Cwm towards Camp 2: a route the Sherpas had completed fixing a day or two before. Aluminium ladders had once again been laid flat over exposed crevasses, the widest of which took five twelve-foot sections lashed together to span its gargantuan and seemingly bottomless chasm. Crossing this particular bridge was unnerving, especially as I was carrying a heavy rucksack. The ladders bounced with each step. When I reached the centre point, it bowed in the middle, taking me down a foot below the level of either side.

In the Western Cwm, also known as the Valley of Silence, no sound went unnoticed, my auditory senses heightened by the minimal input. From this alone it became obvious to me that many other crevasses lay hidden below the surface, spanned by fragile bridges of snow and ice. Their presence was given away by the squeak of my crampons as they bit into the surface. The pitch became higher as the ice thinned and deepened in its tone as I moved onto safer ground.

The occasional stone that fell from high on Nuptse also broke the tranquillity of the Western Cwm. These spun through the air to reach terminal velocity, creating a whistling sound that was followed by a dull thud as they embedded themselves in the snow at the bottom of the face. The route, although close at times, kept a safe distance from this constant reminder of danger.

Behind me, in the distance, I could make out the lone figure of another climber catching me up as I approached the site of Camp 2 at 21,000 ft: a place that this early in the expedition was little more than a series of supply dumps; no tents had yet been erected. The climber turned out to be Anatoli wearing a pair of running spikes. He was making a lone acclimatisation foray to this higher camp. We spent the next two hours sitting on the piles of equipment, passing the time of day.

It didn't take long for our conversation to turn to Anatoli's home city of Almaty in Kazakhstan and to climbing in the Tien Shan: an area that had infrequent visits by Western climbers. Otherwise known as the celestial mountains, they are a large isolated range surrounded by the desert basins of northern China and Central Asia. Placed geographically north of Nepal and Tibet, they stretch along the Kazakhstan–China border. The range has peaks rising up to 24,400 ft, making them the most northerly summits of such a height.

I'd been fortunate enough to visit Anatoli's home city and the Tien Shan four years earlier. I'd spent nearly a whole month there. As luck would have it, I'd passed some of that time both climbing and socialising with another highly respected Russian climber and good friend of Anatoli's, Valeri Khrishchaty. Valeri was a mild-mannered and modest man who'd reminded me very much of my father. From his medium height, build and self-deprecating character, most would have pinned him as a nine-to-five office worker rather than a climber at the cutting edge of high-altitude mountaineering – one who had abandoned a summit attempt, above the Pinnacles, on the then unclimbed North East Ridge of Everest to rescue an ailing climber from another expedition attempting the mountain by a different route. This was an act of heroism that had denied Valeri and his team the first ascent of this highly coveted prize – one that was taken by a very well-equipped Japanese team with a million-dollar expedition budget on 11 May 1995: a milestone in the history of Everest that I'd witnessed from the north side's Advanced Base Camp.

Two years prior to this Japanese conquest, Valeri had tragically been swept to his death by an avalanche while making an ascent of the second-highest peak in the Tien Shan range, Khan Tengri: the same mountain on which I'd first met him.

Anatoli related the story to me of how he'd been chosen for Russia's national climbing team. In 1989, they set out to make the first traverse of Kangchenjunga's four summits, the length of which stands at well over 26,000 feet above sea level. Valeri Khrishchaty had been part of that successful team.

Anatoli had been asked to attend mountaineering training camps from which the national team would be selected. Endurance tests were set whereby the climbers were dispatched from a given height at the same time, to see who would get to the top of a particular mountain first. They began in Pamirs. On the 24,600-ft Peak Communism of Tajikistan, the first one to summit was Anatoli. The competition then moved to the Caucasus Mountains, where they tackled the 18,500-ft Mount Elbrus. Anatoli was first again. The prestige of being named on the national team was so important that complaints soon flew around; he was accused of gaining advantage by using lightweight felt boots. In the interest of fairness, and to avoid future criticism, the selectors set the Elbrus challenge once more. Happy their objection had been accepted as valid, his opponents managed to find a heavy pair of old and rather rigid climbing boots for him to wear. Anatoli, much to his complainants' consternation, was first to the top yet again, firmly securing his place on the national team.

The very personal conversation between Anatoli and myself illustrated the passion he undoubtedly felt for the former USSR and for his adopted home of Kazakhstan following the break-up of the Soviet Union. He was working on Everest, but such agreeable discussions with someone who'd visited his homeland came as a welcome distraction to him. And so we wiled away the time in the warm midday sun before he eventually decided to head back down to Base Camp.

As Anatoli disappeared into the distance, I set about fixing myself a tent. I was the lone occupant in the entire expanse of Camp 2. Everyone else was a few miles away and 3,300 feet lower down. I enjoyed that day immensely. Sitting on a large flat rock on which I'd placed a foam mat, I dreamt away the remaining hours of daylight, immersing myself in the isolation of my Himalayan surroundings. I watched as the sun sank low in the western sky, silhouetting the snow-capped dome of Pumori's summit, which appeared to radiate the rays of light it had interrupted. Far below in the shadows, Base Camp's daylight hours had already come to an end. In the Western Cwm, over 3,000 feet higher, I sat in solitary contentment, bathed in the last rays of a fading sun. The evening clouds rising up the Western Cwm brought with them the sharp cold air of a bitter night. The sudden drop in temperature soon had me scuttling into the depths of my recently erected accommodation.

My sleep was shallow and restless. I sat up at regular intervals to drink from the bottle I'd placed deep in my sleeping bag to keep its contents both liquid and warm. Dehydration is both rapid and severe at these high altitudes. Passing through a night without drinking up to a litre of water brings with it a pounding headache by dawn. Any slight consequential inconvenience of this necessary intake of fluid is far outweighed by the dividends of comfort and acclimatisation.

Shortly after dawn, I emerged from my sleeping bag into the uninviting chill of the morning air. It was 6.30 a.m. After rapidly dressing, I packed my rucksack and made a quick departure down the Western Cwm. No time for breakfast here. There was a far more comfortable and appetising meal waiting for me at Base Camp two hours away. The crunching of my crampons on the hard frozen surface and the clanking of the jumar and karabiners against my climbing harness sounded the eagerness with which I departed.

My return to Base Camp held the reward of hot apple pancakes followed by a chapati with a fried egg on top, which had been skilfully destroyed by our ever-smiling and diminutive cook, Pasang. It also brought a number of questions from my fellow climbers. Although at least six of us had previously attempted Everest from the Tibetan side, none except for myself, on my most recent trip up the mountain, had ventured up the Western Cwm. I described in no great detail the obstacles encountered, the nature of the route and the position of Camp 2. Then the specific question concerning crevasses was raised. I explained there were a few spanned by the familiar ladders, with other sections of potentially dangerous ground fixed with rope, elaborating on how the final crossing over an ice field to Camp 2 was unfixed and appeared safe. As a throwaway line, I joked about how the pitch of the sound made by my crampons changed as they dug into the ice, becoming higher as I crossed over crevasses hidden beneath my feet.

It was during afternoon tea, around 4 p.m., that Henry burst angrily into the mess tent. Looking at me, he demanded, 'What the bloody hell have you been saying to Thomas and Tina?'

I sat upright. Almost totally lost for words, I managed, 'Pardon?'

Henry, who was seething, responded, 'I don't know what you've said, but they are insisting on going up the Western Cwm roped to each other. They say if they "go", they want to "go" together.'

There was an instantaneous roar of laughter from everyone in the tent, one that cleared the air somewhat. From this reaction, Henry suspected there had been an overreaction to something I'd said. Thomas and Tina were not present.

I explained the description I'd given of the changes in sound my crampons made as they dug into the ice. It was an undeniable fact and something everyone would hear, although admittedly not all might notice, as they crossed the Western Cwm.

Henry, with a look of exasperation, rolled his eyes upwards, saying, 'Please don't say anything to them. I've got to deal with this nonsense.'

I looked at Henry. 'No problem,' I replied.

Within a matter of days, Camp 2 was established with a cook/mess tent, affording me the opportunity to make my second overnight stay there in relatively more comfort. On this occasion, an event took place during my return to Base Camp that would lead to my only, albeit brief, contact with Scott Fischer – apart, that is, from the formal leaders' meeting that had already taken place.

Abseiling over the lip of the Khumbu Icefall, I entered the labyrinth once more. Ten minutes into my descent, I came across two climbers moving slowly: a man aged around 30 was assisting an American climber named Charlotte Fox, from Scott's team. Although she appeared uninjured, she seemed distressed. I stopped to offer my assistance only to be informed by the climber aiding her that he'd got the situation under control. He did, however, ask me to head down and find Scott, to let him know of the situation, so that some of Scott's team could come up and take over. Charlotte looked frightened, not of the climbing but of the condition she was convinced she had.

'Tell Scott that Charlotte's in the Icefall. Tell him I've got pulmonary oedema,' she pleaded as I climbed down, leaving the pair to their slow descent.

Her breathing had seemed rapid, her speech laboured. This struck me as possibly a slight panic attack exacerbating the problem she already had, but that was not for to me to decide.

Reaching Base Camp some 25 minutes later, I located Scott in his 'Starbucks' tent. Sitting with a colleague in deep conversation, they were enjoying a cup of strong coffee. This was the first time that I'd met Scott Fischer properly. A man in his 30s, his blond hair tied back in a ponytail, he oozed both charm and self-confidence. I briefly explained the circumstances and Charlotte's approximate location.

Making a quick assessment of the situation, Scott took a sip from his half-finished coffee. 'How did she look to you?' he asked.

I told him it did not appear too serious, although Charlotte was distressed and looked frightened.

Sitting back in his chair with his decision made, he announced, 'OK, we'll have another coffee then I suppose we'd better go and get her.' With a smile of appreciation, he looked across at me and said, 'Thanks for your help, mate.'

A quick nod and I left.

Base Camp's relative silence was broken again around 20 April by the sound of an approaching helicopter. Another rescue had taken place: that of Eamon Fullen from Mal Duff's team, otherwise known as 'Ginge' Fullen. Aged 29, and a serving Royal Navy diver, he'd suffered a heart attack near the top of the Icefall. Enduring severe chest pains, he had been put on oxygen and heroically brought down over this treacherous ground by his Royal Air Force teammate Euan Duncan. After being given emergency treatment by doctors at Base Camp, he was being evacuated back to Kathmandu, where he was to be admitted into intensive care.

However, Ginge Fullen was no stranger to setbacks. He'd taken up climbing six years earlier when a broken neck had finished his rugby-playing career. Against all expectations, Ginge fought his way back from this heart attack to resume his career as a Navy diver. He also went on to become the first person to climb the highest mountain in all 47 European countries, followed by those in all 53 African countries. Currently, he is well under way on the mammoth undertaking of climbing the highest summit in every country in the world, of which there are 194. Everest is still on the list of those he has yet to climb.

The sound of this second helicopter skimming several feet above the Khumbu Glacier with its stricken passenger on board cautioned of the dangers that lay ahead. Such incidents brought an air of unease to Base Camp. Climbing at any serious high altitude had not begun, yet two people had already been evacuated to hospital.

Within a few days of this latest incident came a third. One of Scott Fischer's Sherpas, Ngawang Topche, was struck down with a serious and life-threatening case of pulmonary oedema. Unfortunately, once they got him back to Base Camp, it was decided, for whatever reason, to aid his recovery by moving him to lower altitudes further down the valley rather than ordering an immediate helicopter evacuation: a decision that may have cost him his life. Ngawang was eventually airlifted out of the village of Pheriche several days later. He did not recover; by early June he lay dead in a Kathmandu hospital.

Anatoli's visits to our Base Camp diminished around this time, to the point we hardly saw him at all. Scott, who was reputedly paying Anatoli $25,000 for his services, was complaining that as a guide he was not spending enough time attending to the needs of the team's high-paying clients. In truth, the decline in Anatoli's visits to our camp was because the main reason for them had departed. Linda and Jake had left and were heading back to Kathmandu as planned. As a result, Anatoli now focused his attention on the task ahead.

Towards the latter part of April came my fourth, and last, acclimatisation run through the Khumbu Icefall.

It was probably because I was the oldest of our climbing team, with teenagers of my own, that Henry asked if I would take Mark Pfetzer up to spend one night at Camp 3: the final piece in the jigsaw of our acclimatisation before summit attempts. At 24,000 feet, Camp 3 was placed on some small ledges, only slightly larger than the tents themselves, hacked out of the ice halfway up the Lhotse Face.

Leaving Camp 2 after an early breakfast, Mark and I made our way over the gently rising ground that typifies the upper section of the Western Cwm. The crevasses and other potentially dangerous sections had already been fixed with ropes, as had the much steeper Lhotse Face, as far as Camp 3.

As the sun rose over the top of Lhotse's jagged summit ridge, its dazzling rays burst into the Western Cwm. Within minutes, the sunlight was visibly, and on this occasion depressingly, chasing the shadows faster than I could have run at sea level. The last remnants of the previous night in which we stood were rapidly disappearing. The line delineating the limit of the gloominess, which ran north to south across the Western Cwm, came rushing towards us. There was no escape. Soon we were bathed in intense and highly reflected sunlight, whose instantaneous heat began to drain our reserves of strength. Our pace slowed as this extra burden seemed to force our crampons deeper into the névé. The lifting of each foot to take the next step now appeared to take a more concentrated effort. Slowly, we plodded on.

Within two hours of leaving Camp 2, Mark and I were circumnavigating the right-hand end of the Bergschrund (a geological term referring to a large crack or crevasse where the glacier is pulling away from the mountain). This we did by ascending a tricky 30-ft section of near-vertical ice. Once this was overcome, we gained access to the Lhotse Face proper: a massive rippled sheet of scalloped pale-blue ice that rose menacingly above us for several thousand feet at an angle of 40 degrees. Jutting through this daunting obstacle was the occasional outcrop of shattered rock, whose eroded remains provided the sporadic rockfalls that were a known danger of the ground that lay ahead. Camp 3 from this point was out of sight.

As we climbed higher in the coming hours, we began to appreciate the vastness of the Western Cwm. Stretching out behind us as a gently curving sweep approximately three miles long, it ran between the steeply rising ramparts of Everest and Nuptse, both of which added millions of tons of ice to the already considerable volume of the glacier that flowed along the valley floor. Moving imperceptibly, this river of ice, several hundred feet thick, inched its way downwards from the Lhotse Face to the Khumbu Icefall at its lower end. At the midway point, and far-off to the right, the tents of Camp 2 appeared as tiny specks of conspicuous colour contrasted against the dark lateral moraine. They were some 3,000 feet below us.

Staring down at what we knew would be a one-way ticket, we took special care to be clipped in to the fixed ropes at all times, particularly at the points where the rope was fixed to the face by an ice screw. At these junctures, we took heed to clip in above each point before unclipping from the rope below. Although this is normal practice, the need for it was highlighted in our current location. We knew it would be almost impossible to arrest any fall. Over the years, many a climber and Sherpa had come to an untimely end from this point in the climb, more often than not due to overconfidence or through simple human error brought about by the lack of oxygen supplying the brain at this altitude. Our pace was deliberately steady; the object of the climb was acclimatisation, not the unnecessary use of precious energy. Nor did we want to increase the risk by rushing the simple safeguards.

By mid morning, as we rounded one of the many large bulges formed by the thick sheet of ice grinding slowly downwards over the bedrock of the steep mountainside, the tents at Camp 3 came into sight. Several of this year's expeditions had already erected tents here. Not because they needed them so early on but because tent spaces on these ledges were limited. The ones that remained from previous years saved a serious amount of work in the rarefied air. Each existing tent space that could be 'booked' would allow us to avoid several hours of backbreaking work hacking a level platform out of this frozen expanse. This energy-saving opportunity was purely on a first-come, first-served basis. We were no different from several other teams. One of our tents, with the unmistakable capital letters HG sprayed boldly on the side, was already in place.

Nearing Camp 3, we realised that many of the colours we'd picked out as being tents from several hundred feet further down had been correctly identified but not in the sense we expected. True, they had once been tents, but not from this year. They were the remnants of wind-shredded tents from former expeditions, which had been abandoned at Camp 3. They had been engulfed by the ever-forming ice, through which their tattered remains now protruded. They flapped eerily in an almost constant wind. A ghostly reminder that not all had returned from previous endeavours.

From Camp 3, at 24,000 feet, we were given a glimpse of the Himalaya. Cho-Oyu, the sixth-highest mountain in the world, which had been obscured from view at Base Camp by the much smaller Pumori, now dwarfed the mountain that had hidden it from sight. A myriad of other peaks could be seen from this vantage point: a panorama I knew would increase tenfold from the summit of Everest.

The splendour of what lay before us was spoilt by the nagging headache that accompanied us to our newly gained altitude. The need to gather ice and brew essential fluid drew us rapidly in to our awaiting tent.

Balanced on top of our single-burner gas stove was a small aluminium pan. We watched impatiently as the pieces of ice that we'd feebly hacked out of the slope with our axes gradually melted into a pool of tepid clear liquid at the bottom of the receptacle. The reluctance of the resulting water to boil, which happens at a lowly 80°C at this height, seemed interminable as our heads pounded from dehydration. The need to keep drinking kept us occupied for the whole afternoon.

We spent a cold night – through most of which I lay awake with a persistent headache – keenly awaiting the first signs of daylight. I was ready to depart as soon as possible from this necessary outing, eager to return to the comparatively oxygen-rich environment of Base Camp over 6,000 feet below. So eager were Mark and I to depart from Camp 3 that we arrived back into Camp 2 before other members of our expedition encamped there had risen for breakfast. After a quick bite to eat and a cup of tea, I continued straight on down. Others from our team would head up to Camp 3 for their turn.

Mark, although only 16 years old, took our climb up to Camp 3 and the time we had to spend there in his stride. His previous experience was apparent, shown by his lack of complaint at the discomfort we had needed to endure.

My acclimatisation finished, all I could do was rest, recuperate and wait for the weather to allow us a summit bid. Patience and a bit of luck were what we needed now.

The Upward Move

The end of April, early May, brought what appeared to be better and warmer weather. With this anticipated change came the first summit attempts. Amongst these was the one made on 3 May by Göran Kropp, a Swedish climber ascending alone and without oxygen. He'd estimated the time at which he expected to reach the summit so that the aeroplane he had arranged could depart from Kathmandu and fly over the top of Everest just as he approached this ultimate height. On board would be a photographer. It was an ambitious plan but one, if it came off, that had the potential to give Göran some spectacular photographs for both a book and press releases. However, his progress was slower than he'd hoped, climbers in Base Camp keenly listening to his transmissions. He radioed that he'd encountered deep snow on a section of the South East Ridge between the Balcony and South Summit. Far above him, over the main summit, circled the aeroplane with the photographer on board. It remained in this holding pattern above Everest for some considerable time before finally heading back to Kathmandu, presumably running low on fuel. Göran also had to turn back, just below the South Summit. He was still a few hundred feet short of the top. He descended to the South Col, where he remained for two days, possibly with the idea of making another attempt or perhaps merely exhausted from his first. As this time passed, he grew dangerously weak, until, I was told, one of his fellow countrymen unselfishly, and probably fearing for Göran's life, climbed up to the South Col to persuade him to come down for a complete rest. Summit attempts from other small teams around this time also failed.

By the time these early attempts were taking place, the majority of our team had completed their acclimatisation and were resting in readiness for our first summit bid. The weather had seemed more settled in recent days and we hoped we might be moving towards a period of calm conditions – our weather-window for summit attempts. This was the norm for climbers back then; there was no forecast available to us. Such an incredibly rare commodity was the domain of the occasional military-backed expedition who could pull strings in high-up places. We were reliant on personal observations and looked for trends in the weather; clear skies and a continued calmness in the air were the signs we were hoping for. It looked possible these might be coming.

Several dates were discussed, but in the end 10 May was the date that fitted our plans best. It gave those on the team who had most recently been up to Camp 3 enough time to rest, while not delaying our bid for too long. Nervous tension was building within each climber; the mental preparation for the task that lay ahead was as complete as it could be. It was as though, after years of preparation, we were anxiously pacing about the start line of a major sporting event, eagerly anticipating the starter's orders, in the knowledge that we needed to be in position for the weather window, which we hoped would appear during the first two weeks of May. The date we had chosen allowed time for the second summit team a few days later, and time for still further pushes if bad weather turned us back on either attempt. Although historically the more settled weather usually appeared in the first half of the month, permits for Everest during the spring season ran up until 31 May.

The date we had selected meant that Rob Hall's and Scott Fischer's entire teams along with our first summit team and a few climbers from other expeditions were all going to make a summit bid on 10 May. From our team there would be twelve in all: seven climbers – Ray Dorr, Paul Deegan, Neil Laughton, Brigitte Muir, Michael Jörgensen, Mark Pfetzer and myself – along with five of our very strong and capable climbing Sherpas.

However, following discussions between the leaders of the two guided expeditions, Rob, on behalf of himself and Scott, asked Henry if our team would hang back for one day and go on 11 May instead. This would give their two guided teams a clear shot at the summit. He told Henry the benefit to us was that they would put the ropes in place. Henry considered their request. First, fixed ropes would be a great help, giving our team one thing less to worry about. Second, it would remove the chance of us being held up by their two large teams of over thirty people. We saw no problem with their request, which on paper made a lot of sense. So Henry agreed to put our bid back by one day.

Amongst the other teams, the most notorious was the South African expedition, who, having lost their most experienced climbers through an internal wrangle early on, announced they too were going on 10 May. Rob also asked if they would change their planned summit day but was told rather impolitely that they would not. There were many in Base Camp who considered that the remnants of the South African team were trying to use Rob and Scott to shelter them from their own inexperience.

Once the date of our summit attempt had been moved to 11 May, our climbers began preparing their personal equipment: a useful way to fill the time and calm the nerves. Crampons were sharpened, boots checked, climbing harnesses carefully inspected. Hours were spent familiarising ourselves with the oxygen masks, regulators and the lightweight Poisk oxygen bottles (plus the requisite and previously forgotten spanner).

I vividly remember watching other team members as they practised changing an oxygen cylinder: a procedure they would soon have to carry out at over 28,000 feet, an altitude where thought processes would be somewhat impaired by the low oxygen levels and the exhaustion of the ascent. We all knew these specific tasks well and the answers to many of the questions we kept asking. What was the flow rate at which we should set the oxygen for climbing? How long would each bottle last? How many hours did their total oxygen supply give them? What time should we leave from Camp 4 on the South Col? The concerns were limited in number, but each conversation hit on the same topics. Over and over, these issues were raised in a slightly different way. The answers were by now well rehearsed.

The air of apprehension was similar in all expedition Base Camps that were making preparations for an imminent departure up the mountain. This reaction was quite natural. We'd all spent months, if not years, preparing for this moment at our respective homes long before departing for Nepal.

Everyone hoped nothing would happen in the form of either accident or illness that might stop them from having a clear shot at the top. The weeks of preparation and acclimatisation were now complete. We knew that in a matter of days we would be leaving the South Col at 26,000 feet, just before midnight, to make our final push for the summit of Everest.

The Imax team, led by David Breashears, left on 5 May for Camp 2. Here they would spend an extra day resting and preparing their filming equipment before moving up for their planned summit day on 9 May, one day ahead of the two large guided teams.

Everything appeared normal as we heard Rob's and Scott's teams depart from Base Camp in the early hours of 6 May, to make their way through the Icefall en route to Camp 2 in the Western Cwm. Rob and Scott, like the Imax team, were going to hold their groups there for a rest day. This meant that Adventure Consultants, Mountain Madness and the Imax expedition would all overnight at Camp 2 on 7 May.

We would make the same journey on 8 May. The reason we were setting off then, and not the day after Rob and Scott, was because we would go to Camp 2 one day and on to Camp 3 the next.

I endured rather a restless final night at Base Camp as I recalled my successful summit bid from the north side less than 12 months earlier, wondering how the events of the next few days would compare. What would the conditions be like on the route up from the South Col? Would we encounter deep snow? If so, it might by that time have already thwarted Rob's and Scott's teams attempts, leaving no ropes in place for us to use. We would not carry our own ropes because of the agreement we'd made. These final doubts troubled me as I tossed and turned in my efforts to fall asleep. All these problems could be solved, but still they occupied my mind.

The early start for our climb to Camp 2 brought a welcome end to my fruitless search for rest. I rose at 5 a.m., my rucksack having been carefully packed the previous day. After a light breakfast, I walked the ten minutes to the beginning of the route. My predominant thought was that this ought to be the second-last time I would need to go through this hazardous maze of ice. The last would be on my way down after reaching the summit. Experience had taught me such a positive approach was the way to prepare for the climb. Negative thoughts would only grow in proportion to the effort required.

Now fully acclimatised to the higher altitudes from my previous trips up the mountain, the energy required, although significant, was far less than my first venture into the Icefall a month earlier. This gave me more time to absorb the raw beauty of my surroundings rather than gasping for breath every few steps. The overwhelming feeling was one of being on a journey with a sense of purpose. All the preparation was focused in one direction: up.

Throughout the morning of 8 May, each of our seven climbers arrived at Camp 2. No one was particularly rushing; all were trying to conserve energy. The atmosphere around the camp was one of anticipation as we watched Rob's and Scott's teams painstakingly making their way up to Camp 3. They appeared as dark specks, moving slowly, almost imperceptibly, up the huge ice sheet of the Lhotse Face. One by one, they disappeared out of sight as they reached their tents at 24,000 feet.

Night fell on the still air of the Western Cwm. High above we could hear the roaring of the wind as it was funnelled through the narrowing of the South Col that lies between Everest and Lhotse: a portent of what was to come.

On the morning of 9 May, we rose to a continuing calm within the Western Cwm. Our breakfast here would possibly be the last appetising meal we would have until our planned return here on 12 May. Our task that day was to make our way up to Camp 3 in a reasonable time without burning unnecessary energy reserves. Our leisurely breakfast was matched by the controlled calmness with which we left camp. Paul Deegan, Mark Pfetzer and I set off together.

As we made our way to the head of the Western Cwm, I had my first strong feeling that something was very wrong. Both my instincts and my eyes gave me the same message. Looking high above, I could see a long wind plume from the South Summit that clung tightly to almost two-thirds of the way down the South East Ridge, towards Camp 4 on the South Col. My eyes darted between these unsettled conditions and the specks departing from Camp 3. Rob's and Scott's teams were heading up to position themselves for their summit attempt that night. Surely, I thought, Rob and Scott could see what I could? Up was not the direction we should be heading. The weather was just not stable enough. Weren't they putting their clients at too much risk? There was still plenty of time to leave it a few days and try again later. From where I stood, this looked like utter madness.

I called to Paul, who was nearby, pointing out to him the weather high up. Paul, like me, was concerned at what he saw. We presumed that Rob and Scott thought the weather was going to settle in a matter of hours, especially given the teams they had. Everest is climbed in periods of calm weather. And this was certainly not what we could see.

I listened to my instincts and radioed Henry. From his position lower down, he was unable to see the plume spanning down the ridge: the wind we'd heard howling high above throughout the night before.

'Henry,' I said, 'we are at the top of the Western Cwm and we're looking up to an enormous plume from the South Summit. The weather doesn't look good from where we are. Do you really want us to head up?'

There was a slight pause before the reply crackled back over the radio.

'Keep going,' was Henry's reply.

I queried again, 'Are you sure you want us to head up?'

The answer came back more quickly this time.

'Just keep going,' was Henry's firm reply.

I looked at Paul and then Mark, who had by now joined us to see what was going on. I shrugged my shoulders. This decision put us in no immediate danger, so compliance was not a problem. The firmness of Henry's reply left us in no doubt that he was following Rob's and Scott's lead. Presumably he thought that they had good reason to expect the weather to change into a more settled period, and soon.

Paul, Mark and I slowly separated as we each chose our rate of ascent up the Lhotse Face. As I climbed towards Camp 3, my eyes alternated between the effects of the wind high on Everest and the two guided groups who were by now climbing towards the Yellow Band: a distinctive layer of pale yellow-brown metamorphosed sedimentary limestone deposited many millions of years ago in some ancient sea. I was expecting them at any moment to about-turn and head down. Their progress continued up. Crossing the Yellow Band, they moved slowly towards the long, dark outcrop of the Geneva Spur, the gateway to the South Col. This would be the last time I would see their complete teams.

Nearing camp, I saw three people, in close proximity to one another, coming down the fixed ropes. As they got closer, I could see it was a Taiwanese climber being escorted by two Sherpas. When the moment came for them to pass by me, I clipped in to the rope above the three of them so they could continue their descent. It was at this point that I saw the tortured face of the Taiwanese climber, Chen Yu Nan, a 36-year-old steelworker from Taipei. His eyes pleaded in desperation; he looked frightened and bewildered, almost childlike. He tore his hand away from one of the Sherpas and grasped at my forearm, trying to take hold for reassurance that somehow everything would be all right. I reciprocated by holding out my arm to him, unsure of what he expected I might be able to do. I asked the two Sherpas if they could manage. Their response was positive. Given the closeness of their attendance as the three had come down the fixed rope, the indication was that they had the situation under control. Chen Yu Nan, apart from the distress he was in and his slightly shaky legs, seemed, in his outward appearance, to be uninjured. I tried to reassure him, in a language he did not fully understand, that he was in safe hands and would soon be back in Camp 2. As the Sherpas tried to continue down, Chen Yu Nan held on to my arm tightly. Like a child being dragged away from security, he was trying his utmost not to let go. His eyes pleaded to me as my arm slipped out of his grasp. As they started to move down, his own arm remained outstretched, his stare still focused on me, hoping beyond hope that I might be able to take away his fear. There was nothing I could do over and above that already being done by his attendant Sherpas. Sadly, Chen Yu Nan, probably little more than an hour after we parted company, fell unconscious and died shortly thereafter.

All seven climbers from our team had arrived at Camp 3 by late afternoon. The priority was to keep brewing drinks to remain hydrated. Drinking too much fluid was almost impossible at this altitude. The stoves melted ice slowly while the dry air sucked moisture from every breath. The conversation in the tent I was sharing was of the radio call I'd made to Henry concerning the weather high on Everest. There was a nervous apprehension of what might lie ahead.

During our scheduled evening radio call with Henry, we learnt the sad news of Chen Yu Nan's death. He'd received internal injuries by going out of his tent at Camp 3 to relieve himself without taking the normal precaution of wearing crampons. Consequently he'd slipped and fallen some way into a crevasse from which the Sherpas had rescued him. He had been lucky not to fall the full height of the Lhotse Face by such a reckless action. Initially he was thought to be relatively uninjured but had decided not to continue his climb with the rest of his team, who had then pressed on towards the South Col. By early afternoon, he'd been found lying in his tent by one of the Sherpas from his own team. Concerned by the poor condition he was in, the Sherpa prepared to escort him back down. Fortunately they were joined by a second Sherpa, from the Imax team, who was descending from a load-carry to the South Col. The two Sherpas thought, quite correctly, that it would be best to bring him back down to Camp 2, but it was a journey Chen Yu Nan was fated not to complete.

With nightfall, we cocooned ourselves in our down sleeping bags in the full expectation that when we emerged the following morning either the wind plume would have gone, bringing us a bright still day to make our climb to the South Col, or we'd have to head down and wait for more settled weather. Our instincts told us the latter was the more sensible option.

Unbeknown to us, two days earlier the Imax team had risen at Camp 3 on the morning of 8 May to see the same winds blowing high on Everest. They had decided to retreat and wait for better weather. We were unaware they were now safely ensconced in Camp 2.

As we had watched the two guided expeditions moving up the Lhotse Face on 8 May, the much smaller Imax team had been descending down the same route. This, we had not noticed. Any small group coming down we would have assumed was a group of Sherpas returning from a load-carry to one of the higher camps.

Stepping Beyond the Line
of Better Judgement

10 May

Our plan was to leave Camp 3 around 8 a.m., which would get us to the South Col early in the afternoon. The scheduled morning radio call around 7 a.m. reached us in the depths of our sleeping bags. The night at Camp 3 had been reasonably calm, and everyone was well. As we stepped out of our tents, we were faced with the surprising yet somehow not unexpected disappointment of seeing that the plume was still there. We decided to delay our departure to see if the conditions improved. When the time came for our next scheduled radio call at midday, we were still at Camp 3.

Neil made the call: 'Neil to Henry, come in Henry.'

Henry's voice came back: 'Hi, Neil, could you give me your current position?'

Neil: 'We are still at Camp 3.'

Henry's reply bellowed from Neil's handset: 'What the f**k are you still doing there?'

Neil, in our reasonable defence, replied, 'Henry, we are looking at the weather high up. It doesn't seem very good at all.'

'Rob and Scott are heading for the summit, just get f**king going. Now!' was Henry's unambiguous instruction.

By the strength of his response, Henry thought we were going to blow a good summit chance if we didn't get going immediately. Although we were subject to Henry's control as expedition leader, we each had the final choice. If we continued to witness these unsettled conditions, there would have been little Henry could have said that would have convinced us to make an attempt. The final say would have been ours. At this particular point, we were not in any serious danger. We stared at the rest of the mountain stretching above us. Were Rob and Scott really up there with their teams? As the saying goes, 'Mad dogs and Englishmen go out in the midday sun.' But who on earth would consider taking such a large group of clients to the summit of Everest in these unsettled conditions?

We each placed an oxygen cylinder in our rucksack and departed from Camp 3. The flow rate was set at two litres per minute to supplement the depleted air around us. This was the first use of oxygen on our expedition: a time that required personal adjustment. The claustrophobic feeling of the mask covering both nose and mouth when already gasping for breath had you convinced that you needed to rip it off to breathe properly. Total concentration, belief and calmness overcame this reaction. Only then could individuals achieve the painfully slow rhythm of climbing at this altitude.

Soon we were a sporadically spaced line heading up and across the Lhotse Face towards the Yellow Band. We were the only climbers heading from Camp 3 to the South Col that day. With the agreements in place, we'd be the only team trying for the summit on 11 May.

Within an hour or so of our departure, I glanced over my shoulder and noticed that Paul and Ray had started to drop behind. I presumed both were struggling to adjust to the sensation of being smothered by the masks. In the knowledge that safety in the form of Camp 3 was not far below them, and that they were both capable of looking after themselves, the rest of us pressed on.

I was also suffering – from what I would describe as a turbulent stomach. Nausea at altitude is not uncommon and usually passes, but the cramps I was feeling in my abdomen were a sign of food poisoning. I couldn't work out if the hot flushes that kept coming over me were from the exertion or a sign of problems ahead. On this part of the climb, I was fortunate to be accompanied by Brigitte and Michael, who could see I was struggling and both shouted encouragement. We'd all felt this way at one time or another.

'Turn your oxygen up,' shouted Michael, pulling his mask to one side. 'There's plenty more at the South Col.'

Brigitte and Michael had similar concerns over the weather and questioned what we were doing up there in such conditions. None of us could quite believe that Rob and Scott, along with their respective teams, would have made a summit bid in such unpredictable weather.

By late afternoon, the clouds had risen up behind us in the Western Cwm, with others clinging eerily to Lhotse's summit ridge a short distance above. The only view we had remaining was the direction in which we were travelling: the sight of Everest's upper reaches being battered by an increasing wind. Yet where we currently stood the air was still, with an unnatural sense of foreboding. The intensity of the light dropped; it took on a greyness that gave the ice beneath our feet a mercuric glow. The snow had lost its reflective characteristic. It was as though we were moving unwisely through a transient world, a mystical place, where right or wrong decisions had to be made.

To our right, out of the low clouds and now lightly falling snow, appeared a solitary figure descending from another climb. It was the French Alpinist Chantal Mauduit, who earlier that day had made the first female ascent of Lhotse, the world's fourth-highest mountain. Three of them had set out for the summit of Lhotse that morning, the other two had turned around early on.

They had moved up from Camp 3 to their top camp for this particular climb, which lay off to the right of the route for Everest, on the same day as Rob and Scott's teams had made their way to the South Col. These three would have seen the unstable conditions but must have taken comfort from the two large guided teams moving up to attempt Everest, the higher of the two mountains.

Moving quickly, Chantal soon reached us. There was joyous relief written right across her face. Patting me on the back, she informed us she had just climbed Lhotse; then she hurried on down. The hour was late, around 5 p.m.; she wanted to be in Camp 3 before dark.

I turned and watched as her diminutive outline, set against an eerie Himalayan backdrop, disappeared into the distance. My thoughts turned to Alison, who by this time had been dead for almost nine months; in two years' time, so too would be Chantal.

Falling behind Michael and Brigitte, I reached the top of the Geneva Spur around 6 p.m. Here I was met by a strong wind. Whether it had been gusting this low down on the mountain for some time and we had merely been sheltered from it or it had just dropped to this lower level was impossible to say. Looking towards the South Summit, I could see that the plume still covered the South East Ridge. Everest loomed dark and unsettled above. The opinion I had arrived at over 30 hours earlier remained. My instincts, our radio calls – all were correct.

As I staggered my way along the top of the Geneva Spur, the wind increased dramatically. Bent double, grasping my stomach and coughing violently into my oxygen mask, I struggled to breathe. All I could see was my feet and the blizzard that had started driving snow past my penitent face.

Shortly after 6.30 p.m., I had reached the edge of the South Col. I was the last to arrive. Looking back, there was no sign of Paul or Ray, who I presumed with their problems had retreated to Camp 3. Darkness had fallen, and the brutal wind was driving snow forcefully into my face. Out of the shadows appeared Pemba, one of our most experienced Sherpas. Concerned at the ferocity of the storm, he was making sure we all got safely into the tents.

'This way, Graham. The tents are here!' he yelled through the howling wind. He looked behind me, searching into the darkness. 'Paul and Ray?' he shouted, with an anxious look on his face.

'I think they go down,' I shouted back in simple language so Pemba

Having climbed through the night, Anatoli and I reached the edge of the North East Ridge, at 27,500 feet, shortly after daybreak on 17 May 1995. The rock at the bottom of the image, which is encrusted with snow, is the very last foot before the ground drops away. Ten thousand feet below lies a thick blanket of cloud; Makalu top right, and in the distance, top left, is Kangchenjunga.

Everest on telephoto from Tibet's Pang La Pass. The jet stream, travelling from right to left, is pierced by the summit of Everest, leaving a plume several miles long to the east of the mountain.

Around 6 a.m. on 17 May 1995, looking down the jagged North East Ridge. The climber just below me in the shadow of the ridge is Anatoli Boukreev.

The summit of Everest, 8.30 a.m., 17 May 1995.

View from the summit of Everest looking towards the Tibetan Plateau.
The Rongbuk Glacier flows from the bottom left towards the centre of the image.
Its snout is just to the right of centre; here, Base Camp is located.

Our Base Camp in 1995, at 18,000 feet. The tent conspicuously out of place, covered in printed daises, situated slightly below centre and to the right, was Anatoli's. It had been manufactured for Russian beach holidays not Everest's northern flanks. The line crossing the picture from right to left is a string of prayer flags hung by our Sherpas.

Base Camp for the 1924 expedition. In 1995, our Base Camp had been placed in exactly the same position. All the boulders in my images are in exactly the same spot in Bentley Beetham's photographs; little had changed in over 70 years.

Late March 1996, our equipment begins to be unloaded from the Russian Mi 17 helicopter at the mountain airstrip at Lukla.

In the Solu Khumbu region of Nepal, the Rhododendron Lodge at Deboche. Ang Kanchi Sherpa is about to enter her 'Everest View Shop'.

To the left, Everest's dark summit pyramid towers above
the jagged Nuptse Wall; to the right of centre is Lhotse.

Our Puja ceremony at Base Camp, April 1996.

Two climbers nearing the top of the Khumbu Icefall; tents of Camp 1 top right.

Looking out of the Base Camp mess tent onto the Khumbu Icefall. This mass of tumbling ice is 2,500 feet high. To give an indication of scale, the two climbers in the image above would appear as the smallest of black specks on this picture.

April 1996, looking up and over the huge crevasses that mark the beginning of the Western Cwm. Everest rises to the left and Nuptse to the right, centrally at the far end of the Cwm sits Lhotse, the world's fourth-highest mountain.

During the afternoons in April, Base Camp would occasionally disappear under a blanket of cloud and lightly falling snow, sending its occupants scurrying for the depths of their sleeping bag or driving them into the mess tents.

would both hear and understand over the roaring wind. Eighty feet further on, we were at our tents.

As I was about to remove my crampons and rucksack in readiness to dive into the safety of our tent, I looked up. Considering the conditions, I don't know why I did this. In the distance, on the far left-hand side of the South Col, moving towards the tents but still probably 200 yards away, I picked out the glint of two head torches. I was horrified by what I saw. 'My God, they're getting back late!' flashed through my mind. How on earth could I have known these were in fact probably the first of Rob's and Scott's teams arriving back? Aware that both these teams had a considerable and experienced group of Sherpas along with professional guides, I slid into our tent and out of the driving wind.

Our immediate concern that night lay with Paul and Ray. Had they returned to the safety of Camp 3 or were they caught out in the storm? We had two radios up high: one with us, the other with Paul. Unfortunately, the radio we had at the South Col was having a problem with its batteries because of the freezing temperatures, even though it had been stuffed deep inside a rucksack. Ever resourceful, we wired a head-torch battery into the system and were soon back 'on air'. We established contact with Paul, who we were relieved to hear was by this time back at Camp 3. He'd been struggling with his oxygen mask and had wisely considered his position. We'd set off late, and he'd been falling behind. The weather was of concern. He had plenty of time to make another summit attempt with the rest of our team at a later date. So he took the sensible decision and turned back. It was a shame that Ray Dorr, a climber about whom I'd had doubts early in the expedition, hadn't made the same logical assessment.

Henry came on the radio some time after 7 p.m. A three-way conversation took place between us at the South Col, Paul at Camp 3 and Henry at Camp 2 concerning the whereabouts of Ray Dorr. Paul was watching for any sign of Ray's head torch descending. There was nothing.

I ventured out into the maelstrom, to the larger of our two tents, to tell Pemba that Ray was missing somewhere between Camp 3 and the South Col. The Sherpas along with Mark Pfetzer were in one tent, Neil, Brigitte, Michael and myself in the other.

On hearing this news, Pemba and another of our Sherpas volunteered to go and look for Ray. It was an offer, given the pains in my stomach, I gladly accepted. Bravely, they headed out into the darkness, into the full fury of the storm, the snow driving harder than ever.

Returning about 20 minutes later, Pemba stuck his head through the entrance of our tent where I was crouched. He looked straight into my eyes with an apologetic and worried look on his face. He shouted over the wind, 'Graham, we cannot see Ray. We cannot see in the storm.'

The words rang around the tent. All of us realised the implications of what had been said.

We considered Ray's position. He was on a fixed rope that ran all the way from Camp 3 to the South Col, except for one short 50-ft section on flat ground that ran along the top of the Geneva Spur. He was wearing a down suit and breathing oxygen, plus he was carrying a down sleeping bag and other equipment in his rucksack. If he was below the Geneva Spur, then he was sheltered from the worst of the wind. He had a head torch and was below 26,000 feet. The Sherpas were unable to see in the storm as they headed down to look for him. If we tried, we would be equally unsighted. All we could do was hope that Ray had enough sense to fix himself to the ropes and take shelter in an appropriate place with the equipment he had or that he was already making his way back down. We radioed Henry to give him an update on Ray. He understood the position.

At no time during our scheduled evening radio call was there mention of our summit attempt, either by Henry or by any of us on the South Col. I'm sure none of us thought an attempt was on the cards. Nothing was said; we just knew. More importantly, there was no mention that Rob's and Scott's teams were in difficulty, though their own teams lower down had known a potential tragedy was unfolding shortly after 4 p.m. – nearly three hours before our evening radio call.

At the end of the evening radio calls, the only problem of which we were aware was Ray Dorr. In our tents on the South Col, we prepared to weather the storm. We were all hoping that Ray had made it back to one of the tents at Camp 3. It didn't matter which expedition's tent he found refuge in given these circumstances, any would do.

We transferred our oxygen masks and regulators from our lightweight Poisk climbing cylinders onto the heavier steel ones that contained our oxygen to use while sleeping. These would be set at a rate of one litre per minute. However, here we struck a problem. The regulators all connected without a hitch except one that would not screw far enough in to release the valve that allowed the flow of gas, even though it had worked on the lighter one. Apart from my stomach, I felt fine and offered to sleep without oxygen. I knew I could have used one of our Poisk bottles, but these in my mind were set aside for climbing. Soon everyone, including the Sherpas, was in their sleeping bags with their oxygen masks slowly hissing away. All, that is, except me. I lay curled up in my sleeping bag, grasping my stomach, listening to the wind hammering into the tent for hour after hour. The snow drummed against the side of the nylon tent in driving gusts, the poles bent and strained as the wind tried its best to tear the tent from the ground.

It turned out to be fortunate for me that I was not wearing a mask and was next to the entrance of our tent, as all of a sudden my stomach started convulsing. With just enough time to sit up, and certainly not sufficient to open the tent, I leant over and vomited onto the tent floor. Wiping my hand across my dribbling mouth, I flopped back into my sleeping bag with the thought 'better out than in'. I decided to leave any attempt at cleaning up until dawn. Rid of my unwanted load, a feeling of relative normality returned as I drifted off to sleep.

I woke at first light, probably around 5 a.m. The deafening sound of the wind battering against the tent had subsided. I looked to my side to view the contents of my stomach, expecting to find an unpleasant mess. Instead, I found they'd neatly filled a dip in the tent floor about ten inches in diameter and had rather conveniently frozen solid into what looked like a particularly disgusting pizza. Easing this up from the plastic groundsheet, I was relieved when it came away in one piece. Unzipping the tent, I threw this frozen vomit, as though it were some sort of Frisbee, out onto the South Col. This was one of the very few advantages of being at 26,000 feet.

Despite having a slight headache, I felt significantly better than I had the previous evening. The wind, although still blowing, had dropped considerably. The blizzard had finished. The morning was best described as clear and cold, around minus 20, but very breezy.

Picking Up the Pieces

Morning of 11 May 1996

I can't remember the exact time of the early-morning radio call, but when Neil turned our set on Henry was already waiting for our transmission.

Then came the bombshell: 'Rob's and Scott's teams – 21 people are missing!' Henry's words stunned everyone in the tent.

Neil pressed the button on his radio to reply. 'Henry, can you confirm: you say 21 people are missing?'

The figure was almost unbelievable.

'Correct, 21 missing,' came Henry's reply.

Neil, Brigitte, Michael and myself stared blankly at one another as our brains processed the information and its possible consequences. A moment passed, then Brigitte grabbed an oxygen cylinder and mask.

'What are you doing?' I asked.

'Rob needs help,' was her instant reply.

'Which way are you going to go? Where are you going to look?'

My words hit home. Brigitte sank back, knowing this made sense.

I followed this with some logic: 'Let's find out what's happened and where they are first.'

During the subsequent radio conversation between Neil and Henry, which Brigitte, Michael and myself were party to, it was decided we first needed to assess the situation on the South Col. Rob's and Scott's expedition staff lower on the mountain were by now working closely with Henry and other teams, so all could help in these potentially tragic circumstances.

One of us needed to go around Rob's and Scott's tents to make an assessment. Neil offered to do this and set about the task immediately.

A serious mistake was made at this point, the consequences of which were certainly not the fault of Neil or anyone else. It just happened. The mistake was that we were not given, neither had anyone thought of, either a roll call or the total number of people we needed to count on the South Col to determine whether anyone was missing. In the cold light of day at sea level, rather than having just sat out a storm at

26,000 feet, this would seem glaringly obvious. Unfortunately, it was a vital point that was missed both by the teams lower down and by us on the South Col.

One of the biggest problems in disasters such as the one that happened on Everest in the spring of 1996 is that the urgency of the situation impairs people's ability to think clearly and interferes with unambiguous communication from the outset.

Neil went round the tents both to see and ask if everybody was OK. He found those within visibly shaken by their experiences of the previous night but safely brewing drinks. On asking how they were, meaning their entire teams not just themselves as individuals, they each replied that they were all right. This was the answer Neil got from all he found, the number being well in excess of 21. As a result of everyone's condition, and the replies received, he naturally assumed they had all managed to get back to the South Col during the night and safely to their tents.

Arriving back, Neil radioed Henry: 'Henry, I've been around the tents, they all seem OK and are making a brew.'

This understandably caused complete confusion lower down. No real reply or further instructions came back at that time. Neil had done exactly what he had been asked to do. We were asked to stand by.

Our attention now turned to Ray Dorr, whose whereabouts were unknown. A radio call to Paul at Camp 3 gave us the news that Ray had arrived at the tent Paul was occupying shortly after dawn, minus his rucksack, which had mysteriously fallen down the Lhotse Face. Where and at what time had Ray turned around to head down? How had he lost his rucksack? Had he spent the night out in the open or in another team's tent at Camp 3 before eventually joining Paul? I do not know. Ray never explained to me or any of the climbers or Sherpas I spoke to what had happened to him; it was an explanation I felt he owed us.

Once Ray's safety was confirmed, I spoke with Henry on the radio. Although the wind had dropped considerably in strength, there was a real concern this might be a lull in the storm. The weather around the South Summit still looked ominous. To the east, the tops of unsettled clouds that resembled the surface of a boiling cauldron hung level with the Kangshung side of the South Col.

Despite our incorrect conclusion at that moment in time that everyone was OK, the weather was not settled enough to consider summit attempts the following day – 12 May. We needed to wait.

During my subsequent conversation with Henry, he told me to get Mark Pfetzer down from the South Col straightaway. Mark, although an experienced climber for his age, was still only 16 years old. Given the storm and the continuing poor weather, this was the right decision for Henry to make. Mark, Jabion (the Sherpa who had been assigned to Mark) and I gathered our equipment and headed down from the South Col towards Camp 3 and on to Camp 2 in the Western Cwm.

It was after we'd descended from the Geneva Spur, traversed the Yellow Band and were crossing the Lhotse Face that we met some Sherpas heading up. We stopped briefly to talk. First they enquired if we were OK. Then came the terrible news that Rob had been stuck at the South Summit all night, throughout the storm, and was still there. They explained that two Sherpas were heading up with fresh oxygen cylinders to try to bring him down. Even at that point we knew it had to be touch and go whether he would get down alive. All three of us heading down were shocked by what we'd been told. Staring up at the wind-torn South Summit high above us, we hoped that the two brave souls climbing up to him would make it there in time.

We were, at this point, totally unaware that other climbers had passed away through the course of the night or still lay dying and injured on Everest's upper slopes.

Coming up the Lhotse Face were ten to fifteen climbers and Sherpas who we now realised were moving up to aid in the evacuation of those higher on the mountain. For the three of us, who'd been on the South Col through the night, the worst thing we could do now was to climb back up in some vain attempt to help. The best course of action was for us to continue our descent to Camp 2 and get out of the way of those coming up, rather than risk becoming part of the problem they had to deal with.

Only after we arrived back at Camp 2 did the scale of the tragic events of the night of 10 May and the continuing struggle of the survivors become apparent to us. The following summary, gleaned from the various accounts published by the climbers and guides involved, is set out to help the reader broadly understand the events that took place and the decade of analysis that followed into what went wrong. For those more familiar with this tragic sequence, its purpose is to highlight the key factors.

In all, 34 people had left from Camp 4 at 26,000 feet on the South Col on the night of 9 May for their summit attempt.

From Rob's team there was Rob as leader, guides Andy Harris and Michael Groom, clients Frank Fischbeck, Doug Hansen, Stuart Hutchison, Lou Kasischke, Jon Krakauer, Yasuko Namba, John Taske, Beck Weathers and four Sherpas. These climbers departed around 11.30 p.m.

From Scott's team, leaving Camp 4 at midnight, were guides Anatoli Boukreev and Neal Beidleman, clients, Martin Adams, Charlotte Fox,

Lene Gammelgaard, Tim Madsen, Sandy Hill Pittman, Klev Schoening and six Sherpas, which included Scott's climbing Sirdar, Lopsang Jangbu Sherpa. Neither Dale Kruse nor Pete Schoening made a summit attempt, but had remained at Base Camp. Dale, only a week or so before, had fallen dangerously ill with high-altitude cerebral oedema and was evacuated back down the mountain. Pete Schoening, due to a potential heart problem being identified, had decided to climb no higher than Camp 3.

Makalu Gau plus three Sherpas from the Taiwanese expedition were almost the last to leave, except for Scott, who was to follow his group up an hour or so later.

Rob's team left two other Sherpas in support on the South Col, and Scott's team, one.

The original plan had been that four Sherpas, two from each of Rob's and Scott's teams, would leave the South Col an hour or two in advance of the clients. This would allow them time to fix ropes on the more exposed higher sections of the climb before clients arrived, which would prevent unnecessary hold-ups during the day. For various reasons, this had not happened, and in the case of both teams all the Sherpas left at the same time as the rest of their group.

About three hours into the climb, Frank Fischbeck, from Rob's group, turned around and descended back to the South Col. His instincts told him something that day didn't feel right. Shortly after, Doug Hansen stepped to one side of the ascending climbers. Feeling cold and unwell, he also decided to head down. However, Rob spoke with Doug, and after their short conversation Doug continued upwards. Presumably Rob had persuaded him to keep going for a while and see how the day went.

The progress of Rob's group was slower than that of Scott's, who caught and passed most of Rob's team, which was being kept close together as they moved up towards the Balcony, effectively climbing at the rate of their slowest person. At the very back of this strung-out line of climbers was Scott, who was feeling tired and unwell.

Making steady progress upwards, Beck Weathers, from Rob's team, began to encounter problems with his sight because of a type of eye surgery he'd undergone a year or two earlier, known as radial keratotomy. His vision, affected by the reduced air pressure at high altitude, left him unable to focus. By the time he reached the Balcony at 27,500 feet around 7.30 a.m, it became obvious to him that he would be unable to continue unless his sight returned. This gave him little option other than to suggest to Rob that he wait there in the hope it might when the sun got higher and his pupils contracted; if so, he would catch up. Rob's initial thought had been to send Beck down to the South Col with one of the Sherpas. However, the agreement they came to was that if his sight became manageable within 30 minutes he could follow the rest up; if not, then he was to stay put until Rob returned. In the end, Beck's eyes didn't recover sufficiently, leaving him unable to move either up or down because of his solemn promise to Rob.

As the morning progressed, climbers higher up were being slowed significantly. The ropes they'd expected to be in place over the trickier sections had not been fixed. Bottlenecks of climbers waiting for these to be attached began to appear in the series of rock steps, at around 28,000 feet, slightly below the South Summit.

During the weeks prior to their attempt, there had been numerous conversations within their respective expeditions about a turnaround time on summit day that would leave a sufficient margin for them to return to their tents on the South Col before dark. Both 1 p.m. and 2 p.m. had been mentioned. However, the final decision was to be made by Rob and Scott on the day, depending on conditions – something that in the end never happened. It has been reported since that Rob had, over the preceding week, drilled into his clients 'absolutely no later than two'. This had not been lost on Stuart Hutchison and John Taske, who by 11.30 a.m. were becoming increasingly concerned that they'd not have sufficient time to reach the summit before the safe turnaround time of 1 p.m. they'd set themselves. These doubts were confirmed when Rob told them that the summit was still three hours away.

After Stuart and John had had a brief conversation with Lou Kasischke about their reservations, the three of them decided to head back. Rob sent two Sherpas with them. This left Rob, guides Andy Harris and Michael Groom, clients Jon Krakauer, Yasuko Namba and Doug Hansen plus two Sherpas continuing up.

The rate of attrition on Rob's team was becoming significant, whereas all those on Scott's team who had left the South Col were still climbing towards the summit.

Having abandoned the climb, Stuart, John, Lou and the two Sherpas came across Beck Weathers while making their descent. He was still standing at the Balcony where Rob had left him. They offered to help Beck down with them to the South Col; however, he declined, saying he would wait for Rob as promised.

Stuart, John and Lou arrived back at the South Col during the course of the afternoon, joining Frank Fischbeck, who'd been there for quite some time, having turned around during the early hours of the morning.

Climbers from both groups began to congregate at the South Summit at 28,700 feet at or before 10 a.m. No ropes had yet been fixed above. The fact that the original plan of four Sherpas leaving the South Col ahead of the clients and guides, to fix the route higher up, had not been executed was now causing severe delays. Precious oxygen was being wasted as they sat around waiting for the ropes to be put in place, while the clock ticked remorselessly on. Around midday, the two guides from Scott's team, Anatoli Boukreev and Neal Beidleman, set out from the South Summit to fix ropes on the heavily corniced ridge and Hillary Step. Unfortunately, neither Anatoli nor Neal had been given a radio and were having to use their own initiative. They were unable to communicate with either Scott, as leader, or Lopsang, as climbing Sirdar, both of whom had radios but were somewhere else on the mountain.

Slightly after 1 p.m., Anatoli Boukreev, Jon Krakauer and Andy Harris were standing on the summit of Everest at 29,035 feet, followed soon after by Neal Beidleman and Martin Adams.

Staying on the summit for only a short while, Krakauer, Boukreev, Adams and Harris began their descent. Three hundred feet lower down, they were held up by the bottleneck of climbers waiting to climb the Hillary Step. The clock was ticking. Beidleman had remained on the summit, waiting for the rest of Scott's group to arrive. The first of these, Klev Schoening, reached the top just before 2 p.m.

It had always been assumed that both Rob and Scott would enforce the turnaround time on the day. The guides did not feel it was their place to deny clients who'd paid considerable sums of money for their one shot at the summit. It was not what they'd been paid for or instructed to do.

Shortly after 2 p.m., Charlotte Fox, Lene Gammelgaard, Tim Madsen, Sandy Hill Pittman and Lopsang from Scott's group summited; from Rob's team, guide Michael Groom, Rob Hall himself and client Yasuko Namba. Rob radioed news of their success back to Base Camp. This information was then passed on to the Adventure Consultants office in New Zealand.

In fact, the only climbers to reach the summit before 2 p.m., the latest turnaround time that had been discussed over the preceding week, were the guides Anatoli Boukreev, Neal Beidleman and Andy Harris, and clients Martin Adams, Jon Krakauer and Klev Schoening.

It wasn't until around 2.45 p.m. that the jam finally cleared from the Hillary Step. Last in the line of the ascending climbers was a tired Scott Fischer, who spoke briefly with Adams then Boukreev as they passed him on their way down.

On his descent, Jon Krakauer's oxygen bottle ran out of gas below the Hillary Step. Jon, distressed and struggling to continue without a fresh supply, was assisted by Michael Groom, who was coming down with Yasuko Namba. All were heading back to the South Summit, where the Sherpas had placed their cache of fresh cylinders. It was here they found Andy Harris in a rather confused state. He was convinced all the fresh cylinders were empty when they were in fact all full. In hindsight, it is thought he was having problems with his oxygen supply and that this was impairing his thought processes and judgement. The seriousness of this was not picked up at the time. Michael Groom distributed the fresh oxygen cylinders to Andy, Jon and Yasuko. He was aware that Andy was having problems, but once he saw Andy back on oxygen again his attention was taken up by seeing to Jon and Yasuko. Under different circumstances he would have monitored Andy much more closely, but this was not to be on the day.

On the oxygen flow rate the two teams were running it was expected that by approximately 5 p.m. they would all be out of oxygen. Their safety margin had all but slipped away.

Michael Groom, Jon Krakauer and Yasuko Namba departed from the South Summit around 3.30 p.m. Martin Adams and Anatoli Boukreev were about 30 minutes ahead of them. They descended into a thick blanket of clouds, which had previously gone unnoticed by them. These weather conditions were to worsen considerably by the hour during the course of the afternoon and early evening.

Neal Beidleman, waiting on the summit without a radio, had no way of knowing what was happening lower down. At 3.10 p.m., he left the summit, where he'd been for almost two hours. With him he had Charlotte Fox, Lene Gammelgaard, Tim Madsen and Sandy Hill Pittman.

Scott didn't reach the summit until 3.40 p.m. Arriving around the same time, Makalu Gau and two Sherpas from the Taiwanese team reached the top. On the summit, Lopsang was waiting for Scott to arrive, and Rob Hall for Doug Hansen.

Scott radioed Base Camp to let them know that everyone had summited. He then quietly complained to Lopsang that he was extremely tired, felt unwell and needed medicine. Scott left the summit at 4 p.m., Makalu Gau with his two Sherpas a moment or two after, then Lopsang.

Standing alone, Rob Hall remained on the summit waiting for his last client, Doug Hansen, who wearily appeared over the final rise a short while later. They stood for a few minutes on the summit and then began their descent. By the time they reached the top of the Hillary Step, the oxygen supplies they were carrying had run out. The oxygen cache at the South Summit was a relatively short distance

4 p.m. 10 May

Legend:
1. Summit
2. South Summit
3. Balcony
4. South Col Camp
5. Lhotse Face
6. Kangshung Face

Doug Hansen approaching the summit

Scott Fischer leaves summit

Lene Gammelgaard
Neal Beidleman
Charlotte Fox
Tim Madsen
Sandy Hill Pittman

Lopsang Jangbu Sherpa departs shortly after Scott

Makalu Gau plus two Sherpas ready to depart

Rob Hall waiting on summit for his last client Doug Hansen

Andy Harris

Klev Schoening

Michael Groom
Jon Krakauer
Yasuko Namba

Beck Weathers still waiting at the Balcony

Anatoli Boukreev
Martin Adams

4.
Frank Fischbeck
Stuart Hutchison
Lou Kasischke
John Taske
These four are now back at the South Col

below them, but by now Rob was struggling to keep Doug moving. Around 4.30 p.m., Rob made the first of his radio calls saying that they were in trouble. He was unable to get Doug Hansen down the Hillary Step without fresh oxygen supplies. Andy Harris, who was still at the South Summit, heard Rob's radio call and interrupted to tell Rob that the bottles at the cache were all empty. The conversation was overheard by Michael Groom, as both of Rob's guides had been given a radio to carry. Michael tried to let Rob know that this information was incorrect, that two full bottles were waiting for him and Doug Hansen at the South Summit. Unfortunately, Michael's radio was malfunctioning and working only intermittently.

By 5 p.m., Neal Beidleman, along with Charlotte Fox, Lene Gammelgaard, Tim Madsen and Sandy Hill Pittman were descending from the South Summit towards the Balcony, into the thick clouds and falling snow. Beidleman is quoted as saying, 'Everyone was pretty messed up by that point, but Sandy looked especially shaky. I thought that if I didn't keep real close tabs on her, there was a good chance she'd peel right off the ridge.'

Somewhere between Neal Beidleman's group and that of Michael Groom was Klev Schoening making his own way down.

Michael Groom, on his descent with Yasuko Namba and Jon Krakauer, noticed Martin Adams, from Scott's group, had strayed off the route towards the edge that plummeted into Tibet. Deciding to climb back up to correct this, Michael told Yasuko to follow Jon, who was just below them.

Eventually, some half an hour after Rob's first radio call, Michael managed to get the information to Rob that the bottles at the South Summit were full: a fact that Andy Harris must have then comprehended. On realising his mistake, Andy must have picked up the two bottles and bravely climbed back up the ridge towards Rob and Doug. It was now nearing 5.30 p.m.

Michael escorted Martin Adams down to the Balcony. Pointing out Jon Krakauer and Yasuko Namba, visible in the gully below, he told Adams to follow them down. Initially, Michael had not noticed Beck Weathers standing nearby in the falling snow, a place he'd been all day waiting for Rob's return. Michael was shocked to see Beck still there, expecting that he would have been in Camp 4 long ago. He was unaware of the agreement that Rob and Beck had made. Concerned about Beck's condition, he fastened a short rope between them, six foot in length, and began what was to be a slow and precarious descent back down towards the South Col in a worsening blizzard.

Some distance lower down, Yasuko Namba's oxygen ran out, as had that of most other people by this time. So she simply sat down and was found there by Neal Beidleman and Michael Groom. Because Michael was already struggling with Beck, Neal offered to take Yasuko down with his group.

Visibility above the South Col now dropped down to a few feet. The temperature had plummeted and the wind speed picked up to somewhere between 30 and 40 miles per hour.

The first of our team's climbers, Neil Laughton, arrived on the South Col from Camp 3 around 5.30 p.m., to find strong winds but reasonable visibility. He was followed soon after by some of our Sherpas, who, along with Neil, battled against the wind to put up a second tent. One by one, the rest of our climbers arrived: Mark Pfetzer, Michael Jörgensen and Brigitte Muir, with myself being last into camp shortly after 6.30 p.m. By the time I reached the South Col, conditions had changed considerably since Neil's arrival over an hour earlier. Darkness had fallen and the wind had increased to gale force, carrying with it a blizzard of harshly driven snow. As I bent down to get into the tent, I caught a glimpse of two head torches slightly off the normal route, on the gentle slopes to the left of the Kangshung side of the South Col. I'd stopped for just a moment, stunned by how late these climbers were returning from the summit, before slipping into our tent and out of the biting wind. We were totally oblivious to what was happening outside.

By the time Michael Groom and Beck Weathers reached the easier gradient, about 200 feet above Camp 4, they'd lost their sense of direction. Here, they bumped into Neal Beidleman's group once more, who had themselves become disorientated in the poor visibility caused by the storm that was now raging. The time was around 6.45 p.m., and Jon Krakauer was arriving at the tents on the South Col. Martin Adams, who'd overtaken Jon, had got back there shortly before him.

John Taske, Stuart Hutchison, Frank Fischbeck, Lou Kasischke and Jon Krakauer from Rob's team were now all back on the South Col. Lou Kasischke was suffering from excruciatingly painful snow blindness, having neglected to wear eye protection during part of his descent.

High above, on the Hillary Step, Rob Hall was still trying to coax and cajole a completely exhausted and hypoxic Doug Hansen down to the oxygen cache at the South Summit, presumably at some point aided by a courageous Andy Harris, who'd been having problems of his own. Around them, the storm ravaged Everest's upper reaches.

Anatoli, who'd arrived back on the South Col around 5 p.m., was getting increasingly anxious. Only Martin Adams from Scott's group had returned to the South Col. By 7.30 p.m., Anatoli had begun to climb back up with fresh supplies of oxygen. He knew those above him would have now run out. Unable to locate the exact route and with visibility reduced to almost nothing, Anatoli became concerned he would get lost himself. Eventually, he was forced to abandon this attempt and head back down to Camp 4.

Lopsang had left the South Summit around 5.30 p.m. to catch up with a rapidly weakening Scott Fischer, whom he found just above the Balcony at about 6 p.m. Scott by this time was losing touch with reality, quite possibly suffering from cerebral oedema judging by the comments he was reportedly making. Lopsang, concerned at Scott's worsening condition, fastened a rope between the two of them and began to descend. Bolts of lightning and clashes of thunder began overhead. A short while later, they were overtaken by Makalu Gau and two Sherpas from the Taiwanese expedition heading down. Two hours after that, and three hundred feet further down, they came across Makalu Gau sitting by himself on a ledge, too weak to continue.

Lopsang was beginning to struggle with Scott, who by this time could not walk unaided. A conversation ensued during which Lopsang reluctantly agreed to leave Scott next to Makalu Gau, enabling him to descend alone to the South Col, about 1,200 feet lower down, to get help.

Neal Beidleman and Michael Groom, who'd joined forces on the South Col, were trying to keep Yasuko Namba, Beck Weathers, Charlotte Fox, Lene Gammelgaard, Tim Madsen, Sandy Hill Pittman and Klev Schoening together. With them were two Sherpas. Suffering desperate conditions, they continued their search for Camp 4 in a driving blizzard that had reduced visibility down to six feet or less. They spent hour after hour in their quest, stumbling around the South Col, becoming more disorientated with every minute. Around 10 p.m., Beidleman sensed they were standing in front of a huge void. In a northerly direction, the South Col rises up onto the slopes of Everest, to the south up onto the slopes of Lhotse. However, the eastern side is defined by a drop of 7,000 feet down the Kangshung Face and the western side by a drop of 4,000 feet down the Lhotse Face. The problem was, neither Neal Beidleman, nor any one else in the group, knew which way they were facing. Unbeknown to them, they were in fact a matter of feet away from the Kangshung Face.

In the fear that they might lose someone if they kept wandering around, Beidleman and Groom got everyone to crouch down behind a boulder, a few feet high, to try to shelter from the blast of the wind, forming a group that would later be referred to as 'the huddle'. Amongst these, Yasuko Namba and Beck Weathers were faring worst. Everyone had long since run out of oxygen. Most head-torch batteries had expired, and hypothermia was beginning to set in.

While all this had been happening on the eastern side of the South

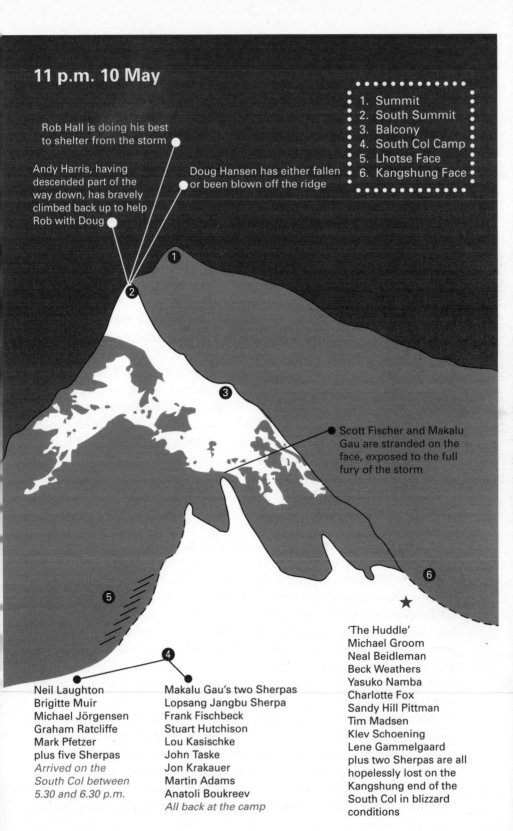

11 p.m. 10 May

1. Summit
2. South Summit
3. Balcony
4. South Col Camp
5. Lhotse Face
6. Kangshung Face

Rob Hall is doing his best to shelter from the storm

Andy Harris, having descended part of the way down, has bravely climbed back up to help Rob with Doug

Doug Hansen has either fallen or been blown off the ridge

Scott Fischer and Makalu Gau are stranded on the face, exposed to the full fury of the storm

Neil Laughton
Brigitte Muir
Michael Jörgensen
Graham Ratcliffe
Mark Pfetzer
plus five Sherpas
Arrived on the South Col between 5.30 and 6.30 p.m.

Makalu Gau's two Sherpas
Lopsang Jangbu Sherpa
Frank Fischbeck
Stuart Hutchison
Lou Kasischke
John Taske
Jon Krakauer
Martin Adams
Anatoli Boukreev
All back at the camp

'The Huddle'
Michael Groom
Neal Beidleman
Beck Weathers
Yasuko Namba
Charlotte Fox
Sandy Hill Pittman
Tim Madsen
Klev Schoening
Lene Gammelgaard
plus two Sherpas are all hopelessly lost on the Kangshung end of the South Col in blizzard conditions

Col, Stuart Hutchison, a matter of 650 feet away at Camp 4, had been getting out of his tent and going out into the storm to flash torches and bang pots in an effort to guide the missing climbers back in. The problem was, he had no idea where they were, or even if the missing climbers had reached the South Col.

It was just before midnight, during a brief lull in the storm, that Klev Schoening, one of the 'huddle', made out the vague outlines of Everest and Lhotse towering high above. From this glimpse alone, he was able to determine the direction of Camp 4. Fortunately, he remained calm and stuck to his guns regarding the understanding he'd reached. He managed to persuade Neal Beidleman and Michael Groom that he was right. Gathering all those who were able to walk, they headed off to raise help. Around 1 a.m., Beidleman, Groom, Schoening, Gammelgaard and their two Sherpas staggered into Camp 4. Still out on the South Col were Yasuko Namba, Beck Weathers, Sandy Hill Pittman, Charlotte Fox and a brave Tim Madsen, who had volunteered to stay with them.

Beidleman went to the tents belonging to Scott's group on the South Col and, along with Klev Schoening, told Anatoli where those they'd had to leave behind were stranded. With the alarm raised and the approximate location known, Anatoli headed out alone to rescue these stranded climbers. He'd been unable to muster anyone to help him.

At the same time, Michael Groom went to Rob's tents, where he came across the tent of Stuart Hutchison and Jon Krakauer and informed them that Yasuko Namba and Beck Weathers were on the Kangshung Face side of the South Col. Stuart, unaware of Anatoli's rescue efforts, got out of the tent again to bang pots and flash torches to try to guide the stranded climbers back in, not knowing the terrible condition they were in by this time.

Anatoli's first attempt was thwarted. He was unable to locate the missing climbers in the blizzard conditions. After returning to Camp 4 for further directions, he headed out into the storm once more, carrying fresh oxygen and hot fluids. First, he brought back Charlotte Fox before going out again later to get Sandy Hill Pittman and Tim Madsen. Yasuko Namba lay unconscious, and Beck Weathers was nowhere to be seen. It was now about 5 a.m.; light was beginning to appear in the morning sky and the storm had started to die down.

Meanwhile, radio calls had continued with Rob throughout the course of the early evening. Experienced mountaineers had been trying to persuade Rob to abandon Doug, who was by that stage beyond help given his condition and their location, and at least to save himself. The last call that evening was made around 6 p.m. It wasn't until 5 a.m. the following day that Rob spoke to Base Camp on the radio again. He was now at the South Summit. By this time, as Rob put it, 'Doug is gone.' Andy Harris was nowhere to be seen, although Rob said he could see some of Andy's equipment nearby and enquired repeatedly after him. Confusion was to reign for a few months after these events over what actually happened to Andy Harris. Rob had said that Andy had been with him through the night, while Jon Krakauer had reported seeing him near Camp 4 on the evening of 10 May. Crampon marks had been found the following morning near the Lhotse Face. It was feared that in the low visibility of the storm the previous night, Andy may have stepped off the edge. It would turn out that it was not Andy Harris that Jon Krakauer had seen near Camp 4 but Martin Adams. It seemed that Andy Harris must have bravely climbed back up to try to help Rob with an ailing Doug Hansen. What actually happened to Andy will probably never be known. His ice axe was found on the South Summit.

Stuart Hutchison and four Sherpas headed out onto the South Col on the morning of 11 May to find Yasuko Namba and Beck Weathers. Both were found barely breathing. The judgement made was that little could be done to save them.

Two Sherpas, Ang Dorje and Lhapka Chhiri, from Adventure Consultants headed up from the South Col with oxygen supplies, in an attempt to rescue Rob. They were followed a short while later by two Sherpas from Mountain Madness and one from the Taiwanese expedition, who set off to reach Scott Fischer and Makalu Gau. Both had spent the whole night on a ledge 1,200 feet above the South Col, exposed to the full force of the storm. Once the Sherpas reached this pair of stricken climbers, both were put straight onto supplementary oxygen. A badly frostbitten Makalu Gau responded and was brought down to the South Col. Scott, who was close to death, did not and was left where he lay.

Also on the morning of 11 May, Todd Burleson and Pete Athans from the Alpine Ascents expedition climbed up to the South Col to assist and evacuate the climbers who'd been caught in the storm the night before. Those in the tents were mostly suffering from shock and only minor injuries. The Imax expedition had oxygen supplies stashed on the South Col; they told Todd and Pete over the radio to utilise these as necessary. Other climbers headed up from Camp 2 to assist those now starting to descend from the South Col. Nearly all expeditions were trying to assist in whatever capacity they could. Medical tents were set up in Camp 2, manned by doctors who waited for the injured to be brought down.

The Sherpas who'd climbed back up to try to rescue Rob were forced back by strong winds at 3 p.m., near the Balcony. They were some 700 feet and probably two hours below where Rob was stranded. Here, they

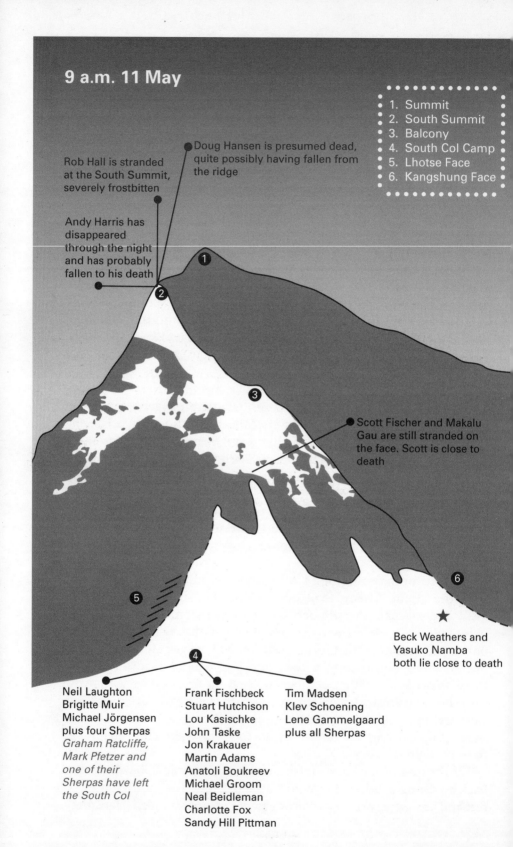

9 a.m. 11 May

1. Summit
2. South Summit
3. Balcony
4. South Col Camp
5. Lhotse Face
6. Kangshung Face

Rob Hall is stranded at the South Summit, severely frostbitten

Doug Hansen is presumed dead, quite possibly having fallen from the ridge

Andy Harris has disappeared through the night and has probably fallen to his death

Scott Fischer and Makalu Gau are still stranded on the face. Scott is close to death

Beck Weathers and Yasuko Namba both lie close to death

Neil Laughton
Brigitte Muir
Michael Jörgensen
plus four Sherpas
*Graham Ratcliffe,
Mark Pfetzer and
one of their
Sherpas have left
the South Col*

Frank Fischbeck
Stuart Hutchison
Lou Kasischke
John Taske
Jon Krakauer
Martin Adams
Anatoli Boukreev
Michael Groom
Neal Beidleman
Charlotte Fox
Sandy Hill Pittman

Tim Madsen
Klev Schoening
Lene Gammelgaard
plus all Sherpas

left the oxygen they were carrying before hurrying back down to the South Col, distraught that they'd not succeeded.

During the course of the afternoon, Beck Weathers, who'd been lying unconscious on the South Col since the early hours of the morning, woke up. Incredibly, he managed to get himself upright and stagger back to a shocked Camp 4. He was immediately put into a warm sleeping bag and placed on oxygen. No one thought he would survive the following night.

Anatoli, seeing that Beck had apparently risen from the dead, refused to give up on Scott. Leaving the South Col at 5 p.m., Anatoli reached Scott some two hours later to discover he was dead.

The final radio call with Rob came at 6.20 p.m., during which Rob was patched through to New Zealand to speak to his pregnant wife. Following that conversation, all further attempts to reach him by radio went unanswered.

Throughout the second night, 11–12 May, the storm raged harder than the night before. By morning, both Beck Weathers and Makalu Gau, who'd both been placed in tents on the South Col, were miraculously still alive. The death toll on the south side of Everest stood at five: Doug Hansen, Andy Harris, Yasuko Namba, Scott Fischer and Rob Hall. Three Indian climbers lay dead on the northern slopes.

The feeling at Camp 2 was one of complete and utter shock. Everyone was drained of emotion. A numb feeling of emptiness settled over the whole mountain. No one could quite believe what had happened.

Evacuation

Over the next 24 hours, all the survivors who'd been caught out in the storm were evacuated down to Camp 2. In light of the serious injuries suffered by Beck Weathers and Makalu Gau, a helicopter was organised to collect them from the lower end of the Western Cwm. This rescue, I discovered later, came about due to immense pressure from the family and friends of Beck Weathers back in the United States and the resultant request of the US Ambassador in Nepal, such was the instantaneous speed of communications across the world. The flight would be a dangerous mission due to the altitude at which the helicopter needed to land. Even more difficult would be the subsequent take-off, with the added weight of its injured cargo. At 20,000 feet above sea level, the problem is the thinness of the air and the resultant lack of lift from the rotor blades. This mission was to be flown by a Nepalese Army pilot Lieutenant Colonel Maden K.C., who, we were informed, had volunteered.

For all teams on the mountain, the planned move was now in the direction of Base Camp. After picking at an early breakfast, I left Camp 2 in a sombre mood to make my way down the Western Cwm. It was 13 May. Half an hour into my descent, I saw to my left, and slightly off the established route, a gathering of 15–20 people. I presumed this consisted of members from several expeditions escorting Beck Weathers and Makalu Gau, who were awaiting the rescue helicopter.

Several hundred feet in front of me, but out of sight, I could hear the sound of rotor blades furiously slicing away, seeking what meagre lift they could find in the painfully thin air. As if part of an improbable scene out of an action movie, the helicopter appeared over the top of the Icefall, dark green in colour and bearing the red star of the Nepalese Armed forces on the side. It continued climbing far above 20,000 feet. The pilot, either full of adrenalin or expertly assessing the control of his machine, or both, flew high along the right flank of the Western Cwm, turning around near the Lhotse Face. The speed at which he flew the length of the Western Cwm indicated the pilot's confidence and ability. He showed no nerves in the manner of his flying; it was confident and precise. Returning eventually to the large gathering of people, he brought his machine into the required position. Keeping the rotors spinning at a controllable speed, he briefly touched down to enable one of the casualties, Makalu Gau, to be loaded. Once the injured party was on board, he took off at a shallow angle using the forward motion to gain extra lift. Without any commotion, the Squirrel helicopter slipped out of the Western Cwm. Silence returned.

A short time later, having safely deposited Makalu Gau lower down, Maden K.C. bravely repeated the operation and collected Beck Weathers. Both of the injured parties were helicoptered back to Kathmandu that morning for immediate hospital treatment before transferring home.

The skill with which he flew the operation would gain him admiration from all those present on Everest that year, his fellow countrymen and from those anxiously waiting abroad. With each patient on board, the helicopter had been dangerously close to its limit. There had been no margin for error.

Makalu Gau, with severely frostbitten feet, hands and face, would go through 15 operations, during which his nose, fingers, toes and parts of his feet were amputated. His nose was reconstructed using plastic surgery and skin grafts. The soles of his feet were reformed using tissue taken from his arms. Makalu's road to recovery was a long, slow and painful process; he needed to learn to walk again and manage even the simplest of tasks. Incredibly, he would eventually return to climbing.

Beck Weathers, badly frostbitten on his face and hands, also had to undergo many surgical procedures. His right hand, which had been frozen solid right up to the wrist, was amputated, as were good portions of his other hand. Similar to Makalu Gau, his nose and surrounding tissue were rebuilt by plastic surgery.

After he had apparently risen from the dead, it would transpire that 10 May and the long road to recovery would have a very positive influence on Beck's life. His marriage had been under considerable strain, in no small part due to his personal climbing ambitions. He was a pathologist by profession, and the events of 1996 gave him a unique opportunity to focus on what was important in his life. These he would realise were his marriage, family and the joy of being alive. Beck, after considerable physiotherapy, returned to his medical career and would become a much sought-after speaker before professional, corporate and academic audiences.

After climbing down through the Icefall, I arrived at Base Camp an hour later. My descent was slow as I woefully reflected on the events of the previous few days. The atmosphere in Base Camp was one of sad contemplation as gradually more facts came to light about what had happened on 10 May through to the morning of 11 May. Mistakes had been made.

The day after my arrival back at Base Camp, a memorial service was held for those who had died. This was attended by almost everyone. Various people spoke remorsefully, some spoke because they felt they had to, but only one stuck in my mind. An older gentleman stood up to speak towards the end of the proceedings. Pete Schoening at the age of sixty-eight was a Himalayan veteran who'd sprung to fame some forty-three years earlier when his quick reactions single-handedly saved the lives of five of his fellow climbers on K2. He made a comparison between the situation of those who'd been caught in the storm of 10 May and an emergency in warfare. In both instances, it was to be expected there would be a lack of communication and difficulties in understanding what had happened before an effective rescue plan could be put into place. He said we all should be proud of the help that was given and to accept that errors will happen when understanding and responding to a disaster. Wise words. I suppose in essence he was saying don't be too harsh on yourselves, you did as well as anyone else could have, given the circumstances.

Homeward Bound

16 May 1996

The topic of discussion in our Base Camp now centred on whether we should continue with the climb or pack up and leave. The feelings were mixed, but undoubtedly the drive to reach the summit was greatly diminished following the tragic loss of so many lives. The decision for each climber was a personal one. My eventual conclusion was that I'd have felt selfish in the light of other people's grief to continue the climb for my own ambition. This was not the year for me to reach the summit of Everest from Nepal. The mountain would be there another year. One by one, each of our climbers would come to the same conclusion: to head home.

Our Sherpas were visibly relieved; the expedition looked as though it was coming to an end. The 'karma' was not good. Everest was angry: a sign the gods were displeased. They too had families to return to. The hard and dangerous work they undertook was difficult enough at the best of times. Preying heavily on their minds were the disastrous events of 10 May.

Unlike those unfortunate climbers who'd lost their lives, I was going home to my wife and two daughters. My thoughts were of the pain and anguish being endured by the families and loved ones of those who'd died. I felt a deep-rooted sense of guilt. Why had no one asked us for help? We had been 50 feet from their tents on the South Col. We could have put out a rescue. Were they hoping the problems would somehow sort themselves out or was this a tragic lack of communication? There are some in our team who felt, after the event, that it would have been embarrassing for these high-dollar teams to ask for help from a low-budget expedition such as ours at an early stage of their problems. If so, they underestimated how quickly and lethally circumstances could change at high altitude. I sincerely hope this was not the case. Once our evening radio call was finished, the radio was turned off, so that avenue of help was closed.

There remained the possibility of getting those of their teams who were on the South Col to raise the alarm with us. We were a team freshly onto the South Col with full oxygen supplies. We were ten in number: five experienced high-altitude Sherpas and five climbers. At no point during the night of 10 May through until early morning on 11 May did anyone ask us for help or tell us there was a problem with the other teams.

Had the storm come in a while later, our team members might have been hit by this fury, not them. Why had fate and misfortune struck their teams and not us? Was it just the luck of the draw? I realised how close we'd come. The difference between life and death can be a split second. In this case, from our team's perspective, it had been the day on which we'd arranged to make our summit bid. Originally we'd been going to make our bid on 10 May: the same day as Rob's and Scott's teams. Then Rob had asked if we'd hang back one day and go on 11 May instead. This agreement with Rob, as it turned out, might have saved us from the ravages of the storm that hit Everest late in the afternoon on 10 May 1996. Why had they kept climbing upwards when lower down we could see the weather hadn't been settled enough for at least two days prior to their summit attempt?

The futility, the hollow feeling that our endeavour was not worth the price that had been paid, brought back painful memories of three years earlier. On that occasion, I was on a post-monsoon expedition on the north side of Everest. We'd been joined by a Shuttle astronaut, Dr Karl Heinz, who at the time was carrying out research for NASA. I was sharing a tent at Advanced Base Camp with Karl. He'd filmed me as I set off to spend a night higher on the mountain. When I returned less than 24 hours later, he was dead. He'd died from altitude sickness or, more precisely, pulmonary oedema. I could still remember being told the devastating news by Jon Muir, Brigitte's husband, as I walked into camp. I'd sat down, without taking my rucksack off, and stared blankly towards the summit of Everest for what seemed like an eternity. Tears had filled my eyes as I tried my utmost to remain in control, the sadness and emotion overwhelming me. What a waste of a wonderful life. A man who'd been into space lay dead from altitude sickness; it did not make sense. Neither did the events of 10 May 1996.

The joy I'd felt while hatching my plan in the far reaches of Argentina to climb Everest that year, all the effort made to bring it into reality, disappeared into a grey shadowy depression. As I picked up various pieces of equipment to pack them away for my departure, I saw them in a dispassionate light. A few days before, each piece had been a vital link in ensuring my survival and well-being. Now they appeared as objects with no significance to my life at all.

Within a day or so of the memorial service, I departed from Base

Camp alone. Not to go back up through the Icefall as others would do in the weeks to come but in the opposite direction: down.

My departure came shortly after lunch and, as it turned out, on the same day that most of Scott's clients had also left to begin their journey home. I arrived at the village of Pheriche in the early evening as the last glimmers of daylight were fading from the sky. Drawn by the lodge with the most lights on, I ended up staying at the same establishment as the clients from Scott's team. Initially, I didn't take notice of the other guests, most of whom were either eating their evening meal or gathered around the hot stove in the centre of the large square dining room. It wasn't until the morning, when I saw some of them had small individual bandages on the ends of their fingers, that I realised who my fellow lodgers were. The dressings were being removed so they could bathe their fingers in warm water containing an antiseptic. Although I could see no significant injuries, they were, from their conversation, suffering from mild frostbite or frostnip. Considering the storm these climbers had endured, their physical injuries were slight. However, I had no doubt the mental scars would remain with them for many years to come.

Quietly eating my breakfast, I observed, several feet away, an attractive-looking lady with short- to medium-length brown curly hair. She was sitting alone in the corner of the lodge nearest the windows. I smiled without speaking, a smile that was returned as she emerged from her trance-like state: a feeling we have all experienced at one time or another when our thoughts are miles away. I didn't know, at that moment in time, the lady's name or who she was. I would see the same person very differently a few days later.

Soon there was a buzz about the lodge: talk of Kathmandu, hot showers, clean clothes and other luxuries of everyday life. Although the mountain airstrip at Lukla was two to three days' walk away, I heard the words 'by this afternoon'. It transpired that the lady who'd been sitting near to me had chartered a helicopter, at a cost of around $2,500, to fly from Kathmandu to Pheriche to collect her. I gathered there was room for up to five passengers, therefore four other members of her group had been offered a quick hop, about an hour's flight, back to the modern world.

Around 9.30 a.m. came the familiar sound of rotor blades approaching. After a quick flurry of activity, I saw the waiting passengers disappear eagerly out of the door. Within minutes, the helicopter had been and gone. The peaceful sounds of everyday life once again descended, as did a look of envy on the faces of other members of their team, who faced a long walk before they could catch their own flight back to Kathmandu.

Over the coming days, on the trail down to Lukla, I was to share both meals and accommodation with some of Scott's team. The events of 10 May naturally dominated the conversation. Their need to talk, to make sense of what had happened, was both necessary and understandable. My role at this time was to listen, not to criticise; the grief and anguish were too recent. The mistakes and blunders that had been made by the two teams had been basic and deadly. No one needed to tell them; they knew it.

Soon I was back in the hot and dusty embrace of a bustling city. Everywhere I looked in Thamel the shops were selling photographs of the Himalaya. What had happened seemed inescapable. The instant availability of modern comforts, the noise of humanity, was such a contrast to the last two months on Everest that it felt as though they had been in a different lifetime. It gave the bizarre sensation that I'd joined an expedition to a different existence and had just returned. In many ways, that was exactly what I'd done. I was back in the 'real' world.

I booked myself into the familiar surroundings of the Gauri Shankar Hotel. It was while enjoying a long-awaited cold beer at the hotel bar that I met the Mexican climber Carlos Carsolio. Aged 33, with neatly trimmed black hair, he was square-set with a strong physique reminiscent of a rugby player. On reaching the summit of Manaslu, he'd recently become the fourth, and youngest, person to climb the world's 14 highest mountains, whose summits are over 26,000 feet. Both Rob and Scott, along with Ed Viesturs from the Imax team and the Finnish climber Veikka Gustafsson from Mal Duff's team, had planned to join Carlos on Manaslu straight after they'd completed their commitments on Everest. Although they expected that Carlos might have completed his climb before they got to Manaslu, they were going to make use of his permit. He'd included their names on the application. These four were going to climb this second mountain as a team, giving themselves a tight schedule to keep. Their self-imposed pressure, particularly in the case of Rob and Scott, seemed endless.

Veikka was a good friend of Rob and Ed, and had climbed with these two on another 26,000-ft peak, Makalu, the year before. The friendship between Rob, Scott and Ed went back further.

Carlos, like the rest of the world, had heard about the deaths of Rob and Scott through the media. He wanted to know why the climb had gone so terribly wrong for his friends. Having been on the South Col during the night of the storm, and through the conversations I'd had with some of the survivors during the trek back to Lukla, I tried to piece together for Carlos what had transpired. I didn't attempt to cover the mistakes that had been made by the teams, the basic errors. Carlos sat astounded as I recounted the events. Almost every question he asked started with the words 'How?' or 'Why?'

It was while talking with Carlos that I became aware of a young man, about 5 ft 6 in. tall, aged around 25, standing at the end of the bar. During a momentary pause, the young man seized his opportunity and asked, 'How is Andy Harris?'

Without stopping to think, I turned to him and said, 'He's dead.'

No sooner had I spouted these words than I regretted the blunt manner in which I'd answered his question. The young man stood there with a look of horror on his face that I will never forget. Stunned into silence by what he'd heard, his eyes filled with tears. He looked at Carlos and me for a second or two, then turned and ran, his grief completely overwhelming him. To this day, I deeply regret breaking tragic news in such a thoughtless manner. I should, at the very least, have enquired first whether he was a friend or relation of Andy Harris so I could have measured my answer more sensitively. Unfortunately, I'd answered his question in a factual way, in the same way I had been answering those from Carlos. Judging by his reaction, he was a good friend of Andy Harris and may well have been a close relative. If that young man now, more than 14 years on, happens to read this book, I would like to extend to him my sincere apologies.

To this day, no one really knows what happened to Andy Harris other than that he disappeared on Everest somewhere near the South Summit on the night of 10 May. A fall seems the most likely explanation.

I can't recall who it was from Scott's team that invited me to an afternoon gathering in the well-manicured gardens of the Yak and Yeti Hotel: most likely it was one of the clients with whom I'd trekked down. This get-together had been organised, I was told, by the lady with whom I'd exchanged a smile over breakfast in the lodge at Pheriche, the one who could afford to charter helicopters and was, as it turned out, a person of considerable wealth; her name was Sandy Hill Pittman.

I hadn't been sure what to expect, but looking back I shouldn't have been surprised. Dressed in no more than casual clothes, I passed through the dimly lit reception area of the Yak and Yeti Hotel and exited via a large pair of glazed doors into the rear garden. There on the lawn I was confronted by what I could only describe as an afternoon cocktail party. Waiters wearing immaculate white shirts, black trousers, bow ties and highly polished shoes were placed at strategic points holding trays of chilled margaritas. Tables of carefully prepared buffet delights, which seemed alien after the month and a half we'd spent at

Base Camp, had been painstakingly laid out to tempt even the most particular palate.

Sandy Hill Pittman was hardly recognisable. She was wearing a tight-fitting black cocktail dress that sparkled with beads and sequins, complemented by matching black high-heeled stilettos. Her hair was tied back and enhanced with long extensions decorated with red-beaded cords; confidently, she drifted amongst the invited guests.

Both the formality of the gathering and the mode of dress seemed inappropriate. People were dressed up, but for whom? Possibly for some of the world's press who'd also been invited. Hardly a week had passed since their fellow climbers had died so tragically in such terrible conditions.

I shuffled my way to the fringes of the throng, away from the hub. Something low key would have seemed more fitting in the circumstances. A final farewell to friends they'd lost.

My instinct was to leave, but incredulity about what I was witnessing welded me to the spot. I stood alone in quiet disbelief. I was shaken from my thoughts by a hand placed firmly on my left shoulder. A hand that was accompanied by the familiar voice of Anatoli: 'Graham, you and I do not belong here.'

Little could I have known this would be the last time I would ever see Anatoli. I did, however, receive two postcards from him during the course of 1996. The first was from Nepal dated 22 October. The card read:

> Namaste from Nepal!
> This autumn as before I spent my time in the high altitude to enjoy the mountains when I climbed Cho-Oyu and Shixspangma [sic] in Tibet. It wasn't easy because of lots of snow made my ascents very dangerous. I don't forget lesson from mountains from last spring.
> Hope to see you again in mountain.
> All the best Anatoli B.

The second was a joint card from Anatoli and his partner Linda Wylie, each writing half. It began:

> Merry Christmas. Best wishes for the New Year!
> Hope to see you soon. Welcome to Tien-Shan area next summer.
> Anatoly.
> Hope this finds you well and that the holidays are a pleasure.
> Toli's spirit is better after a pretty low summer. We have a friends

and family expedition to Khan Tengri next summer – I'll try to write a letter in Jan with more details.

All the Best

Linda Wylie

Sadly the Khan Tengri expedition did not happen for me. As with so much in life, things crop up that conspire to take away these precious opportunities.

On Christmas Day 1997, Anatoli was tragically swept to his death by an avalanche while attempting to climb Annapurna in western Nepal – 12 months after the second card was posted.

Flights back home at the end of May 1996 proved problematic. The date I'd booked for my return when I'd originally bought the ticket had been mid-June. The reason for this was that we'd had no idea on what date our summit attempt might fall, so I'd allowed plenty of extra time at the end. The return flight I was scheduled to take was over three weeks away. A further difficulty arose because Biman Airlines, with whom I'd flown, had only two flights a week back to Heathrow. It transpired they had no available seats on the dates in between for a transfer of my ticket.

I looked into the possibility of buying a one-way ticket on a different airline. Anyone who has tried to book a last-minute one-way air ticket will understand when I say the official full fare I was quoted was eye-watering: nothing like the comparatively modest sum I'd paid for the whole of my original return ticket. The potential cost involved would have been crippling to our already impoverished family budget. In the end, Biman Airlines managed to move my date forward slightly, leaving me another ten days in Kathmandu.

Back in the Gauri Shankar, I spent time at the hotel bar with Carlos, discussing his forthcoming felicitation. This was rapidly being organised by the Nepalese officials in recognition of his recent achievement.

He'd joined an elite group of three people – Reinhold Messner (Italy), Jerzy Kukuczka (Poland) and Ehardt Loretan (Switzerland) – by completing the fourteen highest mountains. The Nepalese authorities were quick on the uptake, realising this presented them with the perfect opportunity to make a public statement of pride. Most of Carlos's success had taken place in Nepal, where the majority of these mountains lie.

Carlos, embarrassed at the attention he was about to receive, asked if I would like to accompany him to the ceremony. Not needing to check my diary over the coming days, I was delighted to accept.

The next day I was presented with an official invite that read:

A DAY TO DIE FOR

Within the same envelope was a brief résumé of Carlos's achievements, giving the year that he'd summited each of the 14 mountains, and a professionally prepared colour postcard that had been printed several months earlier to promote the expedition he'd just completed. This card bore the names of Ed Viesturs, Veikka Gustafsson, Rob Hall and Scott Fischer.

At 4 p.m. on the afternoon of 24 May, Carlos and I were collected by minibus from the Gauri Shankar for our short journey to the Hotel Blue Star. Sitting alongside Carlos, I was slightly taken aback when he asked me what I thought he should say in his acceptance speech.

'Wow, a bit late to be thinking about that,' was my first thought.

In fairness, this quiet and modest man was feeling nervous about the attention that was being lavished on him. His question was searching for the obvious that he might have overlooked.

The felicitation did not disappoint. Taking place in the hotel ballroom, it had all the formality and official speeches that one could have asked for, to the point of overkill. When the time came for Carlos to address the gathered throng, he displayed great modesty, playing down his recent achievement. Rather, he concentrated on the close friends he'd lost along the way. The loss that had affected him most was that of Polish climber Wanda Rutkiewicz on Kangchenjunga, the world's third-highest mountain, in May 1992. Wanda, considered the best woman climber of her time, had been making a summit bid with Carlos. As he covered the ground more quickly, he'd summited first; on his descent, he came across Wanda and tried to persuade her to abandon her attempt and return back down with him. She chose to continue, planning to bivouac and complete her ascent the next day. A storm blew in that night and she was never seen again. Carlos had been the last person to see her alive. He had been devastated. In his speech, he described this as his darkest hour, a time at which he nearly gave up climbing because of the pain he felt over Wanda's death. As he uttered those words, I couldn't help but think they were influenced by more recent events. Deep down he must have been relieved he'd completed his quest before he too became a name on a long list of people who were no longer here.

So eager was I to return home that each subsequent day seemed to grow in length as I waited out the allotted time. Shortly after breakfast on one of these mornings, I heard the unmistakable sound of Elizabeth Hawley's VW Beetle as it pulled up outside the hotel entrance.

Henry and the others had returned from Base Camp. Liz was on her fact-finding tour to collect all the relevant details she needed for her meticulous records. Once again, I sat down to join in the discussion, which understandably took on a more sombre tone than that of the previous year. After Liz had covered some initial questions, she asked Henry how far our team had got up the mountain.

'The South Col,' Henry replied.

'Is that as far as they got?' asked Liz, who'd been surprised by his response.

'That is correct,' Henry answered, in a manner that had an embarrassed tone to it, his eyes not meeting Liz's enquiring glance.

Henry's business was built on success, with each year used to promote the next, much in the way Rob's and Scott's had been. Henry would have preferred to be sitting there telling Liz of success rather than informing her that his team had got nowhere near the summit. However, these were exceptional circumstances. This was anything but a normal year.

Liz Hawley had seen far more than her fair share of people destined not to return. Many a great Himalayan climber she'd interviewed before an expedition had not come back; a good number of these had visited Nepal numerous times before. Now they included Rob Hall and Scott Fischer. She had met these two several times, and Rob on a regular basis for several years in his role as leader of Adventure Consultants. Now she had to place in her records the date of 10 May 1996 for their successful summit, but this time it would bear a small black cross next to their names, along with 'died on descent'.

Sadly, death was no stranger to Elizabeth Hawley. Undoubtedly one of the hardest and most painful tasks Liz had ever undertaken came in 1975, when she had to tell her close and very dear friend, Sir Edmund Hillary, that his wife Louise and their youngest daughter Belinda had been killed in a plane crash in Nepal after he'd helped them board at Kathmandu only a short time before.

When the time came to fly home, I felt relieved to be leaving Nepal. I sensed I could leave the death and misery behind. I could escape from the dreadful emptiness these tragic events had brought. The excitement of travelling home to see Catherine, Angela and Amy almost managed to convince me that this was possible.

One Sentence, Two Lines of Print

It was late 1997, as far as I recall, on an ordinary day like any other, that I was sitting in the kitchen of our home in Whitley Bay having breakfast. Across the adjacent entrance hall echoed the distant sound of our letterbox snapping shut. There followed a thud as the mail hit the porch floor.

In an automatic response to this familiar sound, I slid my chair back across the tiled floor. Standing up, I made my way to the front door to collect the mail, which rarely contained anything more interesting than the constant stream of family bills and junk literature. The bundle that day looked no different from that of any other: a few envelopes and a couple of outdoor-type magazines.

The events on Everest in the spring of 1996, although not forgotten, were drifting into the past. They'd been well documented in a good number of articles; there was no reason to think that anything I read now would significantly change my understanding. For me, life had moved on, as it had for other climbers and people present on Everest that year. All had returned to their families and everyday lives. As tragic as the events of 1996 are and were, all mountaineers live and climb in the knowledge of the dangers of their sport. We'd all come to terms with this loss in our own way.

Settling back down at the breakfast table, I picked up one of the magazines and removed the ubiquitous clear plastic packaging. Whether it was a trade or general publication, I can no longer remember. As I flicked casually through the pages, my eye caught an article about a UK trade show and international climbing competition that had been attended by climbers and mountaineers from around the world. Pausing for a moment before letting the next page slide through my fingers, I spotted the words 'Rob Hall' and 'Everest 1996'. As they seemed so out of place in what the article was covering, my curiosity drew me to read the relevant section.

I was totally unprepared for what I read next. My stomach tightened with a sickening feeling. My mind grappled with the implications of the words as they leapt out of the page at me as though they were printed in letters far bolder than the surrounding text. Before me lay the breakfast table, but the image that filled my mind was the moment I'd arrived at the South Col on the evening of 10 May, the wind and blizzard howling towards me out of the darkness, two head torches glimmering in the distance.

My emotions were torn asunder, between the past and present, as I stared at two particular lines of print. Resentment and anger welled up inside me, feelings that brought with them an internal turmoil and deep sense of shame, as they were, in part, directed at two of those who were dead: Rob Hall and Scott Fischer. To have such thoughts about those who'd paid for their wrong decisions with their lives was alien to me. I struggled with my sense of guilt as it clashed with the shock and anger I felt. Never had I been so stunned by a single sentence.

One of Rob Hall's team, not one of his clients, had been briefly interviewed about the storm and its aftermath at this international show, during which they had said: 'We went on the 10th of May because we knew the weather was going to go bad the next day.'

The next day, 11 May, was the day our team had been scheduled to make an attempt on the summit of Everest.

This meant they'd known the weather on 11 May was going to be totally unsuitable for a summit attempt, and quite possibly dangerous. More importantly, this was the day that Rob and Scott had asked us to make our bid for the top! My mind flashed back to the conditions we'd encountered at the time. The wind and blizzard had hit hard on the evening of 10 May, and although the driving wind and snow died down at the South Col on the morning of 11 May, it had returned with a vengeance that evening.

Up to this point, I hadn't said a word. I'd sat in silent disbelief. Catherine, concerned by the look on my face, instantly sensed something was amiss but had no idea what had caused it. One moment we'd been having breakfast, the next a heavy atmosphere descended on the room.

'What's wrong?' she asked.

I found it difficult to put into words the meaning of what I'd read moments before. As best I could, I explained to Catherine, in a broken and rather muddled fashion, how different the events of 10–11 May could have been. This in itself disturbed me deeply. Was it no more than luck that had allowed me to return to my wife and two daughters that year, and others on my team to their families?

In an effort to reassure myself that my reaction was not unnatural, or in some way disproportionate, I telephoned Paul Deegan. He'd become a good friend through the course of the expedition led by Henry Todd on the North Ridge of Everest from Tibet in 1995. He had been with us in 1996.

Paul had set out with the rest of us from Camp 3 on the afternoon of 10 May but had turned back part-way up when he encountered problems adjusting to his oxygen mask. I wanted his reaction.

Slowly, I read the two lines to Paul. There was a poignant pause of two or three seconds then his voice came reverberating down the phone: 'The b******s!' Paul had instantly grasped the implications of what he'd just heard. The events on Everest in the spring of 1996 could have been very different; the casualties could easily have been ours.

Twice to the Summit of Everest

Prior to this revelation, the only accounts I'd read during the latter half of 1996 were those that had appeared in the British Mountaineering Council's *High* magazine: a publication that put forward the known facts in an intelligent manner, as opposed to some other magazines whose front covers I had seen sensationalising these tragic events. None of the articles I'd looked at had made mention of other teams having prior knowledge of the weather, although one had given a clue that this might have been the case.

A report had appeared in issue No. 164, in July of that year, written by Lindsay Griffin (Mountain Information Editor), and was titled 'Everest 96'.

According to that report: '. . . computer models were forecasting 100 to 120 km/hour winds to arrive at the weekend, leaving an adequate weather window for a round trip to Everest's high point on Friday 10th.'

This article had raised some questions in my mind, but the latter part of 1996 and right through 1997 was a particularly busy time for Catherine and myself. We were in the process of starting two new businesses, one of which was a retail outlet called The Third Eye. We spent the winter of '96–'97 converting the disused and rather derelict lower ground floor of a commercial building we owned in the nearby town of North Shields into a brand-new shop. Here, we intended to sell clothes, jewellery, incense, carvings and other handicrafts that we were sourcing and importing from Nepal. The other was a wholesale business, run from the same property, supplying a wide range of multicoloured novelty hats that we were having manufactured in Kathmandu. Our customer base for these was mostly ski shops, rugby and football clubs, in the latter case including one or two in the football Premiership. This business we called The Crazy Hat Company.

I was so preoccupied with getting these two businesses up and running that the events of 1996 had begun to fade into an episode from the past. My daily schedule was full to the point of bursting. Future plans filled what little time I had left for contemplation. Although being shocked enough to phone Paul immediately when I'd read those two lines of print, my life was running at such a pace that I'd little choice but to let go. Or at least I thought I had. In hindsight, I realise this was never going to be the case. Subconsciously, the events of 1996, along with the statements I'd read, would continue to trouble me.

Everest, however, was still in my thoughts, almost on a daily basis. The goal I'd set myself – to be the first British climber to reach the summit from both Nepal and Tibet – was still there for the taking. I was aware of competition but wasn't sure if any of my rivals might be trying in 1997: a torment that was made worse by the fact I needed to earn a living and couldn't return that year.

This mental pressure I'd put myself under grew substantially due to the fact I had to go to Nepal twice that year on business. The first occasion was in June, shortly after the spring climbing season had ended. I felt uncomfortable, as though I should have been travelling on from Kathmandu rather than spending the whole time in the capital. Climbing shops displaying their equipment and photographs of Everest were everywhere I looked. The frustration I felt, the need to be back in the mountains, was very real. My second business trip in September merely served to reinforce my determination to go back to Everest the following year.

In late autumn 1997, I contacted Alastair Leithead. Since we'd last worked together, he'd moved from being a reporter with the *Newcastle Evening Chronicle* to being one with regional BBC television, North East & Cumbria. My objective was to see if he could entice the BBC into televising the attempt I intended to make that coming spring.

Alastair, seeing the potential this offered, skilfully managed to organise a meeting. Others to be present were Olwyn Hocking, who at the time was head of this region for the BBC, Alastair himself, several of their production team and me.

With my slide projector in hand, I was ushered into a large, well-lit room containing a central rectangular table around which some 15 chairs were placed. At one end, a screen waited in readiness for the images I was to present from the 1996 expedition. The purpose of this exercise, I found out afterwards, was to see if I could actually take reasonable photographs. If not, it would have been an uphill struggle from their perspective and probably a non-starter. Fortunately, I'd foreseen this might happen and had borrowed a couple of slides from Paul Deegan, who I knew had some stunning shots from that year. It was obvious which slide clinched the deal, and it wasn't one of mine. The image was a fantastic photograph of Paul's looking up the polished ice of the Lhotse Face with climbers high up disappearing in and out of a swirling mist. As my audience gasped at this dramatic sight, my mind silently thanked Paul for his assistance. In many ways, I'd undergone a job interview. Sensibly, I had gone prepared.

The questions that followed delved into the practicalities: the equipment I would be required to ship to Nepal, Customs clearance, how I could get the rushes (film clips) back to the north-east as the expedition progressed. With solutions found to these potential difficulties, my interviewing audience seemed satisfied that the undertaking was both achievable and worthwhile.

A further private meeting took place between Olwyn and myself, at which an offer was made. For a sum of money towards my expenses, they wanted me to film my own progress and send back reports via DHL on a regular basis. The amount put forward was very modest for what they expected in return. However, with the BBC on board my chances of gaining commercial sponsorship increased significantly. So agreements and contract were entered into, whereby the film I shot would remain my copyright. The BBC retained the right of first use, an option that would expire after 12 months.

The slight flaw in this ambitious plan was that I had no experience whatsoever of filming. I didn't even possess a home video camera. However, such a minor detail was not insurmountable to this national institution. Wheels were immediately set in motion for me to undertake two days of training. This would take place in the middle of January, on the wild and windswept crags of Northumberland with leading outdoor cameraman Keith Partridge.

The equipment we used for this exercise was one of those large, rather old-fashioned-looking cameras under which a metal stand normally strained. Dressed in thermal underwear and Gore-tex jackets to counter the conditions we faced during my edification, we shot several set pieces, hampered by the legs of the tripod as they sank into the rain-sodden ground. Keith also had me climbing up ropes through a cold biting wind while holding this enormous contraption and filming at the same time. I'd not anticipated the BBC would have been able to replicate so well some of the conditions I might expect to encounter on Everest.

Fortunately, the two cameras they intended to supply for this endeavour were somewhat smaller, lighter and more manageable. As the intended cameraman and subject matter, I was going to be a one-man band once I reached Nepal.

Commercial sponsorship did not follow as I'd hoped. Here, I learnt a valuable lesson. In raising funds to join this expedition, I had to appear calm, as though everything was under control, even when it was not. I was within three weeks of my departure for Nepal and still a long way short of the amount I needed simply to cover my costs. The

BBC was blissfully unaware, as were the other smaller sponsors I'd managed to obtain. Then I learnt my second lesson. Luck can play a significant part.

I was in my local branch of a franchise business called Prontaprint picking up some business cards I'd ordered. Explaining my predicament to the proprietor, John Fleet, whom I knew, I asked jokingly if Prontaprint might be interested in sponsoring me. Much to my amazement, John said he'd ask. I left my contact details and thought no more about it. This was, to say the least, a long shot from which I expected to hear nothing more.

Two days later, I received an email from Dr Kevin Potts, Prontaprint's new CEO, saying they would like to be involved and offering me a sum of money. I was staggered and somewhat relieved this had come in the form of an email, as I was lost for words. Although still well short of the figure I needed, I sent a message back gratefully accepting their offer. I was bewildered when, the very next day, I received a further email from this gentleman, increasing the sum. This was followed by astonishment a few hours later when I received a follow-up offering to cover the remainder of my costs, provided they could rank as my major sponsor. In little more than four days, I'd gone from grasping at straws to having my place on the expedition secured. The key was that the company had a newly appointed CEO who wanted to make his mark, to be seen as dynamic and forward thinking. He had joined the company the month before. My request had been put before the right person at exactly the right moment. It was pure luck and a chance comment that had brought this about.

With days to spare before my departure to Nepal, I was flown down to Prontaprint's headquarters at Watford for a photoshoot. For this occasion, I had been asked to bring my full climbing equipment.

At the arrivals area in Luton Airport stood a driver holding a large card that bore my name in bold printed letters. He was there to take me to their offices and to whisk me back to the airport for my return flight three hours later, such was the urgency of my turnaround. There was much that had to be done before I left for Everest, mostly to do with the BBC equipment and cameras I would be carrying. A Customs carnet would be required for me to bring them back into the country without import duty being applied.

Dr Kevin Potts was an imposing balding gentleman in his late 30s, tall and solidly built. He strutted around the newly laid floor covering, making business decisions as we spoke. In attendance was his number one man, Niall Bryne. Carpet fitters with Stanley knives were trimming the edges of the final sections. They were in the process of settling into their new offices, having recently relocated from Darlington in north-east England. People were frantically rushing around organising what should go where, while answering the phones that continually rang. Fax machines spewed out a constant stream of unattended paper.

In the foyer, a husband and wife team joined the three of us. They had been retained to organise Prontaprint's publicity. The thin bespectacled gentleman, who wore a long trench coat and a broad-rimmed leather hat, had a single-lens reflex camera hanging from his neck. His wife stood nervously alongside with two small cases of equipment. They were out of their depth.

It was soon apparent that no real forethought had been given to the pictures they might take, other than that I would be dressed in the suitable attire. The nearest terrain they had found to a mountain was a six-foot-high grassy slope. It was outside the entrance to the offices.

To the complete bewilderment of those driving past on this modern upmarket business park, I posed in the bright orange Gore-tex jacket and trousers that Sprayway had supplied me with, my ice axe held aloft. Behind me were parked a turquoise Ford Mondeo and a silver BMW 5 Series. I felt ridiculous, but what the heck, they were paying and I was going back to Everest. I would have stood there in my underpants if they had asked me to.

Amongst the must-have photographs they wanted was one of me shaking hands with the new CEO. The backdrop to this picture was their offices, which had Prontaprint World Headquarters emblazoned across the front. It was while we were arranging ourselves for this particular shot that Dr Kevin Potts gave my hand an extra squeeze and pulled me forward slightly. Leaning towards me, he whispered sternly, 'You had better make the top.'

He had uttered these words without an expression on his face. I wasn't quite sure if it was a threat or a joke. I didn't ask.

It was once again one of Henry Todd's commercial expeditions that I joined. His support in my aim to reach the summit for a second time was undiminished.

I found two significant differences in 1998 as compared to my previous Everest expeditions, the last having been 1996. The first was that a high-altitude weather forecast service had been pre-arranged with the UK Met Office at Bracknell. Once this facility was set up, these could be obtained on demand and on a daily basis if required. At a cost of $500 per forecast, they gave wind speeds and temperatures at different heights, which as far as I recall were 16,500 ft, 19,600 ft, 23,000 ft, 26,200 ft and 29,500 ft, which correlate approximately to 5,000m, 6,000m, 7,000m, 8,000m and 9,000m. Second, because these forecasts were widely available, teams were now willing to stay much later in May than they might previously have done. The forecasts had brought with them a huge increase in confidence and the ability to choose the right days for a summit attempt. The downside to this was that the numbers making an attempt during a settled period of weather would logically increase rather than being more evenly spread over the climbing season. Nearly all teams were using, or had access to, this forecast.

The weather was particularly poor that spring as we sat out all of April and most of May. A feeling of resignation settled over Base Camp; time was beginning to run out and little let-up was showing in the forecast from Bracknell. As we moved towards the latter half of May, I was struck down by what most waiting climbers dread. One of the many well-meaning trekkers visiting Everest Base Camp had brought with them a particularly virulent chest infection which some of us caught. After having spent two months in preparation, I was distraught.

About the same time came the first successful summit attempts from the Nepalese side. I had to sit in Base Camp and watch these happen. The consolation was that these were made by a group of gregarious Americans with whom our team had formed great friendships. We were delighted for them. It was unusually late in the season when these first ascents took place: 20 May, far later than is normal. Fortunately, the improved weather held on.

I managed to shake off most of the infection just in the nick of time for me to make a last-ditch attempt at the summit with several of our team before the permit ended. A few were successful, but weakened by the illness I had to turn around at under 26,000 feet, not even making it as far as the South Col. I was left bitterly disappointed. All the effort and sacrifices others had made to enable me to return to Everest that year seemed wasted.

However, the BBC was delighted with the quality and quantity of material I'd managed to send back during the course of the expedition. From this they had managed to broadcast numerous television reports. Prontaprint had placed life-size pictures of me in all their shop windows; their logos had been plastered over the clothing I wore during the filming. Everyone had a return from their investment.

I wrote to Dr Kevin Potts to thank Prontaprint for their support. The reply I received back informed me that he was no longer with the company. His departure had come before I got back from Nepal. He had been chief executive of the company for less than six months, approximately 180 days.

'You had better make the top.' Surely not?

Despite all that had been achieved, I couldn't help but feel I'd let everyone down. I returned to the UK despondent, with the feeling I'd blown a golden opportunity. When asked during a live radio interview what I was planning next, I openly said that I would not return to Everest.

On reflection, I now understand that the intensity of emotions during and after a major expedition are so all-consuming that no decision on future plans should be made for several months. Rather one should concentrate on coping with the adjustment back to what we consider normal life. Success on an expedition has you wanting to plan the next adventure without delay. Conversely, what we perceive as failure can throw you into the depths of despondency and make you feel as if you never want to go back.

Shortly after my return, Catherine and I moved from our large family home in Whitley Bay. The replacement was a pleasant enough two-bedroomed apartment in Tynemouth, overlooking the north-east coast at the mouth of the River Tyne. Our oldest daughter, Angela, had already left home, and Amy, the younger of the two, was looking to head off to university. It was a time of change for me. Everest, I'd consigned to the past. My family was spreading its wings, and Catherine and I were working out what we could keep and what had to go as we squeezed the contents of our large home into this top-floor apartment. This period was not the happiest of times for me.

It was 17 March 1999 when Carol Malia announced on the BBC's regional six o'clock news that: 'The man who said he would not return to Everest departed from Newcastle Bus Station this morning.'

This was followed by a short news piece that showed me saying goodbye to Catherine, then loading several large holdalls of equipment onto the bus that would take me to Heathrow Airport for my onward flight to Nepal.

The BBC revelled in the unusual nature of their opening line and the method with which I started this 5,000-mile journey. I had opted for this simplest form of transport at the onset for three very good reasons. First, National Express had offered me a free ticket. Second, I could take as much luggage as I wanted. There was not the crippling excess baggage penalty that applied on domestic flights. And last but certainly not least, they would drop me right outside the entrance of Terminal 3. Practicality had won the day.

It had been little more than three months after my dejected return from Everest in early June 1998 that I'd started to plan my next attempt. Once the disappointment had faded, the determination and focus returned.

I'd contacted Alastair again, to enquire if the BBC might be interested in covering me for a second time. His lukewarm response of 'I don't think so, as we've already covered that story once, but I'll ask' was hardly the encouragement I'd been hoping for.

However, Alastair did ask as promised. Fortunately for me, Olwyn, who ultimately made the decisions, was far more enthusiastic. I received a resounding 'yes'. She'd been delighted with the material I'd managed to send back the previous year and saw the merits in following the story through, to hopefully a successful conclusion. The sum on offer, although slightly higher than the previous year, was once again very modest, dictated not by Olwyn but by the ever-tightening budget that businesses continually suffer. The terms apart from that remained the same.

Sponsorship was extremely difficult to find, even with the BBC covering the story and despite me managing to secure coverage on the UK Government's Internet-based National Grid for Learning: an educational facility accessed by schools, colleges and libraries throughout the country.

Sprayway, the UK outdoor clothing company that had supplied me with equipment the previous year, contributed towards my costs. They had been Alison Hargreaves' major sponsor up until her untimely death on K2 in 1995.

A few others came in as smaller sponsors, but I was left well short of the amount I needed. I knew before I departed for Nepal in the spring of 1999 that I would return home in debt. I also understood that if I didn't reach the summit this time, another British climber would and the opportunity would be lost.

As the plane banked left between lofty Himalayan peaks to make its final approach, the wide and relatively flat expanse of the Kathmandu valley came into view. Far below lay a patchwork quilt of lush green early crops. Across this landscape, simple traditional Nepalese farm buildings punctuated the ground. Gradually, this rural vista began to change as, one by one, brickworks started to appear, their tall skyward-pointing chimneys belching trails of thick smoke that disappeared into the haze that hung high above the valley floor. The farmland squeezed ever tighter as the flat-roofed buildings, typical of nearly the whole of Kathmandu, began to swamp the landscape.

A sensation of familiarity came over me. The stress of all the planning, the work to get me to this point, evaporated so quickly it was almost as though it had never existed. Moments before the wheels touched the runway, the warm air of late afternoon buffeted the aircraft's fuselage: the final reminder I was back.

That evening, I'd arranged to meet up with Henry for a meal. Joining us were climbers from another team who'd be attempting Everest that spring, two of whom, Jon Tinker and Mike Smith, were also in the running to be first Briton to scale Everest from both the north and south sides. Although these two were friends of mine from previous years, little was discussed about our individual aims – our unspoken competition. Each of us knew we stood an equal chance of being first to the top. I recall being slightly amused that evening, as all three of us appeared to be assessing the opposition's physical condition for the task ahead. Henry, who was well aware of our aspirations, seemed to be taking some pride in me as his contender.

Jon Tinker, whom I'm sure also found this a bizarre situation, turned to me and said, 'Doug Scott tells me you're never off the television nowadays,' referring to my filming for the BBC the previous year.

Not quite sure how to respond to this statement, I only managed to say, 'Well . . .' before Jon interrupted.

'Come on, Graham, there's no need to be modest,' he said, with a teasing smile.

It felt rather like a gladiatorial display before battle commenced. The mind games had begun.

When I arrived at Base Camp in early April, I was so focused that I had more in common with a tightly coiled spring than a climber. Chomping at the bit, I couldn't make progress fast enough to satisfy myself, unaware of how Jon and Mike would play the unfolding game. I felt sorry for Henry, who had to put up with my constant pressure, my continual requests for him to let me climb high as soon as possible. Fortunately from my point of view, and probably for Henry's sanity, both Camps 1 and 2 had been placed relatively early that season.

Most of my spare time was taken up with filming for the BBC and writing the reports to accompany the digital tapes that would be carried to Lukla by a trusted porter. From there, a one-hour flight followed by a twenty-minute taxi drive brought their arrival at DHL's Kathmandu office. Three days later, they would be lying on Alastair's desk at the BBC Broadcasting Centre in Newcastle upon Tyne, the footage they contained often appearing on television the same evening. Reports could be emailed from Base Camp but not high-definition film on the hideously slow Internet speed available on our satellite phone.

My first of only three ventures up through the Icefall that year took me to Camp 1, where I slept before moving up to Camp 2 the next day. After two nights here, I took a walk up to 24,000 feet, where Camp 3 would be placed and where I was to sleep only a week later to complete my rapid acclimatisation.

Not having thought this through carefully, I was, by the end of this period, out of synchronisation with the rest of my team. Fortunately for me, Iñaki Ochoa, a world-class Spanish climber from the Basque region, had only a few days earlier successfully summited Lhotse by himself without oxygen. He now had his sights set on Everest. Iñaki, with his long curling blond hair and fashionable shades, had a rock-star appearance that belied the quiet gentleman beneath. He was a highly talented and self-effacing man who went out of his way to praise the achievements of those around him, no matter how small, rather than his own. His generosity, gregarious nature and effusive humour endeared him to nearly everyone.

Iñaki and I knew each other well from the previous year, when he'd also made an attempt on Lhotse, only abandoning that attempt after the extreme temperatures threatened to freeze the corneas on his eyes.

With Henry's agreement, and a favourable weather forecast, Iñaki and I teamed up to make an early bid. This was to be the first attempt by anyone that season. The plan was for me to make my way up to Camp 3, where Iñaki would catch me up. His preference was to sleep lower down.

On the morning of 29 April, Iñaki rolled into Camp 3, travelling light for our onward climb to the South Col. His intention was to try for the summit without oxygen – an option I'd considered and discussed at length with Henry. The conclusion we'd come to was that if I wanted to be the first of the contenders it was far better to plug in and get on with the job rather than take the risk of missing out. Although carrying an oxygen cylinder and mask, along with the BBC cameras, I followed Iñaki's lead and did not use supplementary oxygen as we climbed up towards the South Col. The logic behind this decision was the higher you climb without using oxygen, within reason, the stronger your body becomes acclimatised. In the event you do run out higher up, the effects of oxygen depletion do not hit home quite as hard, leaving you in a position to cope far better than otherwise might have been the case.

As Iñaki and I made our way along the left-hand side of the Geneva Spur, the South Col came into view: a place I'd last seen on 11 May 1996. Moments before our departure that day, I'd taken a photograph of Mark Pfetzer with Rob Hall's and Scott Fischer's tents in the background. At that time, we were still ignorant of the tragedy that had struck some of those who had left these tents only 30 hours before. Now, three years on, I stood there once again, aware of the events of 10 May. I could not understand why or how this catastrophe had happened.

The sight of the South Col devoid of tents gave me the impression that both time and the wind had cleansed this barren landscape of the images of distant head torches and half-seen figures that still haunted my mind. Now all that lay on the Col were a few supply dumps from expeditions making an attempt that current year.

Glancing at his watch, Iñaki gave me a smile. 'That's good,' he said. 'We made that in Messner time.'

I presumed from this comment he'd been gauging our progress relative to the climbing times Reinhold Messner must have published in his book. I didn't know what those were, nor had I been timing our ascent.

After a quick scour of the separate piles, we located the appropriate supply dump. Soon, our tent was erected, and we rapidly embedded ourselves in the depths of our sleeping bags. It was the warmest place to be. With the stove boiling a continuous supply of fluid, we began to make plans for our ascent during the early hours of the following morning. A midnight start was agreed. Iñaki didn't want to depart too soon. As he wasn't using oxygen, he wanted to do as much of the climbing as possible during the warmer hours of daylight. The time we had chosen also left us ample opportunity in case we encountered sections of deep snow.

Settling down, I began to breathe supplementary oxygen. Alongside me I could hear Iñaki restlessly shuffling about. As the hours passed, I began to fear that he might not have left a long enough gap since his recent ascent of Lhotse. He'd had precious little time to recover before this next endeavour – Everest. If so, this was partially my fault for persuading him to try so soon after. Around 11 p.m., rather than saying 'time to get ready', I asked him if he was up to the climb ahead.

He sounded relieved that I'd asked him the right question. 'I don't think so,' came his reply.

Although setting off alone crossed my mind, it was not a sensible option. No one, not even the Sherpas, had been higher than the South Col that year. If I encountered snow of any depth, I would have to break trail all the way up by myself. Being realistic, it would have been a good way to blow any chance of success.

Shortly after daybreak, Iñaki headed down. I was now the sole occupant of the South Col. During my scheduled radio call with Henry at 8 a.m., I explained my position. I was surprised to be informed that the rest of our team were en route to Camp 2. From there they would climb to Camp 3 the next day and the South Col the day after, in readiness for their summit attempt. As if this wasn't bad enough, Jon Tinker and Mike Smith were moving up at the same time.

'Can you give me 30 minutes? I'll let you know then what I'm going to do,' I asked Henry.

'OK, your choice,' came his reply.

I emerged from the tent to stretch my muscles, aching from a restless night on the unforgiving ice. The plateau of the South Col had not a single tent other than my own protruding above its rocky, frozen surface. It was a spot referred to by many as the most desolate, godforsaken place on earth. For the first time ever, I stood alone in the middle of this lifeless, windswept col, complete with its imaginary border separating Nepal from Tibet. All around lay empty oxygen cylinders discarded in previous years. Their precious gas had sensed the struggles of bygone times, in the precariously fine line between life and death, when noble actions given in the aid of others and those of self-interest had passed in varying measures. Each cylinder's single vibrant colour of yellow, orange or green contrasted starkly against the shards of grey shattered rock. They looked as bright as the day they had been discarded, their thick metal walls untouched by the driving wind, no corrosion from their decades of exposure. They had not sunk into melted hollows that curved with their form but rested on the uneven surfaces where they had last been placed. The temperature here never rose to anywhere near zero.

Small remnants of abandoned tents flattened by the wind and then partially engulfed by ice flapped in the brisk morning air. It was a breeze that was eerily reminiscent of a distant time.

I was totally unprepared for the thoughts and questions that suddenly exploded within my mind. We should have known. I could have helped. These phrases were repeated over and over in my mind. Why had we not been told? How could we have not known? It hit me as hard as I've ever been hit before. Without answers or explanations, they were unable to escape from my head. The empty cylinders lying at my feet were silent witnesses to the events that had happened. Their threaded valves, to which regulators had once been fitted, gave way to empty interiors that long ago had been charged with life-giving gas. The questions that troubled me were all about life, a fragile state to which we all cling. But sometimes to survive, help is needed. That assistance we could have provided – but we had not.

Then, as follows the final loud strike of a drum, BADOOM, my thoughts fell silent. A gust of breeze that blew across from Tibet brought sounds of the past. *'I know you.' 'What are you doing back this year?' 'OK, we'll have another cup of coffee, then I suppose we'd better go and get her.' 'Thanks for your help, mate.'*

What help? I'd lain in my bloody tent and done absolutely nothing. We should have known. We could have helped. The tears fell silently over the stubble of my unshaven face.

Even at this point I was still unable to see the obvious. I was blind to the fact my teammates and I had also been victims of the storm. I naively thought that the only victims were those who had been injured or worse.

I was standing alone at 26,000 feet. Iñaki, the nearest human being, was by now more than 4,000 feet below me in the Western Cwm. I had to confront my demons, to face the scene of the tragedy on my own. It seemed that destiny was taking control. The wind was blowing exactly as it did on the morning of 11 May 1996. The landscape was unchanged. Only a short distance from where I stood, the nearest of the bodies still lay in its icy grave; the others lay beyond, in the exact places they had taken their final mortal breaths. I was haunted by the thought of them praying for help as they clung on to the final vestiges of life. Help that in the end never came. Fate would decree they were to spend eternity where they fell. I was overwhelmed by this alien experience, for which I was ill prepared. The scene was far more powerful, more haunting and real than I was able to bear.

I turned and made my escape to the only place possible: my tent, the very place I'd spent the night of 10 May while the storm raged outside. I knelt on the nylon groundsheet as I tried my utmost to relieve my mind of these guilt-ridden thoughts. They wouldn't go away.

Rescue came by virtue of the handset lying next to me. 'Graham, what have you decided to do?' came Henry's voice over the radio.

This question was the escape I craved so desperately. I had needed to hear the voice of the living. My mind switched instantaneously. It slammed the door once again on these painful memories.

I paused as I hurriedly considered my options. If I were to join the rest of my team, I had two choices. First, I could spend the next two nights alone on the South Col, waiting for them to arrive. Given the emotional turmoil I had just experienced, this was something I really did not want to do. The other problem with this approach was that after so much time at 26,000 feet my chance of success would be greatly reduced. The second option was to leave the South Col and climb back down to Camp 2, in readiness to climb back up to Camp 3 the following day with the rest of my team.

It's what is called Hobson's choice: there wasn't one. I had to move down to Camp 2 immediately. The focus on this pressing agenda helped me break free from my thoughts of 10 May 1996. It allowed me to force them to the back of my mind, to enter yet again the state of denial that had existed for the last three years.

'Are you receiving me?' enquired Henry, as no reply had been forthcoming.

'I'll leave the South Col and start heading down to Camp 2,' I told Henry.

'OK, see you when you get here,' Henry replied. 'Make sure you collapse the tent before you leave,' was his final comment before signing off. The breeze outside rustled the tent.

First, there was work to be done. I set up the BBC equipment and recorded a piece to camera, explaining my predicament. I put it in no uncertain terms that I might well have squandered my opportunity by having to retreat at this stage. I made no mention of my spine-chilling experience.

My final duty was to collapse the tent, leaving it in position for the next to arrive. I hoped I'd be one of them. I removed the end of the tent poles from the eyelets, causing the tent to lie flat. Then I placed some of our other equipment on top to prevent it from being blown away. After gathering up essentials only, I put on my climbing harness in readiness for the descent.

Before me stood Everest, untarnished by human failings. Its upper reaches pierced the cobalt sky. The towering grandeur and jagged ridges were adorned by nature's purest snow and ice. Tragedies could not be caused by such places, rather by the actions and decisions of those who choose to be there. I had been there. Surely I had to accept some responsibility for this terrible outcome of the past? How could we not have known the desperate plight of those caught out in the storm? I was finding it difficult to control my thoughts.

I reached Camp 2 by mid morning. The way I'd hoped to make my ascent was beginning to unravel. My climb up to the South Col had left me weakened with little or no time to recover. This was no time for guesswork. I had to get it right.

I could hear Anatoli's voice whispering advice in the recesses of my mind: *'Power and acclimatisation must balance, too much of one does not compensate for the other. After going high, you must let your body recover.'*

I had not used oxygen in my climb up to the South Col, only on the Col itself. I was acclimatised up to 26,000 feet, higher than most attempting this southern route. But by doing so my energy reserves had been depleted. Ideally I needed to move right down the mountain to allow my body time to rest. I did not have time for that luxury. My competition had arrived fresh for the task ahead.

To make matters worse, I had a bigger problem. I had added a third critical factor to this balancing equation. The climb had reduced the percentage of water in my body. I now had to drink as much fluid as possible to rehydrate myself for the climb back up the following day.

As previously explained, at higher elevations, especially 26,000 feet and above, the rapid loss of fluid results in a build-up of toxic waste products and the blood thickens. It was imperative I drank as much as I could to flush my system and redress the balance. Only then would I have any chance at all.

The downside to this was that I had to drink so much that I was unable to make reasonable headway into the generous portion of dhal bhat the Sherpas had prepared for me. It was a meal they'd witnessed me eat in vast quantities over the preceding weeks. The sustenance would provide the carbohydrates that I so desperately needed to replenish my energy reserves. But at this moment, fluid was far more important: it was required to reduce the viscosity of my blood so it could transport precious oxygen. My body would compensate for the lack of digested food by ravaging its own tissues: breaking them down to supply the huge energy required. The muscle blocks I needed for the climb would be top of its list.

I stared woefully up at the Lhotse Face and contemplated the use of oxygen above Camp 3 for my journey back up to the South Col. Logic made me quickly dismiss the idea. Acclimatisation was the only card I had. Even with the problems I now faced, I wanted to get back up to 26,000 feet unaided.

I spent that night restlessly worrying about the way things had turned out. The resultant lack of sleep only helped to compound my problems. The next day, I delayed my departure for Camp 3 until as late as possible, around 1 p.m., to maximise the precious little time for recovery at this lower altitude. Pacing myself on the ascent back to Camp 3, I caught up with the others shortly after 4.30 p.m. Ray Brown, an Australian climber from our group, had kindly made space for me. He had the stove boiling for when I turned up.

While Ray and I were settling down for the evening, the radio crackled into life. It was Henry, to inform me that someone had been killed in a fall on Makalu, slightly to the east of Everest. The name of the deceased person seemed unclear. He'd heard the name Miguel but wasn't quite sure. The immediate worry we both had was that it might be Michael Jörgensen. Michael had been with us on Everest in 1995 and 1996. He was on Makalu this spring. He had also been with me on the South Col during the night of 10 May.

Henry said he was going to try to seek clarification and signed off. It was no time at all, probably little more than half an hour, before Henry's distressed voice came across the radio.

'Graham, it's Michael. He's been killed in a fall!' Henry sounded close to tears.

I muttered a few words of consolation to Henry over the radio. I didn't know quite what to say. We all knew the risks. Nevertheless, such news always caught us unawares. Probably because it was too close to home.

My words seemed lost in the ether as soon as I released the transmit button. The position I'd hoped to be in was now precariously unbalanced, the news dreadful. My mind was shell-shocked. All I could envisage was to keep climbing. Any cautions, any fateful warnings the news seemed to offer fell unheeded.

Henry and Michael had first met in 1995 and since then had become good friends. Henry had radioed me because I was the only one on our team to have climbed with Michael before, the one person who might understand the senseless loss he felt. Michael had been abseiling when an anchor point above him came out. He was 32.

It was in a sombre mood that I made my way up to the South Col the following morning. My thoughts were consumed by the price paid by those in pursuit of their chosen course. The only conclusion I could reach was that everyone held on to the thought that it wouldn't happen to them. Why else would they be there?

When I reached the top of the Geneva Spur, the South Col came into view. Once more, the sight of this desolate place, and now the news of someone's death, took me mercilessly back to 10 May 1996. However, on this occasion there were a number of people encamped on the South Col. There was no repeat of my shuddering experience when I'd been left on my own. As with eerie sounds on a ghostly pitch-black night, where the mind can play tricks with a lonely traveller, I had been vulnerable. Not so with the current buzz of human voices that drove away the thoughts such solitude can bring. In this situation I could pretend I had control of them.

We spent the night on the Col, patiently waiting for the right conditions. We decided we would wait another day. As the clock ticked, I could feel what was left of my energy reserves slowly ebbing away. Alongside us that first night were the team of Jon Tinker and Mike Smith. Jon had been unwell, and they'd decided to postpone their push for the top. They descended in the morning. This left the way open – my one chance.

We left the South Col at 11 p.m. on the second night. It was dark and still. The oxygen mask that muffled my face hissed gently with its precious supply. My legs seemed to lack any power. I resolved to think only about the next step. Nothing more. If I let my mind wander to the news of Michael, to the events we had both witnessed in the past, then the draw back down to my family would win the day. The effort to continue up and the possibilities of what could go wrong would grow out of all proportion. I switched my mind off to everything except where I would place my next step. Both time and my lofty surroundings were no longer part of the world in which I travelled. My spatial awareness extended little more than three feet in front. Behind me, nothing existed.

Shortly after nine o'clock on the morning of 5 May 1999, with BBC camera in hand, I reached the summit of Everest for the second time. In doing so, I became the first British climber to have climbed Everest twice, and from both north and south sides. This I'd achieved with the support and friendship of many people.

As I took the last few paces, I peered over to the familiar north side and into Tibet, to the route I'd climbed with Anatoli four years earlier, a friend who'd now been dead for more than a year. There was none of the sense of joy or achievement that I had felt on my first ascent. My emotions were melancholy, a mixture of sadness and relief. Sadness for the friends I'd lost as they pursued their dreams, relief because I'd finished what I set out to do and could now go home.

After 20 minutes, I turned and descended. Others I was with dallied to take photographs, to make radio calls and to immerse themselves in the splendour of the views, while I made steady progress back down. Around the Hillary Step, my pace slowed. I understood instantly what had happened. The large oxygen cylinder I was carrying, which was supposed to last over ten hours at the rate I'd set, had lasted less than seven. I was alone at over 28,000 feet and out of oxygen, well aware that to do anything other than remain calm would only make matters worse. I was very well acclimatised, having slept three nights on the South Col during the course of the last week, and had only used oxygen at that location and above. So I had little choice but to resign myself to a slightly slow and cold descent – and to any consequences that might bring.

At the base of the South Summit, bright-orange Poisk bottles stood upright, embedded into the soft snow. These were the fresh supplies awaiting the return of climbers from other teams who were a few hundred feet above me on the summit ridge. This was their ticket back down, not mine. The ones we had stashed were much lower. I pressed on. Some way further down, I passed a Sherpa from another expedition moving up. He was immediately concerned to see my oxygen mask hanging below my chin. Instinctively, he asked if I was OK. I explained in a rather disgruntled fashion that my bottle had run out but that I was fine, that having summited I was on my way back. Before moving on, I thanked him for his concern. In response to this courteous reply, he asked me to wait. Rummaging in his rucksack, he handed me a used bottle that had a small amount of gas left in it. I gratefully fitted my regulator to this fresh supply. Strapping my mask back on, I raised my hand in appreciation and continued down. Within 15 minutes my mask was once again dangling. That bottle too had given up the last remnants of its precious gas.

Relief came at the Balcony several hundred feet lower down, where, as planned, I picked up the half-empty oxygen cylinder I'd deposited there on the way up. Unfortunately, by then the damage had been done. Frostbite had set in to my hands and right foot. I'm sure that my earlier filming on the summit ridge would not have helped in this regard, neither would the dehydration I suffered from my first visit to the South Col.

Two days later, I took my final steps off the mountain to walk the short distance from the bottom of the Khumbu Icefall through various other encampments to reach our own. One of these happened to belong to an American expedition where news of our summiting had already reached. On my arrival there, I was handed a plateful of hot chips and a bottle of whisky with about two inches in the bottom. After eating a few chips, I downed the whisky in one go, an action that brought cheers from my American friends. Aware that I'd suffered frostbite, and showing concern, one of them asked if I was taking anything for it. Full of bravado and the joy of success, I paused for a moment and then replied, 'I'm considering a helicopter.' My response received a huge roar of laughter.

The next day, after careful inspection by the American doctor from this same team, it was decided that I should be helicoptered out, rather than risking further damage to my foot on the long walk back to Lukla.

Three days later, on a bright sunny morning, I was standing alone in the middle of the large, flat sandy area at Gorak Shep: a small outpost a few miles down from Everest Base Camp. In the distance, I could hear the sound of the rotor blades of an approaching helicopter as they sliced through the thin air in the search for some upward lift. It appeared as a small shape high in the distance. Within a matter of minutes, it was hovering overhead, olive green in colour and bearing the large red star of the Nepalese armed forces, the pilot looking for his passenger. No sooner had I waved my arms than the helicopter was brought skilfully to ground level. Looking through the bubble-shaped windscreen, I could see the pilot was wearing a mask. He was breathing bottled oxygen due to his rapid ascent in altitude from Kathmandu, 12,000 feet lower down, less than an hour before. With the beckoning of his left hand, he instructed me to get in. The pilot was none other than Lt Col Maden K.C., the same pilot who had courageously rescued Beck Weathers and Makalu Gau from the Western Cwm some three years earlier.

Apart from this final jolt to my memory brought about by the presence of Lt Col Maden K.C. and the sight of the olive-green helicopter bearing the red star of the Nepalese armed forces, the time had come to make a conscious effort to place 1996 firmly in the past. It had been a dark episode in my Everest adventures, which, despite recent reminders, now seemed long ago. I no longer wanted to look back, rather to look positively to the future.

Back in Kathmandu, Elizabeth Hawley had caught wind that some of the early summiteers had begun to arrive back from their respective expeditions. I received a message from the hotel reception that she would be dropping in the following day at 10 a.m.

Right on time, the dulcet tones of her VW Beetle could be heard as her driver pulled the vehicle up at the hotel entrance. She'd given up driving herself and had employed a chauffeur to whisk her around this bustling city. The manic chaos of motorcycles, lorries, rickshaws, tuk-tuks, cars and pedestrians had eventually become too tiresome for her to deal with. She was held in such high esteem that it seemed fitting for her to be chauffeured around Kathmandu's network of overrun streets in her well-maintained older vehicle.

Before we commenced, I asked Liz if she would mind if I filmed our conversation.

'Of course you may,' she said with a smile.

Manners and politeness went along with Liz, as did a helpful nature.

Initially, Liz wanted to know when I'd arrived at Base Camp and when each camp on the South Col route had been established. Camp 1 was slightly problematic, as I wasn't quite sure which team had slept there first. However, Camp 2 and 3 were easier, as pushing ahead I'd been one of the first to overnight there, and Iñaki and I had been the first to stay on the South Col. Liz looked rather pleased at the accuracy of the information she was receiving, which gave her a head start on the current season. Not quite believing her luck, she then glanced up hopefully and asked about the summits.

'Pete Athans was first, Bill Crouse second and me third. We were minutes apart and the first three to get to the top this year. The date: 5 May,' I replied.

'Well,' said Liz, 'I certainly seem to be talking to the right person here.'

Studying her notes, she continued, 'Your second ascent?'

'Yes,' I replied, 'and the first British climber to summit Everest twice.'

'And the first by two different routes,' she quickly responded.

Her reply took me by surprise. She'd already known the answer before the question had been asked. These facts and figures were at her fingertips, her mind so incredibly sharp.

We sat for quite some time after the official business was completed, discussing the recent find of George Mallory's body on the north side of the mountain, neither of us particularly happy with the photographs that had appeared in the press of Mallory's body frozen face down on Everest's northern flanks. Little thought appeared to have been given to the feelings of Mallory's surviving family. Her compassion and understanding during this conversation came as no surprise from a lady whose home seconds as the headquarters for the Himalayan Trust. Her brusque and forthright reputation belied a much more private and caring person beneath. For Elizabeth Hawley, her meticulous recording of Himalayan expeditions for nearly 40 years had transcended from being a vocation into a lifetime's work, perfectly captured by a book published about her in 2005 titled *I'll Call You in Kathmandu.*

An Escape into History

No sooner had I arrived home than I was out on location filming a BBC documentary called *Mountain High: Twice To the Summit of Everest*. Keith Partridge, who had taught me how to film, was on this occasion behind the camera and Alastair Leithead was interviewing me about my Everest expeditions as we strolled on the rather less challenging but equally beautiful slopes of the English Lake District. The scenes we shot in the Lakeland fells were mixed with the footage I'd taken in Nepal during 1998 and 1999. This encompassing documentary, produced by Mark Batey, with Olwyn Hocking as executive producer, seemed to complete my Everest journey. Articles appeared in both the local and national press. It was a story that was topical for a few weeks, and then it was old news.

However, my return from Everest was to produce ripples, with a most unexpected result. The boarding school I had attended between the ages of 11 and 18, Barnard Castle School, created a display of recent newspaper clippings about my second ascent of Everest. This was prepared for the summer gathering in north-east England of the former pupils' association, the Old Barnardians' Club. My two ascents were seen as a continuation of the school's historical links with Everest, which dated back to the 1924 expedition.

A member of that team was Bentley Beetham, a former pupil and subsequently natural history master at the North Eastern County School, later renamed Barnard Castle School. Organised by the Mount Everest Committee, chaired by Sir Francis Younghusband, this expedition was a joint undertaking of the Royal Geographical Society and the Alpine Club. On this ill-fated trip, George Mallory and Sandy Irvine were last seen high on Everest as they disappeared into the clouds, still going strong for the top.

It was a warm summer's morning when I set out from our apartment in Tynemouth to make the 50-mile journey back to my old school. The date was Sunday, 27 June 1999, six weeks after my return from Everest. I bore the physical scars of my recent adventure. The tips of my fingers on my left hand were hard and black with a thick layer of dead skin. I was wearing sandals. Frostbite had caused the outer flesh surrounding the big toe on my right foot to decay and the toenail to drop off. With bandage wrappings to stave off infection, the return to normal shoes was still several months away.

I parked the car to the side of the school's imposing Victorian stone edifice and made my way around to the rear of the building. The sound of a willow bat striking a hard leather ball echoed across the tarmac road, which passed between a towering gable end and the eight-foot-high perimeter wall that separated the school's grounds from those of the Bowes Museum. In progress was the annual cricket match between the Old Barnardians' Club and the school's current First Eleven. I was greeted by the sight of the club's aged batsmen running between the wickets in an attempt to replicate their more youthful days. From the boundary came polite applause and a shout or two of encouragement from padded-up batsmen waiting their turn.

In the school library, the club's annual AGM was due to begin. A short distance from the edge of the cricket pitch, the single-storey flat-roofed building was set several feet up from the road that ran around the perimeter of the main school building. I entered via the wide concrete staircase. Inside, photographs of me hung alongside those of Bentley Beetham. I was flattered and not quite sure what to say in response to the honour they had bestowed on me with this action. Beetham had retired from teaching in 1949, some 17 years before I first attended the school. It would have been easy for me to say that the exploits of this true pioneer had been my inspiration, but this was not the case. Our connection was down to nothing more than chance. No doubt stories of the school's great adventurer of the past will have been told to us pupils. But staring blankly out of the classroom window, my mind regularly wandered well beyond their bounds.

I had been a young boy who dreamt during the daytime. In those days, adventure for me was not what lay abroad; such far-flung expeditions were the stuff of encyclopedias and picture books. I had never been beyond our shores. For me, journeys of discovery lay in the lands that stretched from Barnard Castle towards the North Pennines. During my free time at school, I would enjoy nothing more than exploring the remote areas of upper Teesdale. Now I was to discover that the same wild areas of northern England had also inspired Bentley Beetham during his formative years.

Despite having little recollection of Bentley Beetham himself, I was aware of these early pioneers and greatly admired their tenacity and self-belief. Having climbed the self-same route attempted by the 1924 expedition, and reached the summit that history suggests eluded them, I could do no less than applaud their outstanding achievements in those early days of mountaineering.

AN ESCAPE INTO HISTORY

Immediately after the AGM, the club secretary, Gay Blanchard, approached me. Accompanying her was Michael Lowes. He had also attended the school and had climbed with Bentley Beetham on the Lake District's Borrowdale Crags. His Lakeland forays had been part of his education. Michael's childhood recollections helped bring to life for me Bentley Beetham himself. He had listened first hand to Beetham's stories of Everest in bygone times and had been enthralled. In more recent years, Michael had been cataloguing Bentley Beetham's photographic collection. He explained that many of the original four-and-a-quarter-inch glass slides were from the 1924 Everest expedition.

Michael and Gay asked whether I might return at a later date to look through the collection. They wanted my opinion. Up to this juncture, I had been unaware of its existence. It had been hidden away during my seven years at the school. Not once during that time, or for many years before, had it seen the light of day. How could I turn down such a wonderful invitation? I was thrilled to be offered the opportunity.

It was three weeks after the AGM that I returned to the school to view the Beetham Collection. I entered the building via a small pair of blue wooden doors at the rear of the property. In front of me, beyond the cosy square entrance hall in which I stood, stretched a long gloomy corridor with a polished stone floor and high ceilings. On either side, doors opened into what had once been classrooms. I recalled, as a child, standing on my tiptoes to peer through their upper panes of glass. Inside had stood rows of old wooden desks, their hinged tops stained from decades of carelessly dripped ink. At the front, fastened to the wall, had been a large blackboard with chalk dust smeared across the surface where the previous lesson had been erased. Thirty-three years had passed since my parents first dropped me off at the school.

Ahead lay the large open space of Central Hall. It contained a solitary figure, that of Gay Blanchard. Term had ended. A building that was normally filled with vibrant youthful voices now stood in deathly silence. The sound of my approaching footsteps alerted Gay to my arrival.

From opposite sides of the large octagonal hall, two enclosed wooden staircases spiralled their way to the floors above. The soles of our shoes tapped against the thick linoleum surface of the four-foot-wide steps as Gay and I made our way up the eastern staircase. In my youth, I had heard the very same steps thunder with the sound of numerous feet eagerly making their way down to the dining hall below. As we passed the exit to the first floor, where the senior dormitories had been, I ran my left hand along the steeply rising banister that spiralled up through the centre of the staircase. Screwed down onto its polished surface and spaced about one foot apart were rounded brass cones. My fingers ran over the top of one. These had been placed to discourage boys from attempting to slide down on their backsides. They looked painful enough to have worked. I'd never tried.

I had first come to the school in 1966, at the tender age of 11. My older brother Robert had moved up into the sixth form. Such pupils were in the higher echelons and our paths rarely crossed. With his name being Robert, schoolboy logic dictated I should be called Bobby. It was a name I would carry until I was 18, despite early attempts to encourage others to revert to my given name. To the schoolmasters, I was a boy with a school number: Ratcliffe 59. I had been a skinny child who wore knee-length trousers, thick woollen socks, imitation tortoiseshell National Health spectacles and a school blazer that had been previously worn by Robert. My parents had struggled to make ends meet while giving their four sons the best education they could.

Life at the school was a harsh world where you learnt to stand up for yourself. I fared better than some but worse than others. Whenever impromptu games were played, such as football, I was always in the last one or two to be picked out of the line-up. This was not because I was inept, rather because I did not fit with the 'in crowd', and because I wore glasses. As time passed, I had less and less time for the pupils who considered themselves more important than those around them. The masters at the school I found by and large a pretty fair lot; the punishments they dealt out were usually deserved. I was often the recipient.

Although I was reasonably talented at sports, these tended to be individual rather than team games. With these, the deciding factor was my ability rather than the decisions of others. Squash and cross-country running came high on the list.

This trait is one that I have seen time and time again in mountaineering. High-altitude climbers, in my experience, are individually driven, self-reliant and content with their own company, often seen as loners. Their preference is to make their own decisions; this they must do while climbing. They are brought together as a team largely through necessity. While climbing on Everest, I'd probably spent 90 per cent of the time on my own. I had been more than happy with this.

In my latter years at the school, I kept hidden a 1953 500cc AJS motorcycle. My brother Stephen, who was studying at a college in Blackpool, had lent it to me as I had by now passed my driving test and could ride a bike of any engine size. To me, it was now the bigger the better. I found what I hoped was a safe hiding place in the bushes at the bottom of what was known as 'prep school lane'. When the unusual parking spot began to raise suspicion, I moved the motorbike into the walled grounds of the neighbouring stately Bowes Museum. The museum contacted the school to ask if it knew anything about the machine that they seemed to have acquired. I was summoned by the powers-that-be. Their first guess as to the culprit had been correct. For the umpteenth time, I had flouted school rules. After being interrogated, I was informed that my brother would need to come and collect his motorcyle without delay, but all this meant in real terms was that I had to find somewhere else to park my new-found freedom – adventure was in my blood.

Every time the AJS's large single-cylinder engine powered the black motorcycle through the village of Cotherstone, I would unknowingly pass the front door of Bentley Beetham's former cottage. And this is how each voyage of discovery began. Skimming past hedgerows along the deserted country roads that extend west from the small market town of Middleton in Teesdale, the needle often eased over 70 mph – rather less than the slightly optimistic 'max 120 mph' that Stephen had marked on the machine's ageing Smith's speedometer. The thundering sound bellowed from the chrome silencer and the fresh air pummelled me as I sat bolt upright on the leather seat. It was intoxicating. I was 17.

This mode of transport opened my horizons; it allowed me to explore remote places that few others visited. High on Great Dun and Mickle Fell, I found the wilderness I craved. The raging waters that roared over High Force, and those cascading over Cauldron Snout, defined the grandeur of these untamed surroundings. The dark-brown waters of the upper Tees river, which slowly drained through the extensive peatlands above, spoke of great adventures on their onward journey. The ancient grey limestone crags heavily encrusted with coloured lichens and damp mosses promised excitement. I would scale these irresistible rugged outcrops, reaching ledges with stunted bilberry bushes that led on to the next stage on my upward journey. The sense of freedom was exhilarating.

The problem with some of my escapades was that I didn't know when to stop. One particular episode, in my last year at Barnard Castle, very nearly brought my school career to a premature end. It was one of epically stupid proportions that could have had deadly consequences. I was about to learn a lesson that I would never forget.

It was January 1973. I was on one of the many cross-country runs that we took part in during the spring term. With me was my best friend, Gordon Clark. The run took us alongside the River Tees, past the local sewage filtration tanks and up onto Abbey Bridge before making a course back to the school. At this point we took an unscheduled break. Staring down from Abbey Bridge's castellated parapets to the dark-brown river water moving slowly through a rocky ravine some 60 feet below, I unexpectedly announced, 'I could jump off that!'

Gordon looked down to the river below: 'You wouldn't dare.'

'No problem,' was my boastful reply.

Over the coming days, the goading and bravado continued. That was until it dawned on Gordon that we could raise some money with such a stunt. Sponsorship from other pupils seemed a good idea. A date was suggested and the numbers willing to part with a small sum to witness the jump began to gather pace.

Two days prior to the main event, we repeated the run, only this time, when we got to Abbey Bridge, Gordon and a couple of willing helpers had managed to drag a large boulder up onto the parapet. Launching it over the side, they shouted, 'This is how you will fall.' Plummeting to the river below, it hit the flat surface with a loud smack, followed milliseconds later by a deep thud as sound reverberated from the depths of the water below. Then it disappeared out of sight. I was having second thoughts about the wisdom of my boast. My self-imposed day of reckoning would take place after lessons on the Saturday morning, at 1 p.m.

Gordon and I had carefully considered the health-and-safety aspects of my proposed undertaking. We weren't complete idiots. We had calculated from our physics lessons that, as the acceleration of gravity was thirty-two feet per second (per second), I would hit the river approximately two seconds after launching myself off the bridge. Hitting the water, provided I jumped off the central parapet, was a definite outcome. The big uncertainty was the depth of the water below, but as the normally fast-flowing river slowed up at this point, we were clinging to the adage that 'still waters run deep'. The problem with the River Tees was its reputation for rock shelves protruding into its dark-brown water. The assumption was that if I hit the mid-point of the river I should be OK. The only unknown we could come up with was: once I had entered the water, would I resurface?

We decided to approach one of the school's top swimmers, Martin Jordan. He had the added advantage of having completed a life-saving course. Martin agreed to be on standby at river level. How he would be able to see me in the dark-brown water if I didn't resurface was a minor point we'd overlooked.

The proposed undertaking bore no hope of the exhilaration I got from my climbs on the limestone crags. On these, fear and anticipation hung evenly in the balance; only when adrenalin tipped the scales would I make the next move. This was the feeling of being alive, the one that would eventually take me to Everest. Had I chosen to jump from the bridge with no one present and without anyone's knowledge it would have held that edge. Why? Because the choice would have been mine. However, the proposed leap from Abbey Bridge was being driven by peer pressure – a deadly force that could easily lead to disaster.

By the time Friday afternoon arrived, and with less than 24 hours to go, most of the school's 500 plus pupils were planning to attend. This was an event that happened less frequently than the passing of Halley's Comet. No one had knowledge of anyone having jumped off the bridge before. But by this point, there was no way out. It was jump or face ridicule and disgrace, of which I wanted neither.

At the beginning of Saturday morning chapel, the headmaster made an announcement: 'I would like to see Graham Ratcliffe in my study immediately after this service.'

Murmurings and glances came my way as those around me wondered what the outcome of this appointment might be.

Standing outside the cream-coloured wooden door that bore the word 'Headmaster' on a metal plate, I gathered my nerves and gave a single knock.

'Come in,' said a stern voice.

Before me, behind his large leather-topped desk, sat Sidney Woods, otherwise known to the pupils as 'Sidney', or more cruelly 'Blotch' because of the large birthmark that covered the entire left side of his face. With wavy grey hair and wearing his black gown, he looked far from happy. He was a kindly man who had taught me chemistry in my younger days; on this occasion, I was not expecting the same friendly treatment.

I stood a respectful three feet away from his desk. I was subjected to a piercing glare. The large rectangular and somewhat austere wood-panelled office with its south-facing windows and their stone mullions was the centre of absolute authority within the school. Many a pupil who had stepped over the line had been expelled while standing in the very space I now occupied.

'I have been told you intend to jump off Abbey Bridge,' were the headmaster's opening words.

For a schoolboy with considerable experience of his teachers' wrath, this was rather easier than I had expected to face. The crime had not yet been committed. I did what any self-respecting pupil would have done: I lied.

'Me, sir? No, sir.'

To my amazement, Sidney was prepared for such an answer. Sliding open the right-hand drawer of his desk, he pulled out a piece of foolscap paper that bore the two shields and motto that made up the school's crest.

The Latin motto of *parvis imbutus tentabis grandia tutus* when translated reads, 'When you are steeped in little things, you shall safely attempt great things'.

'I want you to sign this,' he said, as he slid the paper across to the edge of the desk, along with a pen.

Already typed on the pristine white surface were two sentences. They read: 'I am not going to jump off Abbey Bridge. If I do, Barnard Castle School is not responsible.'

'Sign here,' said the headmaster, pointing firmly to the bottom of the document.

I leant forward nervously and added my signature, hoping that might be the end of my ordeal. Thankfully, it was. I was told I could leave.

At boarding school, the teaching staff, which included the headmaster, were *in loco parentis*; they had a legal responsibility. In asking me to sign this officially prepared letter, the headmaster was attempting to absolve, or at least distance, the school from legal repercussions should I proceed with this ludicrous act. Looking back, I doubt it would have been that simple. By asking me to sign the letter, they had admitted to prior knowledge but had not moved to curtail the possibility of it taking place. I had placed the school, and especially Sidney Woods, in a terrible position. Up to this juncture, he was dealing with boyish bravado, of boastful talk – that a few hours later might have had a dreadful outcome. What good it would have done him to produce such a letter had something gone wrong, I cannot imagine. But I was a teenager. Thoughtless acts without regard as to how they might affect others came all too easily.

The word spread like wildfire that I had been rumbled. Had I ignored the headmaster's warning and proceeded to jump that afternoon, I would have been expelled from the school the same day. This I would have deserved. Had Sidney not intervened, would I have jumped? With the whole school watching, I don't think I would have had a choice.

My unexpected saviour had been the headmaster. I could walk away with my head held high and reputation intact. I had been forced not to jump. Was I disappointed? No – I was relieved. A salutary lesson in life had been learnt, one that I would never forget.

My mind snapped back from these distant memories as Gay Blanchard and I stepped out from the top of the spiralling staircase and onto the second-floor landing that encircled the upper octagonal balcony of Central Hall. I stared over the hefty banister with its tightly arranged balustrades to the matching eight-sided oak table some 30 feet below.

What had once been a battleground of childhood survival I now looked back upon with fond memories. At the recent summer gathering, I had met some of my former schoolmasters who were now retired. In the time since my eventual departure from the school 26 years earlier, they had grown old. I had grown up.

At the south side of this upper floor, a simple wooden staircase led up to a small set of attics, which in my schooldays had been the music rooms. The large open space of Central Hall that rose up through the building had often echoed to the discordant sound of piano and violin lessons.

At the top of the stairs, worn smooth from a century of energetic feet, we entered the office of the Old Barnardians' Club secretary. It was a modest-sized room with a solitary glass window made up of several small panes that looked across the school's slated roof. Bookshelves and cardboard boxes filled most of the available space. Correspondence sat neatly on top of a single pedestal desk that had seen better days.

Positioned nearby, on the floor, were Bentley Beetham's glass slides. The mahogany boxes, approximately twelve inches by nine, were separated into two halves by a central wooden divider. Each side contained a hundred or so squares of glass standing tightly, one against the other. As Gay picked up the first box and placed it onto the desk, it sent a fine film of fibrous dust billowing into the warm dry air. The smell of objects that had been hidden away for decades tantalised my senses. Leaning forward, I nervously lifted one of the four-and-a-quarter-inch glass slides from the box and held it up to the sunlight that beamed through the small grubby window. The definition of the photograph that had been secured between two thin pieces of glass left me speechless. 'Wow,' was all I managed to say.

I lifted one after another to satisfy my growing curiosity. The images portrayed in Bentley Beetham's photographs were of superb quality, far better and more varied in their subject matter than I had expected. Then I randomly selected one particular slide that blew me away. I had never seen this image before, and it would transpire that it was unique to the Beetham Collection. It was of a single A-frame tent clinging precariously to the side of Everest with what looked like a few pieces of thin cord, as though it was going to slide off down the mountainside at any moment. Having climbed this northern route on Everest, I knew from the steepness of the ground and lack of places to put the tent that this had to be over 26,000 feet. It could only be the last camp from which Mallory and Irvine departed for the summit that fateful day, 8 June 1924. I sat back in amazement. I had never seen another image that summed up the audacity and bravery of these early pioneers so well. The thought that these original images, which I now held with the utmost care, had been taken on that historic pioneering expedition all those years ago was mesmerising. History was at my fingertips.

Apparently, Beetham had developed the films at Base Camp in the depths of his sleeping bag. A sudden tingle shot down my spine. George Mallory and Sandy Irvine might have held some of these very same images up to a Tibetan sky before their ill-fated attempt. They too might have admired Beetham's work just as I was now doing. By viewing his work, I was entering into their time, their moment in history.

At the time I had been moving up for my final summit attempt, less than three months earlier – in fact, on the very day that Henry had radioed me with the terrible news about Michael Jörgensen – George Mallory's body had been located high on the Tibetan side of Everest. He had been found where he had come to rest 75 years earlier following a fall. The discovery had brought with it renewed public interest in this historic expedition. Photographs of Mallory's frozen white flesh, with his athletic muscles exposed where the clothes had been weathered from his back, appeared in the press. I felt this publication was tasteless, but the public appetite was for more. Researchers and historians tracked down the Beetham Collection held by the Old Barnardians' Club, hoping to find more images and stories to feed this appetite. Visits to inspect the images were arranged and contact prints had been supplied of certain significant pictures taken high on Everest in 1924, some of which were thought to be unique. They had not appeared in any of the other collections and were unpublished. Permission was being sought from the club to allow use in a forthcoming book due to be printed later that year. This was happening at the time I was beginning my acquaintance with the collection.

I left the attic room that day with my hands still trembling from the excitement of handling those precious images. To see such photographs printed in a periodical was interesting enough, but to hold an original glass slide up to the sunlight was a privilege I had never expected to have.

My advice to the Old Barnardians' Club was that the collection they held was of international importance and that the long-term care and protection of Beetham's work should be a priority. There were those who would be overly keen to make use of this rich archive.

The club was aware that not all the photographs contained within the collection had been taken by Bentley Beetham; his friend Howard Somervell, for example, had given some to him. With these concerns about where the copyright of the slides might lie, the club wrote to the publishers specifically denying permission for the use of these images. The book was published using the contact prints with which they had been supplied. No explicit permission had been given or release form signed by the Old Barnardians' Club.

As a consequence of this event, it was realised there was a pressing responsibility to protect the collection for future generations to enjoy. Within months of my viewing the collection at Barnard Castle School, the club approached me to ask if I would form a trust that was governed by law. I agreed to their request.

Claims over the Beetham Collection appeared to be coming out of the woodwork. Sandra Noel, daughter of the late Captain Noel, claimed ownership, saying they had been lent by her father to Bentley Beetham and never returned. Letters from barristers and solicitors flew back and forth. The commercial value and the potential to exploit this important collection brought other attention as well.

All this to-ing and fro-ing with letters, counter-claims and negotiating the location for the long-term care of this part of our national heritage took up much of my time. Countless hours were spent in my apartment at Tynemouth comparing the photographs from my ascent with Anatoli and Nikolai in 1995 with those of the historic 1924 expedition. I was astounded at how little the landscape had changed. Our Base Camp in 1995 had been placed, unbeknown to us, in exactly the same spot as the 1924 expedition. Large boulders, three feet across, which stood outside their tents in Bentley Beetham's photographs had been in the same position over 70 years later. His images were in black and white; mine were in colour.

Beetham's collection certainly took all my attention and perhaps made up for the lack of it when I had been at school. I spent the next few years refuting claims over the collection and registering The Bentley Beetham 1924 Everest Trust with the Charities Commission of England and Wales. Working alongside me in these voluntary tasks were Michael Lowes and the other two trustees, barrister Alastair Barclay Brown and Justice of the Peace Brenda Joan Gildea. All four of us were determined to bring this historical archive into the public domain, to make it accessible. The entire collection can now be viewed freely online, at www.bentleybeetham.org, as the trustees believe the members of the 1924 Everest expedition would have wanted. The collection itself now resides in Durham University's archives at Palace Green Library.

Although I didn't realise at the time, my immersion in this work came as a welcome distraction from my recent haunting experience on the South Col of Everest. It took me back to a time before the 1996 tragedy, to a northern route on the mountain that brought happy memories and a sense of personal accomplishment. I felt connected to the pioneers by virtue of the fact I had been fortunate enough to tread in their footsteps. The north side of Everest was sheltering me from memories of the southern route.

George Mallory and Sandy Irvine had been amongst the very first to attempt Everest's summit. Their knowledge as to the debilitating effect of altitude had been negligible when compared to modern day; their equipment did not compare to what we had enjoyed. The loss of these two climbers, although tragic, had been at the cutting edge. They had been pushing the boundaries. On the other hand, Rob Hall and Scott Fischer, their clients, guides, and the three Indian climbers who had been lost on the north side, had modern equipment and a better understanding of altitude. They knew of the importance of deadlines over reaching the summit too late in the day. Yet eight of them had perished. The questions for which I had no answers simmered just below the surface.

By the beginning of 2004, the furore over the Beetham Collection had begun to die down. It was long overdue, but at last Catherine and I had time for ourselves. Or so I thought.

The Turning Point

It had been five years since I'd last been on Everest, seeking the summit of a major Himalayan peak. My climbing on lengthy expeditions had, in the intervening time, taken a back seat as I pursued my work in commercial properties. I spent most of my time on refurbishments or dealing with the bureaucracy of planning departments. Paperwork now seemed to fill a life that had not so long ago been consumed by canvas and crampons.

So it was in the spring of 2004 that Catherine and I decided to take three months off, to set out on a journey through Nepal, Tibet and northern India: a real adventure that we'd make up as we went along. For us, such an epic could only have started in Nepal. Here we landed in March of that year.

It was from Kathmandu that we set out on an overland journey across southern Tibet to Lhasa via north-side Everest Base Camp. For this leg of our travels we enjoyed the company of three younger globetrotters: Alberto and Eva, an agreeable young Spanish couple, and Natalie, a rather off-the-wall but very likeable Belgian lady.

The panoramic views from the prayer-flag-strewn high passes of the Tibetan Plateau promised of an adventure to be shared. All five of us held the anticipation of what lay ahead, enthused by our diminutive Tibetan guide, Dorje.

However, when our Chinese driver pulled the four-wheel-drive vehicle up on the outskirts of Base Camp and I got out, my soaring spirit plummeted to earth. The reality of actually standing at Base Camp and staring up at the North Face of Everest rising nearly 12,000 feet from the Rongbuk Glacier brought memories rushing back.

It was from this very spot, a full year before the 1996 disaster, that we'd listened to the radio calls of Rob Hall's Adventure Consultants as they turned around from their attempt.

Of the eight climbers from our team who'd summited from the Tibetan side in 1995, three were now dead, amongst them Anatoli Boukreev and Michael Jörgensen. The third was the talented Brazilian, Mozart Catao, who had been killed in 1998 by an avalanche while attempting the notorious South Face of Aconcagua.

The laughter and camaraderie from our 1995 expedition seemed like only yesterday, but nine years had slipped by since I'd last seen the north side of the mountain.

By the time mid-April came around, Catherine and I had returned to Nepal and were trekking in the Solu Khumbu, following the rugged mountain path that shadows the course of the Dudh Kosi river, its turbulent waters, swollen by the spring thaw, cascading far below through the steep mountain landscape. Towering above us, jagged Himalayan peaks displayed spectacular fluted ribs of snow sculpted by a winter wind. Their seemingly fragile summits contrasted against a cerulean sky. Alpine forests began to give way to the hardy rhododendron, whose woody stems shaded the last remnants of the rapidly melting snow, their heavy, flower-laden buds hailing the arrival of a new season. We were on our way to Everest Base Camp on the south side of the mountain, where we'd arranged to visit some old friends who were climbing again that year.

Our arrival there brought smiles from the Sherpas, many of whom I'd climbed with before. Not least from the Sirdar, Kami Nuhru, who, having known me for almost a decade, had eventually reached the juncture where he felt comfortable calling me Graham rather than 'sir'.

The quarry-like surroundings of Base Camp, along with its amphitheatre of Himalayan giants, felt worryingly like home to me, as though a cradle of security amongst the hidden and often silent dangers of this most dramatic of landscapes. Catherine, although in awe of the beauty, would have quite happily skipped the two nights we spent here. Her tolerance to the plummeting night-time temperatures was somewhat less than mine.

It was while we were here that I couldn't help but notice a large film crew attached to one of the other expeditions. They were working a short distance away. Initially curious at the level of their activity, I sat outside our mess tent with a coffee and observed them. What raised the level of my interest was the number of people they had organising, or attending to, any particular sequence. This in itself was quite unusual. Eventually I enquired with our hosts as to the purpose of this shoot. I was informed that these people were filming sequences for a Hollywood-type movie about the Everest disaster of 1996, based on previous accounts. The budget was reputedly in excess of $100 million. Whether this was correct I didn't know, but with the explanation I'd been given, it did not seem unreasonable. My heart sank at the continued exploitation of this tragedy. It may have been that those who'd already made considerable sums of money as a result of the catastrophe were once again involved. If they were, I really didn't want to know at that time.

I would later discover that David Breashears was taking part in the filming. Also present from the 1996 Imax team were Ed Viesturs and Robert Schauer. Joining them was Veikka Gustaffsson, who had been on Mal Duff's expedition in 1996. The expedition, under David's leadership, went under the name of 2004 WT Everest Expedition. Working Title Films are part of Universal Films. Under the direction of Stephen Daldry, it was planned that the film *Everest* would chronicle the tragic events of 10 May 1996, when a brutal storm on the world's highest mountain claimed the lives of eight mountaineers.

For more than seven years, I'd gone out of my way to avoid the aftermath. Despite this, I appeared to have turned up in the right place at the right time to witness an event that once again connected me to that tragic time. These were reminders that seemed to be moving beyond coincidence, as if my mind was trying to rouse me from my state of denial. My avoidance was edging towards anger. Inside, I sensed a growing unrest. The confusion couldn't continue. I had to know the truth as to what had brought such a terrible outcome all those years ago. I needed to come to terms with the guilt that gnawed away inside.

By May, Catherine and I had moved into northern India, to a place in a bygone era that had been considered one of the most desirable and romantic postings in the colonial British Empire – the far-flung hill station and tea plantations of Darjeeling. Here, we booked into the Tibetan-owned Bellevue Hotel. In the reception lounge, black and white photographs hung proudly on the wall. They were of the Dalai Lama and his entourage during His Holiness's flight from Tibet in 1959. Noticing our interest in these historical images, the elderly owner seized his opportunity.

'That's me,' he said as he pointed to a figure wearing dark horn-rimmed glasses, dressed in a long felt coat with what looked like a Smith & Wesson revolver tucked under his belt.

Looking back at the gentleman, I replied, 'I can tell it's you.'

His face was unmistakable, even from an image taken so many years ago. As was his justifiable pride in the part he'd played. There was no doubt in our minds their escape from Lhasa and the subsequent journey out of Tibet had been a perilous undertaking.

The history that surrounded Darjeeling was undeniable, similarly its connection to Everest. Tenzing Norgay, who made the first ascent of Everest with the late Sir Edmund Hillary, had spent much of his life here, becoming director of field training for the Himalayan Mountaineering Institute based in the town. However, Darjeeling's link to Everest went back much further. The early reconnaissance expeditions of 1921 and 1922 passed through here, as did the ill-fated

1924 expedition. Old black and white photographs of the latter endeavour still hang on the wall of the snooker room in the Planters Club: the place to be seen, the very heart of Darjeeling society in its day. Amongst these images was the unmistakable figure of Bentley Beetham, the schoolmaster from Barnard Castle School, a member of the 1924 expedition whose photographs of the very same are held by the charitable trust of which I am now the chairman. I was no longer an outsider to this continuity. I had, like so many others before me, become part of it.

Immediately outside the Bellevue Hotel lies the Chowrasta: a large rectangular crossroads, a public space similar to a town square. Here, brass bands played, social events took place and horses could be hired – an ideal place to promenade. Two sides of this area are lined by small businesses. Amongst these stands an attractive two-storey colonial-style wooden building, painted in bottle green, the ground floor of which contains a sizeable bookshop, the Oxford Book and Stationery Co.

During an evening stroll, Catherine and I entered this particular emporium, not with any intention of making a purchase but more out of curiosity and to wile away the time. Inside the sparsely decorated shop lay thousands of publications displayed in large shallow trays placed on tables that ran the length of the establishment.

While browsing through one of the many containers, I came across a second-hand copy of Jon Krakauer's *Into Thin Air*. Catherine, standing a few feet away, noticed which book had caught my attention.

'I think it's about time you read that,' she said.

The filming we'd witnessed at Base Camp had made me pick up Krakauer's book. Catherine's encouragement helped me overcome the last hurdle: the decision to finally read it.

The following day, I settled down into one of the many old armchairs in the Bellevue's lounge, with its row of large windows overlooking the Chowrasta. Wafting through the air across this public square were pre-recorded chants of Tibetan prayer emanating from speakers strategically placed around its perimeter.

The celebration of Buddha's birthday, which lasts for a week or more, had been well under way before our arrival here. Beginning at first light, the music woke Catherine and me from our slumber each morning. As the sun's rays rapidly warmed our wood-panelled room, it massaged us from our dreams with a luxurious sense of calm.

Now these soothing recitals brought reassurance as I opened *Into Thin Air* for the first time. Slumping back into the chair, my surroundings gradually faded as I entered the realms of my past.

As I bared myself to what had gone before, I knew I would stir up feelings of sadness and bitter regret, that the deeper I delved, the stronger these emotions would become. And this was the case. They brought with them the disturbingly clear images I had in my subconscious, as though I was back on the South Col that deadly night. Although I was now witnessing these events in my mind, the outcome had to remain the same; nothing could be changed.

I had hardly opened the book when one particular sentence from the introduction sent my thoughts spinning: 'Among my five teammates who reached the top, four, including Hall, perished in a rogue storm that blew in without warning while we were still high on the peak.'

The weather had not been settled for at least two days prior to their attempt; in fact, it had been deteriorating, as indicated by the two radio calls we had made to Henry. Surely this was a warning that a storm might be coming, the one that had caught them high on the mountain? Confused by his opening statement, I pressed on. With the turn of each page, I looked carefully for any mention of a weather forecast. I was searching for some kind of verification of the quote I had seen some years ago: *'We went on the 10th of May because we knew the weather was going to go bad the next day.'* This statement had been made by a member of Rob Hall's expedition, the one Jon Krakauer was part of, so I wondered if he had been aware of it. Page after page there was nothing. In fact, it surprised me how little the weather was mentioned, except when the storm hit. I do not mean weather forecasts specifically but the weather in general.

His book moved its focus onto others, most notably Anatoli, who seemed to come in for quite severe criticism, first for not using oxygen while guiding and then for descending back down to the South Col ahead of the clients.

Rob and Scott were also put under the spotlight for not enforcing a turnaround time to make sure their clients had sufficient daylight to return safely to Camp 4 on the South Col before dark.

However, I was very surprised, and I have to say disappointed, that Jon's book did not seem to question what they were doing up there in the first place. Instead, he went on to say: 'In fact, the gale of May 10, though violent, was nothing extraordinary; it was a fairly typical Everest squall.' Surely they had seen the same deteriorating weather conditions as we had?

Each time I put the book down to partake in the exploration of our colonial surroundings, I sensed a compulsion to continue the read. Deep down I was looking for answers, ones that in the end never came. The book left me disappointed, as though in limbo. More puzzling questions had been raised; of answers there were none.

I returned home to the UK after our trip to Asia in 2004 with a sense of purpose. Now, more than ever before, I needed to understand what had led to the tragic outcome on 10 May 1996.

The Search Begins

In 1996, I had returned home, like so many others, mourning the tragic loss of fellow climbers in the belief that fate alone had taken these lives. The only link, the only clues, to suggest that this might not be the case were the two quotes I had read: 'We went on the 10th of May because we knew the weather was going to go bad the next day' and '. . . computer models were forecasting 100 to 120 km/hour winds to arrive at the weekend, leaving an adequate weather window for a round trip to Everest's high point on Friday the 10th.' These two lines of print would become my driving force.

Unfortunately, it soon became apparent, after a thorough search of our home, that the original magazine containing the first of these two quotes had inadvertently been thrown out back in 1998, at the time we'd moved to our current apartment. The article that stated 'computer models were forecasting 100 to 120 km/hour winds to arrive at the weekend' I had readily to hand. But this was only half of what I thought I needed. Missing the first, I had nothing to confirm that Rob Hall and Scott Fischer knew what weather had been predicted.

If I'd been able to take a long run-up, I would have kicked myself. I couldn't believe I'd made such a stupid mistake. However, I knew the missing quote had appeared in either a UK climbing magazine or UK outdoor trade publication. So began the arduous task of collecting all the copies of every title I was able to identify. In case I'd got my timing slightly out, and to make sure the net was being cast wide enough, I gathered all the ones I could from between June 1996 and the summer of 1999. Unfortunately, the publication I was looking for was printed during the early days of the Internet. Whereas nowadays a simple phrase search might well have pulled it up, as many are now published or stored online, around 1997 this was not the case.

My initial hope that my quest would only take a few weeks to complete was short-lived, as were my expectations that I might find other references to these two guided teams receiving weather information in the spring of 1996. I couldn't find a single thing to substantiate the two quotes anywhere. This in itself fuelled the intensity of my search and yet at the same time perplexed me. At the time, the world's press had been crawling all over the horrifying story of Everest's worst disaster. Why had this vanished off the radar?

Fortunately, by this point in my career my line of business took far less of my time than it had previously done. Because of this I was in a position to dedicate myself, almost full-time, to the task ahead. This was going to have to be done the old-fashioned way: by a lot of hard work.

Countless hours were spent contacting publishers and libraries to discover what copies of publications from that period they still held. It would have helped immeasurably if I could have remembered which one the first quote had appeared in. Piles of hundreds of magazines soon began to swamp the floor of our living room. However, my quest was now for much more than just the missing line of print, it was for any reference to weather forecasts being received into Everest Base Camp prior to 10 May in 1996. Every article I found claimed it was a 'sudden' or 'unexpected' storm, as did the thousands of pieces on the Internet. Many of these latter ones went further and referred to it as a 'freak' or 'rogue' storm. The more I looked, the further I appeared to be from finding any reference to a weather forecast. My task looked impossible.

I spent many a waking hour in the front room of our apartment. Here, I sat in a large armchair with my face buried in one magazine after another. Every now and again I would look up and stare blankly out of the window at the dramatic coastline of the North Sea, mustering the energy to continue with this thankless task. Month after month slipped by as I carefully went through each article. Periods of despondency began to set in where I'd abandon my reading for a week or two until I could renew my determination.

It was as though I was looking for a needle in a haystack; I only wished I knew which haystack to look in. The seasons changed as I sat each day in the same maroon-coloured chair and read every single line in all the issues I was able to obtain. Flowers came and went, as did the summer sun; late autumn rain lashed hard against the windows. Phone calls and visitors became little more than a distraction, and soon one year would turn into the next. Three magazines a day became a good rate of work.

My concern was that as each day wore on and concentration began to wane I might inadvertently skip the paragraph that contained the elusive quote, or I would miss another that might stand in its stead. As I completed reading each magazine, I convinced myself I was one step nearer in my search. Rows of empty coffee cups filled the kitchen bench as I tried to remain alert.

Logic told me that the two lines of print had not been in error, as one supported the other. Each had had a reason for being published. I would, in time, contact Lindsay Griffin to ask what information he had used to write the article that contained the reference to the prediction of computer models. Alas, he no longer held the relevant records to assist me.

Sitting at my computer in the front room, an area that I now regarded more as an office than a living space, I commenced a parallel line of enquiry as I scoured the Internet for relevant information.

Logic took me first to see if Rob Hall had received his weather from the Meteorological Service of New Zealand. A brief search gave me their contact details. With the press of a single button, this phase of my work began.

Having checked their records for May and June of 1996, the reply came back from Consultant Meteorologist Ross Marsden: 'I think it is safe to say that no forecasts or forecast data were provided from Meteorological Service of New Zealand Ltd for that expedition.'

The New Zealand enquiry, although not leading anywhere, taught me a valuable lesson. Each enquiry would narrow the search. Any answer I received had to be used in a positive way: either enabling me to cross a particular line of enquiry off my list, or by utilising the information it contained to make further contact with others. In comparison with the colossal amount of fruitless time spent reading the magazines, even a simple 'no' appeared as progress, a stepping-stone to the next person or organisation to contact.

As Rob's and Scott's teams had attempted the summit at the same time, reason dictated that maybe Scott had been getting a weather forecast from the US. I contacted the National Oceanic and Atmospheric Administration (NOAA) in the States. The answer I received from Research Meteorologist William Brown from the National Climatic Data Centre brought similar disappointment: 'Unfortunately the United States does not forecast climatic conditions for Mt Everest.' He went on to suggest I might try the Swedish Meteorological and Hydrological Institute (SMHI), who gathered their information from the European Centre for Medium-Range Weather Forecasting (ECMWF).

I contacted the SMHI and received a response from Gunnar Berglund of their Customer Services: 'I've talked to some people and sorry to say but we have no forecasts from the year 1996.' He went on to say that they'd first started forecasting for Everest in 1999 and so were unable to help me with my request.

Although buoyed by the relative speed with which I'd received these answers, my initial and obvious lines of enquiry had drawn a blank. Nothing I'd read in my research had given me any indication that I was on the right track. This, I had not expected. I now understood how information could be lost through time. I was beginning to feel that this might be the case or that I was wrong.

Eventually, I managed to get hold of most, but not all, of the various UK periodicals of the time. I was greatly assisted by Allcord, a large wholesaler to the outdoor industry based in Newcastle upon Tyne, who kindly gave me unlimited access to their loft, where box upon box of back issues lay, covered by the dusts of time.

I even resorted to eBay in my search. Here, I committed the cardinal sin of placing wanted adverts for the copies I was missing rather than advertising articles for sale, in the desperate hope that someone might have some old editions stashed away. EBay wrote to me and threatened to suspend my account if I repeated this action, so I opened a second eBay account and tried again.

Certain trade publications, where I was missing issues, had names and addresses of manufacturers and suppliers of sports and climbing equipment listed in an appendix. Catherine and I sent out dozens of letters to companies all over Europe, enquiring if per chance they'd kept back copies of these publications. We offered £250 towards their office Christmas party if they were able to help. Many took the time to reply, but none with the answer we were hoping for. The issues we needed were so far out of date that no one had kept them that long. Like my original copy, they too had been thrown out. The publishing companies of these trade magazines also only held copies for a year or two. Time was beginning to work against me. The trail was going cold.

The search had become all-consuming, but I had never stopped to consider why. I splashed out and placed a four-week-long advert on ukclimbing.com, where I offered a £2,000 reward for any information that might lead me to the missing quote. Most replies ironically suggested I look in Jon Krakauer's *Into Thin Air*. Others hopeful of some money to fund a possible climbing trip actually took the time to have a look through the old copies they held. A blog appeared on the site where discussions began as to why I was looking for the quote. The consensus of opinion appeared to be that I was some lawyer preparing a lawsuit. However, the one that amused me most was when someone emailed me and told me it had all been gone through in great detail in several books already – that I should leave matters alone.

In many ways, it had become a very lonely journey. I was sustained by little more than my own determination and Catherine's support. Although I met friends regularly on a Monday and Thursday evening, they were understandably wrapped up in their own careers and hobbies. The events on Everest in 1996 held little relevance or interest for them. It would have been pointless for me to begin a topic of conversation about a quote I'd read several years earlier, one that I could now not re-find.

There turned out to be only two people who I think truly understood the tortuous task I'd given myself. The first was Catherine, who stayed amazingly positive throughout. I'm sure there will have been many topics she would have rather listened to than this particular one on a daily basis for such a long a period of time. The other was Geoff Scarth, a very good friend, some 20 years my senior, whom I met each Friday evening for a quiet drink in a nearby pub called The Briar Dene. Situated next to the golf course on the seafront at Whitley Bay, it had a reputation as a family-friendly establishment. With comfortable seats and a thick-carpeted floor, it was an ideal venue for uninterrupted discussion and one that served an excellent selection of hand-pulled real ale to add flavour to our deliberations.

Geoff was a lawyer who'd acted on Catherine's and my behalf with regard to our businesses. He'd taken semi-retirement, as he called it, around 1997 when he'd telephoned half a dozen selected clients he wished to maintain on his books, with their agreement, because, as he put it, he 'found them interesting'. We'd been included in the select few – something we took as a great compliment at the time, although I joked with him afterwards that it was really because he made so much money out of us, which he needed for his annual vacation with his wife Enid to Zermatt and Grindelwald in Switzerland each autumn. This comment had made him roar with laughter. A year or two later, he fully retired and had subsequently become a very close friend, whose opinion, not surprisingly, I valued very highly.

Fortunately for me, Geoff, although not a climber, had a passion for the mountains. He'd followed my progress on Everest from the very beginning and had noted well my initial reluctance to talk about the disaster on Everest. He was one of the first to see me after my return from Nepal that year and had left the topic alone. Now, several years on, each Friday, more often than not, we would discuss my fruitless search and the events of 1996. I openly told Geoff that had I not read the quote myself I would have sworn that it did not exist. He played a superb devil's advocate by asking me, in all seriousness, if I might have dreamt reading the quote, in which case it actually might not exist. Fortunately for me, when I'd seen it all that time ago I'd been so taken aback that I'd shown it to Catherine. She too had read the elusive two lines of print and as such gave me the witness that Geoff had to accept.

I would, in time, come to realise that throwing out the magazine when we moved house was probably the best thing that could have happened. If I'd discovered the quote early on in my quest, I might have got some answers on a more superficial level, but I am convinced I would not have dug so hard or so relentlessly. I'd read the quote. I knew it was there somewhere. Had I found it and tracked down the source would they have admitted saying it or would I have been met with a denial? This had only been said once in all that I'd read – from which I concluded there had been a momentary lapse. The real value was that it had become my motivation. The way to the truth was no brighter than a pinprick of light.

One sentence.

Much of the difficulty I'd encountered up to this point had been due to the lack of any official investigation, in the form of an inquiry, into the events leading up to the disaster. In Nepal, for mountaineering fatalities at least, there is no post-mortem requirement, nor does the cause of death need to be shown on the death certificate.

As two Americans had died, Doug Hansen and Scott Fischer, I looked into the US requirements for any of their citizens being killed abroad, in the hope these might be the most stringent.

Since 30 September 2002, the Department of State in the US has been required to record, and make publicly available, detailed statistics of US citizens who die overseas from non-natural causes, including where, when and what category of death. Climbing comes under the heading of 'other accidents of misadventure'. However, in the case of accidental deaths, the host country is responsible for the investigation. Since Nepal has no post-mortem or cause-of-death requirement for the death certificate in such cases, an inquest into the events and circumstances leading up to a person's demise cannot reasonably be held.

I contacted the Ministry of Foreign Affairs and Trade in New Zealand to ask what their requirements might be if a New Zealander was killed abroad. In this case, there had been two: Rob Hall and Andy Harris.

In their response, they wrote: 'If a New Zealander is killed overseas, any investigation into that death is normally conducted by the local authorities and a local death certificate issued. We are bound by the local laws/investigation process of that country.'

The reply from Japan, with regard to the death of Yasuko Namba, was in a similar vein. With an accidental death, the investigation is carried out by, and according to the laws of, the host country.

The short winter days and long dark nights had done little to raise my spirits, nor did the lack of any evidence corroborating the existence of a weather forecast in 1996. Rather than getting overly dejected about the position I found myself in, Catherine and I decided to head off to Nepal that coming spring for a complete break in the hope that when we returned home refreshed my luck might change, although I must admit I was beginning to doubt that very much. The countless hours we'd both spent painstakingly reading and re-reading page after page of the many magazines I'd gathered had produced virtually nothing but a few minor references: ones that might possibly be useful in the future, but nothing of any substance.

We were going to Nepal this time not for climbing or trekking but to indulge our greatest passion: wildlife and the natural world. We'd been to the lowlands of Nepal, the Terai, several times before to visit the world-famous Chitwan National Park. On one occasion, we'd been extraordinarily lucky enough to see a Royal Bengal tiger in the wild. I was hoping we would again, but even if we didn't have a sighting, we wouldn't be disappointed. The change in our surroundings, the very friendly people of the Terai and being in the park itself would be reward enough.

A Lifeline

In late March 2005, Catherine and I touched down at Kathmandu's Tribhuvan International Airport to be met by rising spring temperatures and the mayhem of this sprawling city: a now familiar place that had over the years become like a second home.

We emerged from the terminal expecting to find the usual throng of taxi drivers competing for our business. Instead, we observed all those present lined up in an orderly manner behind a row of metal barriers, each waiting their turn. Slightly taken aback by this dramatic change to the system, I approached the first driver in the queue and said, 'How much to the Sherpa Guest House in Thamel?'

Looking at the trolley carrying our luggage and then to my empty hand, he replied, 'Pre-pay, pre-pay,' as he pointed to the kiosk behind us – the one we'd walked straight past.

Like so many travellers who visit the same destination over a period of time, we'd expected the way things operated to remain the same. They, of course, do not. What travellers remember from their own experience will, over time, gradually change.

Stepping between the entrance pillars of the Sherpa Guest House, we passed from a bustling and rather dusty street into the relative tranquillity of the reception area. Behind the ornately decorated wooden counter stood a lady aged about 35, wearing traditional and very modest attire, her long jet-black hair tied neatly back.

She greeted us with a smile and the words, 'Room 308?' Without waiting for a reply, she turned to retrieve the room key from the appropriately marked pigeonhole directly behind her.

We'd stayed here on previous occasions. In fact, only the year before we'd occupied that room several times, as then we'd used Nepal as a hub from which our travels radiated. Room 308, quietly situated high up at the rear of the hotel, had become our preferred accommodation for a good night's sleep.

Our bags had hardly touched the floor of the establishment before the hotel boy, eagerly awaiting his next task, scooped them up. He'd also been there during our last visit, when we'd given him the nickname, between ourselves, of Speedy Gonzales. He bounded up and down the

Paul Deegan (in red) and myself (in blue) begin to climb through the lower part of the Khumbu Icefall on the morning of 8 May 1996; we are en route to Camp 2 in the Western Cwm in readiness for our summit attempt on 11 May.

Camp 3 on the Lhotse Face, 9 May 1996. Paul Deegan standing on the left and Neil Laughton on the right. These two, along with one of our Sherpas, are taking turns to dig out a platform for a second tent.

En route to the South Col on the afternoon of 10 May 1996, Neil Laughton poses for a photograph at the top of the Geneva Spur. Behind him, Everest's upper reaches are being battered by a wind that has been increasing over the last few days. There is no other image I have seen that so clearly justifies our repeated questioning over the radio as to why we were moving up for a summit attempt. © Neil Laughton

The morning of 11 May 1996. Mark Pfetzer, Jabion and I prepare to leave the South Col. Our team's tents are the yellow- and cream-coloured ones on the left of the picture. Directly behind Mark, who is central in the photograph, are the tents of Rob Hall's and Scott Fischer's teams. Nothing in this image gave us any clue about the disaster that had taken place through the night. Reports say the South Col camp was in tatters; this is not true.

The morning of 11 May 1996. Rob Hall's and Scott Fischer's perfectly intact tents are buffeted by a fresh morning breeze; beyond, the clouds rise up over the Kangshung side of the South Col.

This striking photograph was taken from the top of the Geneva Spur early on 11 May 1996 during my retreat from the South Col. The highest visible point is the South Summit, where, unbeknown to me at this time, Rob Hall was stranded. Doug Hansen and Andy Harris who had been with Rob during the night had already lost their lives. Scott Fischer and Makalu Gau lay close to death halfway up this face, in an area slightly to the right of centre in this image. On the South Col, an area that extends from the bottom right and is out of sight in this picture, Yasuko Namba and Beck Weathers were at death's door.

After I arrived back at Camp 2, on the morning of 11 May, I was shocked to be told the emerging details of the tragedy that took place through the night. © Paul Deegan

Climbers ascending the hard shimmering ice of the Lhotse Face towards Camp 3; some 4,000 feet above towers Lhotse's jagged summit. © Paul Deegan

Catherine and I travelling into Tibet, early April 2004. Pictured is one of the high passes adorned by the Tibetans with cairns and countless prayer flags.

The Epic of Mount Everest by Sir Francis Younghusband:
The following description is of the ill-fated 1924 expedition, as Norton and Somervell move up with three porters, as they are referred to at this time, to establish Camp VI at 26,800 feet – the expedition's final camp from which summit attempts will be made.

'So they progressed till about 1.30, when it was evident that the gallant Semchumbi [one of the porters] could go no further. A narrow cleft in the rocks facing north and affording the suggestion – it was little more – of some shelter from the north-west wind was selected. Norton set the two leading porters to scrape and pile the loose stones forming the floor of the cleft into the usual platform for a tent. On it the tiny tent for the two climbers was pitched; and this was Camp VI, 26,800 feet.'

It was from this tent that George Mallory and Sandy Irvine left for their summit bid on 8 June 1924, never to return. The image is unique to the Bentley Beetham Collection and is the only known image of Camp VI. I have seen no other photograph that sums up so well both the bravery and audacity of the early pioneers.

In the Western Cwm, 13 May 1996. With Makalu Gau onboard,
the Nepalese army Squirrel helicopter RAN-33 heads towards the
Khumbu Icefall. In the background is Nuptse.

The dark summit pyramid of Everest rises to left of centre. Both Everest's main summit
and South Summit, which is to the right of the main summit and lower down the ridge,
are visible. The peak below the pyramid and to the left is part of Everest's West Ridge.
Centre top, the dip with a small amount of cloud hanging over it is the South Col.
From here, the ground then rises right onto Lhotse, which is mostly hidden from view.
The peak on the top right is Nuptse. Between Nuptse and Everest's West Ridge
flows the notorious Khumbu Icefall, seen bottom left.

stairs five or six steps at a time, to the point he appeared as little more than a blur in our vision. The most endearing thing about this wonderful character was that when he stopped long enough for us to actually see him he was always smiling.

'You can fill the forms in later,' said the receptionist, as she pointed to our bags rapidly disappearing out of sight up the polished staircase.

The next day, we surfaced from the hotel to a gloriously sunny morning and made the arduous journey of almost ten yards to the bakery directly across the road that served breakfast in their leafy rear garden. The ease with which we slipped back into this familiar routine was both comforting and worryingly pleasant: a far cry from the frustrations of my research.

It seemed as though each time we turned a corner another happy face would meet us with recognition, not so much to do with my climbing but from the business we'd carried out with the Nepalese. On each occasion we returned, many of the friends we'd made still invited us to their homes to eat with their families, despite the fact we'd long ceased trading.

However, the Maoist problems in Nepal, although not directed at tourists, still posed a risk. Mostly this was if you happened to be in the wrong place at the wrong time. Rather than make our own travel arrangements down to Chitwan, we decided to seek the advice of a Nepalese agent, a 'Mr Fix It' of extraordinary talents who worked for Henry Todd, among other people. The gentleman's name was Iswari. His main business was organising and fulfilling the requirements of large expeditions visiting the country. He was a man small in stature but big on personality, confidence and humour, and he had earned his reliable reputation.

We gained access to the building he was in by passing through an inconspicuous doorway set amongst the many souvenir and jewellery shops that lined either side of a narrow unmetalled road. Confronting us was the familiar sight of a dimly lit concrete staircase that wound its way up to the second floor, where Iswari's business was located. Here, several rooms were set on either side of a long, unlit corridor, their slightly ajar doors giving glimpses of their contents: piles of plastic barrels and boxes full of expedition equipment. At the far end lay Iswari's office.

As Catherine and I entered, we found him sat behind, and dwarfed by, his larger-than-average wooden desk. Filing cabinets bearing the individual names of expedition companies he worked for filled two-thirds of one wall. A fax machine and mobile phone lay alongside neat piles of paperwork on his desk, where a pen lay at the ready. This was the nerve centre of his operation. In the room with him were seated two of his assistants and a Nepalese gentleman wearing Western-style sunglasses and holding a briefcase.

First, we exchanged greetings and a handshake with Iswari, whom we both knew, before each settling down into one of the seven or eight armchairs positioned around the perimeter.

I began by asking Iswari what the best options were for getting down to Chitwan in light of the current Maoist problems. With his typically infectious Nepalese humour, he told me we could go by bus. He followed this with some memorable words: 'If you go by bus, we don't know if you come back. Better you fly.'

As is the custom, we were offered masala tea while one of his assistants went to make arrangements for our tickets. This is a surprisingly mellow beverage made from tea complemented with a mixture of herbs and aromatic spices. It was while I was sipping from my cup that I turned my attention to what was displayed on the walls, amongst which was a large Adventure Consultants poster that I commented on.

Iswari's response took me completely by surprise. He told Catherine and me that the gentleman holding the briefcase, in the office with us, was in fact Ang Tshering, the Sirdar currently working for Adventure Consultants.

Ang Tshering, on noticing my interest in the company he worked for, joined in the conversation. He informed me that he lived in the Solu Khumbu, in a village called Kumjung situated above Namche Bazaar. Then he proudly presented me with a business card from Adventure Consultants confirming his position. As I carefully steered the topic of conversation, I was then handed a completely unexpected pot of gold. He'd been Rob Hall's Sirdar in 1996.

When least expected, I'd stumbled across a first-hand source from within Rob's team, a person with authority and knowledge. A man whose integrity was unquestionable, who was greatly respected in his own community and who I hoped would be willing to discuss these events from the past.

Catherine, sitting only a few feet to my left, could sense my excitement and knew well where I was going to manoeuvre this subject. She sat quietly, not wanting to cause any distraction that might deflect the conversation away from the current topic.

The dialogue opened up further when I told him I'd also been there in 1996, on Henry Todd's team. This led us naturally to discuss some of the events that led up to the disaster. I asked Ang Tshering about the decision-making process within Rob's and Scott's expeditions that had led them to choose the day for their summit bid, about any weather reports they might have been receiving.

His reply was instant: 'Rob and Scott always watching, watching Imax. Imax have the weather!'

He used his hands to accentuate the significant amount of attention he recalled Rob and Scott were paying to these weather reports, ones that might be used to give them a further advantage in bringing their high-dollar clients success on Everest.

I wanted to push deeper into what had happened back then. However, I was aware that Ang Tshering might not be willing to let the conversation progress that far. The fact that deaths had occurred meant we were moving towards a taboo subject he might not be comfortable discussing with a woman present, or maybe not at all.

As Ang Tshering was sipping his tea, I took the opportunity to turn to Catherine and flicked my eyes to one side, signalling for her to make an excuse and leave. This she did superbly and left me the slim chance to glean what information I could.

Once Catherine had departed, Ang Tshering went on to tell me that Rob had very much favoured 10 May: a date that had brought him success on more than one occasion in previous years and on which Rob wanted to summit again if at all possible.

I knew all along I'd been running a race against time, but at that juncture my luck ran out. Iswari's assistant returned holding our plane tickets to Chitwan. These he gave to Iswari, who in turn stood up to pass them to me along with the customary handshake to conclude the transaction. This left me with no polite option other than to depart and catch up with Catherine, who'd been patiently waiting on the road outside. I emerged out into the dazzling sunshine with a look of joyous astonishment on my face.

'How did you get on?' asked Catherine.

'Not as much as I'd hoped, but far better than I could have possibly wished for,' was my exuberant reply.

This small but significant discovery raised my spirits immeasurably. No longer did the spectre of minimal progress hang over our vacation. I was secretly relishing the thought of returning home armed with this latest information.

The sight of Adventure Consultants' Sirdar in the office of an expedition agent was a sure indication that the climbing season was about to begin. The streets of Thamel displayed similar signs. Groups of climbers carrying over-laden rucksacks and large holdalls bursting at the seams could be seen arriving in taxis from the airport, each in search of accommodation for the next few days before travelling on to their chosen mountain destination.

Henry was also in Nepal during the spring of 2005. Once again he was running a commercial expedition to Everest. Despite his hectic schedule, making all the necessary arrangements for his current team, we met up for lunch in Kathmandu. This gave me an ideal opportunity to ask him about our planned summit attempt in 1996.

As I walked into the leafy paved garden, I could see that Henry had already arrived. He was sitting at a small wooden table perusing the menu and bathed in the dappled sunlight that had made its way through the foliage of the overhanging trees.

'Catherine sends her apologies, she isn't feeling well,' I said as I sat down opposite him. In truth, I'd asked Catherine not to come. I felt I had a better chance of getting Henry to open up if there were just the two of us.

'I'm sorry to hear that, give her my regards,' replied Henry as he looked up from the menu, holding a hand up to catch the waiter's attention so he could place an order; I followed with mine.

'You said you wanted to discuss something with me?' continued Henry.

'Yes, I have a couple of queries about 1996 I was hoping you could help me with,' I replied.

'Fire away,' said Henry.

I needed to allow myself the maximum opportunity for discussion rather than bringing it up after the meal only to hear that Henry needed to depart and press on with all the jobs he had to finish before leaving for the mountains. So I came straight to the point.

I explained to Henry about what I'd read in the UK publications and that I was considering writing a book. His wise words of caution were that I should be very careful about basing a book on two lines of print that I'd read in some magazines.

I also told him of Ang Tshering's statement that Rob and Scott were watching the Imax expedition for the weather. This left the way open for me to ask Henry specifically about the storm in 1996. His answer, given what I had just told him, was unambiguous.

'I had no knowledge of weather information being received at Base Camp predicting a storm in '96,' was Henry's response.

In all honesty, this was the answer I was expecting. It would have been most unlike Henry not to share such information with his climbers, especially since we'd had a 16 year old on our planned summit attempt and because he would not have sent us up if he knew a storm was coming.

However, I wasn't going to leave it there. 'I think we were set up by Rob and Scott,' I said, looking at Henry's face to gauge his reaction to this bold statement.

This was not what he had been expecting. Henry rocked back slightly and his eyes opened wider as the implications of what I had said hit home. He moved forward and opened his mouth in readiness to say something, but did not. There was a look of surprise on his face, one I had not seen before. He did not reply.

I pushed the point further: 'It looks to me as though Rob and Scott knew a storm was coming on 11 May. All they had wanted when they asked us to go on 11 May was us out of the way so that on 10 May they had a clear shot at the summit.'

Once again, I looked at Henry for his reaction. I could see his mind was whirling around, but it wasn't in the moment we were in. He was back in 1996. It appeared as though he was trying to recall the sequence of events that had led up to our climbers being on the South Col on 10 May in preparation for our summit bid the following day.

'No, I'm sure you are wrong,' responded Henry, with an uneasy look on his face. It was the look of someone who didn't want to believe what he had just heard.

Rob Hall and Scott Fischer were friends, or at the very least professional acquaintances, of Henry. As expedition leaders, they had spent time in 1996 making a coordinated approach to fixing the route up Everest. Henry had played his part. The decisions they made affected the safety of everyone climbing that year. Rob and Scott should have told us about the serious deterioration in the weather conditions if they knew about them. However, I was making an allegation without necessarily having the grounds to back it up. Henry had relied on his ongoing relations with these two, and with the other leaders on the mountain, as we had little to provide to other teams except for some ropes and Sherpa support to secure these higher up.

Apart from operating a commercial expedition, Henry was a service provider, supplying essential and expensive bottled oxygen to some of the other expeditions. With a price tag of around $300 per bottle, and with each climber requiring several bottles, this was not an insignificant operation. I could understand him not wanting to make further comment on what I had said. Year in year out, he still made a significant portion of his income from his Everest operations, including the supply of valuable oxygen supplies. Adventure Consultants and Mountain Madness had been taken over after the demise of Rob Hall and Scott Fischer. Both still operated on Everest each spring season, as did others who had been present in 1996. It was entirely sensible that Henry would be more cautious than me and be hesitant about getting involved in further discussion on the subject until I had good evidence to support such a claim.

If indeed I was correct, then Henry had been badly let down by those he had trusted, but now was not the time to press him further on this matter.

The appearance of the waiter at the side of the table holding the food we had ordered interrupted our conversation. The aromatic fragrances carried upwards by the steam rising from the freshly prepared ingredients gave Henry his opportunity to change the subject.

'How's business going for you?' he asked.

It was my cue that our previous conversation was over. The next time I raised the subject with Henry, I needed to be armed with much more information.

Through the oval and lightly crazed Perspex window the Terai came into view. A mostly flat alluvial plain containing a mixture of fertile farmland and subtropical jungle fed by mountain run-off, it extends the entire length of Nepal's southern border with northern India. Set only marginally above sea level, this mosquito-infested area is often referred to as the breadbasket of Nepal. Covering one-sixth of the country, it contains more than half of the entire population.

The tyres of the green and white de Havilland twin-engined Otter of Yeti Airlines screeched momentarily as Catherine and I touched down at Bharatpur. The marked increase in the temperature, as compared to Kathmandu, was instantly noticeable as we made our way to the rear of this 20-seater plane. We clambered down the short flight of steps that were suspended from the aircraft's fuselage by a lower hinge and two wire cables.

Collecting our bags from the terminal building, which consisted of little more than one large room overlooking the airstrip, we made our way outside to where several taxis were parked. Amongst this random selection of vehicles there was one particular wreck that stood out from the rest. It was a Datsun that was so old I didn't know the model. Forty years plus would have been a reasonable guess. The driver, an elderly gentleman aged around 65 with a leathery sunbeaten face, scruffy clothes and worn-out flip-flops, began to show off to the younger drivers about how to get a fare, using us as guinea pigs. Enamoured by both his bravado and the condition of his car, we couldn't resist. After a brief negotiation, one that was followed by a grin from our driver to his bewildered young onlookers, I got into the passenger seat in the front and Catherine into the rear.

As we pulled out from the entrance to the airfield and onto the Mahendra Highway, I took time to observe more closely the interior of our transport. It looked marginally worse than the outside of the vehicle. The old plastic seat covers that stuck to our backs were perished and cracked from the intensity of the sun. Carpets and floor coverings had long since been removed, as had the headlining, door panels and anything else that might deaden the sound of the badly patched exhaust. The wiring harness hung down from the dashboard in apparent disarray. Between my feet was what I took to be spare petrol in a plastic container. That was until I spotted fuel being drawn up a tube that passed through the cap and out towards the front of the vehicle. Only then did I realise it was our fuel tank.

After we'd travelled only a short distance, Catherine began to clap her hands intermittently.

'What's the matter back there?' I shouted above the noise of the car – not just of the engine and exhaust but of the rattling windows and doors.

'It's the mosquitoes,' Catherine called back, 'there's more of the damn things in here than there are outside.'

I turned around to see Catherine with dozens of the wretched insects swirling around her head looking for a place to land. It was at this moment that I decided I preferred sitting in the front with the rising petrol fumes and tank between my legs, in the forlorn hope that it might keep them away from me. After all, such a dangerous undertaking was man's work.

Thundering past us in both directions were countless numbers of ornately hand-painted Tata trucks with tinsel, coloured lights and similar decorations garishly displayed on the upper edge of their windscreens. These overloaded monsters of this fragile road system often leant to one side with their uneven cargo as they belched forth clouds of black smoke. Many had large pieces of rubber flailing from the re-treaded tyres, which were utilised to the point of destruction. At regular intervals, we saw lorries precariously balanced on a bottle-jack, as the driver replaced his burst tyre with one that looked little better than the one that had just expired. No one was really safe on this manic thoroughfare, where an accident could befall you at any time.

It was with some relief that we turned off this crowded highway into more rural surroundings. Oxen laboriously ploughing small fields under the scorching sun bore witness to the simplicity of this area's everyday life. Houses and farm buildings constructed from wood and mud with either corrugated steel or thatched roofs were intermittently positioned along the roadside. Ears of corn still on the stem had been placed on the tarmac road to be threshed by any passing vehicles that might inadvertently lend a helping hand.

Nearly an hour after leaving the airport, we pulled up at our destination: the Riverside Lodge at Sauraha. This was a concrete carbuncle of a hotel beautifully situated on the bank of the Rapti river, the far side of which designated the northern boundary of the park.

In the hotel's garden retreat, we settled back into cushioned chairs, Catherine with a neat Bacardi and me with a cold beer to calm our nerves. The slow-moving Rapti, broad and shallow at this time of year, reflected the pace of life. Nepalese women dressed in traditional *khurtas* brought bowls of washing balanced on their heads down to the water's edge. Alongside them, mahouts washed their elephants with scrubbing brushes. Villagers living within the boundaries of the park strolled alongside their bicycles, laden with the day's purchases, as they wheeled them across the shallow water. Long and narrow dugout canoes steered silently up and down stream, the standing boatsmen using a long pole to push against the riverbed.

We watched this ever-changing scene as the large watery sun gradually sank behind the jungle, until its evening colours, which reflected off the Rapti's mirrored surface, gently faded. The sound of peacocks emanated from a jungle coming back to life after the intense heat of the day. It was a timeless scene that only served to raise our anticipation for the jeep safari we'd booked for the next day.

Around 6 a.m., having crossed the river in a dugout, we entered the park in a white open-top Suzuki jeep driven by Bikrum, accompanied by our official park guide, Babu.

For three hours, we slowly crisscrossed Chitwan's network of rough tracks, patiently searching for glimpses of its wary residents, a jungle foray that had been rewarded with the sighting of deer, crocodiles, rhinos and a spectacular array of birds for which this park is famous.

All of a sudden, Babu shouted, 'There, on the road,' as he pointed in front of us.

By the time we all turned to look, it was gone.

'It was very low and might have been a tiger,' Babu said.

Bikrum gradually drove up to the spot Babu had indicated and turned the engine off. The two of them then got out of the jeep, each holding a short piece of bamboo stick little more than a foot long. They proceeded to look for a tiger that would have weighed far more than the pair of them put together.

Deciding that a vantage point could be useful at this time, I climbed onto the roof of the vehicle. From where I was standing I could see the unmistakable black stripes running across the tiger's otherwise orange back contrasting starkly against the dark-green vegetation that rose no more than four feet high and through which the tiger was trying to move slowly away. This huge animal, measuring more than eight feet in length, can't have been much more than twenty-five feet away from me, and only a few feet further than that away from Bikrum and Babu, who were poking around with their sticks.

'It's here,' I said as softly as I could.

The tiger, hearing this, stopped in its tracks and turned its head to look directly at me. I was the only one it could see. Within seconds, we were all crowded on top of the vehicle as this most magnificent of animals slipped deeper into the undergrowth and disappeared out of sight.

We returned home from Nepal in 2005 with my enthusiasm renewed. Our fortunate sighting of the elusive and rarely seen tiger told me my luck was changing.

Walls of Silence

Once back home, I was straight on the telephone to the IMAX Corporation in Canada. Explaining that I was researching into the events on Everest in 1996, the year the IMAX film *Everest* was shot, I enquired who at their head office might be able to help me with some information. The name I was given was that of Adam Edwards.

I sent Adam an email to let him know that my understanding led me to believe the Imax team had received weather forecasts during the course of filming. I asked if he might be able to point me in the direction of the person I should contact to find out the source of these forecasts.

Adam informed me that the IMAX Corporation had not produced the film. The production company had in fact been MacGillivray Freeman Films in California. His advice: 'You should contact them directly to obtain a response to your interesting question.'

At this particular juncture, I decided it would be wise to dig deeper before following his suggestion. I began with a visit to the MacGillivray Freeman Films' website to see if this might shed some light. Alas, it did not.

There was, however, acknowledgement of significant funding for the IMAX film *Everest* out of public funds from the National Science Foundation (NSF). This provided my next port of call.

The point of contact I found at the NSF was Valentine Kass, Programme Director for Informal Science Education. Unable to tell me who might have supplied weather forecasts during filming, he also suggested I contact the production company. More specifically, the name of Greg MacGillivray was put forward as the person who should be able to answer my question.

Considering what precious little information I'd gathered, my hope was to contact the company at a later date armed with much more. Circumstances dictated I took my enquiry there next.

I telephoned their office on five or six occasions in an attempt to speak with Greg MacGillivray. I made attempts to talk to Kathy Burke-Almon, who I'd discovered was their Manager of Special Projects. In 1996, she'd been their 'US-based communication, liaison and facilitator throughout production in Nepal'. I emailed both Greg and Kathy, each on two occasions. I left messages.

Finally, I got Greg MacGillivray's administrative assistant, Susan Wilson, to consider my enquiry about whom they had used for weather forecasting during the filming on Everest in 1996. I think they realised by this point they'd better say something, as I was quite clearly persistent.

I received the briefest of emails. The reply came back: 'Greg does not know the answer to your question. We will try looking through old files and get back to you if we come across the information.'

The IMAX *Everest* film was one of MacGillivray Freeman Films' most successful productions. The gross takings within the first 24 months of release were in excess of $100 million and still rising significantly. It ended up grossing more than $74 million in the US alone and is quoted as being one of the highest-grossing non-fiction films ever screened.

Two of the most critical factors during filming were, first, would the equipment operate successfully in the extreme conditions and, second, would the weather allow filming to take place? Surely it was reasonable to assume that they would know, or at least have near to hand, the name of the organisation or person who'd supplied the weather-related information that had helped in their amazing success. Importantly, they had not denied having a forecast. They had merely said they would get back to me 'if' they found the information.

About the same time, Kathy Burke-Almon also responded:

Unfortunately, I doubt that I will be able to provide any valuable insight or details as I did not accompany the team to Base Camp. The team monitored weather conditions from the Base. I have forwarded your email to Ed Viesturs.

Ed Viesturs had been a climber and film talent on the Imax expedition. His was a name on my list of people I might wish to contact, but I would do so only when appropriate and if necessary. Yes, Kathy had mentioned they were monitoring weather conditions from the Base, but there was no mention of a weather forecast.

To this day, MacGillivray Freeman Films have been unable to provide any more information, but I appreciate that I was asking for information about a film that had been made nine years previously. Nevertheless, it was frustrating that a simple answer to a straight question was so problematic, especially as any high-altitude weather forecasts would have needed to be arranged before the film crew left for Nepal and presumably eventually paid for.

On the company's website was an educational resource for teachers about the making of the film. Surely, I thought, given the significant public funding, meteorology would be well represented here. Not least because it is the movement of the monsoon northward from the Bay of Bengal that nudges the jet stream off the summit of Everest, pushing it north over Tibet. This annual change in the weather pattern is what makes it possible to climb Everest each spring. More important still is the significant effect this moving of the jet stream has on the world's weather. In the 20 pages of this educational resource there were little more than a few passing references to the weather. I list the ones I found:

p. 1: 'Meteorologists want to record its unpredictable weather patterns.'

p. 2: A small section on 'Did you know?' about wind chill factors.

p. 8: 'Everest film team members arrived at Base Camp on Mount Everest fully aware of the land formations and possible weather patterns that might affect their climb.'

p. 18: 'The ever-changing weather surrounding the peak of Mount Everest can also create dangerous situations for all climbers.'

And last on my list but certainly not least:

p. 3: [This refers to the period after the disaster of 10 May 1996]: 'The IMAX Expedition Team rested and recuperated at Base Camp while monitoring the weather forecasts dispatched from points around the globe.'

Now, as there was no mention of the Imax expedition receiving a weather forecast before 10 May, this could easily leave the reader of the educational resource under the impression that none were being received prior to the disaster. That only as a result thereof did they think it might be a good idea to get one.

The Imax expedition had been in the planning and preparation stages for some considerable time – around two years. During this period, they had the body of the IMAX camera specially crafted out of magnesium to reduce weight. In certain critical areas, metal bearings were replaced with plastic, and synthetic drive belts were added for their flexibility at low temperatures. They had a reputed filming budget of $7 million, along with ten scientific advisers. The plan was to cover every possible eventuality they could in advance. Surely an accurate weather forecast, if available, would have been almost top of their list?

A second approach to the National Science Foundation was the next logical step. Public funding brought with it open access through freedom of information.

Sitting at the computer in our front room, surrounded by countless magazines and pieces of paper with my scribbled lists of copies I'd yet to obtain, I made contact.

It appeared the IMAX film had been funded through the foundation's Informal Science Education Programme, of which David Ucko was the current head. He passed my enquiry on to Programme Director Valentine Kass to deal with.

I suppose it was inevitable at some point that I would feel I was going around in circles, as names I'd already contacted cropped up again. I let David know I'd already been in contact with Valentine, setting out the difficulties I'd encountered after following his advice.

David replied:

> We're still following up on this, but keep in mind that once an award is made, NSF is not involved in the implementation of the project, which is the responsibility of the PI [Principle Investigator]. The program officer who handled this award, Hyman Field, has retired from NSF.

I wrote to David once again and pushed the point as far as I dared. I asked him if the work covered by the grant came under the Freedom of Information Act, querying if it would be possible to either pass my email contact on to Hyman Field, or if indeed their own records might provide the answer.

I explained to David my surprise at what appeared to me as the 'almost' avoidance of an obvious and valuable resource – the weather, meteorology and forecasting – in the educational material produced to complement the IMAX film: exactly the sort of material the public money had paid for. This, combined with the apparent inability of MacGillivray Freeman Films to answer my questions fully and without difficulty, for whatever reason, made me uneasy, and I was straight with David about my concerns.

David's response indicated they'd given me as much as they had available to them; there was no cover-up or conspiracy. The information he sent set out the project in clear terms – its aims, the funding and the names of those connected to it. In the meantime, he'd contacted Hyman Field, who in turn had suggested I contact David Breashears, the Imax expedition leader, or Roger Bilham, a geophysicist from the University of Colorado, who'd accompanied the team.

David Ucko concluded his reply by writing:

There is nothing for NSF to hide. The film and ancillary materials produced under the grant are all public. You are certainly welcome to request a copy of the original proposal through FOIA [Freedom of Information Act] if you wish, but NSF does not have access to the records of the grantee nor to those of the other organisations involved in this or any other project it funds.

As a result of my communication with the National Science Foundation, I came away with further leads I could follow up. Roger Bilham and David Breashears had been specifically mentioned.

An All Too Brief Contact

David Breashears, leader of the Imax expedition and the film director, was already top of my list of people to contact, if I could find information to corroborate what I had been told by Rob Hall's Sirdar. Only then could I make a reasoned and sensible approach to open a dialogue with David on the subject.

Following up Hyman Field's other suggestion, I emailed Roger Bilham at Colorado University to ask if he knew the source of the weather forecasts for the 1996 Imax expedition.

Roger replied saying he'd left Base Camp before the storm hit. That he'd needed to return to the US to teach the rest of the semester. However, David Breashears, still on Everest, had contacted him in the US after the disaster to see if Roger could give him any kind of clue about inbound weather. Roger approached Howard Hansen, a colleague and meteorologist at CIRES (Cooperative Institute for Research in Environmental Sciences) in Colorado, where they downloaded satellite images.

> When Hansen and I looked at the satellite imagery, the fatal storm was heading east and the next similar cloud system looked far to the west. But there was no way of knowing how stable the new system was or how it would develop.
>
> I remember thinking that it is relatively easy to recognise problem weather heading towards Everest, but guaranteeing its absence was perilous and would have required the study of many years of data.

Unfortunately, Roger had copied my email to David Breashears, whom I had not wanted to contact quite yet. My hand being forced, I contacted David but at the same time quickly sent another email to Roger Bilham. Again, I asked Roger if he was aware of who had provided the weather forecasts and at what date he'd left the expedition to return to the US.

Roger's response: 'I was unaware of any weather forecast at Base Camp. I left because I had to administer final exams, but I have no record of the date. The person that would remember is Audrey Salkeld, the author and Everest historian.'

Audrey had been a member of the Imax expedition. Later in my research I would come across Audrey Salkeld's reports from the Imax expedition Base Camp. In her report dated 19 April 1996, she stated that Roger Bilham had already left Base Camp. He'd left mid-April, at least three weeks before the storm hit Everest – a time at which the team would not have been acclimatised or ready to start considering weather forecasts for a summit attempt. Therefore, Roger being unaware of any weather forecasts being received at Base Camp was completely understandable. If I'd known at the time what date he'd left Base Camp, I would have asked him if he knew if weather forecasts had been pre-arranged for the beginning of May in 1996. I never did ask him that question.

In the same reply, Roger went on to say: 'My understanding of the phone calls I got from David when I returned was that the intensity of the storm was a huge surprise.' Interestingly, this would indicate that David knew the storm was coming; it was the intensity that took them by surprise.

However, what Roger Bilham and Howard Hansen had confirmed was that the storm that hit Everest on the afternoon of 10 May 1996 was not some 'typical Everest squall', as some authors have suggested. A day or two after the storm had hit Everest, it could still be seen on the satellite imagery heading east.

The original email I sent to Roger, which he'd forwarded to David Breashears, was replied to. Roger passed the response he received from David on to me. In this email, David had written: 'In 1996 I used the London-based Met Office. If Graham would like more information he should feel free to contact me.'

At face value, this appeared a very open and helpful approach. I took David up on his kind offer and sent him a brief email asking if he could help me with a few more details.

In this I wrote:

I presume the arrangement for the satellite forecasts was organised before you left for Nepal and that you received the forecast every so many days by satellite phone? Do you have the name of the person you contacted each time to obtain the forecast? Is there any data that you received from London that you still have on record that I could study?

After nearly two weeks, I'd received no reply. Assuming that David was probably quite a busy man, I sent a polite follow-up.

The reply came back: 'I got your message but will need a little time to locate the nine-year-old Everest Imax files.'

I received no further communication.

Two years later (March 2007), I was to resend my original email to

David Breashears, to once again give him an opportunity to make comment or input into my research.

I neither received, nor expected to receive, any reply.

The Widening Search

The only way I could reconcile the two pieces of information I'd gathered regarding the Imax team – Breashears saying he used the London-based Met Office, and Ang Tshering's declaration that Rob and Scott watched Imax, who had the weather – was if the Imax team had been receiving weather forecasts prior to the disaster of 10 May, because after that date Rob and Scott were dead, leaving what Breashears and Ang Tshering had told me as incompatible. The problem was, nothing I'd read confirmed this theory.

In an attempt to resolve this, I contacted the UK Met Office, under the Freedom of Information Act, to enquire if they'd supplied the Imax expedition weather forecasts in the spring of 1996. My assumption was that they'd be able to determine this from their forecast records and finance department, along with the dates and number of forecasts supplied.

Hopeful this would give me the break I'd been looking for, I was devastated by the unexpected reply:

> We have looked into this matter for you and discussed it with our forecasters, but unfortunately we do not hold any records of forecasts given for Mount Everest prior to 1997. I have also contacted our finance department regarding your request, but unfortunately they are unable to locate invoices so far back as 1996.

It seemed I'd missed the information I needed by one year.

In an effort to sustain my enquiries on both sides of the Atlantic, I carefully went through the detailed information I'd received from the National Science Foundation, amongst which was the name of Peter Molnar, a Senior Research Associate in Atmospheric and Planetary Sciences (now a professor at the University of Colorado). I emailed Peter to enquire whether his involvement with the Imax expedition was connected to weather forecasts or if his role had purely been on a consultancy basis in the US after the filming had been completed.

In his reply, Peter came straight to the point. He felt that those making the film were only interested in sensationalism and that the science within the programme was, at best, very limited compared to what had initially been proposed. In his opinion, the substantial grant of $1.5 million from the NSF had been squandered. I must admit I sympathised with Peter Molnar's sentiments. I found the educational material very disappointing compared to what could have been achieved for such a large sum of money. Noticeably lacking, in my opinion, was the content.

I contacted the National Centre for Atmospheric Research and the University Corporation for Atmospheric Research (UCAR), in the United States. These two, jointly operated by the UCAR, hold a substantial archive of meteorological data.

My initial correspondence was with Joey Comeaux, Leslie Forehand and Will Spangler. I informed them I was researching the disaster on Everest in 1996 and asked if they could look at the information they had archived and compare the forecasts to what actually happened. Joey Comeaux was the one who took over this task, something he did with great dedication.

It was when I received one of the many emails from Joey that my heart sank. It read:

> Graham, in what form do you need the model output? I can provide you with data files either in pure ascii or the original model format, or we can provide you with plots. The model contains a large number of surface variables (temp. at 2 meters above the surface, winds at 10 meters above the surface, precipitation) and variables at different levels in the atmosphere (temp. wind, moisture and others). If you need the actual data, we may have to get special permission from the European Centre for Medium Range Forecasts to provide you with the data.

The phrase that immediately came to mind was 'Fortune favours the brave'. I also hoped it favoured the blindly optimistic, as I hadn't got a clue what Joey was talking about.

Lay persons, like myself, assume that meteorology is merely a way of telling us if it's going to rain, about the wind, the temperature and other such variables that will determine our schedules on a day-to-day basis. Clearly, although I never considered it was quite that simple, this is a very complex subject that well deserves the title 'Atmospheric Sciences'.

I was completely out of my depth. These good people, with an already hectic workload, were going out of their way to make considerable time to research this for me. Joey's suggestion of plots seemed to be the most logical. If I had these, then maybe I could find a meteorologist at one of the universities close to where I lived to interpret them for me. I gratefully accepted Joey's suggestion of receiving them in this form. Despite the many other demands of his own work, this is exactly what he provided me with.

Looking back, the help Joey and others at the UCAR gave me, and the encouraging manner in which they approached the problem, kept me going when my morale was low. For Joey's, Will's and Leslie's support I am most grateful.

I still have the plots Joey prepared for me. I held them back in the prospect that I might obtain further material from other sources before searching out a meteorologist to interpret them for me. In the end, I never used them. The value they had to me when I first received them was probably far greater than the information they contained. They gave me hope.

Lhotse, 2006

In 2006, I returned to Nepal on a major expedition for the first time in seven years. Although my adventures to the mountains had continued in the intervening years, on private trips to more modest peaks with equally majestic summits, I was greatly excited by my return to the Himalaya.

I had joined a commercial trip, organised by Henry, to climb Lhotse. At 27,940 feet, it is the world's fourth-highest peak. Although most of Henry's climbers were there to attempt Everest, a few of us were heading up for Lhotse instead.

By 12 April, I had arrived at the familiar site of Base Camp, the gateway to Everest and Lhotse. Both routes pass through the Khumbu Icefall and share a common line until halfway up the steep ice of the Lhotse Face. At this point, climbers attempting Everest split left across the Yellow Band towards the Geneva Spur. Those for Lhotse continue up into a 2,000-ft narrow gully that sustains steep mixed ground of snow and rock all the way to the exposed summit towering above.

Despite my enthusiastic return to this familiar ground, I was unsure as to the emotions and thoughts that would surface. My previous haunting return to the South Col in 1999 would not be repeated, as our route to Lhotse veered off to the right several hundred feet below this desolate plateau. However, the ground below the divergence was where all the crucial decisions of 1996 had been taken, ones that I suspected but could not yet prove.

I wondered if voices from the past would plague my subconscious once more, or whether I would be tormented by my lack of evidence, cruelly taunted by that which I could not find. I tried my best to block out such thoughts.

As it would turn out, the events of 2006 would have unexpected consequences for my future enquiries into the 1996 tragedy, which at this particular time appeared to be faltering. I had made no real progress since I'd last spoken to Henry.

The routine of unpacking, erecting my tent in a suitable spot and settling in to this inhospitable environment had lost none of its familiarity. Kami was still Henry's Sirdar. A few of the Sherpas I had spent time with before, but the majority were new to me. This was also true for the entire climbing team, except for Geoffrey Stanford. We had been on Everest together back in 1998. My fellow climbers came across as a friendly gregarious bunch with a surfeit of adventurous spirit. I was looking forward to our times ahead.

That was until day three, when I was moving a large propane gas cylinder stored in our mess tent. As I leant forward to lift it out of the way, a pain tore across the lower right side of my back; my legs gave way at the knees. Cursing, I thrust my hand across to the table to support my weight.

'What's wrong?' asked one of the climbers sitting nearby. I can't remember who it was; I too busy wincing with the pain to take notice.

It took me 20 minutes to limp my way back to my tent, where I lay uncomfortably, cursing the stupidity of my mistake. I had done this before at home by casually lifting an object without making a conscious effort not to lean forward while doing so. This was the first time I had done it on an expedition. I was well aware that such injuries do not heal overnight and can take several weeks to recover enough so that normal strains can be placed on the spine once more.

With the Lhotse looming high above, I knew what the consequences might be if, partially recovered, I continued with the climb only to have the injury resurface in an equal or more serious state at altitude. It would place those around me in a difficult and dangerous position as they tried to extricate me from the mountainside.

I skipped the evening meal that day and breakfast the following morning. It was too painful to get up. I spent the night trying to find a position where my back didn't hurt; I failed. Around lunchtime, I inched my way across camp to Henry's tent to discuss this turn of events. He could see the pain I was in and the anguish on my face over what I had done. He had suffered a similar injury in Advanced Base Camp back in 1995, when we had been on the Tibetan side of Everest. He could see only too well the discomfort I was suffering by the way I shuffled gingerly over the ground.

'Your call,' said Henry.

His words were generous considering the problems I could cause him and others on the team if I continued up the mountain.

In bygone days I would have pressed on, but this wasn't wise. After much soul searching, I decided to throw in the towel on this year's climb and informed Henry of my decision. I wasn't sure how I was going to manage the three-day trek back to Lukla, other than one step at a time.

I made a satellite phone call to my insurance company, which I'd organised through my membership of the British Mountaineering Council, to inform them of the incident, in case matters deteriorated on my walk out. To my amazement, they were insistent that a helicopter be sent to airlift me out. An appointment would be arranged at a medical clinic in Kathmandu for when I arrived. In hindsight, I wish that helicopter had not been sent.

Visiting Henry in Base Camp was his nineteen-year-old nephew Oscar, accompanied by another teenager, Tom, who was four or five years his junior. Tom was the son of Dr Mike Brennan, a general practitioner from the Lake District who was attempting Everest this year. They were now due to depart for their walk out. However, the imminent arrival of the helicopter would provide these two with an exciting and rapid transfer back to the capital.

The day before our transport was due, I hobbled my way down to Gorak Shep, from where I had been airlifted out in 1999 by Lt Col Maden K.C. in one of the army's Squirrel helicopters. On that occasion, I had been suffering with frostbite.

We woke the next morning to find a heavy sky and a one-foot layer of dense snow covering the ground. There was no chance of a landing. Twenty-four hours later, nothing had changed.

After a radio call to Henry, we moved further down the valley to Lobuche, in the hope the weather might clear lower down. Mike, who had originally come down to wave Tom off at Gorak Shep, continued down with us, as little climbing could be achieved in these poor conditions. In fact, it would not be until the fifth day that conditions would allow the airlift to happen, by which time we had descended to the village of Pangboche.

Expecting to be boarding a helicopter the next day, I had left Base Camp carrying little more than my wallet, a toothbrush and the clothes I stood in. Clean attire and everything else I needed was waiting for me in a holdall I had deposited in the hotel baggage room back in Kathmandu. Now, several days on, I had taken on a dishevelled appearance: coarse stubble covered my face, my hair was unbrushed and my clothes were beginning to smell from the perspiration of walking and of shivering in the cold night air. I had started to notice my less than fragrant smell. I was desperate for a shower and clean garments.

My back was showing considerable signs of improvement; the walking over uneven ground had gently massaged the injury. It gave me little discomfort unless I stood still for too long. This indicated that muscle damage rather than vertebrae had caused the problem. There was a strong possibility I could have turned around and gone back up to rejoin the expedition. Several factors weighed heavily against this.

First, I had two extra passengers expecting a ride. Second, there had been several aborted attempts to fly in, for which there might well be a considerable bill if I chose to cancel at this late stage. And last, but certainly not least, I did not know how fragile this apparent recovery might be. In simple terms, I was too far down the line.

It was seven o'clock in the morning when we heard the approaching Mi 17 helicopter, visible against a background of soaring Himalayan summits with snow-fluted ridges. Large snowflakes were floating downwards from a sky filled with white billowing clouds, between which dazzling sunshine was breaking through. The morning was bitterly cold.

The landing spot for this colossal Russian machine was a small, dry-stone-walled field on the outskirts of the village. With the nose of the aircraft slightly raised, this gargantuan machine came in to land. The air just beyond the tips of the 70-ft blades sent vortexes of snow swirling upwards. Below, the downdraft ripped freshly fallen snow off the ground, blasting it across the surface in all directions away from the precise spot the pilot had chosen. As the wheels sank through the crusted snow, they touched down on the solid ground below. The small side door was flung open; a dozen local Sherpa people emerged from inside. All flights from Kathmandu to this region had been cancelled because of the weather, and had been for several days. With the incoming helicopter, paid for by my insurance, these few had managed, either through persuasion or personal contacts, to hitch a ride.

No sooner had they alighted than Oscar, Tom and I clambered in. The pilot lifted off without delay. Below I could see Tom's father waving frantically as his son departed. He covered his eyes to shield them from the painful rush of ice particles thrown up by the rising machine.

Passing above the clouds, Oscar and Tom sat on one side of the voluminous cargo hold, myself on the other. All three of us looked out of the round windows that ran down either side of the fuselage, relieved to be on our way. I understood that the last few days had been stressful for everyone, as each day had brought yet another delay.

Within an hour, the pilot had us back in Kathmandu. We landed on the far side of the airstrip, well away from the terminal building. Kathmandu was under military curfew. The country's problems had erupted into violence on the streets. Explosions and deaths had occurred; demonstrations had taken place. In an attempt to bring the escalating troubles under control, King Gyanendra, the absolute monarch, had ordered a clampdown; a series of curfews from 8 a.m. until 8 p.m. had been imposed.

Nepal's unrest had first erupted in February of 1996, when the Communist Party of Nepal (Maoist) declared its intentions to establish a People's Republic of Nepal. In the intervening time, tens of thousands had been killed and a far greater number been internally displaced. For several years, those fighting for the cause – the Maoist rebels – had been seen as violent extremists. They demanded money by extortion and took young boys from villages to swell their ranks; they were feared and outside the democratic process. They struck in small groups causing maximum damage; remote police outposts were often the sites of appalling carnage, vehicles were set alight, Buddhist monks and prostitutes had also been targeted, large numbers had been killed.

King Gyanendra had taken the throne in 2001, upon the death of his nephew Dipendra, who had been king for three days while in a coma. Dipendra had suffered what would later be claimed as self-inflicted gunshot wounds following the massacre of the preceding king, Birendra (Gyanendra's brother), and other members of the royal family. In all, ten people had died in the shooting. Prince Dipendra had been blamed for the massacre. An internal family wrangle over whom the prince should marry was cited as the cause. However, there was a very large number in Nepal who believed the present King Gyanendra, who had been in Pokhara in western Nepal at the time of the shooting, had been behind this wholesale slaughter.

In February 2005, Gyanendra took complete control. He dismissed the elected parliament and declared himself the absolute monarch. This move caused the formation of an unlikely alliance between the Maoist insurgency and the moderate democratic political parties. They united in opposition to his absolute rule. Recent food and fuel shortages had raised the temperature further; civil unrest had dramatically spilled onto the streets of Kathmandu. The stakes could have not been higher – the control of the whole country – and we had landed right in the middle of it.

We sat silently in the helicopter for the best part of an hour awaiting a military inspection. Only then would we be allowed to disembark. They were searching for potential terrorists, weapons and explosives. The airport was eerily quiet. Most aircraft were grounded. Our flight had required special permission from the army hierarchy.

As we exited the domestic arrivals building, a distraught-looking Iswari met us. 'Graham, what has happened in the Icefall? We hear people, Sherpas, have been killed this morning,' he asked, his face wrought with anguish.

These were his friends, the people he worked with. I apologised repeatedly for not being able to give him more information. In truth, we knew nothing of the accident. In May 1996, the teams at Base Camp tried to maintain a news blackout of 24 hours after the tragedy. Now such information spread freely via satellite phones and their Internet connections across the globe, often while rescue attempts were still taking place. The rush to be the first to break bad news brought about speculation and rumours rather than a considered report. No one was quite sure what had happened.

'Big problems in Kathmandu, the army is everywhere, the situation is bad,' Iswari continued. 'The only place you are safe is in Thamel. You will be OK there.'

However, Oscar had been given instructions by his uncle Henry to stay in the Summit Hotel some miles away from Thamel, in more or less the opposite direction from which Iswari wanted to take us. Barbed wire and machine-gun posts barricaded the airport's entrance road; beyond this the streets were deserted.

'My uncle has told me I have to stay at the Summit Hotel,' Oscar told him. Tom stood silently nearby.

Iswari looked at Oscar, not sure what to say, and then turned to me. 'Is Thamel OK for you, Graham?' he asked.

'Absolutely fine by me,' I replied.

'Thamel will be safer for you,' said Iswari, trying to get Oscar to change his mind.

In the back of Oscar's mind were the instructions Henry had given him. Iswari was worried that people he knew might have been killed or injured in the Icefall, we were in the middle of a volatile military curfew, and this 19 year old was struggling to grasp the seriousness of the situation. I couldn't believe it. I stepped to one side while Iswari and Oscar continued their conversation. A moment later, I heard the first signs of common sense when Oscar asked Iswari what Henry would do in this situation.

I leant forward and said, 'He would listen to Iswari.'

I got the impression that Oscar did not like my interference, perhaps because he felt it was his family's affairs. My interruption into their conversation was a mistake. I should have left it to Iswari to talk him round. Oscar told a bewildered Iswari that he wanted to go to the Summit Hotel.

Iswari was in a terrible position. Oscar's uncle Henry, the man who employed him, was the one who had originally told Oscar he had to go to the Summit Hotel. But at the time Henry had given this instruction he would have been unaware of the curfew conditions we might encounter when we landed and what Iswari would be strongly recommending. Iswari was our man on the ground, the person who had our immediate safety in mind.

If I had known what was to come next, I would have instructed Iswari to take us to Thamel. This he would have done. However, I did not. I was trying to stay out of Henry's arrangements. I'm sure if Oscar had known what was just around the corner he too would have accepted Iswari's wise recommendation.

Parked nearby was the Land Cruiser and its attendant driver. 'Can you sit in the front, Graham?' asked Iswari.

I knew instantly that I was to be the token visible Westerner sitting in full view, to steady the jittery nerves of heavily armed soldiers. I had no idea of how right I was.

After driving out of the airport, we turned left along the deserted road, not a pedestrian in sight. Dogs that normally scavenged along the roadside sheltered under cover, unnerved by the deathly silence that hung over this normally busy place. The rasp of our exhaust broke through the air. Faces peered from behind the shutters as we passed by; people were too frightened to stand in their doorways.

Within a quarter of a mile, we reached the first military checkpoint. Other vehicles leaving the airport, in the opposite direction towards Thamel, had been bearing a white flag. We were not; this concerned me.

Possibly because of the close proximity of the airport, we passed through this first obstacle with little delay, eased by Iswari having a few words with the officer in charge. This was not the case at the next crossroads.

Soldiers, protected by sandbags, held rifles hard against their shoulders, their fingers nervously placed on the trigger as they took careful aim at our approaching unmarked vehicle. The driver slowed to a sedate pace. I cannot begin to imagine what thoughts were going through his mind. Oscar, Tom and Iswari sat quietly in the back. This was risky, very risky.

In the last few days, soldiers had been attacked and killed, civilians also; explosions had destroyed properties and riots had taken place. The terrified soldiers we were edging towards had no idea if we might be the decoy for another deadly strike, or where the next one was going to come from. I hoped that beneath my heavy stubble and dishevelled appearance they might be able to see I was a foreigner.

The relief on the young soldiers' faces to see that we were not a threat was matched by my own as they lowered their guns. Once again Iswari began to talk his way through. The officer in charge was less sympathetic than the previous one had been, remonstrating with Iswari for travelling in an unauthorised manner during the curfew. We were let through.

By the time we were approaching our fourth such checkpoint, I lost my temper. Without turning my head, as I didn't want to make any sudden movements inside the vehicle, I said out loud, 'This is getting f**king dangerous.'

Iswari knew how right I was and didn't need to respond. Oscar sat in silence. The soldiers this far out were at greater risk from surprise attack, and their heightened state meant they kept their guns trained on us even when we pulled up to stop, their fingers resting uneasily against the trigger. Their youthful faces were wracked with fear. Their eyes were like saucers as they scanned the buildings around them; others nervously kept an eye behind.

Iswari's words were cutting little ice with the commanding officer. He resorted to making frantic calls on his mobile phone to connections he had within the ministries. His demeanour of a calm 'Mr Fix It' had long since vanished. Panic was written right across his face. No one was more relieved than him when we pulled up at the Summit Hotel, a short distance behind checkpoint number five.

As we clambered out of the vehicle, I turned to Oscar and spat out the words, 'Next time bloody listen to him.' I had nothing else to say to Oscar about what I saw as a ridiculous decision. He wasn't perhaps to know the dangers until he had seen them for himself, although I felt Iswari had given him reasonable warning. There is no doubt in my mind that both Oscar and Tom were fully aware of what a lucky escape we had just had. I felt heartily sorry for Tom. He had not said a single word since Iswari had met us at the airport.

As the two young men went off to get a room, Iswari sat down opposite me in the hotel garden. 'We cannot move for nine hours, until the curfew ends,' he informed me.

'That's OK, don't worry about it,' I replied. I understood what he had just been through.

'Time for some beer and a curry,' I said in an attempt to lighten the conversation. 'Would you like some?'

He declined the offer; he'd lost his appetite.

It was while I was tucking into my meal that the hotel's English managing director approached me. He was aware we had been airlifted that morning. However, the sight of an unshaven and rather scruffy-looking man eagerly consuming beer and curry in the hotel garden was not conducive to the image they were hoping to portray.

'Can I offer you the use of one of our rooms to take a shower?' he asked. 'Complimentary, of course.'

'Thank you, that's very kind,' I replied. 'As soon as I've finished my meal.'

'The key will be waiting at reception when you are ready,' he said before departing.

Iswari wandered off and began making phone calls on his mobile. I presumed he was trying to glean information as best he could from our current location.

News had begun to filter through that a group of Sherpas had been climbing along a narrow corridor in the Khumbu Icefall that morning, at about 18,300 feet, when the accident happened. The reports coming in suggested that one or two of the large ice towers above the area they were in had collapsed without warning; this had caused the wall of ice directly above the Sherpas to partially cave in. The debris struck the last six Sherpas in the line, of whom three were completely buried. Those around were unable to get to these three because of the volume of ice; the others had fortunately only suffered minor injuries. Three more lives, those of Sherpas, had been lost in the notoriously unpredictable Khumbu Icefall. The accident would be felt by the whole of their community.

'We'll be leaving in half an hour,' announced Iswari. 'I've called in some favours.'

'Great,' I said, not quite sure what this meant. My shower was going to have to wait.

He left me to finish my meal and returned 20 minutes later, saying, 'Right, time to go, Graham,' as he beckoned me to follow him out of the hotel entrance and around the corner.

Parked before us was a mid-blue van with thick wire mesh covering all the windows, including the windscreen.

'Get in,' said Iswari, holding open one of the two rear doors. Inside were 15 police officers in full riot gear. I stepped back for a second and glanced down either side of the vehicle. As I suspected, it had POLICE emblazoned on both sides. Yep, I thought, that should let the Maoists and angry crowds know exactly who we are.

I climbed inside and settled on the end of the wooden bench that ran along the right-hand side; on the opposite side there was another. Iswari got in and closed the door behind him.

The occupants, seated along either side, were facing in and with bowed heads they stared blankly at the worn metal floor in nervous apprehension. They looked up as I got in, no doubt wondering what use a tourist might be in a tight situation. The body armour they wore covered the front of the torso, knees and shins. Each had a battered steel helmet with protective face screen and held a thick plastic riot shield. The weapon they had been issued with was a three-foot-long rigid bamboo stick. With these, they had to face hostile crowds of their own countrymen who would hurl bricks, lumps of concrete and heavy metal objects. The officer in charge carried an automatic rifle with a curving magazine of bullets and a handgun at his side. As the van pulled away, I was beginning to wonder where this epic journey was going to end.

With 17 people crammed inside, the windows firmly closed and the oppressive sun heating the metal exterior, the temperature inside the vehicle quickly rose to an almost unbearable level. It was shortly after midday and I had been airlifted out of the Everest region by helicopter. I had been a legitimate target for the Nepalese army by travelling in an unmarked vehicle under military curfew. Now I was a legitimate target for both the Maoists and the violent mobs seeking justice, because I was an occupant in a police riot vehicle out on active patrol. I looked down at the floor, trying to control my overwhelming urge to laugh at the ridiculous situation I was in. I had seen comedy films like this, but this was for real, and it was no laughing matter for my fellow occupants. As we turned each corner there was the possibility that the vehicle might be confronted by a large group of protesters armed with missiles to hurl at us.

The current problems were not seen as involving tourists in any way, and in that lay a precarious safety. I bore no identification to say I was press or anything else of that nature. If the situation arose where the police in the vehicle had to take action and I was spotted, what might the crowd's interpretation be?

Kathmandu was rife with rumours and counter-rumours. What if a protestor in such a volatile situation said he thought he saw I was carrying a weapon? I wanted out of that riot vehicle as soon as possible. This was a very bad idea.

The troubles had first erupted into violence on 13 February 1996, at the time when I had been packing my equipment and making arrangements for my imminent departure for Nepal. This was only three months prior to the disaster of 10 May, an event that gripped the media more than this country's worrying unrest. In fact, three months to the day after the Maoists' 'people's war' began with its brutal killings, the dramatic airlift of Beck Weathers and Makalu Gau from the Western Cwm hit the headlines. I found it difficult to comprehend that ten years had passed since I had witnessed the disastrous outcome of 10 May 1996, yet the images in my mind, the memories of those events, were undiminished. It was a period during which this beautiful country had been ravaged by the bitter consequences of civil war.

After about ten minutes, the blue van swung into a barbed-wired but otherwise open compound. It was full of police vehicles – the sort of place the Maoists would go out of their way to bomb.

Iswari, who hadn't spoken since we had left the Summit Hotel, looked up and said, 'We will only be here for ten minutes before moving on.'

He was right; we were going out onto Kathmandu's deserted streets once more with a new crew of riot police. It was a shift change.

Within a minute of leaving the compound, we had turned two

corners. The vehicle felt isolated in a hostile world; the lifeless streets bore a menacing presence. Suddenly the driver eased his foot off the throttle. The van began to weave. My fellow occupants raised themselves with bended knees and turned to peer nervously out of the windscreen. Their grip on the rigid bamboo sticks tightened. I couldn't see what was happening up front. Peering through the toughened glass window of the rear door and then through the small squares of the thick wire mesh that lay beyond, I saw hundreds of half-bricks and lumps of concrete scattered across the road. Smouldering piles of burnt tyres that had melted the surface of the tarmac road pushed a thin column of black smoke into the sky. The acrid smell of burning rubber filled the air. Only a matter of hours before, it had been the scene of a blood-soaked confrontation between police and protestors.

Three hundred yards further down the road we came to an abrupt halt. Nobody in the vehicle moved.

'This is where we get out,' said Iswari, as he leant over to open the rear doors.

I eagerly scrambled from the wooden bench I had been sitting on.

As the police vehicle pulled away, the sensation I had was that the further away it was from me, the safer I would be. Iswari and I both gave a sigh of relief. We had survived.

A short distance away, I could see a few tourists aimlessly walking on Thamel's unusually quiet streets. A more lenient approach was taken to the curfew in this area. Visitors could move unhindered but were expected not to stray from the district. Businesses were allowed to open. The majority of traders had their shutters firmly closed.

Here, I was confronted by a sight I had not seen in Thamel for more than a decade: that of a cow grazing on a pile of rubbish. During the intervening period, better organised, and more frequent, refuse collections took place. This, combined with a concerted effort to keep cows from straying into the tourist area, had made such sightings a thing of the past – that was until now. With the recent escalation in the troubles, street collections had ceased. Restaurants and shops had discarded their waste on the road outside. Revered by the Hindus, these creatures had wandered unhindered into the relative calm of the tourist quarter; here, they nuzzled into piles of decaying refuse. The cellulose contained in old newspapers also caught their eye. It was not unusual to see a page or two of the *Kathmandu Post* wrapped around their thick muscular tongue as they digested yesterday's news. To the cow, it was no more than a tasty edition to add to their dietary requirements, but for the people of Nepal it brought frightening news of the country's spiralling unrest. However, this bovine intruder brought with it a sense of tranquillity, even normality; a short distance away, humanity's potential for violent conflict hung heavily in the air.

Before going our separate ways, I turned to Iswari and said, 'That was very hard for you today, thank you.' He knew that I meant each and every word.

'People don't understand how difficult it can be. Those army checkpoints, I had to telephone very high up to get us through, very high up.' He felt the need to repeat the last few words. 'I do this so I can send money back to my family in the east of Nepal. People don't understand,' he continued.

I had never seen him so openly distressed. These were difficult times for him. The events of the day had more than taken their toll.

That afternoon, shortly after Iswari and I had got back to Thamel, nearly half a million unarmed pro-democracy demonstrators took to the streets of Kathmandu, chanting for the King to relinquish power back to the people. Alongside other tourists, I watched, for the best part of an hour, as a seemingly endless stream of men made their way through the outskirts of Thamel. Some protestors held banners aloft, all were chanting loudly, but still they came, marching four or five deep. There were so many coming from all directions there was nothing either the police or army could do except stand and watch. Later that evening, 21 April 2006, King Gyanendra announced that he would return political power to the people and called for elections to be held as soon as possible. He was hanging on to his privileged position by a thread.

I spent the first few days back home rueing the early end to my Lhotse climb, which in actual terms had never got off the ground. Also preying on my mind were the events that had taken place immediately after we had met Iswari at the airport. I wrestled with whether or not I should write to Henry.

In more youthful days, a long list of escapades I had undertaken with little or no regard to the consequences they might have on others had been left in my wake. I had been a teenager once and treated those much older than me with a degree of disdain. What could they tell me about life that I didn't already know? Now I knew.

Eventually, I decided that the consequences could have been so serious that I couldn't let it go. I knew Henry could receive emails at Base Camp, so I wrote to him.

This was a mistake on my behalf. Not that it shouldn't have been said, rather I should have discussed this privately with Henry at a later date. Such messages received by email are, more often than not, seen by the recipient as confrontational.

I could see how Henry might have taken it that way. He had been more than generous to me over the last ten years; the manner of my approach had been poorly thought out. He was in Base Camp with teams of climbers on both Lhotse and Everest. With all the attention and mental drain this entailed, my email was the last thing he needed.

I received no reply. I sent two further innocuous emails a week or so later to wish his climbers whom I'd met briefly at Base Camp all the best for the climbs ahead. I heard nothing back.

I didn't regret what I had said to Henry, rather the method by which I had conveyed it. The door of friendship appeared to have been slammed firmly shut: a door that I would need to be open if my enquiries into the tragic events of 1996 proved fruitful.

The Meteorologist in His Garden

Amongst the books written in the wake of the 1996 disaster was National Geographic's *Everest: Mountain Without Mercy* by Broughton Coburn, with an afterword by David Breashears. This publication was the nearest I could find to an official/authorised account describing the making of the IMAX film *Everest*. It was a book in which I hoped to find significant references to weather forecasts being received by the Imax expedition.

With a copy duly ordered, it was only a matter of days before the doorbell rang, announcing the arrival of my parcel and the next phase in my research. It turned out to be a large-format glossy book, adorned with excellent photographs and easy-to-read, well-spaced print: the sort of publication that could be referred to as a coffee table book, that many might flick through, admiring the photography or dallying over a page or two out of curiosity.

However, mine was no passing interest. I wanted to look carefully at the information this contained. It wasn't long before I came across the first reference to meteorology.

On page 28, I read:

> Greg MacGillivray and David Breashears wanted to produce a film that would educate as it entertained. To identify and explore the unique issues that relate to Mount Everest, they carefully assembled a team of ten academic advisers. These advisers, all long-term observers of the Himalaya, portrayed an unusual and dynamic mountain. Geologists described Everest not as a static geological monument but as a mountain in motion; meteorologists explained that the Himalaya and its associated plateau are thought to influence much of the world's weather patterns . . .

These were noble aspirations with a highly commendable purpose. Yet, as I read on, I was puzzled as to why, with a budget of $7 million and ten scientific advisers, I could find no reference to the Imax expedition receiving accurate weather forecasts on a regular basis, in particular for their high-risk summit day, originally planned for 9 May.

Eventually, on page 204, came an unambiguous reference to weather information being received, but from the chronological order of the book, with regards to the 1996 Imax expedition, I took this to be after the tragedy. I could find no specific reference in Broughton's book to weather forecasts being received before 10 May, which surprised me and left me a little confused as to when these forecasts were first received:

> The *Everest* team [Imax] were pinning their hopes on British meteorologist Martin Harris, whose forecasts of Jet Stream movement had so far been remarkably accurate. For additional input, Liesl Clark [who had returned to the US and was at NOVA's offices in Boston] contacted Bob Rice's 'Weather Window,' while Roger Bilham [who'd also been with them, but had returned early to the US because of academic commitments] called weather scientists of the National Climate and Atmospheric Research Centre (NCAR) in Boulder. All were scrutinizing the satellite images . . .

As meteorologist Martin Harris was actually named, then sensibly he had to be my next line of enquiry. Especially as when Martin is mentioned for the second time on page 209 it states: 'On the night of May 20, the team finally received confirmation from meteorologist Martin Harris in England that the jet stream had moved to the north.' Was he the source of the weather forecasts prior to the disaster of 10 May? And why the need for additional input from Bob Rice's Weather Window (a company that provided weather reports for yacht races, record attempts, etc.) and Roger Bilham if Martin Harris's forecasts had been remarkably accurate so far? And if these had been accurate, why was there no mention of their significance in the reports and accounts that followed the disaster?

After a brief search on the Internet, it transpired that Martin Harris was currently working as a director of Oxford Scientific Services Ltd. I telephoned Martin, speaking to him at some length about meteorology and in particular the Everest region, with specific reference to the spring of 1996.

From the information Martin gave me, it soon became apparent he was regarded as a meteorologist with significant experience in mountainous areas. As a specialist in the interpretation of weather satellite imagery, he had some 40 years' experience in the field. In the 1980s and early 1990s, he carried out meteorological research in the vicinity of Mount Everest. In 1991, he looked at the airflow above Mount Everest using radiosonde balloons, satellite systems and other equipment, as part of an exercise called the Mount Everest Meteorological Experiment (MEMEX1991). This work was supported in part by the UK Met Office, and since then they have consulted him from time to time about weather patterns and processes in this part of the Himalaya.

I advised Martin of the references to him in *Everest: Mountain Without Mercy*. He was quite surprised at what these contained. He kindly agreed to answer my questions via email to give him an opportunity to consider them carefully before responding.

In essence, Martin explained he'd received a totally unexpected phone call from a woman called Liesl Clark a day or so after the disaster. She wanted to ask him about the weather in the Everest region, as members of the Imax team were still on the mountain. Following this up, he then telephoned one of his colleagues at the UK Met Office to find out the weather situation.

Martin then received a second phone call from Liesl Clark, on the same day as the first, during which he advised her that the climbers should descend and wait for more settled conditions. According to Martin, this was the only contact he had with the Imax team: that the generalities he discussed with Liesl Clark during those two conversations were the only meteorological information with which he supplied them.

I think this episode is best summed up in Martin's own words:

> I was not in a position to supply the detailed information which Liesl Clark requested, and although I have never met her, she sounded to be an intelligent and sympathetic woman, and she seemed to understand that, even with the best of intentions to mitigate a disaster, I could not provide this information from a back garden in England . . .
>
> I am still more puzzled to know the reason why this expedition thought it was worthwhile phoning me at all, given that they had never contacted me earlier.

Martin's response and confirmation of his involvement with the Imax team was clearly at odds with how his role was portrayed in the book. This surprised me.

That week I went to my usual Friday night meeting with Geoff Scarth, the faith in my research restored and Martin's printed answers in hand. Sitting on the opposite side of a small wooden table supping my pint of real ale, I watched Geoff as he carefully read through the replies. Undisturbed by the conversations of those round about, his head nodded as he absorbed the point each question and its answer made. With a broad nose and distinguished face, his courtroom years had taught him the skill of turning a stern look into a disarming smile in the blink of an eye. The lawyer in him also meant he wanted to see the information for himself rather than hear it second hand. Only a printed-out copy of the exact emails I had received would suffice.

Reaching the end of the document, he paused for a moment, smiled and then said, 'But this doesn't prove anything.'

A long discussion ensued, at the end of which all we could agree was that something here didn't add up. I'd found a difference between what had been written and the facts with regard to the Imax expedition, but deep down I knew Geoff was right.

It could quite easily be said that because Broughton Coburn wrote *Everest: Mountain Without Mercy* David Breashears had no control or say over its content. However, when you consider that David wrote the afterword to this book and that his photography was included, you would assume that he would have read it, but maybe he didn't. Nevertheless, I felt there were gaps in the picture portrayed.

A Need for a Greater Understanding

My findings with regard to Martin Harris made it evident I needed to look carefully through the other significant accounts that had followed 10 May. Having previously read *Into Thin Air*, the next obvious book was *The Climb* by Anatoli Boukreev and G. Weston DeWalt. However, by doing this I would be following a well-trodden path, one that I felt might have accidentally steered everyone away from a more deadly truth. I wanted to look at some of the others beforehand. I would consider *The Climb*, but not quite yet.

First I looked at *The Death Zone* by Matt Dickinson, published in 1997. I wanted to understand how the period leading up to the afternoon of 10 May had been seen on the other side of the mountain.

Matt had been attempting the north side of Everest from Tibet. He had been commissioned to film a documentary for British television's Channel 4 about actor and would-be Everest summiteer Brian Blessed making his third attempt on the mountain. Along with a small film crew, they had employed high-altitude expert Alan Hinkes to operate the camera on Everest's upper reaches. This compact unit had joined a commercial expedition run by a UK company called Himalayan Kingdoms. Amongst their staff was qualified mountain guide Martin Barnicott.

Matt describes the weather conditions at north side Advanced Base Camp on 9 May 1996:

> All day the wind had been building in intensity, and now it was blowing at force four or five – enough to cause me to doubt that we would be leaving the next morning.
>
> 'What do you think the chances of the weather clearing tomorrow?' I asked Al [Alan Hinkes].
>
> 'Not likely at all. From the look of this stuff we're in for a good few days of unsettled conditions,' he replied.
>
> 'We'll just have to wake up tomorrow and see how it is,' Barney [Martin Barnicott] chipped in, 'but I have to say it doesn't look good.'

At approximately the same time as this team were discussing the weather conditions they could see on the north side of the mountain, I had been on the radio to Henry. Matt and his team were at 21,000 feet, a similar height to myself at the upper end of the Western Cwm; the only difference was that they were on the other side of the mountain.

On the north side, Matt relates what they saw on 10 May, the morning they had planned to move to the upper camps in readiness for their summit attempt.

'What's the verdict?' I [Matt] asked them.
'We're not happy about it,' Al said.
'You see those clouds?' Barney pointed up to the north where a milky haze clouded the atmosphere. 'The whole system is unstable.'

At 4 p.m., a ferocious wind and blizzard conditions struck them at Advanced Base Camp. It was only a few hours after Alan Hinkes and Martin Barnicott had given their experienced opinions.

High above them, six Indian climbers had set out that morning from the top camp on their summit attempt. They were caught up in these rapidly deteriorating conditions. Half the team had turned back. The other three, Tsewang Samanla, Dorje Morup and Tsewang Paljor, pressed on, claiming in a radio call to their Base Camp to have reached the summit shortly before 4 p.m. Nepalese time. In doing so, they had foregone their only chance of survival. They had been gripped by summit fever, which offered them the first Indian ascent of Everest's northern flanks. To do this, they had ignored the obvious signs around them that should have told them to retreat. They died on their descent.

Meanwhile, on the south side, we had woken up at Camp 3 on 10 May to observe continuing poor conditions high on Everest. We delayed our departure until after our second radio conversation with Henry at midday, during which we raised our concerns – again. We were struck by the storm on the South Col at 6.30 p.m. that evening. The observations and interpretations of conditions made by Matt Dickinson, Alan Hinkes and Martin Barnicott seemed to match those of our team.

The book I decided to study next was *Sheer Will* by Michael Groom, the lone surviving guide from Rob Hall's team. In fact, he and Jon Krakauer were the only two from that team who reached the summit and lived to tell the tale.

In Michael's book, which is about his climbing career, a solitary chapter is dedicated to the events of 1996. Because of this, he concentrates largely on 10–11 May, and therefore the information about the days leading up to the disaster is limited.

However, one particular point, earlier in Michael's book, caught my eye: his mention of a weather report being used on Everest in 1993, some three years before the disaster of 10 May. I contacted Michael in Australia to ask him if the UK Met Office had been used in 1996.

He responded:

> I first used the information from the British Met Office in 1993 when the British Everest Expedition for that year passed on the forecast to me. It proved to be very accurate, with a predicted weather window of 24 hrs with wind speeds of around 10 kph for 10 May 93. Harry Taylor and I summited as a result. [This forecast had been requested by the British Army.]
> Access to the British Met Office was used again by someone but I don't recall who in 1996.

I sought clarification on this final point:

> Am I correct in assuming this recollection refers to prior to the tragic events, as I'm sure when you got down to Base Camp your thoughts will have been about those who had suffered terrible injuries and the friends you had lost rather than the weather?

Michael answered: 'You are correct, my recollection refers to prior to the tragic events.'

In a subsequent email, I asked Michael if Rob had discussions with, and received weather forecasts from, the Imax team.

Michael: 'Rob sometimes had discussions with other teams and may have received the weather forecast from Imax, but I wasn't involved with this discussion.'

I pushed the point with Michael: 'If you could just confirm whether you recall Rob having his own weather forecasting or not?'

Michael: 'I have had a pretty good memory of the events relating to the summit day of Everest '96, but I can't remember a single thing about Rob's weather forecasting, sorry.'

I understood Michael's reply. I don't think Rob had his own forecast. My belief is that Rob was receiving information from another team that did.

Michael's answers strengthened my belief that the Imax team had been receiving weather forecasts before 10 May.

His account of being lost on the South Col and their desperate attempts to locate Camp 4 I found chilling reading: 'Today, looking back, I realise we had staggered depressingly close to C4 before staggering away in the opposite direction.'

At that time, Michael had with him Beck Weathers, who was to suffer terrible frostbite injuries. Nearby, Neal Beidleman was aiding Yasuko Namba, who would die of exposure the following morning. Had either of these two pairs been the head torches I'd spotted in the distance as I arrived at the South Col that evening?

I already knew what Geoff's response would be, before I showed him Michael's answers.

'Recollections and discussions he was not party to. You'll need much more than this, my lad!' was what I received after he'd read them.

I expected no less from Geoff. He was not deliberately pouring cold water on this painstaking research. Rather, he wanted to keep my feet firmly on the ground. Several people had died in the storm of 10 May, others had been badly injured. If I was going to put anything into print, I had to make the utmost effort to ensure it was correct.

However, for my motivation, it was important to me that Geoff saw I was making progress, albeit slow. Each snippet of information I uncovered would bring about lengthy conversations between us, ones that would in turn give me ideas for further lines of enquiry. The responses I'd received from Michael were no exception to this.

One episode Michael had chosen to tell me about was of an actual event on summit day. I had not asked.

I arrived at the South Summit at 10 a.m. as the lead guide for the Rob Hall group and here I waited for 45 mins for the remainder of our group, including Rob Hall who was last. During this time I noticed the wind speed increase dramatically and suggested to Rob on his arrival that we head down because of it. We did not.

It seemed that Michael was haunted by the events of 10 May. Had Rob listened to him and heeded the signs, had they headed down at this point, then it is highly probable that no one in Rob's team would have died. Beck Weathers might have returned to Camp 4 relatively uninjured.

In view of my suspicions with regard to weather forecasts, I needed to understand the clients' thoughts as they moved up the mountain in readiness for their attempt on 10 May.

Lene Gammelgaard, a client of Scott's, returned from Everest that year to write her book *Climbing High*. This account I found perceptive. She noticed what was happening within her team and its relationship with others.

On 9 May, when I was on the radio to Henry, Lene and her fellow climbers were in the vicinity of the Yellow Band. She writes with reference to this point in their climb: 'The weather has deteriorated – wind!'

As their two teams climb higher, over the Geneva Spur, she continues:

> It is storming big time, and I try to follow the Sherpa in front of me so I'll be certain to find the route around the edge of the slate heap [Geneva Spur] . . .
>
> The gusts are now so fierce I'm thrown off my feet; I have to cling to the rock to avoid being blown off and down the Nepalese side of the mountain.

During the afternoon, Lene and other members of Scott's and Rob's teams reach the South Col:

> Aha! So, this is the South Col. A living inferno. Gale-force winds battle us as we struggle to pitch our tents . . .
>
> The gale is so fierce, we take to wordless communication.

I was particularly interested in Lene's thoughts as she lay in her tent on the South Col, contemplating the summit attempt ahead.

> I wish Scott wasn't taking the risk of being here . . .
>
> Still stormy, I must rest. Wonder if Scott and Rob will decide to proceed if the storm dies out. I hope we'll take off and simultaneously don't want to – not enough of a stable weather pattern so far . . .
>
> 6.00pm – storm. 7.00pm – storm. Hard to imagine it calming down tonight or staying calm for very long . . .
>
> Can't help but admire Scott's decision. This kind of gambling must be what's gotten him to the summit so many times. I would have chosen a wider margin of safety and waited below for more stable conditions. But I want to summit and have no scruples. Apparently nobody else does either.

I was concerned by Lene's use of the words 'a wider margin of safety'. It indicated that the clients might have been aware of the existence of a weather forecast and the information it contained. I emailed Lene to ask if she could clarify what she had meant by this phrase. Unfortunately, I received no reply.

Many unanswered questions had perplexed me since 10 May 1996. One in particular appeared to have no logical explanation. When the climbers and guides of Rob's and Scott's teams were descending from the summit, fighting for their lives and struggling through the storm to get down to Camp 4 on the South Col, why hadn't Anatoli come to ask our team for help?

We were in two large tents, referred to as 'Himalayan hotels', only a matter of 50 feet away. He'd gone round the tents of Rob's, Scott's and the Taiwanese expeditions, so why not ours? Anatoli not only knew us as friends but had climbed with some of us on the Tibetan side of Everest the previous year. We had with us five strong Sherpas. We were fresh onto the South Col that evening with full oxygen supplies. We were his best, if not only, chance.

The days that immediately followed 10 May were not the time to ask such questions. It was too soon afterwards. The pain and anguish, the remorse, were still apparent. Added to this, Anatoli was not on our team, therefore affording me little opportunity to talk to him in the aftermath. Their leaderless expedition was trying to come to terms with what had happened, while simultaneously making plans to pack up their camp and head back home.

Had Anatoli forgotten we were coming one day behind them for our attempt on 11 May, or had he not been told?

I sat back in my chair with a copy of *The Climb* in one hand and an early edition of *Into Thin Air* in the other. The latter had on the front cover a haunting photograph of Anatoli climbing out alone along the steep and precariously corniced upper section of the South East Ridge towards the Hillary Step. The single rope attached to his waist was being lifted high into the air by the strength of the winds through which he was battling. I stared at this image with sadness as I reflected back to early on in the 1996 expedition. Memories came flooding back of me sitting around on the many large rocks that lay randomly around our Base Camp, chatting with Anatoli and my fellow teammates. He'd spent much of his spare time socialising in our camp. The air had regularly been filled with laughter and the sound of our conversations.

I looked to *The Climb* for answers. One of the first quotes from the book that struck me was: 'Boukreev found himself alone, thinking about the decision he'd made to sign on to the Mountain Madness expedition.'

In the planning stages, Anatoli had been going to join our expedition. That was until he was offered a lot more money to join Scott's instead. Anatoli had perhaps been beginning to regret this change. I sensed that he felt a bit of an outsider, not fitting comfortably into this high-dollar guiding.

It was not from *The Climb* but from two independent sources that further confirmation of Anatoli's isolation would emerge. In one of the emails I'd received from Michael Groom, he'd stated:

> I was included in the discussion about summit days. I remember very clearly a meeting with Scott, Neal [Neal Beidleman, a guide for Scott Fischer], Rob, Andy Harris [the other guide for Rob Hall] and myself. What I also remember was the Russian guide [Anatoli] from Scott's team not being there and this I thought a little strange.

The fact that Scott's head guide, Anatoli, was not at the meeting was not only strange but slightly disconcerting, and an observation by Lene Gammelgaard raised the level of my concern. She both saw and understood the relationships that had developed within the hierarchy of the Mountain Madness team. In *Climbing High*, Lene describes an interesting situation around the time Anatoli arrived at Camp 2 on 6 May:

> Anatoli arrives. He's the strongest of all of us, but he has ended up in a weird position in relation to Scott and Neal. It's as if they have bonded like a couple of schoolkids and they are keeping Anatoli out of their club.

I was beginning to suspect that Anatoli had not been fully involved in the planning, and in consequence may have been unaware of all the facts.

In the days running up to summit attempts, we'd seen less of Anatoli. Therefore, I can't be sure he was aware of our summit day, or the fact we'd been asked by Rob and Scott to fall back and make our bid on 11 May. Nor did I know if Anatoli knew of a weather forecast. I was hoping that Anatoli's description of the weather in early May would indicate if he was using his experience or a forecast. I wondered whether there would be any mention of our team on the South Col.

In the following, I have quoted what I consider to be significant observations made by Anatoli, along with thoughts and important conversations he had during the ascent to the South Col. All these are taken directly from Anatoli's and Weston DeWalt's *The Climb*.

LHOTSE FACE, EN ROUTE TO CAMP 3, 8 MAY
Anatoli, on the way up with Rob's and Scott's teams, passed the Imax expedition who were descending. A point at which he spoke with Ed Viesturs, the lead climber on the Imax expedition.

Anatoli:

> 'We're coming down,' Ed told me. He said they didn't like the weather, that it was too unstable and they were going to hang back for a few days and see if the weather would stabilize.

Anatoli:

> Like Ed Viesturs, I was not happy with conditions on the mountain. After more than two decades of climbing, I had developed certain intuitions, and my feeling was that things were not right. For several days the weather had not been stable, and high winds had been blowing at higher elevations.

SOUTH COL, 9 MAY

When he arrived at the South Col, around 2 p.m., Anatoli found the wind gusting in excess of 60 mph. His worst fears were being realised.

Anatoli:

> For me, one of the most difficult things during an ascent of Everest is a squall that tries to rip you off the mountain. It is one of my greatest enemies at high altitude. Almost always, if I can choose, I would prefer foul, calm weather over any day during which the wind is blowing as fiercely as it was at the South Col that afternoon.

As the afternoon wore on, the intensity of the wind grew. Seriously concerned about the unstable weather, Anatoli decided to speak with Rob to find out what he was planning to do. Rob told him: 'My experience is that often it is calm after a squall like this, and if it clears in the night, we will make our bid tomorrow.'

Anatoli:

> For some reason I cannot explain I did not share Rob Hall's optimism, and I thought it highly unlikely the weather would stabilize. My intuitions continued to bother me, and I fully expected that we would not climb the next day.

Anatoli:

> I told Scott, 'I don't think conditions are so very good, and I think we should consider descending.' Then, I told Scott that I had spoken with Rob about the weather, and I told him of Rob's intentions to wait and see if the storm cleared. After our conversation, it was clear to me that Scott agreed with Rob. If the weather cleared, we would climb.

Anatoli was far from being alone in his concerns over a summit bid the next day. According to his account in *The Climb*, there were similar feelings of doubt amongst Scott's clients. This was also true amongst the members of Rob's expedition; of these, four were sharing a tent: Lou Kasischke, Doug Hansen, Beck Weathers and Andy Harris. All but Andy Harris, a guide for their expedition, thought a summit bid the next day was a bad idea.

In addition to the weather, Anatoli was also concerned about the oxygen supply for Scott's team. He was well aware that they had little more than was needed for one summit attempt. There would not be a second. Scott's clients had been told as much. The safety margin of the oxygen was minimal, hardly even enough for the team to spend a second night on the South Col should the planned attempt not go ahead.

They had enough oxygen for one attempt. The weather had not been stable for days. Anatoli had told Scott that he thought they should consider descending to wait for more settled conditions (a sentiment apparently shared by the majority of the clients). Despite all of this, Rob and Scott went on to put both their businesses and the safety of their clients at stake by making a summit attempt on 10 May. One wonders what on earth possessed them to risk an ascent that day when it looked doomed to failure before they started.

The subject of the weather was not one Anatoli shied away from. He wrote of his intuitions and feelings based on more than two decades of climbing. I struggled to think of a single reason why Anatoli would not have mentioned a weather forecast had he known of one.

SOUTH COL, AROUND 5 P.M., 10 MAY (AFTER ANATOLI HAD SUMMITED EVEREST)

Weston DeWalt:
> Boukreev estimates that he arrived at Camp IV somewhere around 5 p.m. As he approached the cluster of Mountain Madness tents, he saw several Sherpas, including Lhakpa Galgen Sherpa, a climbing Sherpa from Henry Todd's Himalayan Guides, who was establishing a camp for Henry Todd. Lhakpa and Boukreev exchanged a greeting.

It is my strong belief that this moment was pivotal in the disaster that was beginning to unfold. It clarified so much that had puzzled me since 1996.

Normally, teams depart from Camp 3 between 6 a.m. and 8 a.m., arriving at the South Col shortly after midday, in readiness to commence their summit attempts that night. However, our team (Henry Todd's) had delayed the expected departure because of the unsettled weather we could see high on the South East Ridge. At midday, when we made our scheduled radio call to Henry, we were still there.

Leaving camp between midday and 1 p.m., the first of our team began to arrive on the South Col around 5.30 p.m., much later than Anatoli, or anyone else, would normally have expected. Anatoli, having seen none of our climbing team at 5 p.m., will have naturally assumed that Lhakpa was there to erect the tent in advance of us coming up the next day. His assumption would have been that once Lhakpa had finished the task he would either stay with Rob's or Scott's Sherpas or quickly head back down. What Anatoli would not have expected is that we'd be arriving a short while later. It appeared that Scott may not have kept Anatoli, his head guide, informed of what would turn out to be crucial facts.

SOUTH COL, NIGHT OF 10 MAY

Anatoli tried his utmost to gather climbers and Sherpas together to put out a rescue party for the missing climbers. He went round the tents of Rob's clients and Sherpas, also Scott Fischer's and the Taiwanese. Those he located, he would later say, were 'either asleep, unable or unwilling to help'. It was an impossible task for him to undertake by himself. Outside, the storm was raging harder than ever, the intensifying blizzard reducing visibility to a few feet.

Anatoli did not know we were there, probably little more than 15 yards away from him.

Early the following morning, 11 May, Mark Pfetzer, Jabion and I departed from the South Col. Some time after, Anatoli emerged to see our two tents with the large letters HG spray-painted on the side. Only this time he will have noticed the activity of our climbers and Sherpas who'd remained behind. At this exact moment, he will have realised we'd in fact been on the South Col all night. This sight must have devastated him, and he would have been haunted afterwards by the thought that, had he known, had he alerted us, more lives could almost certainly have been saved.

I'd seen Anatoli at the 'cocktail party' in Kathmandu several days after these events but not during the intervening period. He hadn't walked out with Scott's clients but had remained in Base Camp for several days. Casting my mind back, I'm not sure why I didn't ask the question of him then. It was possibly because of the bizarre nature of the gathering at the Yak and Yeti Hotel, or the fact I understood that if he'd known we were on the South Col he'd have come for help. Most likely I thought the painful wounds were too recent, that a better time would come where such discussions might sound less like recriminations on my behalf. I had no way of knowing I would not see him again. In the end, the question was never asked.

The UK Meteorological Office

None of the books or magazines I'd read had made reference to an accurate weather forecast being received at Base Camp prior to 10 May. After two years of research, I was left with nothing but hearsay and clues. I had no proof that such a report had been received and acted upon. In research, as in life, sometimes a chance comment brings the unexpected.

I was at the home of our friends Robert and Amanda Newton, talking about the frustrations of my research, explaining how my enquiries at the Met Office had come to an abrupt halt as records were only held for six years to satisfy legal requirements. Amanda, bursting with family pride, announced the fortunate words: 'My brother Mike's a meteorologist. He works in the Met Office. Maybe he can help.'

Within a matter of days, I was in touch with her brother, Mike Harrison, an internationally respected expert in meteorology and climatology, particularly in climate variability. He was still at the UK Met Office when I first contacted him in 2006 but retired the following year from his position in order to consult. Having worked previously for the World Meteorological Organisation, a specialised agency of the United Nations, and earlier for many years in Africa, his interests are in predictability (understanding the extent to which prediction is possible) and in advancing approaches to maximise the benefits provided by climate information (particularly with regard to development in Africa).

Mike looked up my original enquiry to the Met Office from the year before to ascertain at what point, and why, the enquiry had faltered. He came back to me with more or less the same dead end:

I gather that as a result of the 1996 disaster, the Met Office has been providing formal predictions for Everest on request but that a formal facility apparently did not exist at the time of the disaster. But that is not to say that a forecast could not have been provided at that time – it could, and possibly was; we just cannot confirm that. But if you have any contact name for the London office at that time, then we may be able to check on that person's recall.

I asked Mike if he would circulate an email around the London branch of the Met Office to see if anyone recalled dealing with the Everest weather forecasts in 1996. Mike's reply only went to show what an uphill struggle lay ahead:

> I'll forward it and see what I can come up with. But please don't think I'm being pessimistic at the onset – I'd love to sort this out – but the London Centre, as it was constituted in 1996, no longer exists – gone with many others in a cost-cutting exercise with increased reliance on electronic communication.

He explained that the role of the London branch, and other such regional centres, was to support businesses and the public; that although they may have negotiated directly with the customer with regard to the product (forecasts), the predictions were always supplied by the main Met Office through the International Forecasting Unit (IFU) at either Bracknell or more recently Exeter.

Although many of those Mike could recall in the IFU around 1996 had either retired or departed, he offered to see what he could do, while cautioning me that records might no longer exist.

It would be a further three months before Mike would write again:

> I have received responses from most of the names I was given who may have had associations with the IFU in 1996. The most useful, but also typical, was from the manager of the IFU at that time until into 1997.

The response from the former IFU Manager read as follows:

> Although I believe that we issued forecasts for Everest in the last part of my time as IFU manager, I don't remember 'warnings' specifically being part of the service provided . . . it would be necessary to see the original documentation to be able to fully determine the answer to your query – however, as noted before, unfortunately I do not know where this now resides.

Another response from his enquiries read:

> I remember a service for Everest – not least because we were not paid for it! We were instructed to provide the service by the then CE [Chief Executive]. I can't remember the details but believe that we provided a fairly general forecast of wind, weather and temperature for at least two heights – Base Camp (5000m?) and near summit (9000m?). In addition, we provided a forecaster consultancy service on demand.

Mike went on to speculate:

> Does this mean the service was started as a response to the disaster? That at
> least would be consistent with the unpaid for request from the CE.

Following up this lead for me, Mike approached a friend, Julian Hunt,
now Lord Hunt:

> Julian Hunt was the CE at the time, and he's now checked all his notes from
> that period and can find no reference. As he says, that does not mean he did
> not issue an instruction, but with records gone it looks as though it'll be, at
> the least, difficult to find any written confirmation one way or the other.

No payment, no receipt, no official record. But that does not mean the
service wasn't provided.

Time to Go Fishing

With the trail at the Met Office going cold, yet with anomalies revealed by my other enquiries, I decided it was time to turn my attention to those in positions of authority on each team.

On Rob's team, the surviving guide was Michael Groom, whom I'd already contacted. From Scott's, Neal Beidleman was the remaining guide and a person I needed to speak to. With regard to the Imax team, I had yet to contact Ed Viesturs, their lead climber and 'film talent'.

The view from our apartment window of fishing boats heading out to sea hopeful of landing a good catch and of some of the same vessels returning days later with a mass of white seagulls circling overhead signalling their success may have inspired my next move. As I'd precious little to confirm what I believed had happened back in 1996, I decided to go fishing.

I emailed Ed, telling him I had been in contact with David Breashears concerning the 1996 Imax expedition, and that David had informed me the team had received weather forecasts from the London-based Met Office.

I asked him if the original decision for the Imax team to go the day before Rob Hall and Scott Fischer was so that these three teams could take advantage of the brief weather window suggested by the forecasts.

Ed replied:

> I believe that Rob also had some sort of weather forecasting. In fact it was Rob first and then Scott that picked the 10th to go for the summit.
>
> After that was announced by Rob, we decided to try on the 9th – but when we woke up at Camp 3 on the 8th, David and I both felt the weather was not good enough for us, so we went down.

To me this was a glimmer of hope shining like a sliver of light at the bottom of a firmly closed door. Ed hadn't confirmed that Rob was receiving his own forecast, as he'd only used the word 'believe'. The more telling word was 'also', which means 'as well as'. If this were the case, then it put the Imax weather forecast prior to 10 May and Rob's demise. Of equal importance was the fact that Ed had made no attempt to correct me with regard to the suggested use of the forecasts for the period around 10 May.

I remember bursting into the kitchen full of excitement to tell Catherine of my breakthrough, going over and over what Ed had written. Catherine, more than anyone, had witnessed the lengths I'd gone to, the work I'd put into this. She could see by my reaction how important I felt this was. Her support had been unwavering, although at times she must have wondered when our apartment would return to being a home rather than an ongoing place of work. Having told Catherine first, I was straight on the telephone to Geoff. I couldn't possibly have waited until Friday evening to tell him the news.

'Bring it with you on Friday. I want to read this for myself,' was Geoff's uncommitted reply.

Typical lawyer, I thought, too calm by half.

The morale boost Ed's reply gave me was huge. Prior to this, I was losing belief that my work would lead anywhere. I felt I'd been confronted with an impenetrable wall of silence. For one brief moment, Ed's reply swept that aside.

On the Friday evening, I sat across the table from Geoff, watching him intently as he studied Ed's reply. For the first time, I could see in his eyes that he thought I might be making some progress. As he dissected in his mind each sentence of Ed's reply, he went one step further than I had. With a broad grin on his face, he said, '"Also" means "as well as" or "at the same time".'

We spent the remainder of that evening in deep discussion about the implications of the reply and my next planned move.

Buoyed by this small but important breakthrough, I turned my newly acquired fishing skills to Neal Beidleman. However, Neal proved more difficult than most to track down. There were plenty of references to him on the Internet but no contact details I could find. Eventually, after three or four weeks and a number of enquiries to different organisations in Aspen, Colorado, I managed to get hold of his email address.

With a heavily baited line, I wrote to Neal, informing him that I understood prior to the disaster the Imax team had been receiving their weather forecasts from the London-based Met Office and these had been shared with Rob Hall and Scott Fischer; from these, each of the three teams had chosen their summit day.

I also told Neal that I knew of the meeting that had taken place between Rob Hall, Scott Fischer, Andy Harris and himself to make final plans for summit attempts. I asked if during this they discussed any contingency plans in case the Imax team, on their way to the summit, were delayed by a day.

Neal replied:

There was a meeting about the ascents, and you are correct about the original dates selected. I was mildly aware of some weather forecasting that was happening, but frankly, in '96 not much credence was put into the forecasts. Scott did not have specific forecasts from any other source to my knowledge. And the forecasts that I saw never seemed to be very accurate anyway. The big mountains make their own weather as often as large fronts do, it seems. The plan for contingency days and 'what ifs' was not discussed that much. Too many things come in play and I believe it was more a 'wait and see but we'll all work together' type arrangement from my recollection.

After such a long fallow period in my research, I could hardly believe my luck: first Ed and now Neal.

Significantly, Neal had confirmed that, to his knowledge, Scott did not have specific forecasts from any other source. The only source I'd mentioned anywhere in my email to Neal was the forecast I understood the Imax team were receiving from London: the ones he'd said he'd seen.

Once again, Catherine witnessed me utterly elated by these smallest of details. She sensed that I thought I was on the verge of a major breakthrough. My whole demeanour had changed to one bursting with energy and motivation.

I arrived at my usual Friday meeting with Geoff with the sense I'd achieved something important with my newly found fishing skills. Geoff, however, although impressed with what I'd managed to find out, was concerned by Neal's careful use of words and phrases, such as, 'mildly aware', 'not much credence' and 'never seemed to be very accurate anyway'. The words were too vague for him to draw any conclusion that he'd be comfortable with.

I found it difficult to accept this dampening of my enthusiasm. These precious discoveries were so difficult to achieve and so rare that I hung on to them tightly. To relinquish them was not something I wanted to do. They were virtually all I had after two years of work.

I carefully considered the replies I'd received from both Ed and Neal, and wrote to them once more to clarify matters, but in doing so I added into the equation my understanding of Rob's knowledge that 'the weather was due to turn bad the next day', 11 May.

I set out for Neal the sequence of events that I thought was very close to how the summit attempts ended up being planned: that it appeared as though 10 May was the date chosen first by Rob then Scott before the Imax weather forecasts were looked at. When the forecast was seen by Rob and Scott, this confirmed there was a possible window on 10 May with the weather holding until 11 May when there was going to be a change for the worse with a drop in temperature and the wind speed picking up considerably. With Rob and Scott having already announced the 10th, the Imax team decided to go for the summit the day before. I asked Neal if he could confirm that this was a reasonable synopsis of the way the planning for the summit attempts proceeded.

Neal's entire reply was short and succinct: 'Seems reasonable, but this all happened a long time ago. Good luck. Neal.'

I then sent more or less the same email to Ed Viesturs. I received no reply.

For whatever reasons, the avenues of contact with both Ed and Neal appeared to have been closed. They seemed to have joined an ever-growing list of those who either had nothing further to add or simply did not respond. In truth, I was running out of key people to contact. Nothing I'd read had brought me any closer to actually proving my suspicions. It appeared, although tantalisingly close, I'd reached the end of the road. I felt I was so close to the truth, but still it was out of reach. This turned out to be more painful than not knowing at all. The agony of being in this position but not being able to prove my findings brought a depression that I had not expected to feel. My expectations at the onset had been that such information would be easily uncovered. It was not. I was beginning to understand why no one had spotted it immediately after the tragedy of 10 May. I had the crushing sense that my search was doomed to fail, that I would be left isolated, burdened with both torment and guilt.

Proof beyond doubt was part of my journey. Merely knowing within myself was not enough. My deep-rooted feeling was that if I did not expose the full facts about what had brought about this seminal event in Everest's history, then no one ever would.

The press had missed their opportunity to discover it back in 1996. They had been so wrapped up in the gift of a story that they had never looked beyond the surface. Rob Hall was out of reach and dying slowly near the summit of Everest, speaking via a radio link to his pregnant wife in New Zealand; high-paying clients caught out in a ferocious storm; eight people dead – what more could the press ask for? Possibly what had led to this catastrophic outcome? But in the end, the right question was never asked or, if so, it had been asked in such a way that it was easily deflected. Time and the accounts that followed would bury the information almost beyond reach.

Following the highs I'd felt after receiving the replies from Ed and Neal, I'd now hit rock bottom. In hindsight, this was probably a natural reaction, but at the time it was hard to deal with: a problem neither Catherine nor Geoff could help me overcome. On this occasion, I was on my own, in a situation I'd not expected to find myself. Time had marched on.

Although dejected, I knew the only way to deal with the scenario was logically. I wondered how many more years I could end up wasting, going nowhere with this search. I felt worn out. Eventually I concluded that it was in the best interests of both my family and myself if I called it a day and shelved the whole project.

For a short while, I felt a huge burden of responsibility had been lifted from me. My assumption was that I could merely move on with my life.

My newly found free time brought with it a loss of direction; the intensity of my focus had come to an unsatisfactory and abrupt end. It was early April and my 52nd birthday had slipped past unnoticed. Melancholy was in the air, as were the strong winds that accompany this change in season.

The morning was bright and the sky clear as I scuffed my feet along Tynemouth Long Sands: a broad, gently curving golden beach, some half a mile long with a steep grassy sand-dune slope behind and a rocky outcrop at either end, popular with surfers because of the waves that roll in with the predominantly easterly breeze. However, the wind that day was scouring the surface and whisking sand grains up a few inches into the fast-moving air, weaving it in broad trails as it danced towards the water's edge. The hard grains drummed against my trouser legs as though shot from a grit blaster. I leant backwards against this westerly barrage; the roar of air rushing past my ears deafened me to all around. There were no surfers today. Beyond, the sea had been flattened by the onslaught of the west wind. Such was the wind's strength that it was ripping water from the surface and transforming it into fanning columns of dense spray over a hundred feet high. The sea had taken on the appearance of a ferociously boiling cauldron. A mile or two offshore, I caught glimpses of cargo ships travelling north. They moved like ghostly apparitions as they passed in and out of partial sight, obscured by the huge sprays of water being hurled into the air. Rarely could I see a whole ship at once. The bow of a ship appearing in the distance, seemingly out of nowhere, when the rest of the vessel was out of sight, gave the scene an unnatural feel.

At that precise moment, I understood that if the wind blew stronger I would still be able to see the ships; the increase in strength would merely serve to make the vision more ghostly. Likewise, the sight of two head torches flickering on the South Col through the furiously wind-driven snow: they would not fade in time but would become more haunting.

The next morning, I was woken prematurely by the light of the early-morning sun shining through a gap between the curtains of our bedroom window. The howling roar of the previous day's wind had long since subsided. I found myself lying there pondering the huge amount of time and effort I'd put into the whole project and how this would be completely wasted, as nothing had been resolved. If anything, I was in a worse position than when I had set out, as my denial was no longer buried beyond reach. I was tormented by the frustrations in my search. There and then I decided I would write down whatever I had and see where I ended up, in the knowledge that the manuscript I finally produced had the strong possibility of becoming little more than a collection of my personal thoughts.

No sooner had I started putting pen to paper than my enthusiasm returned. Whether this was going to last, I'd no idea, but I sensed rejuvenation in my project. Maybe my mental detachment for that short intervening period was what I'd needed.

For some unearthly reason that I cannot explain, I decided it would be useful if I spent the time when I wasn't writing going through the magazines I'd amassed just one more time. In what way I thought this might have helped is beyond me now. Maybe I couldn't help looking at the haystack, knowing that somewhere inside was the needle, the clue I'd been searching for.

Confirmation from Within

It was while I was grasping at straws, re-reading the first few of the many magazines piled on the living room floor, that I had my luckiest break of all. Whether it was destiny pointing her finger, I will never know. This was the break I had been praying for, but not from a source where I had expected to find it. I'd stumbled across a reference to Audrey Salkeld posting regular updates to NOVA online from the Imax expedition's Base Camp during April and May 1996. I had surely seen this reference on the previous reading but must have been so engrossed in my search for the missing quote that I passed over it without stopping. Now I was leaving no stone unturned.

Visiting the archives of NOVA online, which is part of the www.pbs. org website, I clicked onto the dispatches/reports sent by Audrey. Reading through each and every one of them, my expectations were that I'd find nothing much to help my research. I could not have been more mistaken.

In the report, submitted by Audrey Salkeld to NOVA online on 5 May 1996, the opening paragraph read:

> The team left at 5.45 this morning and are now resting at Camp 2, where they will probably stay an extra night. It is very windy up there. David has reported that the forecast is good at least until the 8th. We are getting regular weather reports from Danish Meteorologists via Mal Duff's camp.

The euphoria I felt when I read these words instantly blew away all the despondency I'd had to endure. The trust in my instincts was vindicated. This was not hearsay: this was on record.

It can still be viewed on PBS's archive using the following link then clicking on to May 5th 1996: www.pbs.org/wgbh/nova/everest/ expeditions/96

I had found weather forecasts and meteorologists, but they were from Denmark. Had I got it that mixed up? Was the source of the Imax expedition's forecasts the Danes? This made the information I'd gathered thus far rather confusing.

CONFIRMATION FROM WITHIN

Despite this, I had confirmation that accurate weather forecasts were being received at Base Camp before 10 May 1996. These were being shared, at the very least, between the Danish climbers on Mal Duff's team and the Imax expedition.

I considered contacting Audrey at this point, but decided it might be more sensible to locate the actual source of these forecasts and to approach members of the Danish expedition first.

Assistance from Denmark

Before drawing conclusions, it was essential that I got verification that these Danish forecasts had actually existed. I'd built up my hopes on previous occasions, simply to have them dashed. Initially, Catherine was the only one I told of my discovery.

Prior to communicating with the Danish climbers from Mal Duff's team, or mentioning this to Geoff, I approached the Danish Meteorological Institute (DMI) to confirm they had indeed supplied these forecasts. This led me to Søren E. Olufsen, a highly experienced meteorologist. From 1981 until 1993, he'd worked as an aviation forecaster with the Danish Civil Aviation Administration/DMI, after which time he was promoted to Head of the Central Forecasting Office. When I contacted Søren, he'd been appointed as Deputy Director of Forecasting Services at the DMI.

In reply to my email, Søren wrote:

> I was the head of the forecast office in 1996 and remember us setting up a service for a Danish Everest Expedition.
>
> We chose to supply wind and temperatures derived from atmospheric models used for weather prediction. Exactly which data we used and supplied has escaped my memory, but I may be able to find out.
>
> We even gave the forecasters information on mountain climbing and routes on Everest based on expedition accounts by Reinhold Messner.
>
> The weather forecast for Everest was, if I remember correctly, done by one of the duty forecasters. Hence it will not have been the same forecaster every day but a group of forecasters.

This, along with Audrey Salkeld's posting of 5 May, confirmed beyond doubt that accurate weather forecasts were being provided directly into Everest Base Camp prior to 10 May.

I contacted Søren again to ask if he knew what source of data the DMI would have used to provide these forecasts. Whether they might have any of that data still stored in their archives.

The reply came back:

I am afraid I cannot help you much on this level of detail. I do not have the instructions to the forecasters any more and the forecasts themselves are no longer in our archive. What I am sure of, though, is that the forecasts were based on data from ECMWF (European Centre for Medium-Range Weather Forecasts) who may be willing to help you with the raw prognostic data. Additionally, the forecasters will have compared the model data with observational data from the area and with positions of jet streams and wind fields from World Area Forecast Centre London (UK-MET OFFICE).

Normally the quality of forecasts for the Himalayan area should be expected to be quite high due to the fact that it is downstream from the data-rich European area. Although satellite data is a very important source feeding into atmospheric forecast models it would be wrong to say that forecast data is derived from satellite data. A huge amount of data from many sources feed the models ranging from data from weather stations on the ground, weather balloons, data collected by commercial aircraft to various kinds of satellite data.

It will have been very difficult to sample meaningful data on the ground in the Everest region. The data would simply depend too much on wind/lee or shadow/sun to be used as a forecasting tool. We carefully pointed this out to the climbers. We said what we probably would be able to predict with some skill was the temperature and strength of the flow at different heights, but not the temperature and wind on a specific location on a face or ridge of Everest. Technically it could be done to some extent, but would have taken considerable amounts of time, effort and all the expedition's money.

Regards

Søren Olufsen

The extra information Søren gave me in this reply would turn out to be invaluable, not least due to his reference to the ECMWF data and the fact that his forecasters would have compared the model data with information from the UK Met Office.

While looking up the names of Danish climbers on Mal Duff's team in 1996, I came across that of Dr Henrik Jessen Hansen, leader of the Danish expedition and, at the time I contacted him, a consultant in the Department of Cardiothoracic Surgery, Gentofte University Hospital, Copenhagen. In fact, it was Henrik Hansen who set up the triage hospital at Camp 2 immediately after the disaster, ready to receive and treat the injured as they were brought down from higher on the mountain. While Henrik was organising this, Mal Duff and one of his clients, Euan Duncan, made a rapid descent to Base Camp to collect emergency medical supplies.

I wrote to Henrik and asked if it was himself or another member of the Danish team who obtained the forecasts from Denmark, and if they compared these with one the Imax team were receiving.

Henrik's reply: 'All the Danes on the Mal Duff team were together and we had an agreement with the Danish Meteorological Institute and we exchanged information with the Imax team.'

Although Henrik's reply hinted that the Imax team had their own forecast, it did not actually go as far as to say this. Audrey Salkeld had made no mention of a second forecast in her report of 5 May, so maybe there wasn't one.

I relished going to see Geoff that Friday evening. The opportunity to land him unexpectedly with something this important was a rare pleasure indeed. This time I'd given him no warning of what was coming.

Leaning across the table, I presented Geoff with the paperwork, consisting of the 5 May report from the PBS archives and the replies I'd received from both Søren and Henrik. I sat back, quietly sipping my beer. Although slightly perplexed by the fixed smile on my face, he carefully made his way through the information before him, nodding to himself as he did so. Finally, after several minutes, he gradually raised his head.

'Good lad!' were his first words.

Praise indeed, I thought, from this retired Yorkshire lawyer – a friend whose opinion I valued so much. Only for him to follow by saying, 'But you know you're going to need more.'

In the knowledge that Henrik provided my best hope, I contacted him again. I asked if the Imax team had also received a forecast from the DMI or if theirs had been from a different source.

Henrik's reply:

Imax weather forecast was from London. I don't remember the institute. I don't remember the details but ours were pretty good but no way perfect. There was a general feeling of immortality and belief in the 10th as a good summit day because Rob Hall had succeeded on this date three times before. Actually several expeditions including Hall and Fischer had a meeting around the 1st of May and there decided the 10th should be the day – and that without any forecast going that long.

Although this confirmed a separate Imax forecast, and suggested these were being received before 10 May, it did not say that unambiguously. David Breashears had admitted he contacted the London-based Met Office, but it was not clear from the information I had read, or from what he had told me directly, if he meant before or after 10 May.

Something else Henrik had said intrigued me. Neal Beidleman had told me that: 'In '96 not much credence was put into the forecasts.' Yet here was Henrik saying that although the forecasts were in no way perfect they were actually pretty good.

I asked Henrik if the Danes had received five-day forecasts and whether both his team and the Imax team had received and compared these two separate weather forecasts, from Denmark and London, at the beginning of May.

Henrik's reply was the answer I had been searching for:

> The London-based institute were quite famous and had a specific name that I do not remember. We did have five-day forecasts, maybe Imax were a bit longer.
>
> We did receive and compare the forecasts throughout May and did not find the 10th good [the Danes therefore scheduled their planned summit bid for 12 May].

Henrik saying that he did not find the 10th good suggested trying to summit even on this day would be ill-advised, let alone on 11 May. First Rob and then Scott had been motivated by their belief in the 10th as a good summit day; this was based on the success that Rob had achieved in previous years.

I asked Henrik if the name of the London-based institute had been referred to as Bracknell.

His reply: 'It might be, it sounds familiar.'

As I had with Ed Viesturs and Neal Beidleman, I put to Henrik my theory about how the summit attempts had been planned. I also let him know that I had been in touch with Neal. I enquired whether Rob and Scott had got the forecast through the Danes or the Imax team, or if everyone had sat down together to consider both forecasts. I went on to suggest to Henrik that Rob and Scott had seen a forecast before heading up for their summit attempt.

Henrik started his reply by saying he remembered Neal very well and could I say hello to him. He continued:

> Everyone did share forecasts and it was correct that they got a forecast as they moved up the mountain but another very important point was that both teams' clients [Rob and Scott] were so weak that there will only be one go and afterwards they will be worn out and go home, summit or not. And the competition between the two and their journalists were very present although there was some cooperation.

I wanted to make sure that there wasn't a point at which these teams might have dropped out of touch with the five-day forecasts. To put this beyond reasonable doubt, I sent Henrik two further questions:

Did you get the five-day forecast you were receiving from the Danish Institute at the very beginning of May 1996 once every five days or did you have the five-day forecast updated each day?

Was it the Danes or the Imax Base Camp that radioed up the weather to Rob, Scott and the Imax team as they moved up for their summit bids?

Henrik's reply indicated the actual volume of information they were receiving:

> We did receive a forecast every day in May. I do not remember who radioed the forecast, but most likely it was the Base Camp managers from each expedition. [The Danes, Imax team, Rob and Scott.]

There was one if not two forecasts being received by the Danes, the Imax team, Rob Hall and Scott Fischer every day in May. Why had it taken me three years to finally get this information?

From the Imax team, I had Audrey Salkeld on record, but I thought it might be wise to see if I could find a second source from within this team confirming that forecasts were being received prior to 10 May. With nothing concrete coming from my direct enquiries to members of that team, I realised my best chance lay on the fringes. I began a search of more obscure articles on the Internet relating to Everest 1996. Amongst these I came across the summit journal of Ed Viesturs, posted on *Outside* magazine's Internet counterpart called *Outside Online*. In its archives, I discovered a fascinating report sent back on 5 May 1996 by Paula Viesturs, the Imax Base Camp manager (and Ed's wife):

> But it's still nice and clear at the summit. The only thing, really, seems to be the winds. We just got an updated weather forecast and supposedly the weather is going to hold. And these forecasts have been accurate so far. The only issue is the wind.

I would later discover that David Breashears had taken part in *Frontline* live online on Wednesday, 14 May 2008; this was reported in the *Washington Post*. I looked at the transcript. During this, David was asked a direct question by someone from Chicago about the weather and turnaround times for the climbers on 10 May. The following is the exact part of the question and David's reply:

> Chicago: How could a cyclone from the Bay of Bengal 'sneak up' on these teams with their support?
> David Breashears: There was no accurate weather forecast back then.

I also recalled a statement made to me by Michael Groom, about his previous experience of a Met Office forecast. This had been supplied to Harry Taylor by the Met Office after a request from the British Army in 1993, some three years prior to the 1996 disaster:

> I first used the information from the British Met Office in 1993 when the British Everest Expedition for that year passed on the forecast to me. It proved to be very accurate, with a predicted weather window of 24 hrs with wind speeds of around 10 kph for 10 May 93. Harry Taylor and I summited as a result.

These two statements relating to the accuracy, indeed to the existence, of weather forecasts for Everest conflicted with David's answer. It also didn't make any sense to me that there wouldn't be accurate forecasts in 1996 if there were such reports in 1993.

Catherine had taken her mother away for a short holiday during the week in which Henrik's last message came through. The person who'd been closest, the one who'd witnessed the highs and lows, who'd endured both our lives and home being taken over for three years, was denied the opportunity to share with me the sense of relief and vindication that this brought. I had confirmation that Rob and Scott had received a constant stream of information from two weather forecasts and that this had even been updated as they moved up the mountain. By the time Catherine returned on the Friday afternoon of that week, I was already pondering my next problem. I realised, in the final analysis, that my understanding of the events that had led to the tragedy of 10 May now hinged on what the forecast data in 1996 had predicted. Most importantly, I needed to obtain this from the same source that would have been accessed to supply the Danes and the Imax team with their forecasts, and through these two teams to Rob and Scott. I needed to compare this to the actual weather that had struck Everest.

I emailed Mike Harrison, the meteorologist who'd been trying to track down information in the UK Met Office, to let him know that the Danish Meteorological Institute had supplied the forecasts based on data they had received from the European Centre for Medium-Range Weather Forecasts.

Little could have I known what would be in Mike's response: 'I have a friend and colleague in the ECMWF. Would you like us to pull all the relevant data from the archives at ECMWF and give you our professional opinion?'

Not one, but two professional opinions. What an offer! 'Absolutely,' was my instant reply.

A DAY TO DIE FOR

I waited nervously for several weeks. Whatever the data said, I would have to face the truth one way or another. Either our team had been put on a collision course with an incoming storm that Rob and Scott knew was on its way, or I was wrong.

Eventually an email came back from Mike: 'I've spent the last few days at ECMWF and my colleague there had very kindly obtained the relevant data and we've gone through it together today.'

I sat motionless as I absorbed every single word of Mike's report:

We had three sets of information to examine:

1. The ECMWF analysis. This is ECMWF's best estimate of the observed atmospheric circulation patterns around the world every six hours – this should be an excellent estimate of reality (which is difficult to measure precisely every six hours across the globe!). In this the development of a jet over a rapidly deepening depression over southern Russia and northern India was clear. Winds in the Everest region increased steadily from about the 8th onwards, to reach maximum intensity on the 11th. By the 12th, wind strengths were reducing quite quickly. It is reasonable to assume that cloud and snow accompanied the strong winds at least on the 11th. Temperatures appear to have remained fairly constant throughout this period, so we are unable to say that the storm was accompanied by any major drop in temperatures – my guess is that the snow plus the winds were the main hazards, although a temperature drop cannot be discounted entirely within the blizzards.

2. The ECMWF forecasts. These were available to the Met Office at the time. As I've said in earlier emails, I cannot tell whether any forecast that the Met Office might have produced took these into consideration. Forecasts went out to ten days and we examined those starting on the 3rd, 5th and 7th. These forecasts were encouragingly consistent, all indicating the strength of the winds on the 11th quite clearly. All also indicated the steady strengthening of the winds from the 8th onwards.

3. The Met Office forecasts. Unlike the Met Office, ECMWF does have an easily accessible archive of these forecasts, and it is on these that I am 99 per cent certain any service provided by the IFU in 1996 would have been based, either uniquely or primarily. Unfortunately the ECMWF archive includes only a rather limited number of details, and those we were examining with the ECMWF data above were not included. Hence we had to interpret from less direct information. Also, for reasons we do not know, it seems that only a reduced number of values were archived for these forecasts, such that the plots we were examining were rather poor quality as compared to those that would have been available in 1996. Thus we had two problems – unavailability of the data we required ideally plus further interpretation difficulties given the poor plots. The forecasts only went out to six days, so relevant ones were

– 274 –

ASSISTANCE FROM DENMARK

not available on the 3rd, and we examined those starting on the 5th and 7th. In both, despite the difficulties, the storm of the 11th was apparent, although we cannot say how the winds predicted by Met Office compared with those of ECMWF.

Hope that helps you.

Best regards

Mike

To summarise:

ECMWF Analysis is the best estimate of the actual weather observed around the globe every six hours. This is what actually happened.

In this, the development of a jet over a rapidly deepening depression over southern Russia and northern India was clear. Winds in the Everest region steadily increased from 8 May onwards, reaching a maximum intensity on 11 May. On 12 May, the wind speeds reduced quite quickly.

ECMWF Forecasts: these covered a ten-day period; the ones for 3, 5 and 7 May were looked at. These were consistent in predicting a steady increase in the wind from 8 May onwards. All indicated the strength of the winds on 11 May quite clearly.

Met Office Forecasts: these covered a six-day period; the ones for 5 and 7 May were looked at. In both, the storm on 11 May was apparent.

The quote I had been searching for all this time was: 'We went on the 10th of May because we knew the weather was going to go bad the next day.' There was no inconsistency between the forecasts and what actually happened. They'd been remarkably accurate. The problem lay not in the forecasts but with those who'd received them.

As far as I can ascertain, this was the first time these teams had received forecasts for Mount Everest. Their lack of expertise in the interpretation of these forecasts in the wider context was apparent.

The weather is a three-dimensional continual system that cannot be divided up into exact twenty-four-hour periods. But the evidence suggested that this was something Rob and Scott had attempted to do, while interpreting differently to others the unsettled weather they could see around them.

As I tried to imagine why they would still want to pursue their attempt after seeing such forecasts, this new information suggested that Rob and Scott had taken their clients to the summit of Everest knowing a Himalayan storm was due. I'm amazed they didn't revise their plans. The weather was generally unsettled and somewhat harsh at times. They appeared to have used the forecasts to say on what day the storm was not predicted to hit Everest, rather than correctly utilising the information they contained: that of steadily worsening conditions over the three days following 8 May.

A leading risk specialist I spoke to told me it was wrong to say that the information (forecasts) had been ignored by Rob and Scott. From a risk perspective, they chose to interpret them differently to others, probably convincing themselves that with their guides, Sherpa support and previous experience they would be able to manage. Nevertheless, surely it was important data? Considering the credence it was being given by the Danish team, and judging from Henrik's answer also by the Imax team, as he had told me: 'We did receive and compare the forecasts throughout May and did not find the 10th good,' this should have been heeded by Rob and Scott and shared by them with other teams, especially ours, which was to be the only team attempting the summit on 11 May.

Meteorologists had supplied the forecasts based on data from many sources. Their predictions weren't supposed to be used in such a manner. By doing just that, Rob and Scott had put their paying clients in significant and unnecessary danger.

I do not believe Rob and Scott had meant us any harm by asking our team to drop back one day and make our attempt on the 11th. They just wanted us out of the way to allow their teams a clear shot at the summit. Once they were aware of the predicted storm, my guess is they probably thought we'd get to the South Col, the weather would turn bad at some point, and we'd be forced to retreat and try again another day. However, we could have gone ahead on 11 May and the storm could have come in underneath us, trapping our climbers near the summit of Everest at 29,000 feet, with wind speeds of 80 miles an hour and blizzard conditions. Rob and Scott had no way of knowing what would happen. They had gambled with our lives and those of their clients.

The evening I presented Geoff with Mike's report based on the material held in the ECWMF archives was one of the few times I'd seen him lost for words. He knew the implications of what he'd read, the importance of the information it contained. However, we understood each other and he didn't need to justify his apparent lack of reaction. The 40 years of being a professional lawyer dictated that he needed, once more, to see all the information I'd gathered, the emails I'd received, to read the previously published accounts again, to ponder the smallest detail before finally drawing his own conclusion.

Southward Bound

It was on 10 April 2008 that a message appeared in my email inbox from Neil Laughton. He was organising an Everest reunion for those whose company he had enjoyed while on his trips to the region. This was to be extended to other 'good eggs', as he put it, who had climbed, trekked, painted or flown over the great mountain. The event was to take place in Surrey, at the Artists Rifles Club, Bisley Camp. Catherine and myself were amongst those invited.

At 6 a.m. on 14 June, Catherine and I departed from the north-east of England for the 300-mile drive south to Bisley Camp, each of us behind the wheel of a vehicle stuffed to the gunnels with goods and possessions for our onward journey to our new home in France. The aged eight-seater people carrier I was driving had recently been bought for this purpose. It had been new when I'd climbed Everest with Anatoli and Nikolai some 13 years earlier. On top of my vehicle there were two metal rails to which I had strapped a set of triple ladders, decorating steps and two 16-ft sections of a large roof ladder. The family car Catherine was driving contained more homely goods and soft furnishings. Behind her she was towing an enclosed trailer containing mountain bikes, a table tennis table and other outdoor activity equipment for the friends and family who had threatened to visit us, many climbers amongst them. These were the last of our belongings; two previous trips in a large box van and flatbed trailer had already taken the majority across the English Channel.

We had sold our property in Tynemouth and the commercial building we owned in North Shields. After concluding that my climbs to extreme altitude in the Himalaya were probably over, I had wanted a new adventure.

For Catherine and me, life had slipped into routine. With my ongoing research there was little in the way of excitement to share, except for our occasional travels abroad. Our daughters had left home long ago, and we were now doting grandparents. Although our four-year-old granddaughter, Sophia, brought us great pleasure, we needed a new passion in our lives. This we had found. It had come in the form of an oak-framed French manor house dating from the mid-1400s that needed some restoration. Although in remarkably sound condition, it was a ludicrous property to buy given that it held France's top listing for a historic building. I had dusted off my climbing harness and bought a 160-ft length of quality rope to use while carrying out the repairs. Scaffold towers had been purchased.

Built some 30 years before Henry VIII was born, the property was one that we couldn't resist. After its construction in 1461, it had been given the title of Château Rouge. This was not because of the green-oak frame that would darken in the years to come, or for the lime-rendered wattle and daub that filled between the framework, but because of the 30,000 hand-crafted red clay tiles, each weighing 3.3 lb, that made up the magnificent overhanging roof. The building sat easily in the French countryside surrounded by oak trees, as it had done for nearly 600 years. It had miraculously survived the widespread destruction of properties owned by the aristocracy in the 1790s, during the French Revolution. This was where our new life was taking us. The fact that neither of us spoke much French posed another small problem we had yet to overcome, especially with the bureaucracy we knew we would have to face. However, in that regard, the fact I had been taught French at school some 40 years ago was on our side, despite my failure in the subsequent exam.

By four o'clock in the afternoon, the heavily laden vehicles that Catherine and I were driving swung through the broad grassy entrance of Bisley Camp. Covering an area of 3,000 acres, the land, owned by the National Rifle Association, National Small-bore Rifle Association and Ministry of Defence, is a conservation area that represents something of an Edwardian timewarp.

After winding our way through the narrow network of tarmac roads that give access to the numerous shooting clubs that occupy these ranges, we pulled up outside the colonial-style Artists Rifles' Clubhouse. The stack of ladders tied to my roof rack and the trailer behind Catherine's car looked conspicuously out of place amongst the other vehicles that were already parked.

The Artists Rifles, as a regiment, was raised in 1859 from a group of painters, sculptors, engravers, musicians, architects and actors. It was part of the great Volunteer Corps movement that grew rapidly that year in response to a threat of invasion by the French, under Napoleon III.

The Corps was officially named 'The 38th Middlesex (Artists) Rifle Volunteers'. Its first effective Commanding Officers were Henry Wyndham Phillips, the painter, and Fredric Leighton, who later, as Lord Leighton, was president of the Royal Academy. Amongst the other famous names that would pass through this highly decorated regiment were Noel Coward and Sir Barnes Wallis.

On the lawn outside, a croquet match was under way. Amongst the players was Henry. He had recently returned from his latest commercial expedition to Everest. We had not spoken since 2006, prior to my episode with his nephew, Oscar, and the subsequent email I had sent to him at Base Camp. I was unsure of the reception I might receive.

'Hello, Graham, or should I say, *Bonjour*,' said Henry, extending his arm to shake my hand.

'Hi, Henry,' I replied, as I grasped his outstretched hand.

As Henry then turned to greet Catherine, Neil came across and asked if I wanted to join in.

'Grab yourself a mallet, we are about to start a new game,' he said.

This gave me an ideal opportunity to gauge Henry's current feelings towards me. We had always got on well in the past, and although there had been the odd minor disagreement, these had blown over as quickly as they had arisen. Catherine stood on the sidelines with others, watching the game.

To Catherine and me, it looked as though Henry had made a wise move by saying hello to me as soon as we arrived: it got it out of the way and we were amongst company that both Henry and I knew. However, there was none of Henry's bullish and exuberant nature towards me that had been an integral part of the past friendship. The reception I received was, in a word, frosty. There was no rudeness on Henry's behalf, merely a reluctance to engage in conversation.

When the game finished, we retired to the bar for a drink before the food was served. Inside, sofas and comfortable armchairs were arranged around low occasional tables. Satirical cartoons, historical pictures and regimental memorabilia adorned the walls. The medium-sized dark wooden bar with the optics behind and a line of select whiskies and hand-pulled ales had a homely feel. It had an atmosphere that one would expect to find in a village pub, steeped in history, quietly tucked away in the English countryside.

In the last couple of weeks, news had filtered through that a good friend of ours, Iñaki Ochoa, had passed away high on Annapurna in western Nepal on 23 May. He was 40 years old. Reports first posted on the Internet had spread like wildfire across the climbing community.

My lasting memory of Iñaki is that of late April 1999, when the two of us climbed our way up to the South Col. We were attempting to be the first to summit Everest that year. From lower down, other climbers will have seen us as two small dots on the Lhotse Face, as we made our way across the Yellow Band and onward to the Geneva Spur. Iñaki had been with me when I stepped onto the South Col for the first time since my departure from that place on 11 May 1996.

We all knew what had happened to Iñaki could have been the fate

A DAY TO DIE FOR

of any one of us; he had been unlucky. For this reason, we did not dwell on the subject that summer's evening.

There were many questions I wanted to ask Henry, resulting from the wealth of information I had uncovered. I had both concrete evidence and confirmation that forecasts had been received into Everest Base Camp prior to 10 May 1996. By pure coincidence, it looked as though one of these had originated from the Met Office's International Forecasting Unit at Bracknell, situated not more than ten miles down the road from Bisley Camp.

Henry had not been able to help me with information on the matter when we had spoken over lunch in 2005, a time when we had got on well. Neither had he been willing to consider that his old friends Rob Hall and Scott Fischer might have placed our team in danger. I'd clearly infuriated him by sending my email about Oscar. So why would he want to talk to me now? I'd had an outside chance of getting him to open up his thoughts to me before the Oscar incident, now I didn't have a hope in hell.

As the evening wore on, I thought he might mellow, but he did not; both conversation and myself appeared to be avoided. I would have to continue my research with that avenue remaining closed.

Catherine and I departed from the clubhouse around 11 p.m. in order to catch the early-morning ferry for our onward journey to France. I was sad about the way things had turned out with Henry.

May 1996: Sequence of Events

As far as our team's planning in 1996 was concerned, Henry wanted to be done with summit attempts by mid-May if possible, because he and others were of the opinion that, as the weather warmed, shifts in the Icefall increased. Such a rise in the activity within this unpredictable mass of ice would effectively place our Sherpas, who climbed through time after time carrying supplies and equipment, at greater risk.

Without knowledge of the forecasts, our team independently chose 10 May.

On hearing that we were intending to make our attempt on the same day, Rob, on behalf of himself and Scott, approached Henry to ask if we'd drop back a day and make our summit bid on 11 May; we agreed.

That said, it is inconceivable that Henry would have stuck to our agreement to go on 11 May had he subsequently been made aware that the weather was going to deteriorate badly that day. This agreement was referred to by Paul Deegan in his article that appeared in the British Mountaineering Council's official journal *High*, August 1996, issue number 165.

Paul wrote:

> Based partly on the report of deep snow, Rob Hall and Scott Fischer (leaders of the Adventure Consultants and Mountain Madness expeditions respectively) together hatched a master plan. Their two large, well-equipped, strongly supported teams would combine forces to summit on the 10th, fixing the South East Ridge above the South Col as they went to make it 'client-proof'. Henry agreed not to clutter the route with our team on the same day but instead slip in their wake on the 11th. On paper it made a lot of sense. A large body of people to break the hitherto unbroken trail to the top, giving smaller teams (like ours) a realistic chance once the route had been breached.

From the book by Brigitte Muir, *The Wind in My Hair*:

> They [Rob and Scott] decided that they would summit on 10

May, a date which had been auspicious for Rob in the past, and asked all the others to follow one day behind, to 'avoid traffic jams high on the mountain'. There were rumours of deep snow, which a couple of renegade groups had encountered on their – failed – summit bids in the last few days. So of course it made sense to someone like Henry, who was an old mate of both Rob and Scott, to comply with their wishes. Their teams of Sherpas were much bigger than ours, and would trench a route to the summit for all to enjoy afterwards. In theory. I was a bit reluctant to have to follow orders, and from the two most expensive trips on the mountain, but I certainly did not feel like going for the summit with forty-odd people, most of whom would probably be very slow and hard to overtake.

However, it is highly unlikely that Rob and Scott knew, at this point in time, that a storm was expected to hit on 11 May, as they were only receiving five- or six-day forecasts.

5 May
The Imax team left Base Camp to move up to Camp 2.

6 May
Rob's and Scott's teams moved up from Base Camp to Camp 2, where the Imax team were spending a second night. While here, their respective Base Camps will have radioed them with the updated forecasts, both of which now covered up until at least the 11th. These will have showed the wind increasing steadily over the 9th and 10th, and a storm hitting on the 11th.

At this time, either Rob or Scott could have easily radioed their Base Camp and had a message passed to our team, advising us to wait because they had information that suggested an incoming storm. They did not. This may have been because at this point we could have easily rearranged our schedule and moved our summit attempt forward one day, to 10 May. This opportunity would have lain open to us until the afternoon of 7 May.

7 May
The Imax team headed up to Camp 3 in readiness for their summit bid on the 9th. Rob and Scott spent a second night in Camp 2.

8 May
At Camp 3, David Breashears and Ed Viesturs got up in the morning to see the wind blowing high on the South East Ridge. Their observations

supported the information in the forecasts: that the weather was deteriorating. Perhaps it began to happen more quickly than they had hoped. Their instincts told them the weather was not settled enough. They were utilising the forecasts more wisely, by adding into the equation their observations of the weather conditions they could see around them. They decided to head down and wait.

The Imax team coming down passed Rob's and Scott's teams, who'd made an early start from Camp 2 to move up to Camp 3. They explained to Rob, Scott and some of their guides that they didn't like the look of the weather higher up. These were the same conditions that Rob and Scott could see, yet these two leaders chose not to revise their plans and carried on up, appearing to be totally reliant on their interpretation of the forecast, one which suggested to them that the storm would hit on the 11th, after they had summited on the 10th. It seemed to be utilised by them as a method of confirmation for the date they'd chosen. In some blinkered fashion, it reaffirmed their belief in 10 May being a fortuitous day.

The question has to be asked: if Rob and Scott had not held the forecast would they have continued up? Or would they have used the experience they'd gathered over many years and followed the Imax team back down?

While this was happening, our team was climbing up from Base Camp to Camp 2. This positioned us one day behind Rob and Scott for our summit bid on 11 May.

Henry had also moved up to Camp 2, although he was not feeling well and spent much of his time in his tent wrapped up in bed. He'd brought with him a radio to oversee our attempt.

9 May

On the morning of 9 May, we left Camp 2 to climb up to Camp 3.

At the same time, Rob's and Scott's teams left Camp 3 for the South Col, where they arrived several hours later. During the course of the afternoon, wind speeds at this higher elevation picked up to in excess of 60 mph.

Rob's and Scott's teams, along with Makalu Gau and three Sherpas from the Taiwanese team, left the South Col shortly before midnight to begin their summit attempt. There was a lull in the weather.

10 May

We delayed our scheduled early departure from Camp 3 until after the midday radio call, to see if the weather improved; it did not. Two hours prior to this, Michael Groom had suggested to Rob that they turn back because of increasing wind speeds, but they continued up.

They were at the South Summit, at 28,700 feet.

Some or all of the Danes from Mal Duff's team had already started to move up to Camp 3 for their summit bid on 12 May. However, on hearing the strength of the winds high up, they quickly decided to abandon any idea of an attempt and descended to Camp 2 to wait for better conditions.

We arrived on the South Col during the early evening – in my case at around 6.30 p.m., much later than was normal. Anatoli, who had arrived back onto the South Col at 5 p.m. from his successful summit attempt, saw one of our Sherpas but no climbers.

The storm that had begun higher up during the course of the afternoon now detonated into full force as it descended onto the South Col: a deadly combination of gale-force winds and blizzard conditions.

Unbeknown to us, Rob Hall, Doug Hansen and Andy Harris were battling to survive near the South Summit, Scott Fischer and Makalu Gau were near collapse 1,200 feet above the South Col, and a group of seven clients, two guides and two Sherpas had formed a huddle little more than 150 yards from our tent after becoming hopelessly lost in the blizzard. There were rescue attempts made through the night, but through a twist of fate none were made by our team.

Michael Groom, who would become part of the huddle, had got his radio to work around mid evening, and Stuart Hutchison answered. It was Stuart who went out into the storm, time and time again, to try to guide them in.

Stuart was sharing a tent with Jon Krakauer that night. Unlike Jon, he'd not summited but had turned around two hours earlier at 11.30 a.m. from 28,000 feet. Rob had told him that the summit was still three hours away, a conservative estimate that put the top well beyond the 1 p.m. cut-off time he'd set in his mind.

In his book *Sheer Will*, Michael describes how, in the early hours of 11 May and close to complete exhaustion, he and a few who could still walk eventually managed to find Camp 4 on the South Col:

> There was a long moment of disbelief on both sides as I crouched outside the door belonging to Stuart and Jon. Did they know who the ice-crusted apparition was? Or was I the one that was dreaming? I am not sure if I spilled out the speech that I had so carefully rehearsed in my mind during those crazy hours wandering around the Col. If I did say something, it probably sounded like a drunken slur. Whatever I said, I hoped it gave some accurate directions to help find Beck, Yasuko and the others.
>
> I was convinced that as a result of whatever conversations

took place between us, rescuers would be rounded up to help me get Beck and Yasuko back into camp.

This conversation was confirmed by Hutchison, who is quoted as saying about Michael Groom:

> He was able to communicate clearly, but it required an agonal effort, like a dying man's last words. 'You have to get some Sherpas. Send them out for Beck and Yasuko.' And then he pointed toward the Kangshung side of the Col.

Only moments after raising this alarm, Michael found himself outside another of the tents. 'I yelled for help and Frank [Fischbeck] responded from inside the tent . . . Frank operated with the efficiency of a battlefield medic and pulled me inside the tent. It was at that point I gave up trying.'

Reflecting on these events, Michael wrote:

> It is my understanding that after alerting Stuart he set out alone to find Beck and Yasuko but once again, like so many times before, he found himself in danger of becoming hopelessly lost in blizzard conditions . . .
>
> I found out these rescue attempts were being made when I regained some degree of consciousness, and I was crushed by a heavy weight of guilt as I lay incapacitated in my tent. No amount of persuasion or money had made Stuart, Ang Dorje or Lhakpa Chhiri [the two Sherpas who'd headed back up on the morning of 11 May in an attempt to rescue Rob Hall] do what they were doing, it was their nature to do so.

Anatoli also went out into the storm several times and successfully rescued some of the stricken climbers. He had been alerted as to where survivors lay by Neal Beidleman, who had staggered into camp with Michael Groom. Unfortunately, Anatoli and Stuart did not know of each other's efforts and so remained uncoordinated.

11 May

Our early-morning radio call and the subsequent check around the other tents on the South Col led to confusion as to who, if anyone, was missing. I spoke with Henry on the radio and was asked to bring our youngest team member, Mark Pfetzer and his designated Sherpa, Jabion, down from the South Col. All three of us departed within the hour. Accounts say that the camp on the South Col was devastated and in tatters. This is not true. Unaware of the disaster at the time, I took several photographs before I left. One photograph is of the tents on the South Col, another is of Mark, while the penultimate one captures the South Summit with the wind blasting off it. In the very last frame there is a Himalayan chough rising up over the lip of the Lhotse Face and onto the South Col, like a harbinger of death. Had the camp been devastated, that in itself would have raised the alarm, but outwardly it looked intact.

On our arrival at Camp 2, we were told that everyone had been asked to observe a 24-hour blackout on news getting out, until relatives of those injured or killed had been informed. Families of climbers who had escaped uninjured were also contacted. Catherine received a phone call from Henry's partner Peta, who was in Edinburgh. She was informed that news would soon be breaking of a huge accident on Everest but that I was safe. Catherine knew before Reuters. Nowadays, I don't think this would be achievable.

Michael Jörgensen, Neil Laughton and Brigitte Muir from our team had remained on the South Col to ponder their options. Their thoughts were to wait and see if the weather cleared for a possible attempt the next night: not an option that I thought was either safe or wise. Once it became apparent to them that casualties and deaths had occurred, they changed their plans immediately and stayed on the South Col to help in whatever way they could. They descended to Camp 2 the following day: 12 May.

The sequence of events has been reasonably well documented concerning the rescues over the 11th and 12th. Some accounts, however, leave the impression that only one or two teams helped in the overall rescue. This is not the case. Ours, like most others, joined in these efforts, although these appear to have received little mention in certain narratives. We did our part, as did nearly everybody else.

Looking back, the summit days chosen versus forecasted conditions speak for themselves.

Team	Summit day chosen	ECMWF archive weather forecast data
Imax	9 May	Wind speeds steadily increasing after the 8th
Rob Hall and Scott Fischer	10 May	Wind speeds increasing
Henry Todd	11 May	Wind speeds 120 kph, blizzard conditions
Danes (from Mal Duff's team)	12 May	Wind speeds forecast to drop dramatically

The Wind of Change

Our first summer in France had ended and autumn was upon us. I was working on the manor. I'd thrown myself into the important work that needed to be carried out before the onset of winter; roof repairs had been top of the list.

Perched some fifty feet up, I leant against the hefty chimneystack that rose from the two broad medieval fireplaces far below. Around my waist was the climbing harness that I had worn throughout my Everest years: my protector, a silent witness to events that continued to concern me. Now it secured me via two karabiners and a strap to the rope that I had tied around the base of the brick chimney.

It was late September and the oak trees were beginning to shed their leaves. Red squirrels scurried through branches collecting acorns and hazelnuts to bury for the winter months ahead. From my unrivalled vantage point, deer and hares could be seen breaking cover across open fields cleared by the farmers working around the clock to gather in this year's crops. A fresh autumn wind was blowing through the air.

Sitting astride the central ridge, my thoughts wandered way beyond my lofty bounds and the distant hills afire with golds and reds to times past. I was reminded of my adolescent escapades when I had sat on top of my parents' three-storey Edwardian house, coughing my way through a cigarette: a time when advertising companies portrayed images of exhilarating sports and tobacco in the same picture. Now, nearly 40 years later, I was straddling a French manor house. Much had changed in the intervening period of my personal time/distance continuum. The ludicrous risk-taking of my youth had moved to one where I took control of dangers based on previous experience – as indicated by the climbing harness fastened around my waist. My adolescent desire to see how far I could push the edge, and the actions I had undertaken without any thought as to how they might affect others, had long since been curbed. I had come to understand that the combination of how we accept responsibility for our own actions, and the willingness to offer assistance to those to whom we have no real connection, defines who we are.

In high-risk sports, of which altitude climbing is certainly one, experience and heeding the danger signs are what protect us. On Everest, where climbing reaches the beginning of the stratosphere and life lies in the balance, such knowledge is critical. In 1996, the signs of potential danger had been there for all to see, as our radio calls to question the weather conditions had shown. But Rob Hall and Scott Fischer were the ones who had undertaken rescues in the past; they were two highly experienced mountaineers. We had no way of knowing that on this occasion the obsession with regard to the competition between their two businesses, the need for success, had turned their strengths into vulnerability.

I was beginning to understand my feelings of guilt. The sign on 10 May that Rob and Scott may have acted irresponsibly was the fleeting sight of two head torches glimmering on the far side of the South Col. From that, I thought I should have deduced a disaster was under way; in hindsight, this might be possible, but at the time, given the excellent reputations of Rob and Scott, there was not a chance. It had not been unwillingness on our part to offer assistance but the lack of comprehension of the situation on 10 May that had given rise to the feelings I carried with me. Willingness, by necessity, must be connected to an understanding of the situation before anyone can benefit. To achieve the latter, if you have not been informed as to the circumstances, then either an element of intuition or fortuitous luck are needed; on 10 May 1996, I'd had neither. No one came to ask us for help that night. Bad luck, misunderstanding and poor visibility had denied Anatoli our assistance. Of the others, Stuart Hutchison alone had tried to raise help; luck and visibility had not been on his side either. We had always had within us the willingness to assist those in desperate need, but through fate the opportunity wasn't to be given to us. Therefore, surely we should not have to bear guilt. I understood we would always carry the regret that we were in a position to have rescued people but had not been able to. This, I had to accept.

However, this was just part of the jigsaw I had been struggling to put together over the last four years, of which our team was but a single piece. Rob and Scott knew this storm was coming, as did others. I needed to establish the significance of this new information and then speak to those who had either written about or publicly discussed the disaster, to find out why they had not mentioned these earlier forecasts.

Our move to France earlier that year had necessitated me changing my email address to one that could be accessed anywhere. I had sent a circular letting friends know of the change; amongst the recipients was

Olwyn Hocking, to whom I mentioned I had begun to write a book about the 1996 Everest disaster.

In a bold move, she had resigned from her position as head of the regional BBC some years earlier and was now a partner in a multi-media company based in Newcastle upon Tyne. This new venture was involved in the making of community-based films and others that tackled serious issues facing sections of society. Environmental issues also formed a large part of her many ongoing commitments, as did her involvement in the local community with her husband Rob. Their enthusiasm, energy and thoughts for others seemed to know no bounds.

Olwyn had replied wishing Catherine and me luck with our new venture and asking if I'd like her to look through what I had written so far. Taking Olwyn up on her generous offer would turn out to be the best move I could have made. A highly intelligent lady who far outstrips my more modest abilities, her vast experience in journalism brought a critical eye that was complemented by advice and positive suggestions. She would remain on board throughout the development of the manuscript and my ongoing research, always approaching problems with optimism.

Whenever Catherine and I had cause to be back in north-east England, Olwyn and I would meet up at a cafe called Jack Spratts for a morning coffee, to discuss the progress being made.

Considerable steps forward had been achieved with regard to the weather forecasts in 1996. However, we were both worried that if I placed my findings in the public domain prematurely, without establishing the importance of this information, I would be seen to be unfairly criticising those who had knowledge of the forecasts and had not placed such information in their subsequent accounts. We knew I needed to show that these forecasts for the Everest region had been taken seriously and been carefully looked at; that they contained specific information for climbing in the form of wind speeds and temperatures at several altitudes.

At Olwyn's suggestion, I contacted Henrik once more. This took the form of several questions and answers by email between Henrik and myself over late 2008 and into the spring of 2009. I wanted to confirm the format in which the two forecasts had been received and to show the importance they had been given. These I have set out below.

Could you tell me if the forecast you were receiving from the DMI and the one Imax was getting from London were both received verbally by telephone, or were they received by email through the satellite phone to a computer and then printed out?

Email by satellite phone.

Was the Imax one also by email through a satellite phone?

Yes by email and it were [sic] usually printed.

Were the forecasts watched quite closely?

Yes.

Henrik's replies demonstrated the serious manner in which the incoming information was treated. However, I needed to know in greater detail what was being received and who was accessing it.

Were these in the format, from the DMI, of predicted wind speeds and temperatures at several altitudes over that five-day period on a day-by-day basis or were they this format on six-hour intervals over the five-day period?

Well I do not remember all details but it was on a day-to-day basis and not six hours. There were several altitudes and the one we used to give info about the summit was higher than Everest.

Was the forecast the Imax team were receiving from London in the same format as the one you were being provided by the DMI?

As I remember it, the London report was more detailed.

Were the Imax forecasts being received on a daily basis similar to those you were receiving from the DMI?

Yes.

When you shared the information you were receiving from the DMI with the Imax team, and compared this with the forecasts they were receiving from London, were the meetings just between you and David Breashears or you, David, Rob Hall and Scott Fischer or you with David, Ed Veisturs for Imax, Rob Hall, Michael Groom, Andy Harris for Rob's team and Scott Fischer and Neal Beidleman for Scott's team?

It was mainly who were in Base Camp and it was for sure the gang of Base Camp managers.

I'd already tried, more than once, to get the contact details of Helen Wilton and Dr Ingrid Hunt, the Base Camp managers of Rob's Adventure Consultants and Scott's Mountain Madness expeditions respectively, by emailing the companies concerned. I'd received no reply from Adventure Consultants, but on the second attempt Mountain Madness did take the time to respond, saying they no longer had any contact details for Dr Ingrid Hunt. However, Henrik's last response concerned me, as this indicated that Anatoli may have been amongst those looking closely at the forecasts, and if he was, then I needed to know. So I asked the straight question:

Was Anatoli involved in looking at the forecasts?

I did not see him around.

Am I correct that you had meetings with David Breashears, Ed Viesturs, Rob Hall and Scott Fischer as and when they were in Base Camp but that each of their Base Camp managers were always present to look at the two forecasts?

Were Rob and Scott's guides present at these meetings when they were in Base Camp or was it just the expedition leaders and their Base Camp managers?

Well, it was quite informal and mainly the Base Camp managers. Leaders and climbers showed up when they were nearby. Hall, Fischer and I think Viesturs talked a lot.

Were the two journalists, Jon Krakauer from Rob's group or Sandy Pittman from Scott's, ever present when the forecasts were discussed or looked at?

I do not remember Jon or Sandy there as those groups mainly got info from their guide.

You told me that you do not recall seeing Anatoli around when the forecasts were discussed, but could I ask if Scott's other guide Neal Beidleman and Rob's guides Andy Harris and Michael Groom were present when you looked at, and discussed, your forecast from the DMI and the Imax forecast from London?

I did see Neal sometimes (I remember him a lot more serious than Scott). The Hall team was run tight by Rob.

Did you, or other Danish climbers on your team, sit down with David Breashears to discuss and consider the two forecasts when they were received?

People from our team including the Danes discussed it with David and others from his expedition. It was not decided before who did it and from the Danish group it was mainly Jan and Bo. They were the computer experts and Bo had made the contact to DMI as I had other duties as team leader and doctor. [Jan and Bo refer to Jan Mathorne and Bo Belvedere Christensen, who were on the Danish team.]

It was apparent from Henrik's replies that Rob Hall's, Scott Fischer's and the Imax team's Base Camp managers had all seen the forecasts. This was also true for the Danes, David Breashears, Ed Viesturs, Rob Hall and Scott Fischer, but in their case, when they were up the mountain this information was radioed up to them. Neal Beidleman had also seen some forecasts. Who else had been in attendance when any of these earlier forecasts were looked at it is not possible for me to be sure.

However, one other thing that Henrik said caught me totally by surprise: 'The Brits Duff and Todd coordinated also sometimes but our Duff/ Danish/Finnish group had the most info due to DMI.'

This suggested that Henry Todd, our own expedition leader, might have been aware of the existence of forecast data. However, he could not have been aware of an incoming storm or he would have told his climbers; our safety would have been his top priority. He'd also flatly denied having knowledge of weather information that predicted a storm when I asked him back in 2005. This made sense, as Henrik had said Henry only coordinated with Mal Duff sometimes. In the case of Neal Beidleman, Henrik had informed me he was present at these meetings on some occasions, which fitted in with Neal's awareness of the forecasts but that he dismissed them as lacking credence. This may have been true in Henry's case as well. However, Henry not knowing about the incoming storm doesn't preclude him from knowing that forecasts were available, and even if Henry was aware of the forecasts it looks likely that he was not kept up to speed with changing events and the approaching bad weather.

From my own perspective, I had no knowledge of our climbers receiving weather forecast information either when choosing our summit day or as we headed up for our attempt. I wanted to make sure others on my team had the same understanding.

I checked with Neil Laughton. He didn't recall receiving any weather information prior to our first choice of 10 May or for our rearranged attempt on 11 May. Paul Deegan looked at the diary he'd kept in 1996 and could find nothing of any relevance at all to my question regarding weather forecasts prior to or during our scheduled summit bid. Both appeared to support my view.

I looked through Brigitte Muir's book, *The Wind in My Hair*. There was no mention of a weather forecast being received prior to 10 May there either, with regard to the spring of 1996.

With all the information I had to hand, I was interested to look at the books of those who should have known about the forecasts, to see if they conveyed the full facts of the events leading up to 10 May 1996.

Omission is the Greatest Lie

The most powerful form of lie is the omission, and it is the
duty of the historian to make sure that those lies do not creep
into the history books – George Orwell

A feeling of guilt was something I had carried with me for the past 14
years: the belief that our lack of understanding of the situation on
10–11 May 1996 had resulted in the loss of innocent lives.

However, with the information I had gathered, I now saw this in a
different light. I understood that the reports written immediately
afterwards were incomplete, because information vital to my
understanding of what had caused the tragedy was missing.

In his book *High Exposure*, David Breashears dedicates a number of
chapters to his filming on Everest and the terrible events of that year. I
looked at his account, to see how it fitted with the information I'd
gathered. In this first quote, he describes the days immediately prior to
5 May:

> There were many things that could conspire to disrupt or halt
> our filming expedition: weather, illness, an accident, a camera
> malfunction, a dropped lens, or lack of will. I was worried about
> what lay ahead . . . We spent the next few days resting, eating,
> and sleeping. Then we checked our barometer, listened to the
> Radio Nepal weather forecast, and watched the clouds. It was
> time for our summit attempt.

From this it would appear that, with a $7 million budget and ten
scientific advisers, the leaders of the Imax expedition had bought
themselves a barometer, a book on cloud patterns and a $50 radio.
Great planning!

I find it rather an oversight, and somewhat misleading, that David
Breashears does not go out of his way to mention either of the forecasts
being accessed at this time. The importance, and relevance, of weather
forecasts being received at Everest Base Camp in the days leading up to
the deadly events of 10 May, which were played out in the fury of the

gathering storm, are undeniable. This day is quoted as being one of the worst in the history of Everest. So why does he not spell these facts out?

On 8 May, the Imax team decided to descend from Camp 3 and wait for better weather, thereby foregoing their planned summit attempt the following day. On their way down they passed Rob and Scott, who were heading up to Camp 3. David comments:

> Rob was curious about why we were going down. There wasn't a lot to say. Two separate sets of experience and judgement stood face-to-face there. I told him it had been too windy the night before and too cold to get the early start we wanted, that we didn't like the weather . . .
>
> He [Scott], too, was curious about our decision. I told him what I'd told Rob, it'd been windy and we didn't like the weather.

Surely it is essential, in order for his readers to understand the importance of this event, that they are made aware these were three of the teams sharing information from the same two accurate weather forecasts?

Like Rob and Scott, the Imax team were also taking a risk, although it can reasonably be argued that such judgements are in the nature of high-altitude climbing. The forecasts had shown the weather would hold until 8 May, but from then onwards the wind speed would increase. The Imax team were planning to summit on 9 May. I can only presume they hoped the forecasts might be wrong in either the conditions they had predicted or the timing of the poor weather front that was heading towards Everest. If this indeed turned out to be the case, it would give them the opportunity to summit in an early weather window and to shoot their film with no one else on the upper reaches of the mountain. However, the conditions they observed on the morning of 8 May told them the forecasts were right. Unlike Rob and Scott, the Imax team needed near-perfect conditions to be able to film with the huge IMAX camera and associated equipment, so they headed back down, passing these other two teams who were moving up.

Rob and Scott, especially with their guides and strong Sherpa support, knew they did not need the same conditions; they must have thought that, provided a close eye was kept on the weather, their vast experience would see them summit safely on 10 May, their chosen day.

That said, it is surprising these two did not heed the implied warning when they saw the Imax team retreating. Along with the deteriorating conditions, it should have told them the forecasts appeared to be correct. All the signs were there to warn them that they were taking their high-paying clients into potentially lethal conditions.

Even the following day on the South Col when Anatoli spoke to both Rob and Scott, voicing his grave concerns with regard to the unsettled conditions, there was still the opportunity to abandon their planned summit bid and descend to wait for better weather.

On the morning of 10 May, David observed the conditions from Camp 2: 'This morning was beautiful, however, not a cloud in the sky. High overhead, the summit pyramid was crystalline and still, without a hint of a plume.'

David at this time was deep in a glacial valley, the Western Cwm, over a mile and a half vertically below the summit. I do not doubt what he and others thought they saw on the morning of 10 May. However, a cloudless sky doesn't mean there isn't any wind. I've seen Everest in previous years on such wonderfully clear days where climbers high up had to crouch down in fear of being blown off the mountain. From his location, David would not have been able to see the changes on the horizon, or the fast-moving incoming weather, until it got close. Around the same time, we were holding station at Camp 3, trying to decide if it was wise to head up to the South Col given the effects of the strong wind we could see high on the South East Ridge.

At the South Summit, around 10 a.m., Michael Groom had told Rob he thought their team should abandon the attempt and head down. The winds, in Michael's words, had picked up dramatically.

On the Tibetan side of the mountain, Alan Hinkes and Martin Barnicott were advising their team to stay put at Advanced Base Camp because of the changes they were observing in the upper atmosphere.

The most graphic image of the weather on 10 May that I have seen is in a photograph taken of Neil Laughton at the top of the Geneva Spur, while we were en route to the South Col. In the frame behind Neil is Everest's South East Ridge with the wind tearing snow off its entire length. I can think of no other image that justifies so well our repeated questioning over the previous 24 hours of why we were moving up for a summit attempt.

David goes on to say:

> Mingled with my sorrow, I must confess, were feelings of anger toward Rob, which I carried all the way from Base Camp. I knew in my bones that the mistakes of May 10 could have been avoided, that hubris had likely doomed Rob and his party.

Yes, the mistakes of 10 May could have undoubtedly been avoided. Maybe it was Rob's overconfidence, not only in himself but also in his personal interpretation of the information contained within the weather forecasts that doomed him and his party and likewise Scott Fischer.

So why doesn't David spell this out? David continues:

> His clients had come for a climb, not to take serious risks. Rob's expertise was supposed to be their warranty against danger and Rob had let them down. There was an ugly premonition of disaster.

The ugly premonition: the forecasts had said the full force of the storm was expected to hit on 11 May, less than 12 hours after their summit bid. Surely this was the perfect opportunity for David to explain this to his readers so they could begin to understand what had caused the tragedy?

David, while describing a period after the disaster, which from his book would appear to be between 13 and 15 May, wrote:

> I contacted a London-based weather service to begin tracking the jet stream. There was very little regional data for them to come up with an accurate forecast. But at the very least it might provide us an overview of our options. The winds at the summit would not abate. Whether it was real or imagined, after the storm the wind seemed much stronger to me.

Although David does not give the actual date he first contacted the London-based weather service, this left me under the impression that he only thought of obtaining an accurate weather forecast as a result of 10 May. This is a conclusion I believe all of his readers will come to.

I asked Henrik Hansen the following question: 'Did the Imax team continue to use the same source for their weather forecasts after 10 May as they had been using before that date?'

His reply: 'Yes they did.'

David's statement also left me with the misconception that because they were in a remote part of the Himalaya, that somehow weather forecasts and data are problematic.

I quote from Søren Olufsen, Deputy Director of Forecasting Services DMI: 'Normally the quality of forecasts for the Himalayan area should be expected to be quite high due to the fact that it is downstream from the data-rich European area.'

The question has to be asked: why would Liesl Clark have telephoned from the US to Martin Harris in England and David have approached a London-based weather service if the Imax team was already receiving forecasts from the UK Met Office? David had also contacted Roger Bilham in the US to try to obtain information.

Then I thought back to one of Roger's replies to me, where he wrote: 'My understanding of the phone calls I got from David when I returned [to the US] was that the intensity of the storm was a huge surprise.'

Then the penny dropped. Intensity can mean either the actual strength of the storm or how long it lasts. When Mike Harrison and his colleague had re-read the information from the archives, the predictions had been for a steady increase in the winds from the 8th onwards, hitting with the strongest velocity on the 11th – and this is exactly what had happened. The maximum force of the storm did ravage Everest on 11 May just as the forecasters had predicted, with wind speeds equivalent to a Category 1 hurricane. However, the increasing wind speed had reached life-threatening force by 7 p.m. on the evening of 10 May. During daytime on the 11th, there was a lull on the South Col, where the wind mercifully dropped to a strong breeze, but it returned that evening with a vengeance.

I needed to understand why we had experienced this temporary drop in the wind during the daytime of 11 May. I asked Mike Harrison if this lull had been due to the eye of the storm passing over Everest.

Mike responded:

From what I recall there was a steady basically westerly flow with nothing resembling a cyclonic centre – nothing such as the eye of a tropical cyclone that you may be thinking of (such tight structures are not seen at those altitudes). There are several possibilities, of which the most probable is something to do with variations in the flow caused by the surrounding mountains – perhaps the flow changed for a while to put Everest in a lee, or perhaps wave structures formed and moved to bring quieter winds around Everest?

I cast my mind back to 11 May. The wind on the South Col that morning was a strong breeze, but some 3,000 feet above us the South Summit was still being battered by much stronger winds. The two Sherpas who bravely climbed back up, in an attempt to rescue Rob Hall that day, got to within 700 vertical feet of him before being driven back by ferocious winds.

There had not been a lull in the storm. The winds the forecasters had predicted were blowing with the maximum force, it was just that they were thundering past a little over 2,000 feet above us. It looks highly likely that the wave structure Mike suggested had formed, putting the South Col underneath the peak of a wave, bringing relative calm. As the day wore on and the wind speed increased, the wave shifted in position and brought the South Col into a trough; with this came the wind, which was even more powerful than it had been the night before. By the 12th and 13th it weakened considerably but was still blowing.

Given that the storm had come from a steadily increasing wind, at what point did it become a storm and when did it finish? Was this the reason for the phone calls to the London-based weather service, Martin Harris and Roger Bilham – to obtain more specific details so they could ascertain what was likely to unfold over the coming days?

David goes on to write in his book:

> It was not the notorious jet stream that had generated the May 10 storm – that had been a localized weather cell, a relatively small, fast-moving storm. But with the jet stream still locked on to Everest, our weather was likely to remain unsettled.

These two sentences, to me, seem contradictory. However, this 'localised weather cell' he refers to, according to the ECMWF archives, was caused by the development of a jet over a rapidly deepening depression over southern Russia and northern India. The winds this would generate had been abundantly clear on the forecasts for almost a full week before the storm hit Everest.

In August of 2010, I sent David an email with the following, in the hope that he would be able to answer some of the questions left open by my findings:

> In the initial communication, forwarded by Roger Bilham, you informed me you had used the London-based Met Office for weather reports in 1996; this is supported by Broughton Coburn's book *Everest*. Unfortunately, his words left me with the impression that these weather forecasts were only arranged and received after 10 May, as did your book *High Exposure*.
>
> My further enquiries led me to the Danish climbers that were on Mal Duff's expedition and I have been in touch with their 'expedition leader', Henrik Hansen. He informed me quite openly that his group were receiving weather forecasts from the Danish Meteorological Institute from the very beginning of May 1996, and that your team, the Imax expedition, were receiving forecasts during the same period from the Met Office in London. He has told me that both your teams compared and discussed these forecasts and that these were also shown to Rob and Scott, or in their absence their Base Camp managers.
>
> Please could I ask why you have not made these earlier forecasts clear in either your book or subsequent work?

I received no reply, so I sent the same enquiry to David by registered letter; I got no response to that either.

There is also the book I alluded to, *Everest: Mountain Without Mercy*, by Broughton Coburn, with an afterword by David Breashears, published by National Geographic. Any book that has a National Geographic endorsement on the front cover is seen by the public as almost beyond reproach, an unerring, truthful account that can be relied upon. As outlined earlier, the only mention of accurate weather forecasts being received in Base Camp appeared, from my interpretation of his book, to be after 10 May. I wondered if Broughton Coburn had been told of the earlier forecasts before he wrote the book.

I contacted Broughton and told him I believed the Imax expedition received accurate Met Office weather reports from the very beginning of May 1996, as did a team of Danes from the DMI; that these were being compared, at Base Camp, prior to the disaster of 10 May.

I asked why his book, *Everest*, which I said as far as I could tell was the official publication about the making of the IMAX film, made no mention of these earlier forecasts.

Broughton replied:

Perplexing, indeed. I may have something on this buried in my notes. Conversations with David Breashears and other IMAX team members were my primary sources; I don't recall being alerted to the Danish forecasts. And, I wasn't aware that the *Everest* book was the official publication about the making of the IMAX film, though it was endorsed by MacGillivray Freeman Films, and was vetted by key climbers on the expedition.

I realised that in his response Broughton had referred to the Danish forecasts but not specifically to the Imax one. So I sent Broughton the following question:

You say you do not recall being alerted to the Danish forecasts when writing your book, but can I ask you if you were aware, to any degree, that the Imax team were receiving their own forecasts prior to the disaster of 10 May 1996?

His answer: 'I think David Breashears would be the best person to answer that.'

Other teams holding a forecast does not make them responsible for the deaths and injuries that occurred on Everest over the period of 10–11 May 1996. Rob and Scott held the same information and were responsible for themselves, their guides, Sherpas and clients. However, the forecasts coming into Base Camp were selectively used by certain teams, and therein lay the danger. Anyone who read the forecasts and was aware of an incoming storm had the responsibility to warn all other climbers.

Liesl Clark, a producer for NOVA online, part of the Public Broadcasting Service in the US, accompanied the Imax expedition in 1996 but had returned to the US before the storm hit. At NOVA's offices in Boston, she assisted in uploading the information they received from Audrey Salkeld and David Breashears at Base Camp.

These reports contained a single reference – the only information I had found in the public domain up to that point – that established David Breashears was discussing the forecasts as early as 5 May. Fortunately for me, the report, once posted on the website and therefore destined for the PBS archives, had become a historical record.

Audrey Salkeld, an eminent historian recognised by many as 'the authority' on Everest, an author and journalist, makes no mention of a weather forecast prior to 10 May in any of her numerous pieces connected to the disaster that I've read. It only appears in her report of 5 May 1996.

Audrey would write her own book, published by the National Geographic Society, called *Climbing Everest: Tales of Triumph and Tragedy on the World's Highest Mountain,* in which she dedicates a chapter to the events of 1996. It contained no mention of weather forecasts that I could find.

Audrey was one of the first to notice the storm coming in on the afternoon of 10 May. She writes:

> I left the Mess Tent, where I had been working (alone), and wandered across to the Kitchen. That was when I noticed an acute drop in temperature and saw the liquid black clouds rolling up the valley. I had never seen clouds like it before outside of time-lapse filming . . . These clouds were racing towards us at tremendous speed, and I called everyone out of the Kitchen to look. They were set to slap into the mountain at any minute, and it wasn't long after that that we began hearing of the deteriorating situation up high.

The storm Audrey had witnessed had come from the south, up the Khumbu Glacier. Yet Mike Harrison had told me from the archives that the approaching bad weather had a basically westerly flow. I wondered if the wind was acting in a similar manner to a tide rising over a rocky coastline, where the shape and size of the rocks can deflect the incoming water, and on occasions force it back on itself. I telephoned Mike Harrison to ask if I was right in my assumption.

'That's exactly right,' said Mike. 'In the upper atmosphere, that would not be the case, but when you get nearer the ground, and especially with the topography of the Himalaya, very strange things can happen. What people witnessed at Base Camp was coming from the west, just it had been forced by the topography of the landscape back up the Khumbu Valley; such occurrences are quite normal.'

I wrote to Audrey and set out, in a similar manner as I had done for David Breashears, the fact I had been in contact with Henrik and the information I had subsequently received from him. I put to her the following questions:

> Your report of 5 May for the NOVA website states David Breashears was receiving weather forecasts from the Danish contingent yet makes no mention of the forecasts the Imax team were receiving from London. Could you explain to me why this is so?

I then went on to ask Audrey why neither of the forecasts were mentioned in her book.

Audrey replied saying she was unable to find her diary for the 1996 expedition due to a recent move but that she would try to work from her memory and the article she had written for the *Alpine Journal* back in 1997.

> I knew we were getting weather reports, but I was not privy to these, nor the advanced planning meetings among expedition leaders and Base Camp managers. What I picked up about intentions and events was from Base Camp talk and radio messages. I was never 'briefed' in any way and there was no PR policy, so far as I was aware.

I looked at Audrey's article in the *Alpine Journal* of 1997. In this she had written: 'I was employed to accompany the 1996 Imax filming expedition specifically to produce accurate reports of the expedition progress for the worldwide web, and my reports joined others put out by Nova/WGBH Educational Foundation in Boston, USA.'

I sent Audrey two further questions, the first:

> Could I ask you to define what you mean by 'Base Camp talk', and with whom did you verify this information as being factually correct before submitting it to the NOVA website?

Audrey replied:

> So far as I remember, there was no formal brief of what I should cover, apart from a request for some historical pieces to kick off with. I regarded my job

as a fly-on-the-wall observer, and interpreted what I learned about in my own way. I was not a seasoned expedition hand, so could easily have missed certain facts and undercurrents. I am not aware that anyone routinely 'verified' what I wrote; Liz just sent them off . . . 'Base Camp talk' means simply what I picked up from chatting to people around.

The second question:

> Why were neither of these earlier forecasts, i.e. before the disaster of 10 May, ever mentioned again in anything I have read? Are you able to shed any light as to why this is so?'

Audrey's explanation:

> And I have absolutely no recollection about getting the weather reports, Danish or British [in Audrey's defence she told me her memory was less reliable nowadays], although since I last wrote to you I have discovered a copy fax from Breashears to Bob Aran of the London Weather Centre, dated 13.5.1996, confirming that the Imax team would like to commission weather forecasts for the south side of the mountain – after the storm, therefore. It looks from that 5th May [NOVA] bulletin that Mal Duff's team [the Danes] could have been the only ones getting weather bulletins before then. That may seem incredible now, but these were early days of satellite technology on Everest expeditions.

Bob Aran was a name I had not come across before. I managed to track Bob down to his home in Northamptonshire and telephoned him.

I was unsure what information I might glean and nervously waited as the phone rang twice before the receiver was picked up.

'Hello,' said the voice at the other end.

'Could I speak to Bob Aran, please?' I replied.

'Speaking,' came back the quiet but confident answer.

I introduced myself and informed Bob I was researching the events on Everest in 1996, more specifically the Imax team's weather forecast. I told him I had been made aware that David Breashears had sent him a fax from the Imax team at Base Camp on 13 May of that year and asked if this was correct.

Without any hesitation came Bob's reply: 'Yes.'

I have to say I was taken aback at how quickly and positively he had answered my question about a fax he had received 14 years earlier.

I continued: 'Were you aware the Imax team were receiving weather information before that date?'

Again his reply was immediate: 'Yes, I was supplying it.'

This I had not been expecting.

For the last five years, I had been unsuccessfully trying to find who had supplied the Imax forecasts. I tried to remain calm, not to let myself get carried away but to maintain the tone of our conversation. In reality, I wanted throw my hands in the air and shout, 'YES!', as loud as I could. I kept my composure.

'Was the supply of these forecasts arranged with the Imax team before they left for Nepal?' was the next logical question I could think of asking Bob while I quickly gathered my thoughts.

'Oh, quite some time before,' replied Bob. 'We had to make sure the model worked.'

In meteorological terms, a model is formed by feeding a wide range of climatic data into a computer and it is from this that the meteorologist will produce the specific forecast. The information that is fed in comes from satellites, aircraft, weather stations, other meteorological offices and many other sources. To ensure the model is effective and will produce a forecast that is accurate to an acceptable level it must be tested and retested against the weather that actually occurs; only then can it be supplied with a degree of confidence.

It turned out that Bob had been a meteorologist for the Royal Air Force and a business development manager for the UK Met Office. It was from here he had supplied the Imax forecasts.

He had served as a senior scientific officer to the RAF's Bomber Command and was no stranger to the jet stream and high-altitude forecasts, or those in difficult or mountainous terrain where low-flying air cover is provided to combat troops on the ground. He knew only too well, and took very seriously, the fact that the lives of others depended on him doing his job to the best of his ability. He told me that forecasting for Everest was not dissimilar to a combat zone in a specific geographical location, where the topography of the terrain and how it affected the flow and speed of the wind, variations in air temperature, moisture and cloud cover were all critical in forming predictions for an accurate forecast.

Bob had retired 12 years ago. Because of this, he made it clear to me that any comments he gave were his and not an official response from the Met Office.

Bob's answers meant, in simple terms, that a forecast on demand from the Met Office for Everest was not available at that time; it had to be prearranged. He confirmed I was correct in saying that in fact a forecast on demand was not available from the Met Office until 1997.

This perhaps explained why he had remembered so well the fax of 13 May, sent to him by David Breashears. I imagine that he must have been very confused to receive such a fax when he was already supplying the forecasts requested in this document.

Bob described how the Met Office had supplied the Imax team with detailed high-altitude forecasts from the very beginning of May 1996. These were five- or six-day forecasts updated each day and contained wind speeds and temperatures at several altitudes along with other specific weather information, exactly what he couldn't now recall.

This was not the first time Bob had supplied weather forecasts for Everest; he had done so by arrangement on two previous occasions for military-backed expeditions. As he said this, I wondered if one of these might have been for Harry Taylor, who had shared the information with Michael Groom back in 1993.

'In 1996, myself and my colleagues at the Met Office carried out an autopsy immediately after the accident, on the forecasts we had supplied the Imax team, to see if it had been in any way our fault.' Bob paused for a moment or two. 'It was not.'

Both the storm and its build-up had been correctly identified within the forecasts the Met Office had supplied. There was sadness in Bob's voice as he told me this.

As Bob recounted this poignant episode, my mind drifted to the transcript in the *Washington Post* of the *Frontline* interview with David Breashears on 14 May 2008, about his latest film on the 1996 tragedy, *Storm Over Everest*.

During this interview, David had been asked two unambiguous questions:

> Chicago: How could a cyclone from the Bay of Bengal 'sneak up' on these teams with their support?
> David Breashears: There was no accurate weather forecast back then.
> New York: Have there been any procedures implemented to avoid the bottleneck near the summit? The climbers lost much valuable time waiting to be able to descend. For the climbers, was there any knowledge that there was an oncoming storm?
> David Breashears: No procedure, and there was no knowledge of the approaching storm.

Even giving David the benefit of doubt, I had previously struggled to see how these answers fitted with the information I had uncovered. And that was before I had spoken with Bob Aran.

I explained to Bob that the DMI had also been providing a high-altitude forecast to a Danish team at the same time and that I had had the archives in the European Centre re-read by two meteorologists, one of whom was a gentleman by the name of Mike Harrison.

'I know Mike,' said Bob. It turned out he also knew Martin Harris.

I confirmed to Bob that Mike and his colleague found the forecasts provided by both the Met Office and the DMI to have been remarkably accurate in both the conditions they predicted and the timing of when these would occur. Although Bob and his fellow meteorologists had found this at the time, I thought he might take some comfort in knowing that the archives backed up what their autopsy had shown.

Bob Aran also confirmed to me that after the disaster of 10 May the Met Office continued to supply the Imax team with updated weather forecasts until they summited Everest in late May 1996. I found this particularly interesting, as *Everest: Mountain Without Mercy* stated Martin Harris had supplied the jet stream information after the disaster, something that Martin had denied doing.

I wrote to Henrik Hansen, Jan Mathorne and Bo Belvedere Christensen and asked, as I had done with Audrey Salkeld and David Breashears, why neither of the forecasts prior to 10 May were mentioned in any of the books, press, articles or films that followed in the years after the disaster of 10 May. None of these three Danes addressed this question or even attempted to, not even Henrik, who had been so helpful throughout. This is probably because they had not been involved in any of the subsequent work and felt unable to answer this difficult question.

Jan did, however, confirm he was aware of the meetings that took place between members of his team and David and Ed from the Imax team, with regard to the DMI/Met Office forecasts, and that Rob and Scott also attended. Jan also told me that as his main role was with the expedition's communications he did not really participate much in these discussions.

Bo had not responded at all to my initial enquiry, so I sent him a follow-up email, to which I received an unexpected reply: 'Sorry, Graham – I cannot recall having weather forecasts except those from the Imax team.'

I was confused by his answer, as Henrik had previously told me Bo was the one who had approached the DMI. I went back to Henrik and asked him specifically who amongst the Danes made the original approach/arrangement with the DMI?

Henrik's reply: 'Bo made the original contact.'

I wanted to give Bo another opportunity to consider the questions I had asked, so this time I laid out the facts, unambiguously, about the Danish forecast, the DMI confirmation these were supplied in 1996 and his apparent involvement. I received no reply, despite following this up with another email. It could be that Bo's memories of the events that year have completely faded and he feels unable to answer my questions.

I asked Henrik one final question: 'When the forecasts were looked at between your Danish climbers and the Imax team, was Audrey Salkeld present?'

Henrik's answer: 'Audrey was present at most times.'

This confirmation of Audrey's attendance at forecast meetings was another inconsistency revealed by my search. Audrey had told me that she was aware of the forecasts but didn't see any, nor was she briefed on such matters. If it were the case that Audrey Salkeld was present, then it is one of life's delicious ironies that she should write an article that appeared in a section called 'High Witness' of issue 191 of the British Mountaineering Council's *High* magazine.

In this, Audrey refers to an article written by Steve Weinberg called 'Why Books Err So Often' that appeared in the 1998 July/August issue of the *Columbia Journalism Review*. Weinberg, having read *The Climb*, tried unsuccessfully to contact Jon Krakauer. Concerned that certain aspects with regard to the role of Anatoli in Jon's account could be either 'exaggerated or plain wrong', and because he was unable to talk to Jon, Weinberg published his article.

Jon, having been accused of not making sure of all of his facts with regard to Anatoli before going to print with *Into Thin Air*, retaliated, accusing Weinberg and the *Columbia Journalism Review* of the very same poor journalistic practice.

This was reported in an article called 'Coming Down', which appeared on 3 August 1998 on www.salon.com under the heading of 'Wanderlust'.

Quoting from this piece:

> When the newspaper and magazine critics who reviewed *The Climb* did not treat the book with what Krakauer thought was proper scepticism, and when Boukreev's co-author [G. Weston Dewalt] continued to knock him [Krakauer] in the press, he grew angrier.

The article continues: '"I take my reputation as a reporter more seriously than I take my reputation as a writer," Krakauer says. "I didn't rely on fact-checkers to catch my errors. I busted my ass to get it right first time."'

It is to Jon Krakauer's *Into Thin Air* that I now turn.

Having read through his book carefully, I agree with what many have said: he is a masterful writer. However, that does not necessarily mean that his account is an entirely accurate or correct portrayal of events.

So as to make sure there are no doubts, I am going to write this clearly and unambiguously. Not hidden in some sentence that infers something without quite being conclusive. Jon Krakauer's book *Into Thin Air* is either poorly researched in certain key areas that relate to

the events leading up to and during the tragic events on Everest in May 1996 or he has chosen not to place this material in his account.
From Jon's introduction to his book:

> Among my five teammates who reached the top, four, including Hall, perished in a rogue storm that blew in without warning while we were still high on the mountain . . .
> The Everest climb had rocked my life to its core, and it became desperately important for me to record the events in complete detail, unconstrained by a limited number of column inches. This book is the fruit of that compulsion . . .

If five people lay dead – four from your own team – others terribly injured or traumatised as a result of a storm and you were a journalist who was determined to get it right first time, you could a) write that 'a rogue storm blew in without warning' or b) obtain a backdated weather forecast to see what happened and where this storm came from.

I wrote to Henrik Hansen and asked him: 'I understand Jon Krakauer was writing about the expedition while he was in Base Camp for the article he was preparing for Outside magazine. Did Jon speak with you about the weather forecasts for his article?'

Henrik's reply: 'No – their group information went through Rob.'

I sent emails to Rob's surviving clients for whom I could find contact details, of those only one replied – Frank Fischbeck, who currently resides in Hong Kong.

I had written to Frank with the following:

> I apologise about the possible surprise of my request but I've been researching into the tragic events of May 1996 and would like to ask if you could help me by clarifying some details.
> As you were aware at the time, Rob Hall and Scott Fischer were receiving information from weather forecasts the Imax team were getting from London.
> Could you tell me how much of the detail contained within those forecasts was known by Rob Hall's clients?
> Did Rob's clients ever have sight of the actual forecasts?

In his reply Frank Fischbeck wrote:

> Forecasts were relayed by radio/phone messages to Rob from Base Camp. I'm unaware of Imax's involvement, as I was not privy to the conversations. He would verbally advise what the general weather conditions were expected to be. Having sight of actual forecasts? I cannot remember ever having seen

a print-out of a weather report at any camp, so I would say NO, clients did not 'see' actual forecasts.

However in the last days of the expedition forecasts were hardly necessary – it was too obvious what the weather was like blowing around our heads. And in those extreme conditions on the col, communications were at best ineffectual.

I found it odd that Jon's teammate knew Rob was receiving forecasts, which were radioed up the mountain from Base Camp and then verbally delivered by Rob to the team, yet Jon, as a reporter on the same team, did not; or did he not think these important enough to include in his account?

From my own experience of several Everest expeditions, such a significant topic as the weather would remain firmly in the conversation and be discussed over and over again. That would be especially so with nerves increasing as they headed up for their summit attempt and with the poor weather they could see around them.

Jon had been sent to Everest that year to write an article for *Outside* magazine. On Scott's team, Jane Bromet was filing reports back to *Outside Online* under the heading 'Summit Journal '96: Scott Fischer'. Although these two businesses are connected, they are based in two different locations in the US – a fact Jon points out in his book. He informs his readers he was unaware of Jane's role for *Outside Online* until he'd reached Base Camp, and I have no reason to doubt that this was the case. However, I later discovered there were also reports being sent back to *Outside Online* from the Imax Base Camp under the heading of 'Summit Journal '96: Ed Viesturs'. I could find no mention of these in Jon's book. Amongst those filed under this second heading was the report sent back on 5 May 1996 by Paula Viesturs, the Imax Base Camp manager:

> But it's still nice and clear at the summit. The only thing, really, seems to be the winds. We just got an updated weather forecast and supposedly the weather is going to hold. And these forecasts have been accurate so far. The only issue is the wind.

The article Jon Krakauer wrote for *Outside* magazine also appeared on *Outside Online* in September 1996, only a matter of a few months after the reports of the 'Summit Journal '96: Ed Viesturs' and that of Scott Fischer had been posted on the same website. As Jon's book wasn't published until the following year, 1997, it surprised me that during his extensive research he'd not read these earlier reports from Base Camp.

Scott Fischer's and Ed Viestur's journals could be seen on the *Outside Online website* until very recently. They now (October 2010) appear to have been removed from *Outside Online*'s archives, as have links to them from Internet search engines.

It is arguably the biggest story that either *Outside* or *Outside Online* have ever covered. In fact, it was, according to Marty Yudkovitz, president of NBC Interactive Media, the first time a major international news story had broken live on the web. NBC's own Everest website had more than a million hits in a single day, and the ones who broke the news to the world, live online on the morning of 11 May, while the tragedy was still unfolding – *Outside Online.*

I struggled to see why *Outside Online* would remove what was a historical record of the days leading up to Everest's worst-ever disaster from their archives. I even emailed them (twice) to ask why they had done this, but I received no reply.

Returning to Jon Krakauer's *Into Thin Air,* the problem I have is that facts critical to understanding what brought about the tragedy are missing. In his book he describes the horrors of the storm well, but prior to 9 May references to meteorological conditions are notable only by their scarcity. Having read *Into Thin Air* carefully, I am surprised at how little the weather is mentioned. His book is so well written, with such content, most would not notice this anomaly.

I was also surprised to read in Krakauer's account of the difficulties he believed other people had experienced with email and Internet communication during the spring of 1996. Henrik had told me they'd received the weather forecasts from the DMI by email. Yet Jon had said in practice emails had been problematic:

> Despite considerable hoopla about 'direct interactive links between the slopes of Mount Everest and the World Wide Web,' technology limitations prevented direct hookups from Base Camp to the Internet. Instead, correspondents filed their reports by voice or fax via satellite phone, and those reports were typed into computers for dissemination on the web by editors in New York, Boston and Seattle. Email was received in Kathmandu, printed out, and the hard copy was transported by yak to Base Camp.

Unfortunately, Jon's statement here is not an accurate reflection of the overall situation regarding email communication at Base Camp. Jan Mathorne, one of the Danish climbers, was a development engineer for Thrane & Thrane, one of the world's leading manufacturers of communication equipment that uses the Inmarsat global satellite system. Jan had managed to arrange sponsorship from his employer, which enabled the Danes to take with them the latest equipment in satellite communications. I contacted Thrane & Thrane to clarify the position with regard to emails being received in Everest Base Camp using the equipment the Danes had available to them in 1996. The company confirmed that the terminal they had both sent and received faxes and emails as well as being used as a conventional phone. So as to make sure there had been no mistake on Henrik's behalf, I double-checked the information he'd already given me.

I asked Henrik the following:

In previous emails you told me the forecasts were received by email. Were they definitely received by email or were they received by fax through the satellite phone?'

Henrik: We did use email.

Could I ask if the emails were a reasonably reliable method of receiving the weather forecasts in 1996?

We did not have any problems. And we were sponsored by Thrane and Thrane, a Danish world-leading company in this business. We did make some money serving many of the other teams.

Did the Imax team make use of your email facility?

Imax used their own system.

Therefore the direct flow of precise information that could be either sent or received 24 hours a day was not only possible but actually took place. A reasonable portion of this information transfer to and from Base Camp, which included the DMI weather forecasts, was down to Jan Mathorne and Bo Belvedere Christensen. Jon, in the second edition of his book, sets out the teams on the Nepalese side of Everest that year but states that 'not everyone present on Mt Everest in the spring of 1996 is listed'. Neither Jan Mathorne nor Bo Belvedere Christensen are on the list. Perhaps Jon was not fully aware of the facilities that were available.

Describing events during the night of 10 May, Krakauer, in his 1998/9 version of *Into Thin Air*, wrote on page 222:

> There happened to be a number of climbers at Camp Four that night [the South African team of three climbers who by this time had been on the South Col for 36 hours] and Neil Laughton, Brigitte Muir, Michael Jörgensen, Graham Ratcliffe, and Mark Pfetzer from Henry Todd's team [we had arrived, with full resources, only a matter of hours earlier] who hadn't yet attempted the summit, and were thus relatively well rested. But in the chaos and confusion of the moment, Boukreev apparently located few, if any, of these climbers. And in the end Boukreev discovered, like Hutchison, that everybody he did manage to rouse was too sick, too exhausted or too frightened to help.

From what I'd ascertained it appeared Anatoli had been unaware of our team's presence on the South Col during the night of the storm. Therefore he would not have been drawn to check our tents, located little more than fifty feet away, on the perimeter of the South Col camp, through a maelstrom that others reported had reduced visibility to little more than three feet as the night progressed.

As far as I am aware, Jon has made no attempt to contact any of us to determine whether we were some of those whom Anatoli had managed to locate, and, if so, why we had not helped.

I contacted Jon's publisher and asked for his contact details. They responded saying they were unable to give these out but that if I forwarded a letter to them they would ensure that he received it.

I wrote to Jon Krakauer to ask why he'd gone public before at least asking us what had happened from our perspective. In writing to Jon I afforded him the courtesy that I considered he'd not shown our team members: the right of reply.

I sent the letter via registered post. I still have the postage slip. I received no reply.

As we were realistically the only team who could have put together a coordinated rescue on the night of 10 May, and when Krakauer's further research revealed each of our names, would it not have been wise to contact us to find out what happened from our point of view and give us an opportunity to set the record straight?

Although we are not named during this episode in the original edition of Jon's book, his further research for the 1998/9 version revealed details of who was where as the disaster unfolded. Yet it appears he was still unable to discover that two weather forecasts were being received at Base Camp each day from the very beginning of May.

There was one particularly important episode I wanted to consider, to see how Jon had described it in his account. It took place on 8 May: the Imax team got up in the morning at Camp 3 and decided to head back down because they didn't like the look of the weather higher up. By doing so they had to forego their planned summit attempt on 9 May.

Rob and Scott, along with their teams, which included Jon Krakauer, passed the Imax team coming down. The route from Camp 2, once it reaches the bottom of the Lhotse Face, is a single fixed rope. So climbers coming down must pass those going up at very close proximity.

Why does Jon make no reference to this event in his book? This is a highly significant episode given what subsequently happened. *Into Thin Air* covers the entire climb Jon made that day from Camp 2 to Camp 3 in four sentences, on page 156. The details of this event were brought to light later by G. Weston DeWalt and Anatoli Boukreev in *The Climb*, and after this in David Breashears' *High Exposure* and later still in Ed Viesturs' *No Shortcuts to the Top*.

Rob Hall's Sirdar, Ang Tshering, whom I'd met by chance in Iswari's office in the spring of 2004, had openly told me, 'Rob and Scott always watching, watching Imax. Imax have the weather!' If I could find this out eight years after the event, and within five minutes of meeting this gentleman for the first time, why did Krakauer not uncover the same information? After all, Ang Tshering was Rob Hall's and therefore Jon Krakauer's Sirdar.

Krakauer wrote: 'Nova, the PBS television show, produced an elaborate and very informative website featuring daily updates from Liesl Clark and the eminent historian Audrey Salkeld, who were members of the MacGillivray Freeman Imax expedition.'

Now given Krakauer's determination to get his facts right first time, one might reasonably assume he would have read through Audrey Salkeld's daily updates from Base Camp as part of his exhaustive research. He does after all refer to the website as 'very informative'. If this is the case, one wonders which part of the report written by Audrey Salkeld, posted on 5 May that read: 'David has reported that the forecast is good at least until the 8th. We are getting regular weather reports from Danish Meteorologists via Mal Duff's camp' did not strike him as important. It had, after all, said they were getting regular weather reports. If Jon Krakauer had investigated properly, surely he would have found that weather reports came in every day in May, covering the whole period from the 1st right through until well after the tragic events of the 10th? Even his teammate, Frank Fischbeck, was aware Rob was getting forecasts from somewhere.

Jon Krakauer was, however, far from alone in not mentioning the topic of weather forecasting for Everest. MacGillivray Freeman Films, a company that went on to produce the IMAX film *Everest*, which grossed $100 million in the first two years alone, was unable to either confirm the existence of, or tell me who might have provided, weather forecasts to the Imax team during filming.

David Breashears' *High Exposure* (foreword by Jon Krakauer), Broughton Coburn's (National Geographic) *Everest: Mountain Without Mercy* (afterword by David Breashears), Audrey Salkeld's (National Geographic) *Climbing Everest*, Jon Krakauer's *Into Thin Air*, Michael Groom's *Sheer Will*, Lene Gammelgaard's *Climbing High*, Ed Viesturs' *No Shortcuts to the Top* – none mention the two, accurate, daily weather forecasts being received prior to 10 May.

The mere mention of weather forecasts being received in Base Camp prior to 10 May dropped off the radar in every single account I have read, although not all authors will necessarily have been aware of these forecasts.

There have been many discussions about turnaround times, and that it was the lack of enforcement of these that had led to the catastrophic outcome. Now, I have to agree, if these had been strictly adhered to it is quite possible no deaths, at least on the south side of the mountain, would have occurred. However, once you are aware of the forecasts, with their increasing wind speeds that within a matter of hours, by 11 May, would reach 80 mph, you begin to realise these two teams were running a lethal gauntlet on the world's highest mountain. An enforced turnaround time would have been little more than a lucky escape.

At least one person had told me that not much credence was put in the forecasts, although this opinion seemed far from universal considering the answers I had received. It could be argued that this lack of credence was proven by the fact Rob and Scott continued with their summit attempt despite what the forecasts had predicted. But the Imax team coming back down on 8 May and the Danes descending from Camp 3 on the morning of 10 May does not necessarily support this argument; in fact, Henrik went as far as to tell me the forecasts were actually pretty good. This last statement is supported by the Met Office autopsy immediately after the disaster and by the ECMWF archives.

If Rob and Scott gave such little credence to the forecasts, why go to the extent of having their Base Camp managers look at the latest forecasts and radio up this information?

Regardless of which theory one wishes to put forward, it is impossible to have a meaningful debate on the subject unless the full facts are placed into the public domain. The suggestion by some that little credence was given to this detailed weather information does not explain why the existence of the earlier forecasts was not made abundantly clear in any of the accounts, written or otherwise, that followed.

I have no problem with someone making a film or writing a book about such events, and in doing so making a profit. That is not only the way of the world but also how the wider public becomes aware of what happened. However, in doing so, all the important facts necessary to understanding what caused the disaster should, in my view, appear in the account.

On Scott's team, Anatoli had guided without the use of supplementary oxygen, a decision that, afterwards, would raise serious questions from some mountaineers and professional guides. I'm not for one moment suggesting that the topic is unworthy of debate. However, regardless of opinions one way or the other after the event, one has to look at Scott Fischer's thoughts on the matter. It was, after all, his right as leader to make the final decision.

I quote from an interview that Scott Fischer gave to *Outside Online*, dated 31 March 1996: 'Anatoli, I know, will not be using oxygen.'

Yet, despite this unambiguous statement, the criticisms in the months and years that followed the tragedy were largely directed at Anatoli, rather than at Scott Fischer for allowing this to happen. Of those involved in this barrage of judgement, either spoken or in the written word, there were some who either knew or should have known about the existence of the earlier weather forecasts. Their denigration of Anatoli's character in a language that was secondary to him, his first being Russian, beggars belief when one considers it was such people who weren't presenting the full facts with regard to the background to the disaster.

I fully understand and accept that there has been an ongoing heated debate as to whether Anatoli had been instructed by Scott to descend ahead of the clients, and this I acknowledge. However, as there is nothing I can constructively add to this discussion it is not one I will enter into.

Anatoli was the one who raised concerns with both Rob and Scott about the weather conditions they encountered on the South Col and their planned summit bid the next day. Unfortunately, little credit appears to have been given to Anatoli in the accounts that followed the tragedy for at least trying to get Rob and Scott to reconsider their plans and to descend and wait for more settled conditions.

The following statement was made by Anatoli, translated from an interview that he gave at Everest Base Camp the following year, in May 1997: 'And people forget about everything when they speak about money – you can rewrite history as you like.'

Arguably, with the weather being explained away as 'a rogue storm that blew in without warning', a disproportionate burden of blame was unfairly placed on Anatoli's shoulders. It weighed heavy on this very private man. His reputation, the respect he had earned over many years of climbing, was left in tatters.

He set about trying to rebuild his life and regain the reputation that he had once enjoyed. He did this the only way he knew how – by climbing. He hoped he might be able to gradually move away from guiding and earn his living by being sponsored on more interesting climbs. Now more than ever before he needed success; failure would only raise questions about his ability. It was not an option. I recalled his postcard to me dated 22 October 1996:

> This autumn as before I spent my time in the high altitude to enjoy the mountains when I climbed Cho-Oyu and Shixspangma [*sic*] in Tibet. It wasn't easy because of lots of snow made my

ascents very dangerous. I don't forget lesson from mountains from last spring.

By his own admission Anatoli was making ascents when his considerable experience told him the conditions were far too dangerous. To raise his profile, he wanted to finish the three outstanding peaks over 26,000 feet he had yet to climb. This he wanted to complete as soon as possible. Annapurna was going to be first, in December of 1997. The following year he hoped to climb Gasherbrum I and finally Nanga Parbat. Such an achievement would further distance him from the tragic events of May 1996. It would place him with the elite of high-altitude climbing; only a handful had achieved this feat.

As with Alison Hargreaves, Rob Hall and Scott Fischer, he was under pressure and this was forcing him into decisions against his better judgement. His reasons were different from theirs, but the outcome would be the same.

He came down from his preparatory climbs on Annapurna for a rest. It was a mountain that he knew was precariously laden with snow that winter season. By 18 December 1997, he reported that at lower elevations they had 11 feet of new snow. The need for continued success must have been preying on his mind because he went back up onto a mountain that he knew was far too dangerous to attempt in such conditions. One week later, on Christmas Day of 1997, Anatoli was swept to his death by an avalanche while making his attempt on Annapurna.

Had the full facts behind the 1996 disaster been placed in the public domain would Anatoli have faced such fierce criticism? Would he still be alive today? Was Anatoli Boukreev the final fatality of the 1996 disaster?

The Final Analysis

It was early spring 2009. Peering out through the window I could see nothing on this moonless night. I switched off the light that hung from the oak-beamed ceiling and opened the front door. A sudden draught of cold air rushed past. Using my fingertips to guide me through the doorway, I stepped outside into the inky black. My feet crunched against the large gravel stones as I ventured blindly further on. I counted out 15 paces and then stopped. The large pond with its resident carp and murky waters lay just ahead. Holding my right hand up in front of my face, I was unable to see any sign of it.

After several minutes passed, my eyes began to adjust to the dark. Spread right across the heavens were distant specks of shimmering light. The still air held a sub-zero temperature. As I turned around, the manor house, my next great adventure, stood as a towering featureless shape set against a sky filled with countless stars. It was reminiscent of a night from my past. The night that Anatoli, Nikolai and I had emerged from our tents at two o'clock in the morning to stare up at the challenge that lay ahead: the upper section of Everest's North East Ridge. It all seemed so long ago: 14 years to be precise. I had left the mountain that year under the assumption that my Everest journey was complete. I was wrong. So many lives had been needlessly lost in the intervening time.

With the uncovering of the facts behind 10 May 1996 came my first glimmers of comprehension as to what had driven me in my search: an emotional roller coaster of a ride that in an instant could launch me from the depths of depression to euphoric excitement, only to have my hopes dashed once more. I knew I'd had an overwhelming desire to know the truth, but I had not understood the reason why I had needed to embark on what would appear to have become a self-imposed, soul-destroying journey. It was because if I didn't, I could never release the burden of guilt I carried with me. In truth, I'd borne this from the moment I'd lifted my head to look into the raging storm seconds before I'd clambered into the safety of our tent on the South Col. That was at 6.30 p.m. on 10 May 1996. The image of the two head torches glinting feebly on the far side of the Col through the ferociously wind-driven snow remain as vivid as the moment I saw them. To my eternal regret, I had not comprehended at the time the significance of what I was witnessing.

In everyday life, I get on quietly, sorting out problems as and when they arise. This was the approach I had taken to running my business. The setbacks that often arose were solved in an intelligent manner, and through this I had learnt both to negotiate and to stand my ground. However, in the period that followed the disaster of 1996, I pushed the tragic events into the dark and inaccessible recesses of my mind. This was a problem I was unable to solve. The outcome of 10 May was fixed; nothing I could say or do was going to change it. The guilt I carried could not be negotiated or bargained with, neither could the finality of death.

None of the accounts in the climbing press that followed in the summer of 1996 made any reference to prior knowledge by way of a specific altitude weather forecast for the Everest region. So when I read the two quotes my initial feelings were a mixture of bewilderment and anger. I felt these not simply for myself and those on our team but also for the casualties of the storm. I sensed that this should never have happened. What I failed to realise was that those of us who had sat out the storm on the South Col had also been victims.

I had departed from Everest that year convinced that in light of the conditions we had observed high on the mountain on the afternoon of 10 May we should have anticipated that events might spiral out of control for these two guided teams. My mind dealt with this alien experience in the only way it could: by shutting it out. This was my denial.

In the years that followed, I turned my back on the whole episode and read none of the books that began to appear. In consequence, I gave my feelings no chance to be aired, no opportunity for me to release the resentment and guilt that I felt, so they stayed with me.

The sight of a large film crew at Everest Base Camp in 2004, when Catherine and I were visiting some friends there, was the final straw. I'd had enough of what I instinctively felt was a deception. My anger and dismay were reinforced by what I saw. My denial was trying to break free from its shackles, but I was yet to realise it had existed at all.

On reflection, at the onset of my personal journey, all I had wanted to do was expose the truth behind 10 May 1996, about why it had happened. In reality, people already suspected that the cause had centred on poor decisions and the unspoken rivalry between Rob and Scott looking towards their respective future businesses in this lucrative guiding of Everest, but I had wanted to go much further than this, to expose the true depths of this whole sorry affair.

Once I had proof that weather forecasts were being received into Everest Base Camp prior to 10 May, and the information the archives said these contained, it opened up a whole new understanding as to what had actually led to the disastrous outcome.

With the information I now had, I pieced together the events leading up to 10 May, but this time with the truth in place. It read like a Shakespearean tragedy. Rob Hall and Scott Fischer had cast themselves in the lead roles by announcing that their two teams would make a summit bid on this day. It pre-determined the position of each of the players when the storm hit Everest. By asking us to go on 11 May they had even supplied our curtain call to walk onto this deadly stage. In the west, a spectre was gathering, one that had appeared on the forecasts nearly a week earlier, one that Rob and Scott knew was coming. But they had not taken enough account of the days either side of the peak of the storm, of twists in fate, communications faltering or of opportunities missed. These were compounded by a blizzard during which visibility all but disappeared, leaving would-be but uninformed rescuers out of sight. Their rivalry had made them vulnerable: a trait that others on the mountain had not expected to see from these two highly experienced climbers and one that would put their two entire teams in danger. Nor had they told us of this maelstrom rushing towards Everest.

It was apparent that those in possession of the most advanced weather information ever available for an Everest expedition had ended up walking their high-paying clients straight into the rising storm. Somehow it had deluded them into thinking they could tread ever closer to the edge of risky judgements. Their stubborn decision to make their summit bid on 10 May, despite the weather forecasts, suggests they seemed to think the storm would hold off in its entirety, without any build-up, until emerging almost in an instant on the following day. But that is not what the forecasts predicted.

I began to realise that what Rob and Scott had effectively done by asking us to go for the summit on 11 May and then not telling us about the subsequent information they received predicting a storm on that day had been foolish. This selfish act on their behalf could have easily put us in mortal danger. But they had done so because they'd lost touch with reality; they were no longer in full control of rational thoughts. Their self-imposed pressure had brought them to decisions that were totally out of character. Rob and Scott had stepped far beyond the line, not by asking us to go on 11 May but by doing so with tunnel vision. They were focused only on their competition. They took no account of the consequences of their request and the responsibility this placed on them should information come to hand that suggested we would be put at risk.

So, history took its course. The storm, which the forecasters had said was to be fronted by increasing wind speeds, ones that Rob and Scott had observed gradually building up over the preceding days, struck on the afternoon of 10 May with life-threatening force. The intensification of the wind to this level had occurred some 12 hours earlier than they had gambled on, and, to make matters worse, a sudden drop in temperature and blizzard conditions accompanied this howling gale.

Described as the worst day in the history of Everest, 10 May 1996 had been an appointment with fate already set in stone several days before it happened. Vital information was there on the mountain, but it was not drawn upon to protect lives; instead, it was played in a high-risk strategy. It was a game my fellow teammates and I had unwittingly become a part of. Only luck had saved us from a similar end.

The anger I'd originally felt towards Rob and Scott had long since faded; now I felt only sadness. Sadness that the competition between them for a successful season, success that would be reported back in the US and which could be the key to their future business, had brought them to a series of uncharacteristic decisions, ones that in the end had made them authors of their own demise and that of Doug Hansen, Yasuko Namba and Andy Harris. Had they stepped back for one moment to heed the signs, to consider their decisions, their course of action, no one need have died.

Scott, although slow and feeling unwell on that fateful day, knew that all his clients were on their way back down to the South Col. He was unaware of events yet to unfold. It appears from the accounts I have read, that Scott, during his descent, displayed behaviour that would indicate he was suffering from cerebral oedema. Scott realised he was sick but was unaware he was losing touch with reality, as shown by the report that he asked for a helicopter. Hopefully as this detachment accelerated it spared him the final comprehension of the terrible circumstance he was in.

Rob, on the other hand, was completely lucid as he struggled down the heavily corniced South East Ridge towards the Hillary Step in gale-force winds with a rapidly ailing Doug Hansen. Desperately radioing for help, Rob, over several hours, managed to drag or cajole Doug most of the way towards the South Summit. Tragically, Doug, a much-loved father of two, was not destined to complete this short distance. At what point during their epic struggle to survive, battling against the ferocious winds, did the relevance of Rob's knowledge that 'they went on 10 May because they knew the weather was going to go bad the next day' tear at his very soul? Was it when he knew Doug had passed away? Or when his concerns turned to the whereabouts of Andy Harris, who was nowhere to been seen the following morning after he'd bravely climbed back up through the storm to try to aid Rob in Doug's rescue? Or was it when he lay badly frostbitten in the realisation he would never see his wife again or set eyes on his unborn child?

How could I feel anything but sadness for the anguish he must have felt as he lay there waiting for death, perhaps in the comprehension that only he had brought himself to this point?

It may have been the biting cold that eventually took these five desperate souls, but it wasn't the storm that really killed them.

Like so many tragedies that have in the past been thrust into the public domain, closer analysis reveals a series of wrong decisions. At each fork in the road, those in charge made the incorrect choice time after time, so drawing them towards an inevitable conclusion. May 10th, the day that first Rob, then Scott, sought above all others, would cloud their judgement. They'd ignore their more cautious natures borne out of previous experience, setting a course that would steer both of them and three others to their deaths.

In the aftermath, both survivors and victims carried with them a feeling of guilt that they could have done more. I now realised that what had transpired on 10 May was not our fault. From our team's perspective, we bore the anguish that had we been told of what was happening outside our tent, or been asked for assistance, then we could have put together a rescue. But this is regret, not guilt; the pain of this will fade in time. Rob Hall and Scott Fischer knew the storm was coming; they should never have been up there in the first place. The two loaded dice they rolled that day each had six faces, five of which warned them of the dangers that they knew lay ahead. The remaining faces, one on each die, read 'competition' and 'future business' respectively. These lightweight sides faced uppermost, the only ones they chose to see and the ones on which they gambled everything.

In my search for the full facts, it became apparent that some of those who'd been unclear in their responses to me or reticent when questioned on the issue of forecasts were amongst those who it seems had full knowledge of the accurate weather forecasts received at Everest Base Camp prior to 10 May, but they had chosen not to put this clearly and unambiguously into their accounts: a decision that had continued for more than 14 years and one that had been veiled behind a human tragedy.

I lost count of how many hundreds of emails I sent, the number of letters posted, to give those concerned the opportunity to have their say, their right of reply. Nobody, and I mean nobody, has ever attempted to answer my question of why the earlier forecasts were not made clear in any of the accounts that followed the disaster of 10 May.

Looking back at my own emotions in the days immediately after the disaster, I had felt empty, numbed and an overwhelming sense of sadness for the families of the deceased. Only a month or so previously they had waved goodbye to their loved ones, who now lay as frozen corpses on Everest's upper reaches.

Clearly I understood at this time that the events would be in the news, but I had no idea it would be such a huge story that would give rise to films and books that would sell in their millions, then more books and more films. In truth, I don't think anyone who was at Everest Base Camp that year could have predicted the public would have such an appetite for the story.

Within a matter of days, members of the press from all over the world were heading for Nepal, some of whom helicoptered into Base Camp; telephone interviews had taken place. It seems likely that this was how everyone came to talk about a 'rogue storm' that had 'blown in without any warning' and had caught out these teams near the summit of Everest. And so, it seems, the story was born. The questions about this particular aspect ceased.

The press were so preoccupied with Rob and Scott's teams, the Imax team and one or two others, mostly Americans, that a small Danish contingent on a commercial expedition appeared to be of little interest in this highly volatile media scrum, and so they were never questioned. Once they'd called an end to their expedition, the Danes simply packed up and went back home to their normal careers and stayed out of the furore that followed.

Had the press been made aware that forecasts were received in Base Camp prior to the tragedy, the questions would have come thick and fast. Surely chief amongst these would have been 'Had these forecasts predicted a storm?' Other questions would have quickly followed, such as:

Had Rob Hall's and Scott Fischer's high-paying clients been given full details of what the forecasts contained and therefore climbed with full knowledge of the risks they were taking?

Had other teams put rescue plans in place and were they prepared to react quickly?

Were the forecasts and what they contained shared and disseminated widely, and, if not, could such information have reduced fatalities?

The sequence of decisions leading up to 10 May suggested Rob and Scott had exposed their teams to an unacceptable level of risk. Surely this would bring worrying implications for grieving families? How might they react to such news? These are all questions a rational person would ask.

As it was, newspaper headlines splashed across the globe announced

'Rogue Storm Kills Climbers Being Guided Up Everest' and 'Eight Die in Everest's Freak Storm'. The press soon latched on to the financial aspect. Cynical headlines appeared about people paying large sums of money to be guided up Everest, as though it were some new form of tourism for the well off. They showed little mercy and took no account of any previous climbing experience that Rob and Scott's clients might have had. Yet, notwithstanding this initial rush to get the breaking news of Mount Everest's worst-ever disaster on the front page of newspapers, magazines and Internet websites, it seems that no real investigative, probing questions appear to have been asked to see if the climbers had any prior knowledge of the incoming storm. As a result, the fact the storm was forecast has lain out of the public domain ever since.

I can't be sure why those who knew about the earlier weather forecasts didn't correct this error in any of the numerous interviews they have given, or in their films and published accounts. I've had no answers from those involved that explains their reasons. There is a range of possible motives, some more damning than others. Only those who were fully aware of the forecasts being received at Base Camp prior to 10 May but who decided not to mention this crucial fact can truly know the answer to that question.

Over time, my emotions have changed from being incensed to disappointment – disappointed that the truth had not been told from the very beginning, that the grieving relatives of those who'd perished had not been shown this final dignity. Instead, they and everyone else were led to believe that those who had died were the victims of a rogue storm.

The tragedy of 10 May 1996 was a cruel blow to the families and friends of those killed, injured, traumatised or otherwise affected by these events. All were victims to a varying degree and suffered pain and anguish as a result of that disatrous time. Through my own personal journey, I have now come to terms with that fateful day on Everest. However, I have also come to the understanding that as catastrophic as 10 May 1996 might have been, those who knew of the earlier forecasts and have not placed the full facts clearly and unambiguously in their subsequent accounts had delivered the cruellest blow of all. For without the truth, victims can have no meaningful foundation from which their healing process might begin.

Bibliography

Boukreev, Anatoli and G. Weston DeWalt. *The Climb: Tragic Ambitions on Everest*. New York: St Martin's Press, 1998.

Boukreev, Anatoli and Linda Wylie. *Above the Clouds: The Diaries of a High-Altitude Mountaineer*. New York: St Martin's Press, 2001.

Breashears, David. *High Exposure: An Enduring Passion for Everest and Unforgiving Places*. New York: Simon & Schuster, 1999.

Coburn, Broughton. *Everest: Mountain Without Mercy*. National Geographic Books, 1997.

Dickinson, Matt. *The Death Zone: Climbing Everest Through the Killer Storm*. United Kingdom: Arrow Books, 1998.

Gammelgaard, Lene. *Climbing High: A Woman's Account of Surviving the Everest Tragedy*. London: Pan Books, 2000.

Groom, Michael. *Sheer Will: The Inspiring Life and Climbs of Michael Groom*. Australia: William Heinemann, 1997.

Krakauer, Jon. *Into Thin Air: A Personal Account of the Everest Disaster*. New York: Villard Books, 1997.

Krakauer, Jon *Into Thin Air: A Personal Account of the Everest Disaster*. New York: First Anchor Book Trade Paperback Edition, November 1999.

Muir, Brigitte. *The Wind in My Hair*. Australia: Penguin Books Australia, 1998.

Rose, David and Ed Douglas. *Regions of the Heart: The Triumph and Tragedy of Alison Hargreaves*. London: Penguin Books, 1999.

Salkeld, Audrey, 'Emergency on Everest', *The Alpine Journal* 1997, vol. 102, no. 346.

Viesturs, Ed. *No Shortcuts to the Top: Climbing the World's 14 Highest Peaks*. New York: Broadway Books, 2006.

Weathers, Beck with Stephen G. Michaud. *Left for Dead: My Journey Home from Everest*. London: Time Warner, 2003.

Index

The following abbreviations have been used: b. – brother; d. – daughters; GR – Graham Ratcliffe; s. – sister; w. – wife

Dorr, Ray 81, 120, 127, 128–30
GR's doubts about 88, 89–90, 102,
129, 133
Duff, Mal commercial expedition
(Danish/Finnish/UK team)
Khumbu Icefall 94–5, 115, 154,
197, 284, 313
satellite communications 309–10
weather reports 266–7, 269–70,
286, 291–2, 298–9, 302, 305–6,
312
Duncan, Euan 115, 269

ECMWF (European Centre for
Medium-Range Weather Forecasts)
269, 273–5, 276, 298
see also Danish Meteorological
Institute (DMI); UK Met Office
Edwards, Adam 21
Everest: Mountain Without Mercy
(Coburn) 242–3, 244, 245, 298, 299,
305, 312
Everest
1924 expedition see Beetham,
Bentley
commercialisation and trip charges
65–7
disabled ascent, first 57
litter problem 100–1
post-monsoon expedition (1993)
31, 88, 152, 248
successful ascents 68, 69, 80, 81, 90,
112, 168, 178–9, 181
see also Nepal headings; Tibet
Everest expedition (1995)

Field, Hyman 221, 223
Finnish team see Duff, Mal (Danish/
Finnish/UK team)
Fischbeck, Frank 68, 134, 285, 307–8,
312
descent before summit 135, 136,
139, 141, 143, 146
Fischer, Scott
K2 climbs 50–1, 65
Manaslu plans 154
Sagamartha Environmental
Expedition 100
tragedy, events leading to 134–47,
154–5

Fischer, Scott, Everest expedition
(1996)
Base Camp formal meeting 99
competition focus 66, 67, 314
death of 147, 159
leadership style 114–15
maps showing stranded climbers
and rescue attempts 139, 143, 146
official investigation into death,
lack of 206
and Outside magazine 66
Outside Online reports 308, 314
oxygen supplies, concerns over 98,
254
rescue attempt 145, 146, 147
summit attempt and choice of date
120, 152, 161
summit attempt and turnaround
time 136, 137, 199, 203
summit descent 129, 138, 139–42,
143
summit reached 137, 138, 139, 284
team members 69–70, 134–5, 137
team members, news of missing
132–3
team survivors after descent 153–4,
155–6
weather forecast, GR's research into
knowledge of 203, 210–13, 250–5,
260–3, 270–2, 280–4, 286, 288
weather forecasts, prior knowledge
272–6, 290–300, 305, 307, 312–15
Fleet, John 166
Forehand, Leslie 227, 228
Fox, Charlotte 70, 114–15, 134,
137–9, 140
rescue of 142, 143, 144, 146
Frontline (website) 272, 304
Fullen, Eamon 'Ginge' 115

Gammelgaard, Lene 70, 135, 137–40
Climbing High 249–50, 252, 312
rescue of 142–4, 146
Gasherbrum II 70
Gildea, Brenda Joan 193
Griffin, Lindsay 163, 203
Groom, Michael 68, 134, 136
descent and helping other climbers
137–44
radio malfunction 140

CMWF cooperation 273, 274–5
and pre-arranged forecasts 167–8,
257–9, 302–4
see also Danish Meteorological
Institute (DMI); ECMWF
UK National Grid for Learning 170
ukclimbing.com 204
University Corporation for
Atmospheric Research (UCAR)
227–8
US expedition 38, 39, 42, 44–6

Viesturs, Ed 19, 65, 67, 69, 99, 101,
154, 158, 197, 219
and IMAX *Everest* film 219
No Shortcuts to the Top 312
Outside Online reports 308
and weather reports 252–3, 260–3,
272, 282–3, 290, 291
Viesturs, Paula 67, 272, 308

weather reports
Everest 1993 expedition 248
Everest 1996 expedition *see under*
Hall, Rob; Fischer, Scott; Ratcliffe,
Graham; Nepal, 1996 expedition

Nepal return trip (1998) 167–8
see also Danish Meteorological
Institute (DMI); ECMWF; UK Met
Office
Weather Windows 243
Weathers, Beck 69, 134, 135–6, 139,
254
descent 140–7, 285
evacuation to hospital 148–9
frostbite injuries 149, 249
Weinberg, Steve 306
Whittaker, Cindy 47
Whittaker, Lizzy 47, 54, 56
Whittaker, Tom 36, 47, 54, 56
Wilson, Susan 219
Wilton, Helen 68, 290
The Wind in My Hair (Muir) 281, 292
Woods, Sidney 189–90
Working Title Films, Everest film 197
Wylie, Jake 107, 116
Wylie, Linda 107, 116, 156–7

Xegar, checkpoint incident 41–2

Yudkovitz, Marty 309